CW00541914

SHERMAN'S WIFE

SHERMAN'S WIFE

*A wartime childhood amongst
the English Catholic aristocracy*

JULIA CAMOYS STONOR

First published
in 2006 by

DESERT♥HEARTS

www.deserthearts.com
PO Box 2131
London W1A 5SU
England

© Julia Camoys Stonor 2006

Typeset and designed by Desert♥Hearts

Printed and bound by
Newton Printing, London, England

British Library Cataloguing in Publication Data
A catalogue record for this book is available from the British Library

ISBN 1-898948-79-8 • 978-1-898948-79-7

Caution
This book is sold subject to the condition that it shall not, by way of
trade or otherwise, be lent, resold, hired out, or otherwise circulated
without the publisher's prior consent in any form of binding or cover
other than that in which it is published and without a similar
condition being imposed on the subsequent purchaser.

Dedicated to
Sherman & Mildred,
Crista, Jock & Donald

Contents

Sherman and Jeanne
on their wedding day, July 14, 1938

From 1939 until 1945, Stonor Park and its annexe Assendon Lodge were war zones. Jeanne made sure of this. Deprived (but only to a certain extent) of the full drama of life in the raw in London, she recreated its heady atmosphere as nearly as she could in the country. And this she did most successfully, using all the props of the large, prosperous, ancient lands, villages and mansions that belonged to her husband (absent on active service and, as Jeanne pointed out, "in foreign parts, thank God!") and his family . . .

I

Mama

"Heil Hitler!" shouted Mummy as she pushed Daddy down the stairs at Assendon Lodge. He stood at the top of the stairs, slim, with long hands, and a gold ring on his little fingers, his uniform khaki wool, with bright brown leather straps crossing from shoulder to chest, a silver bugle badge on his shoulder, laced shoes burnished to the same chestnut as his belt. I could smell the sweet aroma of his hair oil—he poured it from a silvered lime glass bottle surmounted by a small crown—from where I crouched beneath the stairwell, stopped in my tracks on the way to the kitchen.

"Get the hell out of here and back to your battlefield, Shermie. You're totally useless and absolutely *de trop* round here. The sooner I'm rid of you the better!"

Mummy rubbed her hands together, her scarlet finger nails glittering. A lighted cigarette clung perilously to her clenched lips.

Daddy flew backwards down the stairs.

At the bottom, he picked himself up off the floor and dusted himself down, smoothing the crease on his trousers. Slowly, carefully, he walked back to the war through the tradesmen's entrance. A small gust of air blew by me as he went.

2

'Don't Be Such an Effin' Bore!'

One rainy day in 1945, before we had left Assendon Lodge for good, I was on my morning walk with Nanny and the second nanny, Nana to ever-enticing sewage works at Lower Assendon. As the bus from Pishill and Russells Water to Stonor sped by past us I caught sight of Mummy's face, frozen in fury and embarrassment, glowering out of the window.

I couldn't hear my mother, but I could see her lips moving as she continued to glower and scowl at me. Seated bolt upright alone on a seat in the grey-painted wartime bus, Mummy was dressed in full uniform, her pageboy hair smoothed into place beneath a navy blue peaked cap, a silver whistle on a white lanyard was draped over her shoulder epaulettes. Bright scarlet patches of rouge matching her lipstick rose high on my mother's dead white cheeks, lightly dusted in palest green powder—a mixture, which she had specially prepared at Elizabeth Arden on her visit to London. Blue spectacle lenses glittered in their blond tortoise frames and Mummy's hands tapped impatiently at the window ledge as the bus sped past. I cringed at her stare.

But Ruby Heath could explain nothing to me in the kitchen of Assendon Lodge. "There, there, Miss Julia," she said soothingly. She couldn't bring herself to tell me that this was the first time in her life that my mother had travelled in a bus with the "common people" as she called them.

Instead, Ruby rubbed her hands on her flowered pinafore and continued making jams and jellies and feather-light sponge cakes. I licked the yellow pudding basin clean with greedy fingers.

" 'Victorias'—those cakes are called," explained Ruby busily dusting them with icing sugar.

A few weeks later I found myself in a similar position, standing close to Mama-who-was-Mummy in the green and cream kitchen of Assendon Lodge as I watched her every move as she attended to a new batch of scones. Only recently had my mother announced her change of name: "In future and startin' immediately, WE are to be called MAMA. Daddy is now PAPA. And both with the accent on the final A!"

The few children I occasionally saw from the Rainbow Inn or at the Catechism classes and Sunday services at Stonor chapel who stood from one foot to another frozen with cold and fright, only ever called their parents "Mummy and Daddy". It puzzled me, and the person I used to know as "Mummy" receded into the distance.

But now, in the kitchen and hovering close to the hem of Mama's navy-blue serge police skirt, I edged ever closer to the magic of her presence. She reached down into the oven to scoop up the sand-coloured scones baking there. Very slowly she swung round with the white-hot tray of perfectly formed golden cakes, then drew without warning the thin tin rim across my lips, sending a searing pain into my mouth.

I lurched sideways, dressed in my best smocked linen frock, a hand clutching my scorched mouth, my heart shaking. Mama laughed casually, a light tinkling sound. Sharply she called to Ruby: "Come immediately and cope with the child!"

Turning on her heel, my mother laughed over her shoulder, a cigarette leaning out of the corner of her mouth. "For God's sake, Julia dear, stop makin' such a fuss about nothin'. You really are nothin' but a God-awful borin' brat. Just shows what useless stock Sherman's Stonor blood is, and all your useless inheritance to boot."

And once again Ruby, with her curling red hair and comforting arms, consoled and soothed me. "There, there, poor Doodo," she said as she bathed my tear-stained cheeks and blistered lips.

Mama herself cried only rarely. The first time I saw her cry was after her experience falling off a bicycle that caused such a crisis. But she seemed more angry than sad as tears streamed down the rouge, making rivulets and runny lines in the thickly applied Elizabeth Arden green powder.

Dressed in an afternoon frock of green and white seersucker, Mummy, now Mama, had taken her seat bolt upright on a brand-new black bicycle. It stood on the gravel beneath the drawing-room window at Assendon Lodge. A lighted cigarette ("my Philip Morris, ha, ha, *olé!*") leaned sideways out of Mama's scarlet-painted mouth. Her long fingernails were an even more intense red as she leaned over the curved handle-bars.

I had watched intently as she wobbled forward unsteadily on the bicycle a few feet before Uncle Eric St Johnston, Chief Constable of Oxfordshire, gallantly gave her a push and encouraging shove from behind. There was a shrill shriek as she skidded wildly and crashed to the ground. There followed a cascade of tears and a torrent of words, mostly in Spanish.

"If this is your idea of playfulness, Eric, then you are more of a goddamned fool than I already know!" Mama stormed.

I started crying too as I was more upset that Mama had cut her knee. And even more since her contraband American silk stockings were laddered from heel to toe.

Supported by Uncle Eric, who was such a frequent visitor, his arms supportively around her, Mama staggered into the kitchen shouting at me as she went: "Shut up, shut up! You're such a humiliation to me you silly brat. Don't you dare tell anyone. And stop cryin' this minute. Fetch the first-aid box you effin' idiot. And get me a Horse's Neck at once. You'd better make it quick," ordered Mama. She put her bleeding leg up on the kitchen table.

The only people I could dare to tell would be Ruby or Joyce my day nanny. Several other nannies had just recently been sacked with louder-than-usual shouts from their employer. "You're sacked, you're sacked. You can leave in half-an-hour. On second thoughts that's not soon enough, you can leave immediately," Mama would announce scornfully. "References you said? Certainly not. How dare you? Get out, get out!"

Nannies, one after the other, packed and left rapidly. But they still had to stand outside the gate at Assendon Lodge, come rain or shine, to wait for the Pishill and Stonor bus to take them into Henley. Joyce would then come to fill in, from the Rainbow Inn, a black-and-white Tudor beamed building opposite the gate of Assendon Lodge. Its low-hung brilliantly painted sign of a rainbow in a glowing arc swinging in the breeze was magic to me.

Daughter of the pub keeper Archie Froud, Joyce was pretty with dark curly hair, vivacious and kind. I loved her dearly, and the day she left to be married to Arthur, a demobbed airman, I cried. But she had me for her bridesmaid, dressed up in one of Granny Camoys' wartime presents from Newport, Rhode Island. It was my favourite, a striped yellow and white cotton dress, thickly smocked the breadth of my stomach and chest, a long sash tied tightly above my bottom. I had white buckskin strapped shoes, also from Granny Camoys.

"That ridiculous child of Sherman's has inherited Mildew Camoys' impossibly narrow American foot," laughed Mama scornfully. "Triple-A, for God's sake. What a nightmare Julia is!"

My white ankle socks were neatly folded over for the wedding at Bix Bottom church. I went to the wedding alone with Ruby as Mama had other emergency engagements on wartime activities with the ARP (Air Raid Precautions). The reception was held at the Rainbow, and there were white bread sandwiches spread with Gentlemen's Relish bought at Fortnum & Mason (or, Mama would say, "*Fortún y Masón* as it's called in my aristo Spanish!"), which Mama released from the heavily locked pantry store cupboards. The wedding cake was made from carrots, though surprisingly, it had brilliant white icing sugar and silver decorations.

I cried again when Joyce promptly vanished from my life. She had gone away on honeymoon but I had no idea what that could be and I was convinced she'd never come back. Curious, I asked Mama what a "honeymoon" was, but all she did was hum. Anxiously I asked her again.

"Oh don't be such an effin' bore, you silly little ignoramus," she replied finally. "You understand absolutely nothin'!" She paused briefly to light another in her chain of Philip Morris and Camel contraband cigarettes from America. "Thank God for your father's darlin' Cousin John Nicholas Brown, and that darlin' colleague of his, the Tiny Tin commander Ted Macauley. What would I do for my fags without them in this goddamned nuisance of a war?" Mama sighed reflectively. "Another darlin' boy in uniform is droppin' in for lunch, that darlin' Archbishop Frank Spellman. Early bed for you my girl. You're not to be heard and not even to be seen!" she added and inhaled deeply.

Mama somehow managed never to take the cigarette from the corner of her scarlet mouth. She passed the fire off the end of the old one to the tip at the longer end of a new one. This immediately grew a funnel of long grey ash scattering itself this way and that as she walked briskly along.

Frequently the ash found itself tossed straight into the antique copper Bostonian pots that Mama used. She would briskly click her fingers, impatient with Ruby who was busily washing up saucepans and innumerable kitchen utensils in the scullery.

Stirring the ash further into her recipe, Mama would laughed merrily. "I've done all this before. FAG-ends indeed. Ha, ha, *olé* and heil Hitler!" She continued to stir briskly, her newer cigarette cascading ever more ash.

Jeanne (pronounced "Jun") was a superb cook. Everything she touched became transformed and, if truth be told, the cigarette ash made no difference to the taste on the rare times I was allowed to eat the creations which she made for the grown-ups.

Usually I had nursery food on Peter Rabbit china plates in the nursery dining room. Mama seldom allowed women into the big dining room unless, as she said, "they are those useful foreign grandees, my Spanish and South American aristo cousins, *olé!* And they've got to be in the money, with PLENTY of titles to boot. Quite useless to me without. I'm simply not interested."

But Lady Helen Dashwood was an exception. Besides, as Mama pointed out: "Darlin' Helen Hell-Bags is a Canadian cereal millionairess and a damn good shot with her 20-bore gun. Always most frighteningly accurate."

Mama appeared to be slightly alarmed by Hell-Bags, though her more gentle husband Sir Johnny Dashwood was far more beguiling. Jeanne found Hell-Bags' gentle husband Johnny irresistible. A King's Messenger during the Second World War, and member of the Balloon Squadron, Jeanne was vastly intrigued by the "official secrets" that he held. Secrets, secrets and more secrets—Jeanne wanted all divulged to her.

Johnny's several thousand acres and glorious butterscotch Palladian house West Wycombe Park was set in a landscape designed by Capability Brown. Its sheer grandeur, alongside a beautiful lake, enraptured Jeanne. The heavily married Johnny was an enticing challenge, an elegant man who habitually dressed for dinner in bespoke, frogged green velvet, faced with watered green silk.

Johnny and Hell-Bags Helen's daughter Sarah had been one of seventeen hand-picked, scarlet-gloved bridesmaids at the Wedding of the Year, Bastille Day, July 14, 1938, Miss Mary Jeanne Stourton to the Hon Ralph Robert Watts Sherman Stonor. Hell-Bags Helen also attended this spectacular marriage of one of the most chic and glamorous women in society of the time. A cereal heiress, and a great beauty of what Jeanne pronounced to be "very common Canadian stock, hardly bred at all", Helen had a fine eye for the various gentlemen who substituted for Johnny Dashwood's "inadequacies", as his wife would explain with scathing delicacy.

But, unusually, Jeanne was considerably in awe of Helen with her razor-sharp tongue, and sparkling, biting sarcasm. Surprisingly for a society woman of those days, Helen was an extremely good shot. She habitually carried a 20-bore handmade Purdey gun, packed with her luggage for the various country house parties and smart weekend shoots.

But far more exciting for Jeanne, ever more enticing than the rather soft charms of the gentle Johnny, were the "Amorous Knights of Wycom", the infamous Hell Fire Club, so long established in the Hell Fire Caves at West Wycombe, of which Jeanne had heard so frequently, and through the dubious, experimental occult activities of the black magician Aleister Crowley.

These dark, damp catacombs were hidden away beneath the family church, besides the River Styx. Rumour had it, throughout the late Thirties, that wildly exciting sexual orgies and black masses were ritually practised there once again. And there was an additional excitement of the "Mollies Club"—a cross-dressing group of fashionable, worldly rich men dressed as women—and vice-versa. The Mollies were notorious as gin sippers, giggling behind feather fans.

Known from the 18th century as "Satan's blessed darkness", sinister devils' heads were carved into the chalk walls of the caves, in rooms known variously as the Inner Temple, the Buttery, the Banqueting Hall. Off these rooms led Nuns' Cells, Robing Rooms and a Cursing Well on the underground River Styx. Here, to Jeanne's ever-increasing excitement, scarlet Venetian gondolas ferried "nuns" and "monks", masked and robed across the water.

My mother, a superstitious woman despite her fanatical Catholicism, had long been attracted to the excitements—and the dangers—of both the erotic and the occult. Excitedly she saw herself as a reincarnation of one of the original "Nuns" of Medenham, perhaps Charlotte Hayes (a successful London bordello-keeper), or more likely the rather grander Frances, Viscountess Fane, authoress of *The Memoirs of a Lady of Quality*.

Deeply bored with her husband Sherman, and her useful father-in-law "Pop" Camoys (renowned as a colossal bore), even more bored by the stupefying provinciality of Henley, and country life, in Johnny's caves Jeanne could ogle the memory of the "Twelve Apostles", the nobility of the "Inner Order of St Francis (Dashwood) of Wycom". She was irresistibly compelled towards the heady exotica of the Hell Fire Club and the Dilettante Society.

The descendants of the original patrons, bearing such illustrious names as Frederick, Prince of Wales, the Earl of Bute, head of the millionaire Crichton-Stuart family, a keen admirer of pornography and Jeanne's near ancestor, the Earl of Westmoreland, the Earl of March—a great rake—all members of the Mollies Club, remained richly emblematic of all power, and throughout her life Jeanne was consistently intoxicated by power, consistent in pursuit of its lucrative gains.

Despite the amusement of her entanglement with the Hell Fire Caves, and her fling with "one of my *old* beaux", Johnny Dashwood, Jeanne became increasingly alarmed by Hell-Bags Helen—who had been married since 1922 and into a situation which well-suited the wife of the 5th Baronet.

A beautiful, compelling, highly-intelligent member of the aristocracy, Helen Dashwood was quite able to deal with Jeanne's unscrupulous sexual threat. So undermined did Jeanne become by Helen—who always addressed her as "you *funny* little thing, you!"—that, defeated, she hastily awarded her the sop of being the only woman to participate in the famous Stonor Park shooting parties.

These Saturday shooting parties, accompanied by sumptuous luncheons, fine wines and vintage ports poured from Sherman's cellars, continued in the presence of foreign royalty and ageing colonels throughout the Second World War and the period of ration books—which frequently went quite unheeded in well-heeled country mansions.

Even despite its criminal illegality, and the certain prospect of a prison sentence and heavy fine, Jeanne was never averse to flirting with the fire of the black market so prevalent in Henley-on-Thames during the war. Indeed she and a carpet-dealer, a certain Mr Affia, were eventually bought to court to answer certain "unfortunate" and extremely accurate charges of profiteering.

But Jeanne had always flirted with the finer points of the law. And, as a protégé of Commandant Jean Allen, a well-known Hitler admirer, when she enlisted as a police constable in wartime Henley—becoming uniformed driver to the heavily handsome, blue-eyed Chief Constable Sir Eric St Johnston—Jeanne, ever meticulous, honed her technique, and the finer details of the laws of England supremely to her own increasingly ambitious advantage.

But nevertheless she tried not to think too much of the ever-watchful, deeply suspicious Helen Dashwood, perhaps the only living person of whom Jeanne was genuinely frightened.

*

My second attempt as a bridesmaid, not long after Joyce's wedding in 1942, was even more exciting. The bridegroom, a diminutive "Uncle" known as "Carlos from Bogotá", was splendid in RAF uniform, blue-grey with a peaked, braided officer's cap, shiny black shoes with thick soles to make him look taller, two rows of striped medals on his chest.

Said Mama with a sneeze: "That pipsqueak cousin of mine is doin' something awfully essential for *mon général* You-Know-Who—dear old de Gaulle himself, actually, and I'm sworn to secrecy. Top secret and in absolute confidence." She winked and pealed with laughter. "Such a dear boy, my *primo* Carlos, he really has come a very long way from the family tin mines and shoot-outs in Bogotá, Biarritz and Bayonne. And to think of all our own adventures together up and down the Spanish lines. *Viva El Rey De España—V-E-R-D-E, olé!*" She poured out a long list of Spanish grandees with laughter. "It most certainly was 'heil Hitler!' in those divine times. This goddamned war is irritatin' the hell out of me. Gas masks aloft, *olé!*"

Mama brushed aside my sudden concern at her cold caught while on night duty with the local police. "My channels and canals are all blocked up, and that certainly hampers my pure Castilian accent," she said crossly. "What's more, my COIL has dropped out again, in Bell Street, right outside those chemists, Cartwrights, the bastards, goddamn it. Still, the 5th Baron Camoys knew all about that. He picked it up but Ralph's performance was almost worse than useless in the event." My mother reached for a Horse's Neck cocktail. "All your grandfather can do is to fuss about his haemorrhoids, hernia, and gas. Common or garden wind I call it. Effin' pills and balls to all that. The 5th Baron will be totally redundant to my needs once I get my hands on the 'entails and entrails' of those Bosmore and Cock's Leas estates." Mama paused in thought.

At the other end of the room, Bangpa-Pop Camoys' loose cheeks' flashed a dull purple again. He guffawed and cleared his throat.

Continued Mama: "As far as I am concerned, Ralph Camoys, I hope it all falls orf with frostbite. Your latest attempts are hardly up to scratch or snuff. You've been eatin' too many overcooked greens from Father Cereal's very questionable kitchen, and Miss Broslem's undesirable cuisine." She laughed, overcome with amusement at her own comments. "Onions, onions, and more onions. Less gas and hot air might help you to get your act back together old boy, *olé*, heil Hitler! And don't you ever forget it. Hot air's very much part of the family inheritance, after all, and don't think I can't remember YOUR family history and how you 'performed' during the Great War."

Bangpa-Pop pulled up his-baggy grey worsted trousers, and tried to fasten the belt buckle into place beneath a paunch which swelled well outside a tight white shirt.

"And just what were you up to in Madrid, Pop dear, as a hot-air aide-de-camp?" asked Mama. She did not wait for his answer. "'You were certainly hot on the job and that was long before you conned that tedious and common American millionairess Mildew Constance Sherman in New York."

Bangpa-Pop explained, that he was only doing his duty as best man to Lord Decies.

Mama leaned back and clicked her elegant dark red finger nails, swinging her heavy gold bracelets into one another with a crash. Reflectively she powdered her face. "If you can't take the competition, old boy, you can beat it. As far as I'm concerned you're merely the borin' beekeeper from the Bosmore Estate, and you don't even own it, blast your four balls and your damned stupid coronet, *olé!* But I shall own Bosmore and Cock's Leas, very soon. So you can take your gas-mask, and tinpot helmet, and piss orf out of here up to Piss-hill if you can't take the heat!" Mama roared with laughter.

The wedding of *Primo* Tio Carlos, bored my mother. As she said: "It was SO English, really dreadfully dull, especially when you consider our times together Cousin Carlos and I racin' about, up and down those Spanish borderlines." She yawned. "Of course I was there in the Civil War, with my darlin' De Zoo and Merry del Val cousins. Not to mention my darlin' old brother-in-law Mon del Moral—only a common or garden Marqués you know. And my very own divine swashbucklin' Cousin Rupert Bellville smugglin' a few arms in his aeroplane. Ever so slightly inebriated, if you know what I mean and got effin' caught in the wrong lines, ha, ha, *olé!* The British Navy had to send in a frigate to avoid a diplomatic incident, ha, ha, and it was all very much heil Hitler in those merry days I can assure you." Mama glared around at everyone. "And, of course, my very own darlin' Dick Sheepshanks was bumped orf right in front of me by that wretch from our Anglo-German Fellowship, Kim Philby. Just another bastard to add to a long line of bastards—my aristo self included. *Olé* and *viva el rey de España!* I'm not a Royalist for nothin'." Mama dabbed a tear from her eye. "Get me that atlas immediately, Julia you tiresome child, and I'll show you just where Madrid and Teruel are."

As Mama jabbed at the map of Franco's Spain, all these new borders fascinated me. Mr White, the head gardener and a devout Plymouth Brethren member, cultivated vast herbaceous borders in the walled garden at Stonor Park. He told me the names of the flowers: "They's delphiniums and hollyhocks and peonies, Miss Julia, and larkspurs."

Other borders which Mama so frequently mentioned were the heavily printed black ones around all the death cards, announcements and obituaries that she kept with a pile of holy pictures in a black leather-bound St Andrew's missal. Without doubt, this was her favourite prayerbook. "It was given to me by my beloved boyfriend, such a saint of a man, super-spy in Special Operations, darlin' Cousin Andrew Constable Maxwell. A proper Maxwell you know, very nearly a Fitzalan Howard. He just missed bein' the Duke of Norfolk by a whisker, dammit!" Mama paused for a sip of elevenses before continuing happily. "So damned annoying that darlin' Andrew missed out but at least his Swiss bank account has proved such a boon to me in all my agonisin' poverty and terrible sufferin' in this damned annoyin' war." She sighed deeply. "Oh the inconvenience!" She sniffed into a delicately embroidered and richly scented handkerchief. "Valencia lace, most certainly. Only the very finest for me," she purred. With a limp hand she lightly dabbed at her brow.

Bellville, Maxwell, Fitzalan Howard . . . I spent many hours pondering the litany of names that I heard so often recited. Irún, Teruel, San Sebastián, Biarritz, Bayonne, Madrid, Manzandeo, del Moral, Merry del Val, and Mugaburu de Zulueta were among the ones I heard most, frequently rolling off my mother's tongue with "my divinely aristo Castilian accent, a very *racée* pronunciation you know!" Perplexing it may have been but at least it helped me to understand whenever my Spanish grandfather Pedro de Zulueta came to see Mama, his eldest child.

Like Bangpa-Pop, Pedro de Zoo too had a moustache, but not so white. My mother was very proud of her Castilian ancestry, the de Zulueta Mugaburus and Counts of Torre Diaz, and, as she said, "darlin' old Pedro really is a most frightfully important go-between these days, most terribly busy doin' something vitally important for that divine Franco. He's up to his eyeballs in it with your ancient Uncle Mon del Moral. Up and down those 'Portugoose' borders to boot. *Olé!*" Mama sat back on the cut yellow velvet sofa in the drawing room at Assendon Lodge next to her father, smoking happily. "Too bad I'm an aristo bastard, but someone is going to pay for it in no uncertain terms. Come to think of it, that deadly dreary bore, my demi-semi-sister Gytha, has been duped and dumped her husband by the Marqués himself. Fancy that! The Marquesa left on her own to starve in a Portuguese convent with their two brats. Frightfully good riddance to bad rubbish and religious mania. To say nothing of all those useless rosary beads." She laughed happily, throatily.

Bangpa-Pop did not seem happy to see my Spanish grandfather Pedro and he burped uneasily as Mama regaled him with details of what the visiting "Guns" and "Uncles" at Assendon were doing for war efforts. Too old for active service, they seemed to be very busily occupied.

"War motions and manoeuvres are such frightfully important matters," said Mama brightly.

But my English grandfather gave the impression that he did not do very much during the war, he occasionally was to be seen in a sloppy baggy uniform of khaki felt with a beret perched on one side of his head.

"Pop-goes-the-Weasel is frightfully active in the Home Guard and the Air Raid Precautions," explained my mother. "Based at Assendon Lodge and up at Bosmore you know, keepin' close watch on things and just waitin' for the all clear from that damned siren. Sounds just like that crashin', deadly old bore of a witch Lady Ovey wailin' again over at Assendon Sawmills."

My Spanish grandfather seemed ever anxious to leave for his house at Old Windsor. Usually he came with his sister—tall, gaunt, white-faced Aunt Tia María. But this time she was indisposed at the Onslow Court Hotel with the shingles.

"Where's the money?" Mama would demand indignantly. "I simply can't be kept waitin' yet again. Short of a bob or two you know. Frightfully awkward, if you see my meanin', for an aristo Castilian bastard like myself. I will just have to put someone else out on the street like those other damnnuisance nannies. And I ALWAYS keep my word," Mama would tartly warn as Pedro retreated through the gate at Assendon Lodge. "With any luck you'll catch the pox!" she screamed furiously over the fence at his departing figure.

My all-English grandfather Bangpa-Pop wore an important tin helmet and had a gas mask permanently at the ready for emergencies and for a dash to the Assendon Lodge air-raid shelter, though in reality it was only a cellar occupied by a solitary mouse. Occasionally he did things with his bees and beehives together with the florid-faced parish priest Father Seyres, whose name Mama seemed to have difficulty in pronouncing.

"That André Cereal needs to go straight to the cleaners, lock, stock and barrel," my mother often sniffed, looking out of the window.

Father André Seyres, or "Cereal", was a plump French cleric officially in residence at Stonor since 1931. A member of the order of the Fathers of the Sacred Heart, he had managed to have a house built for his own use in Stonor village. Constructed in orange brick, it was in the style of a miniature French seaside villa. His housekeeper was an Irishwoman Miss Broslem, who played the harmonium in the chapel at the Park.

I could see that some of Father Seyres' scrambled egg breakfast had landed halfway down a black ribbed silk encased stomach.

"And just where did he get those contraband eggs in wartime?" exclaimed Mama. "Most of us are just existin' on water-glass and all that powdered muck. I shall report him immediately to the powers that be for black marketin'. I've done it before and I'll damn well do it again. Just look what happened to Sherman's cousin Countess Peel at my last denunciation. No one crosses my path without payin' for it." She dropped her cigarette end onto the nursery dining-room floor and ground it into the lino with her heel.

Father Seyres and Bangpa-Pop were dressed up in voluminous green hairnets, an anti-bee sting device beneath large and floppy white linen hats. These they pulled loosely down over their very pink faces for protection. Thick black clouds of bees hummed round hives in the unkempt, nettle-strewn garden of Bosmore, which was wild, windy and untidy. The house stood starkly on top of a hill with a far-distant view of Windsor Castle.

Bangpa-Pop always said he "much preferred to knock something up at Assendon rather than garden". He had brought his carpentry kit with him, down to stay at Assendon Lodge "in case the little woman needs some emergency repairs". On these occasions Bangpa-Pop seldom had to wear uniform, only his tin helmet and once in a while the gas mask.

"We've been aidin' the war effort and practisin' with the new gas chambers as it's Pop's day off from the ARP. He's even giving the Home Guard a rest, *olé!*" Mama saluted. "Heil Hitler!"

Summer or winter, my English grandfather would invariably be found in a baggy jacket of tweed or crumpled linen, and creased worsted trousers. This was Bangpa-Pop's daywear. At night times—I was put to bed firmly at 6pm—he was known to don a navy-blue double-breasted suit and to take Mama down to Henley for an outing.

"We're orf to that hideous town hall of silly Billy Hambleden's for a hop," Mama explained hastily one night as she rushed out of Assendon Lodge. "I'm wearing one of my little black numbers tonight and just a sprinklin' of darlin' Barbara Hutton's rubies."

Mama swung round towards the front door in a pair of high-heeled patent leather shoes with peep toes. I could see scarlet-painted toe-nails through her evening stockings, made of very fine blond silk.

"I really can't take synthetics next to my sensitive aristo skin," laughed Mama. "Quite plainly I simply have to have silk and nylon in the day. That's where Sherman's American side can be made really useful. Don't you agree Pop dear?" Laughing, she continued: "A little encouragement in this area really produces rapid results. After all I have to keep the supply ship goin'." Throwing open the door she propelled my grandfather in front of her. "I'm damned if I am going to go without after all my agonisin' sufferin's, effin' inconvenient war or no war!"

Bangpa-Pop guffawed, missing his step. Mama gave him an impatient shove. "Jump to it I said, Ralph you crashin' old bore. And you'll just have to lump it tonight because you're sharin' the hop in Henley with my own darlin' member of parliament Sir Gifford Fox. And that's that, whether you like it or not. Too damned bad if you don't, and don't you ever forget that you're a kept man, TAGGIN' on to Mildew's American millions."

I watched timidly out of the nursery window as Mama, still laughing and shouting, slid into the car beside Bangpa-Pop.

"Don't you ever forget it was old Mildew Camoys who bought you out of the bankruptcy court in 1937. So watch your step. Or you might queer your own pitch," she warned him with a dangerous smile.

Mama looked beautiful night or day, habitually smelling of exotic perfume, rich and heavy. One day I asked Mama what it was but she wasn't in the least amused: "Don't you EVER forget, borin' brat that you are, that my very special French scent is never, EVER called 'perfume'. That really is most frightfully common and *cursi*—that's Spanish in case you forget my aristo Castilian ancestry—ever to say anything as nouveau as 'perfume'." Sighing with exasperation, Mama flicked her cigarette ash in my direction. "Just what I would expect comin' from you. As it is, my SCENT comes straight from a very well known beau in Bordeaux. And there's a lot more to come. I've seen to that, and make no mistake."

Ever mystified by Mama's statements and expressions, I asked Ruby again to explain them to me. But Ruby only sighed and, as she always did, said soothingly: "There, there, Miss Julia."

And when I asked Mama why her stocking seams sometimes wobbled up the backs of her legs, and sometimes didn't, and what a "beau' was, her reply to me was brief: "Stockin's? Sherman's ridiculous brat that you are, you can put a SOCK in it and eff orf. Can't you see that I'm extremely busy and that you are extremely stupid. Feckless to boot!" She delivered a cuff round my ears.

I blinked hard as I tried to keep the tears from welling up but Mama just laughed. "For God's sake, stop complainin' child. You bore me to tears myself. But what can I expect of Sherman's once-orf brat?" She winked again at Bangpa-Pop. "Do stop just hangin' around, Pop, and get back to those vital entrails. You bore me almost as much as Julia does these weary-makin' days!"

So saying my mother stamped out of the room, banging the door shut as she went.

3

A Memory of Jeanne's Childhood

Jeanne Mary was born in London on 22 May 1913, the daughter of the Hon Frances Stourton, the only daughter of Viscount Southwell, of Castle Mattress, County Limerick. Her birth certificate registered Jeanne as the daughter of Major Herbert Marmaduke Stourton, army officer and lieutenant in the Oxfordshire Yeomanry Cavalry.

In actuality, Jeanne was the illegitimate daughter of a Spanish grandee, the bachelor diplomat Don Pedro de Zulueta, whose uncle the Marqués Merry del Val was Spanish ambassador to the Court of St James. Another uncle, Cardinal Rafael Borja Merry del Val, was to become secretary of state to Pope Pius XI, and mentor and teacher to Cardinal Pacelli, later Pope Pius XII.

Jeanne's mother Frances, widely known as "Feckless Fanny", had lost her father as a very small child when Viscount Southwell had committed suicide. He shot himself in 1878 when his daughter was four years old, her elder brother but six. Fanny, as the girl became known, became an heiress-at-law, a large fortune to become hers on attaining the age of 21.

Feckless Fanny Southwell was a very pretty child and young woman: Irish, French, Welsh and Scottish by blood, her mother the elder daughter of Sir Pyers Mostyn, baronet of Telacre, Flintshire, and the grand-daughter of Lord and Lady Lovat of Beaufort Castle, Beauly, Inverness. Fanny's French ancestor was the Countess Walsh-Serrant of Château Serrant in the Loire Valley. These families had always been Roman Catholic despite the Reformation at the time of Henry VIII and his daughter Elizabeth I.

Thus Fanny's own background was that of strict, austere Catholicism, and tainted by the Mortal Sin (as the Church deemed it) of her father's suicide. Her mother Charlotte was a young widow who had perforce to live out her life in widow's weeds, wedded to her rosary beads. And so Fanny was sent away aged twelve to the newly formed convent of St Mary's, Ascot, where her best friend, a future reverend mother of the Order of the Institute of the Blessed Virgin Mary (an international order of teaching nuns founded in the 16th century by the Yorkshirewoman Mary Ward), was Cecilia Marshall of Lancashire banking fame. There is at the convent a charming photograph of the first dozen girls there in 1886 showing the prettiness of Fanny herself.

But in fact Jeanne Stourton suffered humiliation and deep indignity from being forced as a young woman to live with her mother in a humble flat over a butcher's shop. Throughout her life this humiliation and insult stayed with her. She talked, mocked and scoffed about it frequently. And smouldered with resentment since Fanny Stourton had taken to drugs after Jeanne's birth, and desertion by her husband. This depleted her fragile finances and increased the pressure on Jeanne to "do well", to better herself from a sorry, somewhat sordid experience. It made her all the more ambitious, the more ruthless in her technique with men. And, unlike her mother, Jeanne actually made money from sex.

Most of Jeanne's immediate Roman Catholic circle of family, whether English, Welsh, Scottish or Spanish, were extremely right-wing, conspicuously anti-Semitic, anti-communist. Many English Catholics of the Establishment were openly anti-Semitic, encouraged by outspoken policies such as those promulgated by Jeanne's own Spanish great-uncle Rafael Merry del Val and Cardinal Pacelli (there are substantial anti-Jewish quotes from the cardinal in the British press of the time).

Most prominent among these distinguished families were the Earls of Bute, bearing the name of Crichton-Stuart, of Mount Stuart, Isle of Bute, and of Algeciras—whence an immense family fortune. As closely related to Jeanne were the families of the Duke of Norfolk (FitzAlan Howard), the Earl of Perth (Drummond), whose wife was born Constable Maxwell, and Lord Lovat of Beaufort Castle, Beauly.

Jeanne grew up surrounded by eligible bachelors of these closely related, intertwined relatives. Between them they held vast tracts of land in England, Wales and Scotland, Ireland and very considerable fortunes. Many of the pre-Reformation Catholics—of Recusant family fame—had the added lustre, privilege and prestige of owning their own private chapels. This too had, and still has, considerable snob value and elitism.

Furthermore most of these castles and estates still had private chaplains living in, attending the family meals, the various social functions. An added dimension of this denomination was a fascination with, and competition in the numbers of hiding-holes that houses such as Stonor, East Hendred (Eyston) and others could be found to contain, left over from the persecution of the Reformation years.

To the serried ranks of these eligible young men, Jeanne was as Continental as they were, to a large extent, provincial, narrow-minded and lacking culture despite their fortunes. However, Jeanne in her religious outlook more than concurred with her male and female relatives, Princess Blücher included. The Spanish Civil War further enhanced extreme views of the British upper class, some of whom, including the journalist-writer Peter Kemp (*The Thorns of Memory*) went to fight for Franco.

Jeanne was also influenced by her direct French ancestry through her own Irish-French descent: the Counts of Walsh-Serrant, of Chateau Serrant, a stunning castle in the Loire Valley. To her group of Roman Catholics, ancestor worship or, at least, the worship of their own pedigrees was and remains essential. And yet, by and large, it was also important that there should not be the taint of too much foreign, Continental blood—especially in the men.

The combination in Jeanne of extreme orthodox religious, thus political, views of the far right in combination with her glamour and conspicuous sex appeal was, therefore, more acceptable to her male contemporaries than to her female ones—many of whom were, with justification, extremely alarmed from the early days by Jeanne's precocity and innate sense of revenge, vengefulness. And she triumphed in her own extremes of Catholicism, pleasing to the hierarchy both in London and at the Vatican, where various of her immediate family other than Cardinal Merry del Val held powerful positions.

Throughout her life Jeanne was a superstitious woman whose main weapon against her own immediate family was the over-use of both the Catechism and the Bible. She was therefore as she had always been, a ruthless religious fundamentalist whose paradoxical enjoyment, as she herself expressed it, was the knowledge that the head of the village priest had been kicked down the street of the de Zulueta family estate of La Alcaría early on during the Spanish Civil War. Jeanne would relate the tale with relish, taunting and tormenting uneasy lunch guests at her famous shooting parties, whether at Assendon Lodge or Stonor Park. The chaplain at the time, Archbishop David Mathew, would clear his throat, hapless betweeded men would turn uneasily in their Gothic Revival heavily spiked chairs, while a frequent guest, Graham Greene, would remark quite mildly on Jeanne's cruelty—which always elicited an amused, throaty laugh from Jeanne and complete silence from Sherman.

Jeanne certainly saw herself as an expert on the topic of Mortal Sin. As also on the punitive yet purgative powers of the Sacrament of the Confessional. One of her manias, oft expressed, was that I myself, from the age of six, was in perpetual danger of this condition. A powerful terrifying technique, Jeanne was proud of the Spanish Inquisition, the blood of which seemed to course through her veins.

She was especially close to her Crichton-Stuart and Constable Maxwell male cousins. Their sister Ursula executed a remarkable terracotta likeness of Jeanne in the mid-Thirties when she was up in Scotland for the traditional Highland Meeting, a ball where the men wore full-dress kilts and the women long white ballgowns with the family tartan draped across a shoulder.

On such occasions, Jeanne would also meet her cousin-by-marriage Captain Maule Ramsay, married to Ismay Crichton-Stuart. He was a great-grandson of Queen Victoria and the only member of parliament to be imprisoned, together with his wife, along with Sir Oswald Mosley under Regulation 18b during the Second World War. It was Captain Ramsay who founded the Right Club in May 1939, the extreme views of which led to others of Jeanne's immediate circle and friends, such as Sir Barry and Lady Domville, being imprisoned for their openly admiring, wildly anti-Semitic, openly pro-Nazi standpoint. This group, several of whom came both to Assendon Lodge and Stonor Park as friends of Jeanne's from 1939 onwards, among them Lord Lymington (later Earl of Portsmouth), the Duke of Wellington, Colonel Moore-Brabazon, Lord Brocket, Lady (Nancy) Astor, her son Lord "Bill" Astor, Lord Darnley, openly despised and detested Jews and feared their purported financial power. Jeanne's cousin, the Hon J. J. Stourton, MP, was also among this group.

Mollie Hiscox, a member of the British Union of Fascists, one of several right-wing bodies, wrote to Hitler as follows:

31/8/39
The Führer & Reichskanzler
Adolf Hitler
Reichskanzlei
Berlin

Dear Herr Hitler

As an Englishwoman who was very often in Germany,
I wish you to know that I have unlimited trust in you.

Yours,
Mollie Hiscox

The mistress of Jock Houston, Miss Hiscox was just one of Jeanne's circle of acquaintances and close friends, many of them cousins, with the same political philosophy. Prominent among all Jeanne's friends and influences were those of Ribbentrop's circle—as openly announced in the social and court circulars in *The Times* round which high society revolved, together with magazines such as *The Tatler & Bystander* and *The Sketch*.

Jeanne's politics were coloured and informed by her immediate family foremost. Her real father came from a staunchly monarchist grandee Spanish family with strong South American connections—they were landowners on a vast scale, supplying ambassadors, cardinals, army officers. Like Jeanne's close relatives of the Mowbray and Stourton family and other distant cousins, the Hon Sir Henry ("Harry") Stonor and his brother the Hon Edward Stonor, they belonged to societies called The Anti-Communist and The Anti-Socialist Leagues.

"Yids", "Niggers", Poor White Trash", "Eyties" and "Frogs" were widely reviled and despised and socially rarely acceptable, unless there were special, redeeming circumstances. Relatives who had served in the Colonial Service often came to be regarded with suspicion.

Even such an illustrious military figure as Major-General Sir Hugh Pereira was considered to have "a touch of the tar brush" from his ancestry in Macao. The white Maharajah of Sarawak, Sir Charles Vyner de Windt Brooke, however, was considered most pure-blooded—possibly because he was a king in all but name.

This Roman Catholic minority was, therefore, inward-looking, conservative, narrow-minded and priggish. After the Reformation, it was not until the nineteenth century that there was far more opportunity when the prime minister Benjamin Disraeli successfully brought out of abeyance five Roman Catholic peers to serve in minor office. The 3rd Lord Camoys, as Mr Thomas Stonor, was elected the first member of parliament as a practising Roman Catholic since the Reformation for Oxford. Unfortunately he was found to have won his election through rigging his votes and was forced to resign within less than three months. Nevertheless, he would achieve entrance to the House of Lords.

Jeanne's politics were also coloured by pedigrees, as evidenced at the College of Arms, in the superb books of reference including the respected *Debrett's* and *Burke's Peerage*, kept in all the best drawing rooms across the nation. She wanted and aspired to what could be thus attained: vast wealth, a title, servants (mostly "Kept In Their Places"), large estates, and best of all wonderful family jewels, jewellery such as Barbara Hutton had supplied Jeanne with but on an even grander scale, at least one diamond tiara included.

British society in the Twenties and Thirties was strictly hierarchical, and politics among the group which Jeanne moved in were brutal and simplistic. Like those around her, Jeanne was convinced that she had the "Divine Right of Kings", directly inherited from King Charles I. This divine right later convinced her that she was entitled to take her own King Charles spaniel to Mass in private chapels. This attitude allowed too the condonance of capital punishment, flogging, and imprisonment for homosexuals.

In all these matters, Jeanne was considered an "orthodox" Roman Catholic whether during the Spanish Civil War, where she was openly Falangist as her immediate Spanish family, or during the run-up to the Second World War. Even during the Second World War her close friends, many of whom belonged to the Anglo-Spanish Fellowship and similar organisations, were frequently to be seen in Jeanne's company, including the local Henley MP, the pro-Fascist Sir Gifford Fox (well known to have had an affair with Jeanne). She openly cohorted with the various cardinals, Hinsley and Heenan especially, and the various archbishops of Birmingham (the diocese in which lies Stonor) as also the American archbishop, later cardinal, Frank Spellman. Her close relatives included at least one archbishop and a monsignor, and she was well acquainted with the papal court of Pope Pius XII in Rome.

Above all, these English Catholics were tight-knit, and, being a small group comparatively, everyone knew everyone else. Furthermore they knew all about one another. They were a clique, predictable, almost Calvinistic in outlook, inbred, inward-looking – very far removed from the European Catholic. Additionally, they were inbred sometimes to the point of inheriting deep emotional psychological problems, as with the Acton family where one great-uncle and bachelor, the 63-year-old Lord Acton was unusually given dispensation by the Pope in the latter part of the 19th century to marry his niece of only 16 years old.

Sadly, any such dispensation was expressly forbidden to Julia Stonor, the granddaughter of Sir Robert Peel, when permission was sought from the Vatican so that she could marry her fiancé the Duke of York, Prince Albert George, then the second son of King Edward VII but later to succeed him to the throne. No devout and dutiful Catholic could ignore this refusal. So Julia Stonor could not, as the king had fondly hoped, elope with Prince Albert George and marry him while he was still a younger son. Instead, she married an eligible if slightly mysterious Frenchman, the Marquis d'Hautpoul from Toulouse.

4

'Straight from the Horse's Neck'

At Assendon Lodge we had dogs that we called bitches. Mr Machin, the vet and Mama explained they were "females of the species". These great danes and labradors had soft, gentle personalities which I found at odds with my mother's most emphatic use of the word in her language and phrases. I had asked about this but decided not to ask more questions for a while after my mother had surreptitiously pinched me sharply on my bottom, followed by a slap across my equally plump cheeks.

"Your figure is quite gross," she had added crossly as she hurried out to another hop at Henley town hall. "Totally out of proportion. And furthermore, you promise to be top-heavy, tiresome, demandin' child of Sherman's that you are. You never fail to blight my pleasures."

The following morning Mama was again indignant: "That dreadful Miss Cooper with the ginger hair who smells like a polecat and thinks she's a reincarnation of Queen Elizabeth the First—though, come to think of it she does have a lot of money—blighted my time at the hop in that hideous Edwardian pile which Billy Hambleden's father built. That barrow-boy made his entire fortune sellin' newspapers on the street corner you know." She paused for breath. "Such a frightfully nouveau peer, only being W. H. Smith and a vulgar discount viscount at that," she sniffed derisively.

Uncle Billy Hambleden was another short-statured Gun and a kind and friendly Uncle for whom I had to pray each night. Like many of my other Uncles, he had a moustache, a red one. I supposed there to be some connection to Miss Cooper's own ginger-red hair, but Mama's response to this was terse: "And Miss Cooper can keep her nosey-parker habits to herself. Too bad she owns the best lawyers in town."

On one afternoon Mama took me with her on a drive to Hambleden in Granny Camoys' blue and silver Chevrolet brake. The Hambleden estate had been sold off by my American grandmother, she busily explained as we hurtled down the narrow lanes. "Your tedious American grandmother, old Mildew, Lady C, actually bought it from poor, penniless—useless too, come to think of it—Bangpa-Pop to save his skin."

Now Uncle Billy owned not only Hambleden valley and the village within it but also Greenlands, a large mansion house by the Thames. This impressive white Twenties residence with green shutters was set right on the edge of the river. Down its long, curling drive Mama drove fast and furiously, in jolts and starts, thundering in and out of dangerously deep puddles making the wheels spin wildly round in the slime. The window wide open, her cigarette smouldering wildly in the wind, she roared with laughter as she talked.

We skidded to a halt in front of the house and I was promptly jettisoned from the car and left to wait on a narrow bench outside a pair of dark green tall shutters, mysteriously firmly closed. "My darlin' Billie's very own slatted shutters," chuckled Mama as she disappeared inside the house.

I did what I was told—there was nowhere for me to go. Marooned by the river, I waited. In due course Mama re-emerged, smoothing her skirt.

Once more back at Assendon Lodge, she ran to the drawing room and commenced slitting open the day's post with a heavily coroneted silver paper knife.

One letter in particular had caught her attention . . .

"The trouble with that nosey-parker Miss Cooper, and her bossy-baggage sister too, is that they think they know everythin' round here. And it comes from owning a third-rate firm of lawyers in West Street—of all suburban places. How dare she insinuate in this letter that I'm having it orf with a peer of the realm, my father-in-law Ralph Camoys—of all people. Boot's on the other foot come to think of it, Pop's got a terminal case of brewer's droop if you really want to know. And that foxy old gel dares to mention darlin' little pipsqueak Sir Gifford Fox in the same breath, dammit."

Rushing to the boiler Mama tore the offending document in shreds and hurled it into the flames. And calmly sat down to read *The Daily Graphic*. "It belongs to my old beau Kemsley," she would explain. "I'm frightfully keen on the strawberry leaves in his coronet. More than a bob or two inbetween the darlin' Berry boys. We all went orf to the Olympic Games together in 1936 with dear Chips Channon—a frightfully successful MP you know, Chicago millionaire married to one of those crashin' bores of the Guinness family. Too bad about Chips's BOYFRIENDS, ha, ha!" Mama's laughter tinkled around the kitchen and nursery quarters. It was followed by a deep, throaty cough as she inhaled more cigarette smoke.

Even when my mother had no official calls and callers, and Bangpa was away ("Bangpa-Pop's just popped up to Bosmore for the afternoon bee round"), without stopping Mama would continue her conversations to an exclusive audience of Ruby Heath and very small me. But we were expected neither to reply nor pass comment. Ruby Heath sighed deeply as I took a deep breath of delight—at least Mama was talking to me even if I wasn't permitted to join in. But she barely acknowledged Ruby, who was busy down on her hands and knees scrubbing stone-flagged floors.

"Scrub harder and get a move on with it Ruby," ordered my mother sharply as she finally left the room. "And make sure you keep the stupid brat with you. I'm orf back to the study and not to be disturbed in any circumstances. And should there be a telephone call, you may knock at the door and wait until I answer. Most strictly out-of-bounds to you, child," she said tartly, turning to me. "You can bugger orf now, Julia, young lady. You're just borin' me to tears as usual."

Deftly kicking my shins, Mama swept past in a aura of exotic scent, slamming the door as she exited.

*

While "Papa" who had been "Daddy" was away in the war, Bangpa-Pop lived mostly at Assendon Lodge and when he wasn't there he would be at the nearby Bosmore estate where Mama would drive up to visit him in Granny Camoys' car.

This 2,000-acre estate and house belonged to Granny even though she lived in Rhode Island. It was barely two miles away up a narrow lane through banked beech trees and layer upon layer of leaf-mould at the top of a steep gravelled drive. The road passed the mysterious, very dirty, run-down farmyard of Old Mrs Phillips and her ragged pack of howling, snarling dogs.

"Squalid old hag!" Mama shrieked one day as she hiccuped through the gears of Granny's Chevrolet, making the car shoot forward in the centre of the Fawley Bottom Lane that led to the square orange brick house of Bosmore, standing starkly in knee-high weeds and unmown grasses.

Granny Camoys' brake fitted eight people with ease into its three rows of brown leather seats. The car had several doors and was painted a light blue with panels of narrow wooden slats. The radiator, mudguards and finish were a bright chrome. But this cheerful 1938 vintage vehicle had come to a premature end during the war, finishing its life a lonely wreck under a wizened crab-apple tree. Here it lay rotting in the park at Stonor, not far away from the moat, nuzzled by a bone-thin ragged grey donkey.

"One of my favourite geldin's, that dear old donkey Ned," exclaimed Mama. "Used to pull my pony trap down to the Lower Assendon Sewage Works. On a good day that is," she added hastily.

In reality, Ned had been a recalcitrant puller, known to hurl the human contents of Mama's pony trap into the nearest ditch.

Meanwhile Mama manoeuvred through the ruts and potholes of Bosmore drive until the car shuddered to a halt with a lurch and a jolt outside a tin barn piled high with straw bales.

"Hurry up and get out immediately child," ordered my mother. "I've absolutely no time to waste on you. You can amuse yourself inside the barn until I call you, and stay put there until then."

Obediently I installed myself in this barn filled with bright-yellow straw bales. It was also filled with bluebottle flies and thick dark cobwebs. I hid tremulously between the bales while bats fluttered round the beams of the ceiling and swooped towards the floor. Several of the flies were caught up in spider's webs while chickens busily scratched at themselves and pecked at the frosty ground foraging for food. With fresh peals of laughter, Mama had already explained that "those are Granny Mildew's very own Rhode Island Reds, complete with roosters to boot, ha, ha!" This was all the more confusing as I knew that Granny Camoys lived in America and not here at Bosmore. I was curious that Bangpa-Pop seemed to belong to Mama and lived in an English house, which belonged to my American Granny, and so I asked Mama.

As usual Mama was infuriated. Ceaselessly, unsuccessfully, I had always tried to please her. I was excited when and if I occasionally made her laugh. I could never understand why this happened, nor could I ever anticipate when my mother would be amused. She was obviously far happier angry. I tried increasingly to please her, and to keep physically as close as possible to her side. This was not a success.

"Small wonder you bore me so," she said in reply to my question. "You remind me of one of the dogs. Absolutely infatuated, over-devoted and completely idiotic. What you need my child is a good quick kick in the backside."

So saying she took a flying leap with a smart new Delman shoe. Made of a dark-brown corrugated leather, it was "the very latest new-look in crocodile. Your divine Uncle Charlie Aramayo from Bogotá caught me one specially." She laughed merrily.

Mama could only wear hand-made shoes, and always strong ones. "My well-bred, aristocratic Castilian foot is far too sensitive to wear ready-mades," she would say grandly, throwing off Newmarket boots, brogues, sandals, and high heels in a random clatter.

She would order Ruby to put the shoe-trees in, but only after polishing the footwear with a silk cloth (or "clorth" as Mama pronounced it). There were row upon row of shoes, sandals, boots in her cupboards in the summer and winter bedrooms. Enraptured I would gaze and count secretly.

Mama was always prepared for an emergency underfoot, such as the serious problem of mud during and after early morning walks with Uncle Jack Rutherford at The Warren, a derelict Victorian house hidden high up in the park at Stonor. Once returned, Mama would don a shiny white plastic overall and hasten to clean her shoes in the kitchen, scraping soil swiftly into the sink and washing it away.

"Don't you dare look, Ruby Heath!" she shouted as she scrubbed. "And keep that brat Julia well out of my sight."

Mama hated to be observed by me in her personal perambulations unless invited. I rarely was. "You're starin' at me AGAIN, Julia," she had snapped on one occasion as I watched her put on a surgical apron. "I've caught you redhanded. What impertinence. I simply won't have it. Fetch the catechism *muy pronto*, and *I* will decide which of the Mortal Sins you have committed today."

As usual, she lit another cigarette and poured from a bottle of dark brown liquid into a broad-stemmed glass. The vessel, one of Papa's, was a translucent green, its stem slightly crooked but, as she explained, "I can only use hand-made glasses for my delicate constitution. Furthermore everything that once belonged to Sherman is now mine and absolutely MINE alone. *Olé!* Heil Hitler!"

She tossed the Horse's Neck cocktail down her throat, ignoring the cigarette that still hung from the corner of her mouth. Turning on her heel to leave, she snapped back: "If you MUST know where my surgical apron came from, it was my very own medical periodical *The Lancet* no less, which had a special offer: six for the price of one. Frightfully useful for when I'm on duty and in the night wards seein' to this and that."

There was as little chance of sharing Mama's attention when she was on the telephone. Between the clutter of cocktail glasses, brogue walking shoes, stiff black shoe brushes and a cascade of cigarette ash, she juggled the ever-ringing telephone with dexterity.

Reaching over the kitchen table she shouted merrily down the mouthpiece to a Harpsden "Uncle" and "Gun", Colonel Guy de Pass, Papa's regimental commander, a tiny man of Spanish-Jewish origin. He too had a bristling moustache with black eyes set too close together behind a sharp nose. But, as Mama pointed out, "the darlin' man may be minuscule, but he is a millionaire and owns all that land at Harpsden and Huntswood. Too bad his giantess of a wife, that Anne—Afrikaner heavily lapsed Cartholic to you—is such a pill. So disapprovin' she bores me to tears. I'm jugglin' between you and darlin' old Alan Hartley," shouted Mama down the black Bakelite receiver. "Just plannin' for another outin' to a hop at Henley in that monstrous town hall of Billy Hambleden's."

Alan Hartley was our doctor sometimes at Assendon Lodge. He was the son-in-law of Old Mrs Selwyn, the wife of the Protestant minister at Remenham Rowing Club, and had "come South" before the war from the Scottish Lowlands. The Selwyns were also co-members of the Anglo-German Fellowship.

"Too bad Alan is not distinguished enough to wear anything more than tartan trews. No kilt for him," my mother laughed throatily down the telephone before shouting: "Corf it up and spit it out, I always say, *olé!*" The dense haze of cigarette smoke surrounding her smelt of rich perfume. "Coco Chanel, actually," said Mama. She sniffed.

Of course, there was no mention of a Mr Chanel. Nor indeed of the wives of many of my numerous "Uncles". They seemed to be just as Mama described them, "bachelors of my whims, convenience and comfort".

Early on at Assendon Lodge, Mummy-who-had-become-Mama from the earliest days was busily occupied in her study each morning with Bangpa-Pop.

"I'm toilin' away at my essential war work. And Old Pop-goes-the-Weasel is tryin' his hardest to concentrate his pin-brain on those vital entrails and entails." She had spied me peering through a gap in the door and shouted to get her another Horse's Neck. I had been taught how to mix these essential cocktail elevenses quite early in the war. The telephone dangling in her hand Mama shouted again: "No time to waste between my vital estate work up at the Park and my emergency night duties at Maidensgrove."

These wartime duties took up a great deal of my mother's time and energy, night and day. So mixing her drink correctly to aid her concentration on such duties was not an easy task.

"For God's sake, go easy with the ginger ale! You'll DROWN the brandy you hopeless little fool. But not before I drown YOU, Sherman's tedious brat that you are."

Mama's wartime duties invariably took her away at night. Smartly dressed in the silver-buttoned hand-tailored uniform of a Special Constable, she would disappear in the later afternoon or early evening into a local police constabulary car together with a colonel—Uncle Eric St Johnston—sometimes in mufti but mostly in full-dress uniform.

Mama was always happy to explain her hush-hush role: "My actual beat covers a wide field: Nettlebed, Russells Water, Piss-Hill, Henley, all the way to Oxford and that sort of thing. Absolutely top secret in this goddamned war of course. My lips are sealed. GUARDIN' AGAINST ENEMY ACTIONS, olé!"

Inbetween times, she dashed around the countryside in Granny Camoys' Chevrolet before its demise, perched high up at the driving wheel on a smart cushion, a cigarette hanging out of her mouth as she bent intently over the wheel. She would take me with her, flitting between Bangpa-Pop, Bosmore, Stonor Park and the knacker's yard at Benson Aerodrome.

Sometimes Mama took me, or sent me alone, to nearby Nettlebed for tea parties at Merrimoles. Here lived another of her fellow police officers, the young actress Celia Johnson.

"Married to my old beau that darlin' boy Peter Fleming—darlin' old Ian Fleming's brother you know," my mother sniffed derisively. "Far too good for Celia of course. Just such a crashin' English bore and thoroughly Goodie Two Shoes. And just the very PLAINEST of cooks to boot."

Already famous for her performance opposite the dashing Trevor Howard in the movie *Brief Encounter*, Celia was a pretty woman with thick plain glasses, habitually kind and welcoming. Like my mother, she too had a dark blue police uniform. Her husband, Uncle Peter, was a brother officer of Papa's and another colonel in khaki. And, like my father, he had the insignia of the regimental silver bugle on his shoulder.

As Mama explained: "I've known these darlin' boys Ian and Peter Fleming since the Twenties. We are all most frightfully close to darlin' Cecil—Beaton, you know. And that darlin' dashin' brother of his Reggie Beaton and I were even closer. Until that rather unfortunate incident . . . we won't go into that now. Bumpin' orf on a railway platform is so frightfully inconvenient. The greater the truth, the greater the libel, I can tell you!" Mama cackled.

Home on leave from his regiment, the Oxfordshire and Buckinghamshire Light Infantry, Peter was a silent, taciturn man. He sat one afternoon with Celia in the drawing room of their Merrimoles home, smoking a rosewood briar pipe, gazing intently and inscrutably at my mother from behind a cloud of blue smoke.

Mama too wore the bugle badge, which glistened brightly on her uniform. Ruby had whispered to me: "That there bugle is made out of diamonds, Doodo darling, like all her other brooches." At this she gave a sniff and a deep sigh.

As the tea was brought in, I remembered Mama's hissed command beforehand: "You can tell your borin' Aunt Celia that you 'NEVER eat BOUGHT cakes'."

Obediently I repeated this at the Merrimoles tea party and falteringly explained to Celia that "I cannot eat BOUGHT cakes". She was decidedly bewildered and not over-amused.

Never caring who heard, in the horrified silence that followed, Mama commented out loud: "That Fleming woman is such a pill, and really a damn nuisance at police HQ. Gets in my way, and just bores me to tears. But I hear Celia is frightened of me, *olé!* And heil Hitler!' she exclaimed triumphantly. "Plain as a pike-staff, and her Anglo-Saxon complexion is not a patch on my own exquisite aristo Spanish skin." She turned Uncle Peter: "Pity your wife is as Anglo-Saxon as the day is long. And so is her cooking. Just like her, fit only for an army canteen."

She sniffed contemptuously.

5

A Memory
of Reggie

On the evening of Wednesday October 18, 1933, Reggie Beaton and Jeanne had been together at a cocktail party for 150 guests at Dennis Anthony Bradley's office in Old Bond Street. Dennis was an art dealer fashionable at the time.

Afterwards, as Jeanne so frequently boasted, she had dinner alone with Reggie. In urgent need of money (despite her liaison with Gordon Selfridge amongst others), during the course of the meal Mama turned to Reggie, an RAF officer, and laughed as she threatened to reveal his secret.

He was gay and, at a time when homosexuality was still illegal, any revelation of his sexuality would have meant that Reggie would be immediately cashiered and probably imprisoned.

'Reggie, darlin' boy," Jeanne said, "tomorrow will be almost too late. But, as I've mentioned before, for a certain sum—always in cash of course—you'll be quite safe. Mind you," she continued smoothly, "in your case I prefer the instalment plan."

Rapping briskly on the restaurant table Jeanne ordered more champagne. "And we'll meet again tomorrow at your place for tea, Reggie old boy. And all that . . ." Jeanne finished with characteristic confidence. She laughed again and inhaled, exhaled clouds of blue smoke.

Cecil Beaton's brother, Reggie, was killed by a Tube train at Piccadilly Circus that night. According to newspaper reports, and the evidence of the driver, Reggie dived beneath the approaching train with his arms outstretched. He was 28 years old.

The following appeared in the London *Times* on Monday October 23:

Flying Officer R.E.H Beaton.
Inquest. Saturday October 21, 1933
Miss Jeanne Stourton of Fulham Road, said she saw Mr
Beaton at 7.55 p.m. on the night that he died at Old Bond
Street. He complained of having trouble with his eyes. He
said he would come and see her at tea time the next day, and
seemed in very good spirits.

The coroner said he had a pretty shrewd idea that Mr
Beaton was worried about his sight. [Another witness had
mentioned conjunctivitis, commonly known as "pink-eye".]

And Mr Beaton gave way to a sudden impulse to get rid
of anxiety and trouble and end his life.

Verdict: suicide whilst of unsound mind. Age 28.

The actual cause of Reggie's suicide was well known to a troubled inner circle of family and friends—though the knowledge was kept from the broken-hearted Mrs Beaton herself.

In his biography of Cecil Beaton, Hugo Vickers said that there didn't seem to any particular reason for Reggie's suicide. Vickers described him as "a reasonably happy person, he had many friends . . . and was his father's favourite son. He loved his career with No. 101 Bomber Squadron."

Vickers said that Reggie had health worries and was worried about his health and the danger of losing his commission, but does not make it clear on what grounds. He adds that Reggie occasionally "dated" Jeanne Stourton.

However, if Jeanne's persistent boasting was true, then Reggie had displayed more courage than she had reckoned upon, making this one of her rare failures. He had not waited until the following day for the tea-time extortion which he understood he could neither negotiate nor win.

Jeanne's actions set off alarm bells for those in her circle. Inevitably the friendship between the younger Beatons and her cooled but the social connection had to be continued. Jeanne's threat to the family could still not be underestimated—the Beatons did not have the necessary social position to brush away the inevitable rumours, terrified that the ruthless Jeanne would tell Mrs Beaton the truth, making similar trouble for the equally vulnerable Cecil in his budding career as a brilliant photographer, the heights of fashion.

The fearful Cecil hastily took a flattering, beautifully composed society portrait of Jeanne. Significantly, 1933 is the date on the photograph. The sepia portrait of a demure yet exotic Spanish beauty, arms folded, nails a deep, deep red—soon to be painted a shocking green in emulation of the Bloomsbury Group—with a large diamond solitaire ring and an even larger diamond brooch. Jeanne could not look more plausible.

She wore the same dress in which she presented herself so convincingly at the inquest in Fulham on that autumn Saturday.

6

Land Gels
and Pussies

Papa's brigade colonel was the foxy-looking Uncle Guy de Pass, who came frequently to call and to shoot. He looked the twin of the Henley member of parliament Sir Gifford Fox.

Chatting to Uncle Guy, Mama pointed out that: "Peter Fleming, Sherman and you are all in the same regiment for this goddamned war, which has gorne and upset all my well-laid plans. But really, you must admit that my darlin' IAN Fleming cuts such a dash in his naval uniform, quite divine and most frightfully virile." She winked at Uncle Guy. "Too damnable for Peter that he's become impotent after bein' thrown from a Polish horse, ha, ha! Straight into the Nettlebed woods. Hardly surprisin' nothin' functions in those parts anymore. And didn't Shermie came quite a cropper himself with my darlin' Joachim Ribbentrop's spur at Sonnenburg in '38? Never been able to get it up ever since. But one just has to resort to other methods . . ." Mama sighed. "No one could ever accuse me of lack of resources, or supplies!" she added triumphantly, lighting another cigarette.

She spun round to glower at Bangpa-Pop as he came through the door. "I'm most frightfully put-out, quite *fâchée* in fact—French in case you didn't know from your short spell in the Corps Diplomatique, Pop-goes-the-Weasel—that you sold orf those Nettlebed woods to such common-or-garden bankers as Fleming. Quite frankly Ralph dear, yet again you've sold what doesn't belong to you. I want to know—and I want to know NOW before I have it out with you—where the hell has all that dough gorne to for those thousand of acres?"

Mama gazed hard at Bangpa-Pop with narrowed eyes, sucking in her cheeks. Her scarlet mouth pursed downwardly.

Uneasily Bang-Pop cleared his throat and belched noisily in reply.

"And you can certainly eff orf out of it if you can't PERFORM any better than that. Quite frankly, Ralph Camoys, even Fred Machin's veterinary motions and potions are superior to your own miserable efforts in that department," my mother commented scathingly.

We left once again to hiccup up the narrow winding road to Pishill, Mama leaning well forward over the steering-wheel and into the windscreen, her blue spectacles glittering, the usual cigarette glued onto the corner of her mouth. We were on our way to a nursery tea party at another purloined Stonor property, Watlington Park.

"Damn it, I'm in the wrong gear," shouted Mama as Granny Camoys' brake slowed down, rounding a curve in the hill and passing the smallpox isolation hospital. She put her foot down hard on the accelerator and we rushed forward in a series of leaps and bounds.

"Goddamned germs and germ warfare. A damn nuisance they didn't carry your grandmother Mildew Camoys away with them," shouted my mother above the roar of the revving engine.

As we sped by, I thought of Granny as I gazed in fascination at the green-roofed single-storey wooden isolation unit up on the side of the hill. We swerved suddenly through an open gate opposite the hospital.

"Cherry Orchard!" announced Mama above the noise of the car grinding up the Pishill slope on the wrong side of the road. She swerved from side to side laughing merrily, blowing clouds of cigarette smoke through her nostrils and spitting out of the window. "Corf it up and spit it out I always believe!"

Cherry Orchard was where Papa's Aunt Marjorie Bryce and Cousin Gwennie Sladen lived with their many Manx cats.

"Some cherries ripe for pickin' up there," said Mama, waving a hand towards the house. I knew we were still on the Stonor estate, and that this was one of Papa's properties. At the front door she ordered: "Hold your nose hard, and don't breathe in!"

Obediently I did as I was told and held my nose against the overpowering fug of cat hair and piddle.

"Merry old pussycats and PUSSIES, Gwennie and Marjorie. Land gels together in the First World War. Met, side by side, diggin' up spuds. Up to their armpits and other places quite unmentionable in their knee-breeches." Mama laughed merrily. "And, what is far more important to me, is that all your father's family are deep in the dough together. And so shall I be when I've finished. As it is, I've hardly even begun, ha, ha! *olé!* I'll snap all their members orf." She clicked her fingers briskly.

I pondered the image of my family "deep in the dough". I always loved whenever Ruby made her magical dumpling dough for Irish stew, puddings and pies. I helped her mix it with flour, water and pieces of flaked lard in a yellow china basin, and what she didn't use for the stews Ruby rolled into pastry and shaped lady's finger biscuits for Mama's drawing-room teas. Mama would show unexpected if uproarious appreciation. "These beige biscuit *números* of Ruby's creation certainly look like MEMBERS to me," she would announce to the polite company of the tea party guests. "What imagination she does show from time to time!"

The connection with "dough" continued to elude me as we arrived at the hidden opening to Cherry Orchard. Nor could I connect Mama's descriptions with the chubby figure of Cousin Gwennie. The only small resemblance I could see in her shape was to one of Ruby's white suet steamed puddings for the nursery dining-room. This came wrapped in a large white floury linen serviette, all tied around with string.

"Poor dear Gwennie has never even heard of a brassiere," observe Mama cuttingly. "Quite obviously she thinks it makes her look sexy to resemble a sack of potatoes, old ones at that. But of course dear Marjorie must like it like that once she drops her slacks. Full of S-A—sex appeal, Julia, you fool—and all of that."

Aunt Marjorie Bryce and Cousin Gwennie continued to puzzle me as Mama would never stop mentioning their "sex-appeal, old chestnuts, sweet and otherwise, bras, brassieres and screamin' hot braziers".

These comments were usually directed at Bangpa-Pop, then living in at Assendon Lodge. Mama would address him with winks and throaty giggles, and generally starting the day at breakfast with a flurry of such questions as: "And how are your own particular parts warmin up this mornin', Pop? Plenty of other competition out there my boy, so you'd better hop for it. More goose for my gander. Rather less goose for your gander comes to think of it, and *olé!*"

I regarded Aunt Marjorie with with ever increasing bemusement. Once an accomplished stage actress, she was taller than Cousin Gwennie, her spare figure quite flat and prominently boned. Her shape and form of dress was that of whiplash energy. Marjorie's figure-hugging hacking jacket was made out of the very stiffest tweed, tightly patterned in freckles and speckles of brown and black.

"Northern Ireland, Donegal—and Protestant to boot. Marjorie's been hackin' to quite another tune than just the hounds," Mama would comment. "She can hand over that divine Garnish Island of hers to me. And the sooner the better."

Aunt Marjorie wore a very different hat to the floppy green-knitted round one of Cousin Gwennie. A stiff brown-green trilby it reminded me of Mama's favourite German hat, tilted at the same sharp angle with an angular cock pheasant's feather sticking up over the brim. "My darlin' Joachim gave me this divine hat at Sonnenburg," Jeanne had explained to Aunt Marjorie, whose own hat was really khaki in colour, while Mama declared hers to be a more authoritative darker shade of loden green.

The waisted Donegal tweed jacket fitted Aunt Marjorie to perfection. A long vent was cut sharply down over her behind showing off a trim narrow waist above the tightly-cut beige cavalry twill slacks and brown lace up brogues. One of her feet was permanently turned sideways in its shoe. This had been the result of a riding accident in Ireland and was obviously painfully twisted.

"Just look at those bugger-puzzles," shouted Mama, gazing at the hacking jacket intently. "Most appropriate too. Marjorie no longer has to pretend. 'Land gels' indeed!"

Cousin Gwennie's figure by contrast was plump and shapeless, the soft clothes loose around her. The hem of her long skirt was crooked, and she wore brown schoolgirl's shoes with a single bar and a button. Her stockings, which were thick, flesh-coloured lisle, had slipped into long creases beneath her knees.

Gwennie's father, Uncle Gerald Sladen, was an important general in the North-West Frontier and Sikkim Field Force with the Indian army. She had several of his ceremonial silk umbrellas open and standing in rainy corners of Cherry Orchard to block the leaks.

"Gwennie's father was a general you know. After all he went bombin' around in Burma on an elephant with his umbrella. And a lot of wind 'phletus' come to think of it, *olé!*" laughed Mama. "So it all makes sense that his gel and Marjorie simply fell into one another's arms diggin' up potato tubers in the First World War mud."

That made me remember that there was a brass plaque in Stonor Chapel to one of Bangpa-Pop's two brothers, Uncle Howard Carew Stonor, who had died in the conflict. So I reminded Mama about our connection with the Great War.

"I know, I know all about it," came the hissed reply. "Drowned in the MUD at Givenchy. But no DOUGH, only £8,000, in 1915. Quite unsuitable to talk about it, child. The only Givenchy of any interest to me at all is the one that makes that divine scent. So you can put a sock in it, you stupid meddlesome brat of Sherman's."

Then she laughed again, flicking ash out of the car window after our visit was over and we bumped back down the rutted drive away from Cherry Orchard.

We had made this detour on the way to Watlington Park, as Mama said, "just to check up on the gels". She had stopped the car at the entrance, clambering down the step of the brake to smell the empty milk bottles to see just how much gin Gwennie had been drinking.

"Old soak," commented Mama acidly. "Gwennie will consume anything in sight that's alcoholic." So saying, she took a quick sip from her silver hip flask, a present from an Uncle and Gun. She continued in the car, swaying it this way and that through the wet leaves, the heavy wheels skidding round and round.

Several Manx cats, all tailless, sat along the rain-sodden drive and on the grass verges gazing at us. Jamming her foot hard down on the accelerator, Mama drove straight at them through the rutted track.

"I'm in 'four-wheel' drive!" she shouted.

I held tightly onto the side of the car, the tyres screaming through the water-filled potholes. Mama spat again out of the window. A torrent of Spanish poured forth but I was busily concentrating on keeping hold of my seat. As we careered through the darkness of Pishill woods in the direction of Marjorie and Gwennie's my mother turned towards me.

"Don't tell me you're frightened of me, Sherman's borin' brat that you are!" she scoffed "Such a totally borin' brown mouse of a child." One-handedly, she lit a Philip Morris from her previous cigarette end without interrupting her tirade. "You really are quite as borin' as your father, and just as tedious too as that tiresome bitch, my mother-in-law, Mildew Camoys herself. Just too bad that you look exactly like Sherman," Mama added, suddenly reflectively. "You are, all three—Sherman, Mildred and you—such bloody damn nuisances in my life. And, what's more, you get in my way. I shall see to all of you!" She inhaled and blew out a series of perfectly formed smoke circles. "And I'll make sure I put you, Julia, out on the pavement. Like all the other women, I'll make you pay the price too."

She laughed softly, taking a yet deeper puff on her cigarette before blowing smoke into my face. "You are to be seen, but seldom, if ever, to be heard in this life, do I make myself quite clear?" She dug a long red fingernail deep into my ribs as we swung round the corner and came to an abrupt halt and shuddering stop once more in front of Cherry Orchard.

Pausing before she unlocked the doors of the car to let us out, Mama concluded briskly: "And never forget Julia what a smashin' bollockin' bore you are, the once-orf end-product of my thankfully brief time with your father in '38. At least I was able to be with my own darlin' red-blooded Joachim Ribbentrop at that divine Castello Sonnenburg of his. And the return ticket was cheap at the price—12 guineas there and back, first class! Heil Hitler!"

Once in the house, Aunt Marjorie and Cousin Gwennie had brought cherries along with our tea.

"Tinker, tailor, soldier, sailor, knacker and THIEF," said Mama idly, flicking away the cherry stones from the side of a Peter Rabbit china plate as she counted. "Church, chapel, Methodist, freethinker—of course the latter is just me," she laughed. "Coach, carriage, wheelbarrow or dung-cart . . . and that just suits you, child," she hissed.

Aunt Marjorie and Cousin Gwennie had their backs turned while they combed their cats.

"I've just popped by again to collect the deeds of your house," purred Mama at them. "Dear old Pop—that is, your Cousin Ralph—and I are just fixin' up all the family entrails and entails."

Cousin Gwennie gazed round at my mother through pink plastic spectacles. Her cheeks were also very pink though she wore no rouge.

Aunt Marjorie, her own cheeks well rouged, and wearing bright mauved pink lipstick applied slightly at a slant, said briskly: "Come, come Jeanne Mary dear. Isn't this rather inappropriate in front of Julia? After all she IS Sherman's child." She paused before continuing. "I do think we should leave it for another day, once our poor dear Sherman comes finally back from the war. Let me pour you out some more of our favourite Indian tea from this splendid old heirloom."

Aunt Marjorie picked up a large heavy and tarnished silver teapot, embossed with roses and a crest which she had located behind a plant. This plant flourished on top of a Regency table where sat even more Manx cats.

"Such a problem the poor darlin's can't go out-of-doors too much in this disagreeable weather," said my Aunt, explaining away some of the more curious stains on the furniture.

"Wee-wee and pee-pee is far worse from your cats than it is from my dogs," said Mama grandly. "I simply have to let mine piddle away on the Aubusson rug in the Library, poor darlins', when the weather is so bad. It's their noble pedigree and royal prerogative you know. Fortunately, Ruby Heath finds it all quite easily washable. And HOW do you and dear Gwennie cope with your smalls?" asked my mother smoothly, her voice silvered. "Ruby simply hangs all my new rubber two-way stretches over the kitchen Aga these days. I find them such a great economy during wartime, two at a time, ha, ha, and *olé!*"

"Well Jeanne my dear I'm most frightfully busy in full rehearsal with dear Gladys Cooper," replied Aunt Marjorie in stentorian tones.

Replied Mama: "Gladys is just as much of a damn nuisance in my life as that actress cousin of Sherman's, old Bee Lillie—Countess Peel you know. Another of those tedious widows. She lives far too close to the towpath at Marsh Lock too. And Bee's only son and heir has been most inconveniently drowned in the war, and not even an officer," she continued irritably. "The Peel fortune comes from Lanarkshire lino, and I've missed out on a considerable fortune." She flicked her ash impatiently.

Aunt Marjorie relinquished Cousin Gwennie's hand and strode purposely up to Mama looking her straight in the eye. "And while we're about it, keep right off the subject of 'lizzies' and 'lessies' when speaking to me, Jeanne Mary. You have obviously quite forgotten about your own affair with dear Enid Bagnold. And how about poor Barbara Hutton, the Woolworth millionairess, poor little rich girl that she is, whom you milked for all that she's worth?"

Uncharacteristically, Mama paused before replying in a mollifying tone: "And how are you and dear Gwennie orf for firewood and vital supplies? I'll get Sherman's foreman Freddie Shirfield to bring some logs up on the tractor *toute suite*—though *muy pronto* is even more appropriate, *olé!*"

She lit another cigarette, and demanded that a Horse's Neck be prepared to help her "indigestion".

Cousin Gwennie sipped a little gin to calm the Indian tea. She had propped one of her father's fringed silk ceremonial umbrellas up in the corner of the Cherry Orchard drawing-room to block a leak in the ceiling. The Georgian cottage itself was not in the finest of states and was not even on the water mains: all drinking and bath water had to be drawn up by bucket from a well.

"Perhaps you could see yourself to seein' to some of these holes and showers round here, Jeanne Mary?" suggested Aunt Marjorie with a know-ing wink. "I'm sure Cousin Ralph could bring his carpentry kit to help out once more. Between his Home Guard duties and the 'All Clear'." So say-ing, she suddenly blew a whistle on a lanyard to demonstrate her meaning to Mama. "Summons my nephew Camoys forthwith!" Aunt Marjorie intoned in a commanding voice.

Startled, Cousin Gwennie looked up. "But we always had the native ser-vants to carry our umbrellas," she said suddenly. "Is that why you've sum-moned Ralph, Marjorie dear? I simply can't imagine where all the natives have gorne to these days. It's all so worrying."

She hiccuped, blushing at Aunt Marjorie, who put an arm around her shoulders and gazed sternly back at Mama. "Well, Jeanne Mary dear," she warned, "we don't forget our dear Enid and the Others."

Abruptly Mama got up to go. She seemed in the greatest hurry as I scampered to catch up with her.

"Damn and blast Marjorie's infernally infallible memory," said Mama crossly, getting quickly back into the car and slamming the door. "So frightfully inconvenient to be caught out in my moments of passion."

She gave a sob, a gulp and a large hiccup and got out to swing the engine of the Chevrolet. Down the drive we bolted, on to the main Pishill to Watlington road, and collided with an oncoming car.

"How dare you, how DARE you!" screamed Mama at the old couple in their vehicle that now lay motionless and wrecked on the verge. "Don't you know who I am? You goddamned fools gettin' in my way!"

By now I had piddled in my knickers, and my mother had knocked her spectacles into the windscreen in frustration. "Poor Mama has broken her glasses," I explained to them.

"Don't you dare say 'glasses'," shouted Mama. "I've told you over and over again it is common and *cursí* not to say 'spectacles'."

We took refuge in a retainer's cottage opposite the car crash while Mama telephoned Watlington Park. "I'm tellin' old Aunt Oinette and rolypoly Uncle Oliver Esher that I'm unavoidably detained by an episode most certainly not of my makin'."

Mama glowered at the couple shaking with terror in their crumpled vehicle as the tenants and retainers comforted them with cups of tea laced with sugar.

"Get me my brandy bottle," ordered my mother. "And get me out of here quick. And for Gawd's sake at least stop all that squeakin' and squarkin', Julia. What a borin' coward you are, and fancy wettin' your knickers in public. What a disgrace. Mine are quite dry."

Mama dabbed a lace handkerchief into the brandy and pressed it to the bruise under her eye. Raising the brandy bottle to her lips she tossed back the rest, before loudly addressing the aged couple from the side of their wrecked car. Overwhelmed, the victims were by now cowering in the kitchen of the cottage.

"Now then, just you listen to me," declared Mama imperiously. "I'm an officer in the police, and this is strictly orf the record, so just you keep it there. And how dare you mention compensation indeed. Completely and absolutely out of the question." Stamping her foot, she glowered at the occupants of the cottage. "And don't you ever forget who and what your landlord is!"

The elderly tenants looked fearful as Mama marched smartly out of their cottage with me, still very wet and without my underwear which had been thrown into a bag on the back seat of the car.

"We can't afford to waste those," said Mama briskly. "As it is, I simply cannot afford any more knickers let alone shoes for Sherman's brat. Nor spectacles, indeed."

Mama's glasses, which she called "spectacles", came from a heavy-breathing stern and silent "Uncle" in Wimpole Street, Sir Stuart Duke Elder. I had the opinion that this Uncle was yet another of Mama's favourite royals. She often referred to one called "*mon cher ami*, Monsieur Bar-le-Duc from Biarritz, *olé!*" Mama had many Cousins there, mostly from Colombia and Brazil, and I waited in anticipation to see which of the Uncles he would be. Tall perhaps, like the blue-eyed Pepe, Marqués of Manzanedo, or Pepe Primo de Rivera, soon to be an ambassador. Or would Monsieur Bar-le-Duc be small and swarthy with black currant eyes like the Uncles Carlos from Bogotá, Tio Enrico Marone from Turin, or Ambassador Raul Regis de Oliveira from Brazil? The possibilities for my night prayers became boundless.

I was taken by Mama to have my own eyes "seen to", as she put it, by the ducal Uncle Stuart in his hushed and darkened consulting rooms off Cavendish Square. Next door was my mother's dentist, also called Stuart. "But only a Smith, rather common actually but most frightfully good at his trade what with all that tackle and his laughin' gas," Mama giggled brightly.

As I sat in his consulting room, Uncle Duke Elder told me: "Your dear

Mummy is wrong. After all my investigation, you do have a nasty astigmatism in your left eye. But no, you don't have a squint."

My mother was infuriated. "Damn nuisance all of this 'stigmata'. I've got to go to the quite unnecessary expense of orderin' spectacles for the brat from my favourite chemist in Wigmore Street."

She chose thick-framed blue plastic glasses for me, adding brightly: "Those specs make you look just like Lord Robin Phillimore's governess at Shiplake Hall. Miss Lynes, poor dear must be a hundred if she is a day. Very suitable for orphan Cousins of course. Such a disaster his frightfully glamorous father the ever-so dashin' Anthony was killed in this god-damned war."

My mother's own blue-shaded "specs" had hand-made curvaceous blond tortoiseshell frames. These were a surprising contrast to the aged soot-black tortoise at Assendon Lodge. And to the two American ones which Granny Camoys had brought with her from Newport to the ponds behind the potato beds in the back garden at Stonor itself. A deep and dingy black with unpolished shells these two tortoises lurked beneath water lilies surrounding two islands of mud—as Mama explained, "a legacy of that nightmare character Mildew Cee, Rhode Island Red as she is. These are my frightfully special prescription spectacles. I've absolutely had to wear them for my splittin' migraines ever since I banged my head with my darlin' old beau Dickie Sykes at Sledmere. The 14th baronet you know—owns thousands of acres of Yorkshire. Quite a catch in his day. Worth millions, and more."

I asked what a "Sledmere" was since I remembered that Papa had made a wooden snow sledge for me when he was home on leave from the regiment.

Mama was in an unusually kind mood when she answered my question: "Darlin' Richard and I were comin' down from Sledmere in a big hurry before my weddin' to have my appendix out. And I banged my head in the rush." She sighed. "I could have sued him in the High Court of course. The greater the truth, the greater the libel . . . The mere threat of a breach-of-promise case sent dear Sir Richard simply runnin' to Cartier," she said, gazing lovingly at one of her many sets of diamond brooches, ear-rings and bracelets. "Quite simply I had to make do with a bit of dosh and a few rocks. Settled out of-court—the publicity could have destroyed old Dickie. Ha, ha, ha!" she concluded triumphantly. "If anyone is a past master at Cartholic scandals you've got the right person here. *Olé* and heil Hitler!"

7

'My Soon-to-Be Four-Balled Baron'

Many of Mama's bracelets were of diamonds. Others were of emeralds, sapphires, rubies and pearls. Yet others were heavily linked gold chains, hung with large medals and a stout gold swastika charm. "The Macarena Madonna from Sevilla, olé!" said Mama, swinging her heavy bracelets cacophonously around her wrists.

The swastika hit me behind the ears as she gave a random slap in passing. "For askin' such damned darin' impertinent questions," she snarled, her mood changing. "I'm not takin' any more cheek from Sherman's effin' bore of a brat. You know what you can do, Julia, so piss orf out of it." Mama narrowed her eyes and pursed her lips. "I'm always most FRIGHT-FULLY close to the Vatican, so don't you ever forget it. You're in Mortal Sin as usual, so get down on your knees immediately—and *muy pronto!*—and make an Act of Contrition before I allow you to get up."

I knelt hastily. Mama was not in the best of states and tempers before I had finished reciting my contrition. This was one of the occasions when she frequently had to lie down in a darkened room.

"My ongoin' concussion from the crash at Sledmere," she would explain. "Such an effin' bang from darlin' Dickie causes me these blindin' headaches ever since. Gives me such goddamned splittin' migraines."

Witch hazel had to be applied to her forehead, and Pond's cold cream in a wetted green waterproof bandage. "My cold compress," she would say.

On these occasions the three doors to her bedrooms were even more firmly locked. "On no account am I to be disturbed in my agony," she always ordered.

Up and down the stairs went Ruby carrying trays laid with coroneted silver, lace cloths and light meals for the restoration of Mama's delicate constitution. Deep down in the pantry, Ruby had prepared a linen serviette and a silver pepper-pot in the shape of a castle turret. This was surmounted by a large, bulbous coronet.

"My soon-to-be very own four-balled baron," explained Mama sitting up in a white bed-jacket of satin bordered silk. "Straight from the White House" as she explained to male callers.

Mama's bed was draped with a blond vicuña fur rug from the family in Bogotá. She always wore her pearls, diamonds and full make-up for visitors.

"I'm receivin' child, and I'm certainly not receivin' you today. So you can just bugger orf out of here and make it pretty damn quick, *olé!*" Mama clasped her forehead with a beringed hand over the cold green mackintosh compress of witch hazel and cream. "You can get the hell out of here Julia, but not before you have brought me up my elevenses!"

I hastened downstairs to mix an early morning Horse's Neck.

"And take that damned stupid expression orf your ridiculous face—you look just like the Phillimores' bedraggled spaniel Winkle. Though nothing like as nice. All you are is Sherman's borin' brat," my mother sighed angrily.

On tiptoe Ruby and I left her darkened bedrooms, her summer one alternating with winter quarters with Mama once again pointing out my Mortal Sin for not "hoofin' it quick enough" for her liking.

She dwelt a lot on the subject of sin. And most of all on the subject of Mortal Sin. My worry grew over her firm conviction that I was suffering from such an excess of the latter. I would explain solemnly that I was doing my best but all Mama said in reply was: "Your best is simply not good enough. Nor will it ever be good enough young lady. And it is more than high time you made your First Confession. Your quite disgraceful arrogant attitude makes it such an emergency that I'm arrangin' this absolutely immediately with dear Uncle Alfonso de Zoo. He will make quite sure you're kept firmly down on your knees makin' amends to me with Acts of Contrition and a rosary or two," said Mama, sobbing suddenly.

Desperately I asked Ruby what I had done wrong. But Ruby just sighed wearily and said as always: "There, there, Doodo darling."

Mama leapt on her words of comfort scornfully. "You're just another low-church Protestant, truly borin' to boot . . . and you know eff all about such matters. Since when did you tedious Prots know anything about

Mortal Sins? That bastard King Henry the Eighth conveniently did away with the confessional box. Aristo bastard that I am in my Spanish calendar it features, and loud and clear. Julia will pay on this earth. I will make sure of that, I shall see to it. Just you watch me," she said menacingly.

Ruby sighed again and wrapped me protectively in her arms when she saw that Mama was looking the other way. It was a transgression for which Ruby would pay dearly in later years.

Night prayers became ever more fervent as I tried to find a way of telling God how sorry I was for causing my mother such pain. I had also worked out a plan for saying "thank-you very, very much Mama" for all that she was doing to help save me from Mortal Sin. But not before I had prayed for Bangpa-Pop, and all the Uncles that Mama kept changing on a weekly basis.

It was exceedingly confusing for a little girl, but I always was so grateful for my mother's magic and beauty. And for her tinkling laughter and the alluring smell of the rich perfume with which she was continuously drenched.

Mama had listened impassively, imperviously, to my fervent night prayers, dressed in her little black number on the way to the flicks at the Regal cinema in Henley. Bangpa-Pop stood at her side in his double-breasted navy blue suit belching slightly.

"Phletus and flatulence all over again," said my mother merrily.

My brand-new prayer thanking Mama and seeking her forgiveness seemed to be quite successful, and each night I repeated it to Mama as she stood silently at the foot of my bed. Overcome with impatience one evening, she flicked off the electric light with a long fingernail and left me alone in the dark.

Summer or winter she would throw open the window wide and tonight was no different. "It's much too hot in here child, except for invalids, and you're certainly not pretendin' be one of those. Orf with your blanket and let's have some proper discipline round here. You're wastin' my valuable time, and borin' me to tears."

So saying Mama yanked the pink woollen blanket off the bed. I was left shivering with cold.

"Your grandfather and I are orf to the flicks for the evening" she said over her shoulder, slamming my nursery door as she went.

My penance would be worse whenever I was found reading my favourite storybook, *Uncle Wiggily's Adventures in Rhode Island*, by the light of a small silver tin Woolworth torch beneath the bedclothes. Hovering above me silently Mama would wait to pounce once I had come up from under the sheets for air. The cause of so many "early bed for you" punishments, I would spend days expelled earlier and earlier to the night nursery. Ruby would tiptoe up and read to me, whispering lest Mama arrived back early from the flicks or from police "excursions" with Uncle Eric St Johnston. Her return from night duties was frequently noisy as she would fling open my bedroom door with a mighty wrench and a flying kick.

"Where the hell has Pop gorne to this time," she shouted at me late one night. "Where, in Gawd's name is your effin' grandfather? Sound asleep in his Bosmore beehives again, no doubt. That will give him brewer's droop if nothin' else does the trick. I've already had to 'export' one baby too many down that convenient Vatican corridor. Pop-goes-the-Weasel really is as randy as any cock and bull." So saying Mama took a foot to my behind as I lay in bed. "Get up this minute and look in the bomb shelter!"

Rubbing the sleep from my eyes, I went down and threw open the cellar door to see if Bangpa-Pop was sitting there as usual in his rubber gasmask and tin helmet.

"That 'stigmata' thing in your eye really makes you squint, tedious brat that you are," Mama said briskly when I reported back.

It always puzzled me since she frequently mentioned "that stigmata thing" as in the "stigmata stuff-and-nonsense that ridiculous Gytha, my least favourite demi-sister, suffers from. Such a crashin' bore she is, marquesa or no marquesa. All that bosh and bunkum she insists on talkin'. Complete religious mania, of course, just up her street. Wouldn't bother to listen to a word Gytha says. Makes up for her entire lack of a sense of humour." Mama opened her mouth wide and yawned. "That tedious Gytha really bores for all China—except you've only been to Japan, Pop!" Mama laughed and winked at my grandfather.

He guffawed, blowing a mauve nose into one of many off-white handkerchiefs and pulled up his grey worsted trousers.

"Such a pity Pop you don't go in for flannel. Such a divine texture, though I do say it myself, worn by many of my beaux," said my mother reflectively. "But I, of course, can and do completely out-flannel most people." She gazed at Bangpa-Pop. "I really can't think why you must wear such truly borin' worsted trousers. Personally I've always gorne in for flannel bags."

Aunt Gytha's husband was the Marqués Ramón del Moral. He had worked with my Spanish grandfather at General Franco's embassy during the Civil War.

"Antique as my brother-in-law old Mon is, he really is frightfully important and terribly busy with his new spyin'. Quite an expert after all that Civil War practice and safe conduct passes in San Sebastián, and up and down the borders," said my mother knowingly.

Grandpa-Pop belched.

"And don't be so impertinent as to bother to cross-examine me, Pop, you old fool," she snapped. "I, for one, should certainly know from my own professional experiences in that neck of the wood. After all it is my territory."

Mama despised Aunt Gytha and felt warmly enthusiastic for Uncle Mon. "Such a rosary-freak marquesa, dreary old Gytha. Serves her right that she all but perished from starvation in Portugal with your dear Uncle Mon's two unfortunate Spanish afterthought brats. Penniless the whole lot of them. They bore me to tears. All but kicked the bucket starvin' in that convent in Coimbra, ha, ha and *olé!* Hitler's very own signed portrait hangin' in our very own embassy to boot. In the drawin' room too!"

Uncle Mon, the Marqués de Bertodano y del Moral, was tall, blue-eyed and chisel-chinned. He habitually dressed in navy-blue on his visits to Assendon Lodge with Grandpa Pedro de Zulueta (or "De Zoo").

On one such visit Mama had taken them both hurriedly into her private study, and then into the drawing-room where I could hear tinkling laughter. Ruby was ordered to bring in a silver drinks tray laden with glasses, brandy, gin, ginger ale, ice and a bottle of pink bitters. As Mama was fond of pointing out, "my old beaux really prefer the gin", and she kept several bottles in the locked sideboard where they could be seen behind glass panels. Frequently I heard the clink of coins and the rustle of notes. Followed by silence. And the clink of glasses once more.

Mama's confidence was less evident with her own womenfolk. Her other English half-sisters, Magda Stourton and Barbara Bellville, were blue-eyed blondes, handsome but far less pretty than Aunt Gytha with their hooked noses, imperious expressions and supercilious behaviour. Both poured clouds of cigarette smoke from their nostrils. They were extremely elegant.

"Magda and Barbara's voices really are most frightfully upper-class and classic English Catholic," Mama would opine.

But she seemed to be in some awe of these two rich, grand and imperious women, who looked at my mother with consternation and considerable disdain and sniffed. They smoked long cigarettes in elegant tortoise-shell holders, and their make-up was like Mama's—except that both Magda and Barbara plucked their blonde eyebrows to an even finer line. And their finely shingled hair was very blonde indeed.

Aunt Magda, who had caught an American millionaire in 1935 ("Magda has hooked and netted a frosted pea magnate from Detroit, ha, ha!") soon came to abandon her holder and so her cigarette habitually hung from the side of her mouth.

"I saw to it myself in the sheer emergency of the situation that sister Gytha dropped that flash-Harry major domo who picked her up at the Ritz Carlton," Magda had said one day when visiting. Pausing only to take a deep puff, she continued: "Went straight over to Washington DC myself and fetched her right back immediately. Imagine the shame cast upon our Stourton name if Gytha had made orf with a common foreigner. And an Eytie called Mario to boot."

Mama agreed hastily: "Only a common-or-garden Eytie waiter and totally penniless, my own diplomatic resources tell me," she laughed nervously.

Magda and Barbara joined in the laughter, exhaling clouds of scent-drenched smoke. My heart bled for Aunt Gytha as the three sisters conspicuously disliked her and were even happier that she had so little money. In contrast Magda and Barbara both wore sizeable diamond brooches and rings, and heavy gold bracelets like my mother's. Round their necks each sister had row upon row of large, evenly matched pearl chokers.

They talked earnestly to my mother. "Really Jeanne, we must protest about all your most undesirable boyfriends. And there's more than a rumour about all your dangerous black-market stuff that we wouldn't be caught dead gettin' involved with. We are, after all, Barbara and I, livin' up to the Stourton motto: *'Loyal I might, or might not, remain, during the whole of my lifetime'*."

Ruby, in her best uniform, brought in china tea on a large silver tray, and a Horse's Neck for Mama, at which both half-sisters stared with incredulity and sniffed again.

Barbara said: "Don't you think it is rather too early in the afternoon, Jeanne Mary dear, for cocktails . . . ?"

After her Plantagenet blonde half-sisters had hastily left—Magda for Lowndes Square and Barbara for Sunningdale—Mama turned, quite obviously disconcerted, to Bangpa-Pop.

She glowered angrily from behind her blue-shaded glasses. "They can both piss orf out of my life. But there's nothin' these gels don't know about the world, damn it. They started on a star-studded trek durin' the First World War—if you get my meanin'? Two red hot potatoes on the ambulances you know. And they've been hard at it ever since, Magda and Barbara. And you can say that again. Always get the goods no matter what!"

Her humour restored, Mama roared with laughter, and winked at my grandfather. "Just exactly what were you up to, Ralph dear, durin' all those years of the First War? Simply flyin' around the trees at Blenheim Palace in your little flyin' machine, *olé*? Up in the air with darlin' Sonny, Duke of Marlborough!"

Nor did my mother's Aunt, Tia María de Zulueta, choose to stay the night at Assendon Lodge. She came down for the day from the Onslow Court Hotel with her lady-in-waiting, the rosy-cheeked stepdaughter of Aunt Gytha, Mónica de Bertodano.

Tia María was from Madrid and looked strikingly like my mother with her dark eyes and strong widow's peak. Resolutely she wore no make-up save for a heavy white lead powder. Her chiselled chin was an exact replica of Mama's, her hair the same jet-black, austerely cut and trimmed.

Aunt and niece played duets on Tia María's Steinway baby grand piano. "All part of my Spanish inheritance for when I am the Condesa of Torre Diaz. Mine, and mine alone," explained my mother imperiously. "No one takes my rights away from me. Anyone who does will pay one hell of a price, God damn them. And that applies to my demi-sister Gytha for gettin' in my path. She is far more suited to the convent life, and I'll see to that on her behalf . . ."

Mama's rights greatly preoccupied her. Several of the grand houses where she took me to tea parties round Stonor were situated on large estates which Bangpa-Pop inevitably seemed to have sold "by mistake".

"Pop would never have dared to sell orf such valuable assets if I'd been around. As it is, it's a great pity I wasn't around even earlier than '33," she said emphatically. "Mind you, Ralph's actual bankruptcy didn't hit home till '37—and I should know, what with Sherman inheritin' so soon and all. Freehold stuff. Ralph broke the entails, *olé!*"

Locally, these manor houses were now lived in by Guns, new Uncles and their wives. "Rather nouveaux bankers like the Flemings and the Hamburg Barings," commented Mama.

And whenever we went up the Pishill Hill road to Watlington Park, paying a visit to the Cherry Orchard Aunts as we went, Mama took special delight in personally telling Viscount and Viscountess Esher, known to me as Aunt Oinette and Uncle Oliver, that she considered them "EXTREMELY nouveau-riche".

Mama explained scathingly to Uncle Oliver: "Not only do you come from the suburbs of Epsom and Esher, and Brussels to boot—sprouts you know, and rather rotten at that—but you are only a third-rate third viscount, and most frightfully recent, who believes in euthanasia. Furthermore you're decidedly impostors, you and Aunt Oinette, because Watlington Park is basically MINE. It was built by the Stonors some 300 years ago, and I want you OUT!"

Neither of the Eshers seemed at all appreciative of my mother's comments, but she continued regardless: "And as for you Oliver dear, president of the Euthanasia Society as you so appropriately are, you know just what you can do, and start right away with yourself, ha, ha! Just from Bruxelles and lower Surrey as it is—*olé* and heil Hitler!—you need never forget what I know. And how about Aunt Oinette's questionable New York origins, eh? 'Borston' did you mention? I very much doubt that, Heckshaw-Rickshaws indeed!"

Watlington Park seemed a magical house to me because the Eshers grew rose-coloured peaches indoors. I thought these far superior to the greenhouse grapes Mr White the Plymouth Brethren head-gardener grew at Stonor next to the earth privy. I was very excited the day I was asked to stay at Watlington as I had only ever been away to Bosmore with Bangpa-Pop and Mama until then.

The Eshers' Nanny Brett was a more fascinating nanny than my own at Assendon. She looked like a kindly pirate, peg-legged, with one eye half-closed beneath a drooped eyelid. One leg was much shorter than the other giving the nanny a staccato-like limp in her neatly laced stout black leather walking shoes from Milwards, the smartest shoeshop in Henley. The rhythm of her walk reminded me of the ghosts that I heard at Assendon and Stonor.

Excitingly, Nanny Brett organised musical chairs for me and Aunt Oinette's grandson in the stone-flagged hall of Watlington Park. I became over-excited by the sheer speed of the music played on the hand-wound gramophone. Falling dizzily I hit my head hard and painfully on the flagstones as the Brett boy pulled the chair sharply out from beneath me. I had thought him so handsome that I had already considered proposing marriage. Now mortified with shyness and timidity this made me cry and long to go home to Ruby Heath and Mama.

The angular paintings on the walls at Watlington were strange to me. They were "abstracts", as I was told by Aunt Oinette, and highly intellectual. I was in awe of Lady Esher, who from early on in the war had broadcast on the BBC.

That night, in those strange surroundings, I repeated my night prayers even louder, remembering the sequence of Uncles all the more fervently and anxiously together with Bangpa-Pop and Mama, hoping for the magic of her approval and love.

The night before going to stay at Watlingtons, as on so many other occasions, I had had been made to stand to attention in the shallow, tepid bath water of the freezing cold nursery bathroom at Assendon Lodge.

"Up on your feet immediately for the National Anthem, you tiresome brat," my mother had ordered me. "Just too bad if you're starkers. God save the King, *olé* and *viva el rey de España!*"

And then the wooden radio would be turned up all the louder, for the National Anthem.

"And now," Mama sighed, "we've got to listen to that frightfully affected American accent of Aunt Oinette Esher's from Borston—if that is where she really comes from. So much stuff and nonsense all that spurious poetry that she's readin' . . ." Mama laughed merrily. "Such a yawn and you can tell that to your Watlington Park hostess. I will make VERY sure that you do."

Obediently I strived to do as I was told. Clearly Mama wanted Aunt Oinette to know how she really sounded, and so, wanting to please, I tried all the harder to remember my mother's comments.

In reply, the Third Viscountess Esher merely sighed heavily and crossly.

"Well," I added in desperation at my lack of success, "Mama says I am to tell now that you've been going to far too many fancy-dress parties with Peter Fleming dressed up as the Barefoot Contessa Aunt Oinette."

My efforts were not well received, but the Watlington Park indoor peaches remained exotically exciting after the sour Stonor grapes—which gave me wind.

Bangpa-Pop and Mama had said in unison: "This is all gas and hot air, and don't we know all about that!" and they winked at one another.

*

Very occasionally my mother was silent. This was so unusual that I would worry that she was not well, understanding that she suffered from something constitutionally deeply delicate other than her concussion and migraines.

"My nerves," Mama would sigh.

These attacks necessitated concentrated attention and nursing in a darkened room, the blinds drawn with a red-hot fire of rationed coal. As usual it was laid and lit by Ruby, who brought up her trays laden with delicacies for Mama's condition.

Flicky, who in reality was Sister Gertrude Flick from the depths of Loch Ness—*"ma sage-femme"* as Mama mysteriously called her—came up the many stairs with the trays too. Habitually dressed in nurse's uniform, a green linen dress with white linen cap, apron and rolled-cuffs, Flicky came down from Scotland quite frequently.

"Quite indispensable at these frightfully inconvenient moments," Mama declared. "But, of course, after I dropped that damn nuisance coil in Henley High Street, I got in touch with the Vatican right away—old boy, or should I say, old lady Sir D'Arcy Thing-and-Osborne better look to his merits, murky as they are in this department. I need action, and I need it quick." She seized the telephone. "Get me Monsignor Mostyn right away," she shouted into the receiver. "On second thoughts that won't be soon enough, so you can clear the line and give me my usual diplomatic clearance. Special Constable the Honourable Jeanne de Zulueta Stonor, Countess of Torre Diaz and shortly-to-be Baroness Camoys here, so you'd better make it quick. And no muckin' about," she shouted again. "No, I certainly did not say *fuckin'*! How dare you, how DARE you make any such insinuation. No coarse word ever sullied my lips, and you'll pay for such down-right impertinence young woman," Mama vowed scornfully to the operator at Turville Heath. "Just set to, there's a darlin'," she said, softening her tone "And get me that brigade of boys at the Vatican *muy pronto*, or you'll lose your job young woman," she added menacingly.

Lady Dashwood came unexpectedly to call on Mama.

"That damn nuisance Hellbags Helen is here again from West Wycombe Park," snapped my mother irritably.

But she was in awe of Hellbags, the Canadian grocery tycoon and the only female Gun my mother had allowed to shoot with the Uncles and Guns at Assendon and, later, Stonor. After any encounter with the beautiful Lady Dashwood my mother looked peculiarly green, the rouge faint on her dead-white skin. Her moist scarlet lips clenched into a thin, grim line as she drummed long red fingernails in obvious contemplation.

"'I'd take two Johnny-Go-Lightly-Dashwood baronets for any one of old Hellbags and her sharpened razor of a tongue any old day'" said my mother bitterly.

This was after Helen had alluded yet again to my mother's connections to the "scandalous" goings-on at the Hell Fire Club. The rumours about my mother continued to be rife. After all, rumour-mongering, salacious gossip and character assassination were among the many hideous excitements of life in the countryside.

8

A Memory
of Gytha

Gytha Stourton was nine years old, the youngest of Fanny and Herbert's four children, when Jeanne was born in 1913. Gytha would also become the prettiest of her sisters Magda, Barbara, Jeanne: blonde, blue-eyed, gentle, innocent, and truly devout.

But from the moment of Jeanne's birth, Gytha's life was blighted. She was to become an instant scapegoat, most of all at the behest of Jeanne—who early learnt to torment her hapless half-sister. Nevertheless it was Gytha who truly understood her character, her whims; and it was she whose heart was big enough to forgive the half-Spanish Jeanne, who ruthlessly, systematically beggared Gytha into grinding poverty and deep humiliation.

Born in 1904, Gytha it was who saw most closely her mother Fanny's feckless, reckless affairs of the heart. Thus she was completely bewildered to find herself banished, aged nine, to stay with her maternal grandmother Charlotte, the dramatically widowed Viscountess Southwell, who lived in a damp, dreary house at Ramsgate, where much of each and every day was taken up on one's knees, praying the mysteries of the rosary and litanies of the saints.

A naturally devout child, Gytha was not so upset by this rigour of religious discipline as by a singular lack of clothing, ashamed every item casually given to her, or "passed down" by patronising Crichton-Stuart relatives, was conspicuously second-hand, shabby, ill-fitting—even down to the obligatory school uniform and woollen cami-knickers—when she followed her sisters Magda and Barbara to the convent at Ascot in 1915.

These slights made an indelible impression on the sensitive Gytha, bewildered, homeless, casually passed from one relative to another making her feel as second-hand as her clothes. Almost completely unwanted, the increasingly pretty young woman became equally lonely.

Gytha's mother, Frances Stourton, or Feckless Fanny, had great difficulty in budgeting with the extremely inadequate trust fund administered in her name by the head of the Mowbray, Segrave and Stourton family. After Fanny's irresponsible, indifferent, absentee husband Herbert had dissipated his wife's considerable Southwell inheritance, this paltry, inadequate allowance was reluctantly agreed only in order to avoid embarrassment to the notoriously parsimonious, deeply sanctimonious, fervently Catholic Stourtons. Eagerly aware of their place in high society, within the English aristocracy, this pompous family was ever-anxious, and not for the first time, to avoid even the whiff of scandal.

The hapless Fanny's trustee was the bullying, violent, and eccentric William, Baron Mowbray, Segrave and Stourton, premier baron of England. It was he who was frequently to be seen in House of Lords livery—bespoke black and silver-striped trousers, single-breasted black woollen jacket, stiff white shirt with its fashionable highly starched collar, round-edged, black silk tie anchored with a gold stickpin, hand-rolled cream silk handkerchief nonchalantly stuffed into a breast pocket—scrounging in the rubbish bins in Belgrave Square.

William Mowbray, Segrave and Stourton, poked into these rubbish bins of Belgravia with considerable fervour and force, randomly, deeply, with a stiffly-rolled black silk stick-umbrella, gold-feruled and handmade at Swayne, Adney & Briggs—as famous for its umbrellas as Purdey & Sons for their hand-crafted guns.

In the course of his pursuit, the baron retrieved all manner of objects, not least rotting copies of old newspapers avidly perused. Sometimes even the remains of an ageing sandwich would be enthusiastically rescued, consumed on the spot, the elegantly dressed eccentric with popping blue eyes and receding chin, leaning against an old dustbin, supported by the gold feruled umbrella. William regarded this too as a possible weapon, a worthy substitute for the habitual shooting-stick and hand-axe with which he was notoriously equipped on his Yorkshire estate at Allerton.

Indifferent to the humiliating poverty forced upon Fanny by the spendthrift Herbert, William—himself soon to be had up, arrested by the police, on proven charges of grievous bodily harm and criminal assault with the very same Yorkshire axe—was always in a position to help this most hapless woman, his near cousin, abandoned by her husband. But, just as cruelly, William chose quite otherwise and remained parsimonious to the end of his life, thus inflicting even further damage on Fanny, already in embarrassingly reduced circumstances

The unexpected arrival of Jeanne, nine years Gytha's junior, in 1913 meant that all the funds of the miserly trust fund were now devoted to the new baby. Gytha was left completely stranded, abandoned, penniless.

Leaving St Mary's Convent at the age of seventeen, the poverty-struck Gytha without either academic qualifications or income, had immediately to make her way in the world. She sought work as a social secretary and found a job at the Foreign Office, proving herself a good linguist both in French and Spanish, languages in which she would become fluent.

Quite unlike her handsome, chic, soignée elder sisters Magda and Barbara, more than worldly-wise from their experiences as dashing, underage ambulance drivers in the First World War, Gytha was a considerable innocent of exceptional sweetness, deeply devout, a true believer in the Catholicism which had sustained and nourished her unhappy, lonely growing up.

Magda and Barbara, on the other hand, were self-possessed, hardened by their experiences in the war and highly ambitious. Socially distinguished, both as blonde as Gytha, with similar blue eyes, elegantly hooked noses, and a creamy clarity of skin, which they claimed to have inherited from their Plantagenet ancestors and French great-grandmother, the Comtesse Walsh de Serrant, the two sisters had hastily dispensed with active practice of Catholicism, whereas Gytha, to their intense irritation, would never falter.

Continuously aware of their "aristo" breeding, their superior social class and the brittle insecurity of their home background, so completely dominated by the demanding, attention-seeking Jeanne, conspicuously spoilt and a most precocious child, Magda and Barbara had married handsome army officers. The mid-Thirties found them each remarried to richer, more eligible men—out of the church. Between marriages the two sisters embarked on heady, heavy affairs.

In the early Thirties, Gytha reached Washington, DC. Here she became social secretary to the British ambassador, on whose embassy staff she met two very different men: career diplomat Jock Balfour and the as yet unmasked spy Kim Philby. The former, a brilliant, multilingual, talented if slightly eccentric Scotsman, later knighted as a distinguished ambassador, was a family acquaintance, deeply sympathetic to the naive but charmingly pretty Gytha.

And so it was Jock who had to see to the sorry task of Gytha's quite unexpected and precipitous return to England in the early months of 1934. "Outrageous, quite out-of-the-question, just a common Eytie!" had shouted the scandalised Mowbray, Segrave and Stourton family from the far side of the Atlantic. For news of Gytha's engagement to Mario, an Italian waiter with whom she had fallen deeply in love, had reached them via Magda, to whom Gytha had written of her happiness and joy at the reciprocal love of her fiancé, of their forthcoming marriage on the "wrong side of the Pond" as her sisters laughingly described America.

That the hapless, darkly handsome and able Mario would before long become the highly successful, prosperous maitre d'hotel, then manager, at Washington's most prestigious hotel was of no significance to Gytha's infuriated sisters. "Career indeed! What career could a common or garden waiter—and a frightfully charlie Eytie at that, common as muck—possibly have?" they taunted Gytha scornfully. The proposed union was immediately forbidden.

That the comely, kindly, innocent Gytha and Mario were deeply in love, deeply sincere, was a matter of sheer indifference to the Stourtons. In their eyes he would always remain just a waiter, a cause of frightful scandal, wrecking their heraldic escutcheons.

Initially it was the outraged Magda who sailed first-class on a Cunard liner to fetch Gytha back. Her poor sister, though deeply reluctant, would have no option but to obey, she reasoned. After all, at thirty years old, Gytha was considered "on the shelf" but, unlike her three sisters, she was still a virgin and a catch for an older man, preferably a respectable widower, a Catholic of course, in need of a new wife—in all likelihood a convenient step-mother to a brood of motherless children. And Magda already had just such a suitable, deeply respectable person in mind.

In contrast to the threatened shame which Gytha's "liaison" represented, it was a matter of considerable pride that the head of the family, axe-wielding William, and his similarly violent younger brother, Conservative member of parliament for Salford, the Hon John Joseph Stourton, were jauntily rumbustious, vociferous, pro-Nazi followers, members of the highly fashionable Anglo-German Fellowship and its affiliated clubs.

That these brothers, both valiant officers in the First World War, had been bound over to keep the peace after a particularly violent episode of grievous bodily harm, was considered as "just a bit of a lark, ha! ha! Nothin' to be too ashamed of'!" amongst their fellow aristocracy, some of whom had already enrolled in Oswald Mosley's baton and brick-wielding British Union of Fascists.

Jock Balfour witnessed with horror the heartbreak and anguish of Gytha as he helped arrange the liner ticket for her immediate return to England with Magda. Wreathed in blue smoke, in her most commanding, and ever imperious manner, Magda caused considerable alarm to the young diplomat, sharply barking orders down the length of an elegant tortoiseshell cigarette holder.

Gytha never ceased to mourn the love of her life. To be forcibly parted from Mario, her great love, broke her heart. But she was to be made even more wretched upon setting foot in England once again.

Magda, aided and abetted by Barbara, now the third wife of Frank Bellville, a Bembridge magnate, took matters once more into her own hands. With the approval of William Stourton, she set about arranging Gytha's engagement to an eligible but aging widower, the sixty-three year old Ramón del Moral, 8th Marqués del Moral. And Ramón, known as "Mon", came complete with family, six in all, the youngest of whom was the same age as Gytha.

Marriage to this austere, handsomely-boned and tall Spanish grandee came as a considerable shock to the dismayed, innocent Gytha. This sociably suitable, suitably Catholic wedding took place on August 23, 1934, its consummation causing shock and immediate misery to the increasingly bewildered new bride, horrified that her husband had the bedtime habits of an old man and needed to keep a chamber pot ever ready beneath the marital bed. Nevertheless Gytha soon found herself pregnant, her first child arriving in May 1935. A second baby, a son, arrived in early December 1937 to whom the Spanish king Alfonso XIII would be godfather.

Alone amongst the Stourton family, Gytha was both ignorant of, and disinterested in high politics or politics of any sort. Once married to the highly political Marqués del Moral, Gytha found herself plunged into the centre of a whirl of political activity, and circumstances socially which revolved around the London court of Queen Ena of Spain, her daughters and courtiers. Mon del Moral was a fervent Royalist, a close friend of King Alfonso, and, from the onset of the Spanish Civil War in July 1936, a staunch supporter and friend of General Franco whose personal representative to the British government he immediately became.

Mon was equally a close friend of Count Joachim von Ribbentrop, Hitler's ambassador, whom he frequently encountered in London and in Spain with mutual friends, many of them important businessmen, industrialists, manufacturers of arms and armaments, Lord Brabazon of Tara, Lord Weir, Lord Portsmouth and Lord Illingworth amongst them.

Before long Gytha found herself accompanying Mon to the grandeur of 44 Grosvenor Square, a magnificent mansion of Waterloo fame, where "Puss", Lady Illingworth, entertained in considerable grandeur and stately style for her husband's friends, the Duke of Alba and Berwick, the Marqués de Portago, the Marqués de Santa Cruz, the Marqués de Manzanedo—the latter a contemporary of Mon's at Stonyhurst College in Lancashire. There were the British peers too, such as Brabazon and Weir, who were as heavily involved in supplying arms to Spain: to the Nationalist cause, to the followers of Alfonso XIII.

Gytha was horrified by the politics of these men, by Mon's open friendship with committed admirers and such enthusiastic followers of Hitler. But she was unable to do anything—as an obedient wife, and very Catholic woman she could hardly oppose her husband, let alone his friends so well disposed to the German and Spanish regimes. Any such protest would have been completely ignored. Besides, her three sisters, who had very little time for Gytha and her unworldly impracticable attitude, had long declared their own colours, their shared extremes of political views nailed conspicuously to the mast of social expediency.

The new Marquesa therefore found herself a pretty, occasionally useful ornament to her older and very busily occupied Spanish husband. Mon was particularly and enthusiastically in charge of propaganda for the Nationalist Cause in London, together with the Duke of Alba, both personal appointments of General Franco. Their base was the Dorchester Hotel. Mon's duties encompassed a passionately delivered speech on Franco's behalf at the House of Commons, and the handling of conveniently selected diplomatic passes over the French border into Spain. There documents, several involving accredited journalists fervently dedicated to the Nationalists such as Peter Kemp, Dick Sheepshanks, Kim Philby (playing his convincing double game) and even rogues like Rupert Bellville, were handed out by Mon and his deputies.

Bewildered though she was at the beginning of her own, harshly arranged marriage, Gytha could not be other than deeply sympathetic to

Jeanne when she lost her only true love and unofficial fiancé Dick Sheepshanks, Reuters' special correspondent to General Franco.

Killed on New Year's Eve, December 1937, the able Dick had previously been assigned to Abyssinia—a contemporary of Evelyn Waugh there—and hand-picked by Reuters' owner and managing director Sir Roderick Jones. Brutally murdered with a hand-grenade hurled by Kim Philby in the days of civil war carnage at Caude (a village on the outskirts of Teruel) in the cruel winter of 1937, this dashingly handsome, highly accomplished sportsman and aspiring journalist Dick Sheepshanks was truly the love of Jeanne's life.

But, as Gytha was later to tell me, Jeanne abruptly rebuffed her sister's spontaneous sympathy and deeply genuine concern at her tragic loss. That Jeanne detested such sympathy, despised such a genuine emotion as "sheer sentimentality, God damn it!", merely fuelled her own deep resentment, and jealousy of Gytha's newly-acquired Spanish title and undoubted social status. Despite her genuine grief at the tragic loss of her fiancé Dick, Jeanne had no time to waste in mourning. Within six weeks of his murder Jeanne had set her cap at a rich young landowner, half-American and fellow Catholic: Sherman Stonor, new owner of the Stonor Park Estates and a millionaire.

Gytha observed Jeanne's ruthless pursuit of this naive, gentle and good-looking man with considerable dismay. By March 1938 her engagement to Sherman was announced, officially followed by the curious date set for the wedding, Bastille Day, July 14, 1938. For this quite extraordinary social spectacle Gytha and Mon's small daughter would be a bridal attendant, carrying the pearl-strewn satin train, many yards long, up the aisle of the Brompton Oratory together with other progeny of Jeanne's erstwhile lovers.

Deeply embittered and aware of her own more than questionable behaviour too frequently witnessed by Gytha, Jeanne embarked on a carefully executed strategy of long-term revenge against her unwitting sibling. In this, as with so many of her vendettas, she would succeed even beyond her wildest expectations.

Jeanne knew that the 8th Marqués del Moral was a spy, and an important one. Furthermore, Jeanne considered his new bride Gytha to be standing in her way. In embarking on this prolonged vendetta, Jeanne had already learned a technique well-honed not only by the Stourtons, but by others in her set, Protestant as well as Catholic—and only from the top drawer—Bowes-Lyon, Clinton, Stonor among these exclusive families. And there was already a well-tried formula, guarantee of success. Its frequently repeated mantra was: "Abandon, Isolate, Deride, Victimise, Vilify, Abandon to Impoverishment, Exterminate!" As important was the obligatory codicil: "Madness: Quite off his—or her—Head. Deeply Insane, Mad, Bad, The Sooner he—or she—is Dead and Buried the Better!" With the frequent aid of the hierarchy of the English Catholic church this had seldom, if ever, been known to fail.

So busily occupied was Mon, so frequently away on "official duty" that at the beginning of the Second World War, Gytha found herself completely stranded in Portugal. Abandoned, she was parked in a convent with her two very small children, without money and entirely forgotten by Mon. Once again Jock Balfour, *en poste* as minister at the British embassy in Lisbon, came to Gytha's rescue, astonished yet again to find the young woman in such dire circumstances.

But it would not be until 1941 that Gytha and her children were rescued from this nightmare, which grew grimmer by the day. All but starving, they returned home steerage aboard a merchant vessel from supposedly neutral Portugal to Tilbury Docks.

As for so many, the Spanish Civil War had cruelly changed life for Gytha. Following the brutality of the bombardment of Guérnica and other Nazi dress-rehearsal bombings throughout the blood-letting of the war, Mon was frequently away, travelling between France, Portugal and Spain, organising and issuing safe conduct passes. Peter Kemp in *The Thorns of Memory* reveals himself as one of several recipients, a young intelligence officer and writer, a fervent Nationalist.

Certainly Mon's sister-in-law, Jeanne Stourton benefited during these hectic, heady, savage days. She boasted vividly of her own frequent trips to her fiancé Dick Sheepshanks, to her de Zulueta y Merry del Val family, and the Falangist officers—"up and down the lines, so frightfully excitin' "— her very closest friends during hectically violent times. Mon and Gytha's swashbuckling, extrovert nephew Rupert Bellville, an erratic amateur pilot and conveyor of guns and sherry, also benefited from this official safe conduct pass—although he finally had to be rescued from his wilder adventures by a British frigate in 1937.

Gytha was increasingly seized with deep unease. She was almost certain that her beautiful but unscrupulous and manipulative half-sister Jeanne had had an affair with Mon. A deeply attractive, deeply seductive young woman, endlessly amusing with throw-away lines of Spanish repartee, most men and many women found Jeanne quite irresistible. And even if Mon had done no more than to place his hand on her knee this would give Jeanne more than enough ammunition for more successful practice of sexual blackmail. Gytha was increasingly fearful.

As with other men of similar age, and even older, with whom Gytha had observed Jeanne's sexual entanglements—among them Sir Roderick Jones, Sir Austen Chamberlain, Lord Camoys and Gordon Selfridge—Mon del Moral was all too vulnerable to flattery and temptation, and the inevitable, deeply consequential, expensive blackmail which ensued,

The aging Spanish diplomat was deeply conventional in such matters, aware of his reputation and good name—a distinguished Catholic, a Spanish grandee, an important, accomplished spy and equal admirer of the Duke of Windsor and Count von Ribbentrop. Gytha was convinced her husband had succumbed to Jeanne's all-but irresistible charms and deadly wiles—as time proved so to be.

Quite certainly in the Fifties, once Jeanne was more than safely installed at Stonor as chatelaine and commander-in-chief of such grandeur, property and vast inheritance, she resorted again to blackmail. This time it was of Gytha and and her two children.

Jeanne drew up a strategy of "divide and rule", threatening damning revelations that her Spanish brother-in-law had "all but raped me, the bastard, tore my new nylon stockin's to a shred". Her terrifying technique worked to perfection, ensuring that Gytha was kept at even greater arm's length as far as possible, completely out of sight, let alone earshot.

Jeanne had certainly entertained Mon at her wartime residence, Assendon Lodge where she lived with her father-in-law Ralph Camoys quite openly, providing a cause of excited local gossip and scandal. Sherman had been swiftly marginalised, far away, fighting in the war. Here too at Assendon, Jeanne entertained Archbishop Frank Spellman, Chaplain General to the U.S. Forces, and Count Enrico Marone Cinzano, husband of the Spanish Infanta Princess Maria Cristina, whom Jeanne had made my godmother.

As it later transpired, Enrico, the able businessman and Cinzano tycoon, was negotiating with the Foreign Office for considerable monies, some £2,000,000, to be released for the Italian partisan movement. Upon receiving this payment the count lodged the money in his Swiss bank accounts in Geneva and Lausanne. Yet again Jeanne was privy to this secret, an expert weedler of important men, and the occasional, usefully important woman.

Mon himself owned a successful family business in Surrey that made fireplaces. He also owned farms in what was then Rhodesia—now Zimbabwe. It was here, after the Second World War that he took Gytha to live. Their nearest neighbours were the Acton cousins, at Umvukwes.

Perhaps Mon had to seek a safe, or safer, cover. But Gytha was heart-broken, torn between wishing to be with her children and yet persuaded against her own better judgement and instincts to send them away to English boarding schools, unhappily reliant on her prejudiced sisters Magda and Barbara for help at such a distance.

Gytha was deeply miserable, deeply lonely with her children so far away. Life in Rhodesia with an aged husband—thirty-three years older than she—became increasingly isolated. Moreover the fireplace business was failing and money had become scarcer, School fees had to be paid, school uniforms purchased, school holidays funded.

So when Mon died in February 1955, age 84, Gytha, only 51, was already too poor to buy a ticket to accompany her husband's body back to England for the solemn Requiem Mass celebrated at the Spanish church of St James's. From this moment on, her life became a series of unending dis-asters, humiliations and personal suffering.

Yet Gytha was a relatively young and still pretty woman, an impecunious widow with two children from a conspicuously wealthy, aristocratic fami-ly. But, in their eyes Gytha had seen too much, witnessed too much. The Stourton family had to make quite certain that by keeping this tragic woman poverty-struck they could also keep Gytha silenced, without a voice of any consequence.

In this cruel vendetta and crudely successful strategy her youngest half-sister Jeanne was the principal ring-leader. But both Magda and Barbara, well-married and well-established financially, were as much to blame for their tireless persecution of their only honourable sister Gytha. Even their humourless half-brother, the chief of Colonial Police Colonel Sir Ivo Stourton, acquiesced in the merciless persecution inflicted upon the pen-niless widow of the 8th Marqués del Moral. At the same time certain of Gytha's stepsons joined in this cruel, semi-silent, all-English revenge.

Gytha's widow's pension was a derisory pittance, a paltry £9 per week, administered by a de Bertodano stepson. This sum was never be reviewed. She was mercilessly reduced to grinding hardship, barely able even to turn on the heating.

Jeanne was acutely aware that Gytha had witnessed her involvement with the Nazi ambassador, war criminal Joachim von Ribbentrop, close friend to so many English aristocrats and important members of the Royal family. And a vitally important ally to Mon. Like Jeanne, Ribbentrop had counted amongst his pre-war friends the gay Duke of Kent and his beautiful wife Princess Marina, daughter of the prominent Nazi, the Duke of Brunswick. Many of their collective activities, glamorous house parties, socially extravagant and triumphalist Nazi celebrations of the 1936 Olympic Games in Berlin, had been wittily observed in the Diaries of Chips Channon, member of parliament and doyenne of London society, his wife a beautiful Guinness millionaire. Besides the Court Circulars of the London *Times* carried full listings of the aristocracy who most happily accepted the invitations to the German Embassy at Carlton House Terrace, so magnificently refurbished by Albert Speer.

Jeanne was determined that none of this should leak out. She chose to view Gytha as a danger—though it was highly unlikely that a woman of such conspicuous loyalty and discretion, such a truly devout Christian and Catholic would betray the secrets which also implicated her late husband. Besides, Gytha did not want her children damaged by their ruthless, piti- less aunt, widely known by her own frequently trumpeted statement as "The Aristo Spanish Bastard".

Ever titillated by acts of cruelty, Jeanne targeted Gytha, taking supreme advantage, once again of the unhappy woman's integrity and honour, mak- ing sure that her everyday life was as miserable as she, Jeanne could make it. "Such a crashin' Anglo-Saxon bore—just look at her crumpled figure, *olé!*" Jeanne exclaimed merrily. "Religious maniac to boot—Gytha's caught that stigmata thing, sayin' the rosary over and over again."

Arrogantly confident in her campaign that Gytha would not reveal the depth of her involvement with Ribbentrop, executed in 1946 for war crimes, Jeanne remembered scornfully and loudly her brother-in-law Mon's own deep involvement politically and socially with the suave Nazi diplomat and the armaments sold through their joint auspices to Franco and the Nationalist. She well remembered and with a boastful, ever- excitable relish, her own much deeper involvement with the sordid, erotic, sinister intricacies of the Thirties, and those of her near family and closest friends, intimately involved with Fascism and the pro-Hitler Movement.

Even more explosive, long to be hidden and secreted away by Scotland

Yard at the orders of the Home Office, was the notorious "Red Book" containing a list of the members of the Far Right Club founded by Jeanne's cousin, the wildly anti-Semitic member of parliament Captain Maule Ramsay. As war was breaking out, Winston Churchill had him imprisoned under Regulation 18B along with his fellow fascists Sir Oswald and Lady Mosley. A handsomely leather-bound, scarlet morocco, gold-tooled volume and illuminating record, this explosive book of distinguished names and signatures, including the Duke of Wellington, and details of stewardship and membership dues, now resides at the Weiner Museum in London's Devonshire Street.

Jeanne bullied Gytha unmercifully, aggressively, scoffingly. Derisively not only did she refuse to help her impoverished sister, she now refused even to see her—except for a very rare Sunday lunch by command at Stonor Park. Again she made it clear to her bewildered guests, Graham Greene amongst them, that: "The Marquesa, that colossal bore Mrs del Moral, bores me absolutely to tears. Besides I'm not in the slightest bit interested in her sorry tales." Mercilessly she mocked poor Gytha's Spanish title, reducing willing listeners to titters of mirth at bitingly witty imitations that further humiliated her sister, reduced to silence in Jeanne's crucifying punishment delivered so publicly.

Gytha had been reduced to such poverty after her humbling return from Rhodesia that she was forced into becoming a landlady in deeply straightened circumstances. She took in lodgers at her first cottage in the grounds of the Ascot convent, some of them her own nieces, heartless, pitiless and deeply unkind. They mocked the hapless woman's frugal cooking, her excellent needlework, her knitting, her worn clothes and out-of-fashion motor car. They derided her as-unfashionable moral code.

Gytha grew increasingly poorer. She now took a tiny cottage at Malmesbury, followed by a cottage in Ramsbury. Between whiles, already in her late fifties, Gytha with her excellent command of French and Spanish was forced into a dismal, live-in job as a governess in Greece, a misery-making experience. It only added to her lonely grief.

The family which employed this distinguished governess was merciless, indifferent, condescending and deeply unkind. Gytha was bewildered by this newest cruelty adding immeasurably to her loneliness and isolation.

To add to her humiliation, the sisters Magda, Barbara and Jeanne would simply laugh out loud at her predicament. Perhaps, as the only practising Catholic of the four of them, the tragic Gytha uncomfortably represented their consciences—a truth so boring as to be totally unacceptable to these selfish, spoilt, wilful, worldly women.

Inevitably she became increasingly bitter about the ghastly circumstances and penury of the daily life that she was forced to live, fearful for every penny of her existence, daily sinking into ever greater frugality. Increasingly Gytha, a deeply prayerful woman, relied on the rituals of the Catholic church for comfort, scant as it was. But still her courage and dignity far surmounted the shabby viciousness of the hydra-headed vendetta gradually swamping her life.

Her health diminishing, Gytha sought for a way to live within her ever more miserable means. As her niece, I pleaded with the immediate family for financial assistance for her. The answer—by letter—was a mocking, scoffing "NO."

My aunt found subsidised accommodation in ancient almshouses at Froxfield. Then she found even more scant lodgings at St John's Convent very near to Jeanne's lover Dr Jack Kempton at Rushington, near Maidenhead. Here she was only a few miles away once again from Stonor, and yards away from another niece. But succour came there none—calculated indifference was Gytha's daily, indigestible diet.

Increasingly arthritic, a finger amputated, and in continuous pain, Gytha became quite housebound, desperate to find a solution to her housing crisis. As ever courageous, always dignified, she applied for and found refuge in a charity, in the form of sheltered housing with the Royal United Kingdom Benefit Association. Here she was to remain for several years, moving at the last into their nursing home near Farnborough.

The gallant Gytha was an old-fashioned lady of principle. Despite the squalor of the punishment so mercilessly meted out to her in this bizarre Stourton family vendetta and its willing cohorts, Gytha's magnminity of character, her deeply devout, prayerful persona enabled her to forgive all those around her who had so deliberately inflicted endless years of privation, poverty and humiliation.

Despite her agony of loneliness, to the end of her life Gytha never lost her good manners nor thought and consideration for those around her. And she maintained a quite extraordinary bond with all eleven of her grandchildren, French and Spanish alike.

Gytha Stourton, Marquesa del Moral, died on March 12, 1992. Fortified by the Rites of Holy Mother Church and still wearing the miraculous scapular medal, she is appropriately buried opposite to the

Empress Eugenie of France at the Benedictine Abbey of Farnborough.

Some years before she died, Gytha stayed on various occasions with me in Fulham. On her last visit she brought with her remains of an exquisite set of bone china, the finest French porcelain, teacups and saucers. An eloquent reminder of Gytha's remarkable character and noblesse of spirit, the elegant porcelain is delicately flower-strewn: *"Blessed are the poor in spirit: for theirs is the kingdom of heaven; Blessed are the pure in heart: for they shall see God."*

9

The Joyful Mysteries of the Swastika

From my earliest childhood Mama had busily taught me the Roman Catholic Catechism, set out line by line in a scarlet-covered booklet. "Nothin' like draconian enough for you, silly brat of Sherman's that you are and permanently in a state of Mortal Sin. Somethin' must be done, and done *muy pronto!*" said Mama, swinging a slap at my head with a heavily braceleted arm. The sharp gold swastika caught me on the ear.

"Really Julia dear, it is high time you offered up all your so-called sufferin's. Make an immediate prayer of ejaculation, *olé!* And you can add to that at least two decades of the Joyful Mysteries of the rosary in contrition. Down on your knees I said, child!"

My mother gave me a sharp push and set her watch to time the Decades of the Joyful Mysteries, settling down in an armchair with an Angela Thirkell novel and a cigarette.

The word "ejaculation" I found difficult to pronounce and I had no idea what it could mean. Perhaps, I thought, it was in some way connected to the violent scenes that had recently so frightened me at a Punch and Judy show at the local lunatic asylum on the Henley Fair Mile. It might even be related to the "evacuations" Mama mentioned ceaselessly.

"Pops really has such extraordinary problems with his motion, and all such interesting evacuation," she would say thoughtfully. "As it is. I've had to consult both dear Fred Machin, my vet you know, and dear old boy Sir Archie McIndoe, though he does tend to specialise in the upper half of the body come to think of it, ha, ha and heil Hitler! Old Archie is one of my better Guns, and quite an expert in mendin' burnt-out, burnt-orf faces, quite the other end of the anatomy in this goddamned war, which is ruinin' all my plans."

I considered the possibility that the evacuations and ejaculations—which Mama said "are ejaculatory excavation and evacuation, ha ha!"—could be connected to the two red-headed East End evacuees whom Stanley West, the minuscule estate carpenter at Stonor had adopted. Stanley had a walrus moustache, bright yellow from nicotine. He and Mrs West, a fierce, stout and silent lady, looked after these two shy evacuees in their village cottage, and brought them up to Mass in the chapel on Sundays.

There was a lot to puzzle a little girl in those days, but I knew that much of the confusion around me had to do with the War and its strange regime of beige ration books and coupons for food, fuel, clothes, brandy, cartridges and petrol. Mama always had "special" additional ration books and several extra coupons, which she could exchange at will. This meant she did not have to suffer from the scarcities or shortages of rationing experienced by the rest of the population.

"I'm absolutely vital to the war efforts; and I'm most frightfully badly orf into the bargain. And BARGAIN it is, I'm tellin' you," she would say, sniffing into a lace handkerchief as she busily loaded a store-cupboard with packet upon packet of sugar, banging shut the door and locking it firmly with keys from her chatelaine silver-linked belt.

It wasn't only food that seemed to appear copiously from nowhere at this time of national hardship and crisis. Mama's rich Chanel perfume, she explained, "comes straight from France and You-know-Who at Biarritz and Bordeaux. Our lips are heavily sealed." Meanwhile the strong scent of Philip Morris cigarette smoke attached itself to every room at Assendon Lodge. I smelt the excitement of her presence even after my mother was swept away for night duties in the chauffeured police car. And for me there was also the sheer imposing perfection of Mama's Best Bedroom, one of two, each with its three exit doors—"My essential escape hatches; just right for matches and dispatches with my tutors."

Faced with Mama's clear and obvious sufferings, I was determined this beautiful, clearly fragile person must be protected from any further slight. I wanted to break into intercessionary prayer and decided that "Hail Holy Queen, Mother of Mercy!" would be the prayer Mama would most like me to ejaculate.

In the altar of her bedroom I tried this as hard as I was able, gazing spellbound at the mountain of silk and satin-edged cushions and lace-bordered pillows atop an elaborate crocheted bedspread. Everywhere I could see there were ribbons, bows, heavy flounces of flowered chintzes on top of the four-poster bed, a further deep-flounced chintz petticoat beneath.

Mama was unimpressed. "Don't go out of your way to upset and irritate the hell out of me," she declared angrily from the bed. "I'm most frightfully busy consultin' my old friends Colefax & Fowler and it's far too soon for you to be released from your Mortal Sins. So back to the rosary, my girl. The 'Sorrowful Mysteries' will do this time."

Mama patted the sleek vicuña rug draped over her feet, two black claws facing towards the ceiling. "South American, my family from Bogotá of course, *olé!* Far superior to cashmere too." Lovingly she stroked the vicuña claws.

I supposed the yaks and llamas whose photographs I'd seen in Papa's yellow-bound *National Geographic* magazines to be obvious cousins to this vicuña of Mama's. But she said: "As usual, as always, again and again, Sherman's totally tedious, tiresome brat that you are, you're totally out-of-place, ridiculous, and quite absurd. Furthermore you bring on one of my misery makin', totally cripplin', and agonisin' migraines." Sighing, she passed a weary hand over her brow. "Don't ever bother to tell me again you're doin' your best. Let me make it quite clear, child, that your best is simply never goin' to be good enough. Mark my words, and listen hard!"

Mama suddenly threw off the bedclothes and rose to her feet in a green nylon White House nightgown. Flicking her fingers she continued: "Not only are you a damn nuisance in my life, but you're a positive vulgarian to boot. I could, and I will get that darlin' boy Cardinal Hinsley—and all my other pals at the Vatican—to EXCOMMUNICATE you for sheer stupidity." Pausing to light a cigarette, she continued reflectively. "After all, the cardinal owes me more than a favour or two—or three. *Olé* and heil Hitler!"

So saying Mama gave me a resounding slap round the ears, my hair pulled in a series of jerks as she aimed a vigorous kick at my bottom. Taken by surprise I could not stop my tears.

"Oh, for Gawd's sake Julia, shut up, shut up!" hissed Mama scornfully. "You're such absolute rubbish, you borin' brat of Sherman's. If only I could rid of Mildew Camoys, I'd be shot of the both of you, and that goes for Sherman too."

I obeyed as fast as I could and stood there shaking with silent sobs. I knew there would be worse in store for me.

*

All through the Second World War, daily life at Assendon Lodge was filled with callers, and Mama was constantly busy. But Papa was mostly away with his regiment. Several sundry Guns, royalty and foreign "Uncles" came and went with regularity. But some stayed put, and my night prayers were constantly changing although they invariably started with a prayer of fervent gratitude "for Mama and Bangpa" followed by the Guns whom I tried to remember in sequence so that I could truly please my mother. Her turnover on the rota of Guns and Uncles was swift indeed.

"Absolutely *de rigueur* of course to pray for your grandfather and me first and foremost. Look at all I do for you, silly brat," sniffed Mama through my litany of names. "And don't forget those quite divine royal boys Uncle George and Uncle Paul—the Greeks you know. Though, I have to say, 'boys' is just their taste, ha, ha, *olé* and heil Hitler!" Brightly she continued: "Some frightfully nice jewellery in that pipeline, and comin' my way shortly down the Claridge's pipeline. That will help keep Certain Events under wrap—chastity belt, lock and key too, come to think of it, and I keep the padlock, ha, ha, and *viva el rey de España!*" Mama swooped up a pair of black ebony castanets and whirled them round her head.

Some of the Uncles and Guns wore khaki uniform like Papa's. My mother said "most of these divinely gallant boys are Sherman's fellow-officers from the Oxon-Bucks, *olé!*" This made me dream that night of oxen and bulls fording the Thames at Henley bridge, led by the regiment's officers, their glamorously braided caps still on their heads. Mama would insist these caps were removed whenever they came into the drawing-room at Assendon Lodge. And in my dream, the officers still kept their trousers on in the Thames water that rose to their waists.

The next morning, I told Mama eagerly about what I had dreamed. But the reality was quite different: at Assendon Lodge the officers kept on taking their trousers off as this was the way Mama preferred it. "Pants orf," she would command imperiously. "Don't let's waste any time, boys, *olé!*"

In the latter part of my dream these Officers, Uncles and Guns dragged with them weapons and ammunition, their bright orange cartridges bought from the royal gunsmiths opposite Mama's favourite London hotel, the Connaught. Here their glamorous 12-bore guns were hand-made and hand-carved.

Others of Mama's callers wore the British dark-blue naval uniform or the American pale beige. The burly blue-eyed hook-nosed Uncle Dick

Ovey was Papa's best friend and already a commander in the Royal Navy. Living at Middle Assendon Mill, he was our closest male neighbour and a habitual pipe-smokin' Gun. Old Lady Ovey, his mother, shouted stridently and frequently at my mother. Uncle Dick's young American wife from New England was blue-eyed and pretty with curly hair. Mama did not seem to like her

"What a borin' rich bitch from Boston your prim Betty is," Mama would comment, "and with a great penchant for the sherry bottle."

And when Uncle Dick's equally blue-eyed brother-in-law Cuthbert Sheldon came to call at Assendon Lodge, my mother mocked him. "You're just constantly runnin' from Orstralia to Downside Abbey and back again in this goddamned war. Typical conscientious objector, Cartholic coward and shirker, and just another effin' nuisance in my life!" Mama looked now to Uncle Dick. "I've been tellin' Cuthbert to take that frightfully common colonial tweed jacket orf immediately. Just too bad he removed one of your sisters so swiftly, Dick darlin' boy. She never deserved quite such a sod, ha, ha and *olé!*"

My godfather Uncle Libby—Lebbeus Hordern—wore a similar uniform to Uncle Dick, though he was in the Fleet Air Arm of the Navy. His chest was covered with medals and frogging.

Said Mama: "My darlin' Libby is most frightfully brave, even though he does have a case of gallopin' tuberculosis. He's divebombed the *Tirpitz* and a lot of other Hun ships straight to the bottom of the ocean, *olé!*"

Papa, now home after being invalided from the army, sat silently and alone at the far end of the vast table intricately laid with heavily crested silver cutlery. Georgian silver hunting cups, candlesticks in the shape of Corinthian columns and Carolean candelabras festooned the dining table at the other end of which sat my mother covered in jewels and wearing a Tyrolean hunting hat.

She caressed the hat as if a memory came to her. "My own divine blue-eyed boy that darlin' Joachim," she murmured, her hand sliding neatly into Uncle Jack Rutherford's beneath the folds of the stiffly starched linen tablecloth.

Seated at her other side, the slim-figured Lebbeus was gentle and shy, with long, delicate hands. He seemed to be in some awe of my mother and his hands shook as he ate.

"Libby is your vastly rich Orstralian godfather, and such a dear old beau of mine," said Mama, gazing at Uncle Lebbeus. "Of course he's in most frightfully fragile health, not long for this world," she sighed. "Ragin' TB!"

I wondered about the fate of my shy godfather as my mother busily explained that he owned every store in Sydney. "But your darlin' mother Olga Romero married to that mini Don Juan Spanish diplomat who plays cards with your grandfather at St James's Club—and Brook's come to think of it—is most frightfully rich too. Such a bosom friend of mine, the darlin' old girl," Mama told Uncle Libby cheerfully. "That randy Rafael, tied to Olga's coat-tails of course, looks like a Belgian rat that should have been drowned at birth. Except that he owns a flat in Belgrave Square to die for," she added reflectively. "Not a patch on number 24 and my *abuelo* old Marqués Cardenal Borja Merry del Val's palazzo, my very own Spanish Embassy."

I couldn't help but notice how beautiful Uncle Libby's hands were. Like Papa's they were slender with long fingers. He too wore a signet ring, of lapis lazuli and yellow gold.

"And that," said Mama, "is an aristo family crest, Julia dear. Mine has just been made up in 18-carat gold of course, by my own divine Monsieur Louis at Cartier's. Quite frankly I simply cannot abide cheap gold. Nothing less than the best, and I mean the VERY best, in my agonisin' poverty will begin to do . . ."

She looked approvingly down at her ruby and diamond double-clip brooch and matching watch-bracelet. "My own darlin' Barbara Hutton certainly got my message," she said happily, winking at Uncle Libby.

The little finger on Mama's left hand was entirely encased up to the knuckle with a thick wide band of solid gold. A design in miniature of a skylark and a rock was sunk into its centre, like a plush pin-cushion. "This is my very own puddin'-stone you know," said Mama admiringly, gazing down at her family ring. "Quite prehistoric and absolutely phallic don't you think? It's that Druidical Stonor blood-line, ha ha!"

Her new signet ring seemed to be used more frequently as a weapon than even the de Zulueta crest which she had now abandoned. "Some old *castillo* near Cádiz called La Alcaría will shortly be comin' my way as it is," she announced emphatically. "And just a nip and a tuck from my sportin' activities at my cousin the Marquess of Bute's place in Algeciras over to Tangiers," she added happily. "A frightfully rich smuggler, the old boy. Into porn. Absolutely."

I straightaway rushed to tell Mama how beautiful I thought her new acquisition was. Emphatically she raised her entire arm and shoulder and brought the newly crested ring onto the dining table with a bang to signify her displeasure that I had spoken.

"You are strictly to be seen as seldom as possible, Julia and never ever to be heard you tiresome child. Did you hear what I said?" Another crash of the Cartier ring. "Furthermore, the conversation round this table bores me to tears. All change gentlemen, please. On with the Oporto *muy pronto*! A toast to my darlin' boy, the gallant Colonel Jack Rutherford!" She picked up an antique silver handbell, shaped like a lupin, waving it in the air as she rang briskly to summon Ruby for fresh provisions from the pantry.

Of all Mama's callers, my second godfather Uncle Al Russell had the loudest and heartiest laughs. His skin was olive and his dark brown hair had a rich shine. "Dear old Al has more than a dose of Bosch blood because his mother, Lady Odo, such a dear, comes from Vienna. And that explains darlin' Al's sweaty, swarthy looks. Almost Dago."

Uncle Al was cheerful, sturdily built and plump. He bounced around, and his loud voice and fruity conversation, peppered with German phrases, made Mama laugh so I too was very happy. And this second godfather—"Just like having the First Prince Paul of Greece, and Second Prince you-know-who of Holland," explained Mama cheerfully—gave me some pretty glass animals.

There was a long brown dachshund followed by a fat green cat with a curly tail and a colourless dull white pig. These were given to me by Uncle Al wrapped in expensive tissue paper. "They're Eytie from that funny little island orf Venezia," Mama couldn't help explaining on Al's behalf. "Murano-Burano, you know."

I was deeply disappointed when this flow of presents came to an abrupt halt. One day, Mama had instructed me to tell Uncle Al firmly that his presents were "nothin' but a bore" to me. Obediently I did as I was told as we ate, but I was confused when he seemed hurt and rather surprised. Watching our conversation, Mama laughed before giving me a quick nip and pinch from beneath the tablecloth.

Then there was "Count Brown who makes herbal tinctures in Turin and Lugano", as Mama called him laughingly. A caller whose complexion was as khaki as Uncle Al Russell's and something of an unsmiling little man, Count Enrico Marone Cinzano had a thin, trim, pencil straight moustache stretched over safety-pin tight lips. His trousers were baggy, and his jacket looked more like a box. There were none of the bugger-puzzles and tailor's vents so favoured by Mama at the back of his squarely-cut brown suit.

Uncle Enrico and my mother conferred and talked together in the locked study, their voices lowered. I could not hear very much of what they said except the once when I heard Mama's laugh as she shouted: "You can screw that smug, inscrutable expression right orf your snug face, Enrico Marone Cinzano. I must know absolutely now and immediately, this very moment just where the money is. And don't you effin' dare to keep me waitin'." I could hear her bracelets jangling as she laughed excitedly. "Dollars or Swiss francs are all the same to me. Either currency does the trick. *Olé* and *viva el rey de España!*"

Opening the study door suddenly, she marched towards the stairs, calling over her shoulder: "Just come this way, darlin' boy. You haven't seen my bedroom yet."

When the count reappeared from Mama's Best Bedroom, Ruby Heath had prepared tea and scones in the yellow drawing room. I was called in to be inspected. "And this, then, is Sherman's thoroughly tedious brat who is the Infanta Cristina's god-daughter, Julia Maria Cristina Mildred, completely gormless, brainless and quite idiotic. So you can report that back to the royal marines in Turin and Lugano, and to your wife, *olé* and heil Hitler!"

Uncle Enrico sat upright on my mother's stiff-backed, mustard-yellow cut-velour sofa. His minute feet dangled, just touching the parquet floor. From this angle, where I had been placed to sit, I could see that he was wearing a cream silk shirt, silk tie and long dark-brown socks matching his suit, with black patent leather shoes. Uncle Enrico's stomach was tightly but neatly squeezed into his double-breasted jacket. His face looked like a thundercloud.

"I see you've been diggin' deep into a solid gold Swiss trough since you so inconveniently removed yourself from Torino, Enrico, old boy. Lugano and Geneva banks obviously still just your thing," said Mama cheerfully. "And how is darlin' Queen Ena herself? Such a frightfully close friend of mine all these years. Such a poppet your mother-in-law. Must be about the same age as you, Enrico darlin' come to think of it? Gawd knows the Queen and I have gorne through it together since even before that goddamned Spanish Civil War, *olé!* We've always had SO very much in common."

Wearily my mother passed a heavily bejewelled hand languidly across her forehead, taking a further deep puff on a contraband American cigarette. As she smoked she mused: "Do be sure to ask your Infanta just how her dear old uncle, the Marquess of Carisbrooke is. I'm really most frightfully keen on his coronet decorated with strawberry leaves. Fewer balls than most other peers come to think of it. All those divine velvet robes of his suit me down to the ground. I've worn them almost as frequently as my darlin' Cousin Peter Derwent if my infallible memory serves me well."

I dared to ask Mama about the whereabouts of all these interesting people and places.

"Don't bother me with such trivia," came the cold reply. "Surely by now you can remember that Cousin Peter is the Lord Derwent of Hackin' Hall, Scarborough and all of that. And dear old Carisbrooke is the Marquess of Castle Carisbrooke, and Keeper of the Key to the Isle of Wight, a very important diplomatic postin', what with the Royal Yacht Squadron and the Bembridge Dingy and Sailin' Club, my old huntin' grounds. Enrico's own huntin' grounds could be a little differently described of course, dependin' on just how he thinks fit to treat me in these awkward circs. He could leave himself rather compromised, *olé!*"

Mama rustled a wad of notes she had been holding tightly in one hand, flicking each one over as she counted out American dollars and Swiss francs.

Mama hastened to explain to her next afternoon caller: "Al, darlin' boy, these absolutely absurd Eyties have such funny names, foreign of course, like Macaroni and Marone, ha, ha! Basically Enrico is just common Mr Brown who manufactures herbal tonics for my dry martinis." Another deep sigh. "Of course he is a millionaire come to think of it. Explains why the Cinzano title is really so recent and totally nouveau. Unlike dear Ralph Camoys whose title is hundreds of years old, just like him." Mama winked at Bangpa-Pop, who was sitting the other side of the drawing-room. "I shall most certainly be Lady Camoys the moment that bitch Mildew Lady Cee drops ORF her perch. And the sooner the better as far as I am concerned, don't you agree Pop, old boy?"

Breaking wind more lightly than usual, Bangpa-Pop guffawed in reply.

10

A Memory of the Commandant Mary Allen

Jeanne met Commandant Mary Allen, co-founder of the Women Police in March 1934 when she was guest speaker at a London dinner of the right-wing January Club.

This introduction to such a stalwart supporter of Hitler, an enthusiastic member of the Ladies' Carlton Club, annexe to the important all-male Carlton Club on St James's Street, was to have profound consequences for Jeanne and her future and burgeoning career in the Women Police Force.

Enrolled in 1940 under the auspices of the Chief Constable of Oxfordshire, the handsome blue-eyed Colonel Sir Eric St Johnston, an acquaintance of Joachim von Ribbentrop, and a beau whom Jeanne had not discarded, she was appointed, officially, as a woman police officer, uniformed, spankingly smart, even bemedalled, serving in various roles throughout the Second World War.

Jeanne, whose first heady excitement had been the signing of the Official Secrets Act (despite her quite extraordinary involvement with the Ribbentrop Büro) continued to parade in immaculate and bespoke full-dress uniform, into the even more promising years and aftermath of the Second World War, triumphantly, regally, imperiously installed as the Commandant of Stonor Park, 1945 onwards—and only thirty-two years old.

Recently returned from Germany earlier in 1934, where she had been studying the methods of German policewomen, the burly, uniformed and bemedalled Mary Allen was a profoundly committed enthusiast of Hitler by whom she had been received in audience and with whom she was officially photographed, the image duly autographed by her Berlin host.

Guests at the glamorous January Club dinner of March 1934, chaired by

Sir John Squires, included Sir Oswald Mosley, Sir Donald and Lady Makgill, William Joyce (later to become the notorious propaganda broadcaster Lord Haw-Haw, judged a traitor, executed after the war's end), Sir George Duckworth-King, Wing-Commander Louis Greig, Lord and Lady Russell of Liverpool, Sir Philip Magnus, General the Hon Charles Bruce, Major "Fruity" Metcalf, closest friend and confidante of the heir to the throne, the Prince of Wales (later the Duke of Windsor). Jeanne's own prestigious women companions on this occasion were Lady Alexandra Metcalf, Lady Ravensdale and Lady Houston, the extremist pro-Nazi newspaper editor. Another of the clique was the Russian emigrée Anna Wolkoff, later tried with Tyler Kent of the US embassy, accused of spying—just part of the many intriguants deep in the heart of this influential high society.

From early youth Jeanne had always been fascinated by the elegant footwear of the men around her. Her cousins and "beaux" habitually wore spats, bespoke shoes, hand-made thigh-high, highly glossed, gleaming leather military and hunting boots. She was all the more hypnotised by a passion, shared with Unity Mitford amongst other contemporaries, for uniforms, medals, and the swashbuckling, right-wing, male-dominated clubs. Politically and socially dominant amongst these was the Carlton Club and the Ladies' Carlton Club of which Mary Allen was a member.

Like Unity, Jeanne increasingly turned to the blood-lust, sex appeal and violent glamour of the Nazis, several of whose active English sympathisers, excitedly anti-Semitic, were both related to and close friends of Jeanne's.

As the Thirties progressed other clubs sprang up, including the extreme New Right Club, the Link, as also the January Club. Emphatically anti-Semitic, they were fully supported by the Catholic hierarchy of the day, encompassing politically extremely active and powerfully successful men and women—as the infamous "Red Book" would further endorse in 1940.

Solidly cemented in amongst these several well-funded power brokers were the Cardinal Archbishop of Westminster Cardinal Hinsley, the still youthful priests Monsignor Alfred Gilbey and Canon Alfonso de Zulueta, the 16th Duke of Norfolk, the 22nd Lord Mowbray Segrave and Stourton, his brother the Hon John Joseph Stourton, Lord Ralph Camoys, the Hon Sir Harry Stonor, the Hon Eddie Stonor and Jeanne's maternal uncle Archbishop Mostyn of Cardiff, his portly brother Monsignor John Mostyn, well dug into the corridors of power at the Vatican. The English

Catholic Establishment of the day was an openly active supporter both of Fascism and the Nazi regime. They saw the dictators Mussolini and Hitler as bulwarks against the advance of obnoxious socialism and evil communism, the former as detestable as the latter. But these exclusive English Catholics were driven mostly by greed for the capitalist system and financial and personal gain rather than by any principle. Overwhelmingly, the Establishment across the board irrespective of denomination was utterly determined to hold onto property, estates and inheritances. This ambition was largely achieved through the dysfunctional law of primogeniture, exclusivity of birth and wealth, and any available means legal or illegal in combination with the skilled, wily, highly-paid lawyers with whom these ambitious, ruthless persons surrounded themselves.

In the Catholic world of the day there were a number of law firms, solicitors and canon lawyers (approved by the Vatican) who specialised in services such as annulments and asset stripping. It seemed that few scams were too small for them in their quest to seek yet more lucrative income. The skilled manipulation of wills and entails was a particular speciality, and these complacent lawyers would robustly and angrily spring to the defence of the church hierarchies of Westminster and Birmingham whenever scandal threatened—of which there were many.

But it was normally the hapless victims of these calculated campaigns who were promptly marginalised, mocked, silenced and publicly trashed. A particular discrimination was practised, with very rare exception, against the women who, seemingly, stood in the way of these ruthless men of the English Catholics, the very Establishment itself. This was never a fate which the skilful, deeply skilled Jeanne would remotely contemplate— though she never hesitated in its cruel implementation even against her own mother, "Feckless Fanny" Stourton, deliberately abandoned to die in lonely squalor. And enacted as vigorously against Mildred Camoys, her hated American mother-in-law from 1938 until her untimely death in 1961.

The ultimate, habitually successful weapon wielded by this cabal of unscrupulous lawyers was the very real, ruthless threat of poverty, preferably absolute poverty, whereby the hapless, innocent victim was reduced to a life of privation, living in an unheated grace and favour cottage with an unsound, leaking roof and an external lean-to toilet. Hidden away on a lonely common on the estate as far removed as possible from public transport, the hapless victim's cries, pleas for help could not even be heard from behind the thorn thickets, bramble patches, dew pond and wringing wet, mud-strewn dirt track that served as a so-called drive to "The Cottage". These dependencies were habitually called after the family that owned the estate and seat—Camoys, Drummond, Norfolk, Perth, Tichborne, Weld, Witham, Stourton, Stonor.

As self-seeking, harsh-hearted, hypocritical men, it would be the lawyers who would be inevitably called upon to loudly declare their terrified quarry as "totally mad, quite insane, off his/her head—a lunatic whom we shall have committed". Invariably this scandalous device succeeded in creating misery, chaos and abject poverty—and, additionally, a gratuitous, dismissive scolding from a triumphantly perfidious, deeply unscrupulous Catholic Canon Law Tribunal, shielded by such contemptible terror tactics from ever making recompense for terrible wrongs enacted in its ceaseless search for yet more inquisitional cruelty, yet more influence, yet more power. Such a vicious, calculated—and lucrative—means of vendetta was yet another abuse of power that invoked all the unholy pleasures for those pulling the reins.

Another such useful legal device was the proving of peerages, the revival—at huge expense—of defunct baronies, a speciality encouraged by Queen Victoria. At the Queen's suggestion, and granted for payment of the then princely sum of £15,000 in 1839 Thomas "Old Tom" Stonor, applied to the College of Arms for this privilege, enabling him to inherit a title several hundred years out-of-date, originally used at the Battle of Agincourt.

This somewhat dubious but useful inheritance, the Barony of Camoys, doorway to the House of Lords, came specifically through the female descent of the blood line, a pre-Reformation Barony of Writ, legally, armorially, in the female entail. The title had been in abeyance since the 15th century.

The 3rd Lord Camoys, Old Tom, a hunting contemporary of the Duke of Wellington while both were students in France, was however blessed with little sense of humour and so the fact that his new title Camoys equated with "Cam Eas", a Welsh name denoting "crooked nose, crooked river", seems to have passed him by. Nevertheless Old Tom did quickly abandon the newly-acquired somewhat spurious motto: *"I stoop not."*

The literary set of Hilaire Belloc, himself half-French, and the Catholic convert G. K. Chesterton gave great support to the anti-Semitism that had also become fashionably rampant during the Thirties in France and Spain. This highbrow but narrow-minded, deeply opinionated, arrogantly articulate, well organised group joined together with much of the English ecclesiastical hierarchy and its Establishment of grandees, in giving fervent support to General Franco's fascist Falangists in the Spanish Civil War. Some members of this powerful group were happily and not always covertly supplying lucrative armaments to Franco and his Nationalists.

The compelling lure of the Spanish royalist factor in London was dominated by the court of Queen Ena of Spain. Illustrious ambassadors, close personal friends of the Queen, the handsome Brazilian diplomat and gold bullion merchant, doyenne of the diplomatic corps, Raul Regis de Oliveira, the dashing Duke of Alba and Berwick, reigned supreme amongst the courtiers.

The regal "English Queen of Spain", as the granddaughter of Queen Victoria was known, lived in the surrounds of an elegant, worldly, well-born entourage of devout Spanish and English Catholics. The intoxicating atmosphere enabled the dazzling Jeanne with her dashing, provocative Spanish allure, beautiful couturier clothes and witty glamour to be a centre of this glittering stage. She glided vividly effortlessly, supremely self-confident through these gilded circles with consummate ease, ceaselessly, suggestively seductive, in an elixir of hedonism and restless ambition.

Besides, Jeanne could rejoice in the conquest of the still handsome, albeit aging millionaire Brazilian ambassador, the infatuated Raul Regis de Oliveira, his long-suffering wife Dona Georgina Patiño Olinda, submissively ever-loyal, despite Jeanne's continuous flaunting of her rich, glamorous grandee prize—a prize shot to boot, with deep, angulated roots at the powerful Vatican court in the heart of Rome.

Jeanne spent much time together with her dashing but short-statured cousins, millionaire smuggler, the 5th Marquess of Bute, and his son and heir, Lord John Crichton-Stuart, both fervent Knights of Malta, enthusiastic members of the Anti-Socialist League, and the Anti-Communist League, and equally enthusiastic members of the popular and well-funded Anglo-German Fellowship, highly successful and vividly active under the auspices and patronage of the Duke of Brunswick and Hitler's ambassador, Count Joachim von Ribbentrop.

The Thirties were for Jeanne a period of intense excitement. And they were years which she would endeavour to replicate in the Forties and

Fifties at Stonor Park—of which Assendon Lodge, Jeanne's wartime bivouac was merely an adjunct of expediency, and local convenience, an immediate gateway to the Park, to the Bosmore Estate, to the Henley town hall, to the knackers' yard at Benson. And to Turville Grange, the house of Julia Stonor, the Marquise d'Hautpoul—whom, initially, Jeanne regarded as Royalty.

Jeanne saw a lot of another close relative, President of the Potato Marketing Board, Captain Archibald Maule Ramsay, Conservative member of Parliament for Peebles and Mid-Lothian. First cousin to HRH Princess Victoria, Lady Ramsay, and the 14th Earl of Dalhousie, "Archie", was a founder member of the pro-Nazi club, the Link, in active collusion with the 7th Marquess of Londonderry, the 11th Marquess of Lothian, and E. M. Tennant, tycoon businessman, co-founder of the Anglo-German Fellowship, and member of the Glenconner dynasty closely related to Cecil Beaton's notorious friend, Stephen Tennant.

Archie was also married to a Crichton-Stuart widow, Ismay, a fervent Catholic. Both husband and wife were vociferously anti-Semitic, both inside and outside the House of Commons—to the point where they would be imprisoned during the war. So too were others of Jeanne's mutual friends, the maverick Admiral Sir Barry and Lady Domville amongst them. After the war, the latter would later become near neighbours of Jeanne once she had returned to Stonor.

Amongst this set there were not only the political Stonor brothers, Eddie and Harry, but also Lord Tavistock, later the 12th Duke of Bedford; the 1st Lord Brocket—a successful tycoon and a close friend of prime minister Neville Chamberlain from whom Joachim von Ribbentrop rented a house in Eaton Square while the German embassy in Carlton House Terrace was refurbished by Hitler's personal architect Albert Speer; E.M. Tennant, close friend of Ribbentrop and founder member of the Anglo-German Fellowship; the 8th Duke of Buccleugh; the 1st Lord Mottisone, Minister of Munitions, another confidante of Ribbentrop's; the 19th Lord Semphill, a dour, inhibited and secretive Scottish peer. Whilst they emphatically shared the same extreme political views as the unfortunate Captain Maule Ramsay and Admiral Sir Barry Domville, as also the more worldly Sir Oswald and Lady Mosley, nevertheless they were exempt from detention, imprisonment under Regulation 18B even despite their openly anti-Semitic, pro-Nazi views.

The great round-up of Enemy Aliens occurred in 1941. It touched this arrogant group of power brokers not one whit. Nor was the liberty of most of their number in any way infringed, indeed they shot their way through the Second World War, the most of them, it seemed, as knickerbockered Guns and Uncles at Assendon Lodge and on the Stonor Park Estates, well rewarded with the favours of the day accompanied by many a wink, many a nudge—and occasional embarrassment when their required "perform-ance", as with the 5th Baron Camoys, was "not quite up to scratch, *olé!*"

But the pay-off, the essential cover-up, the bribery proved curiously expensive, and seldom in a single payment. Disconcertingly the Guns and Uncles all too soon discovered their beautiful, intoxicating hostess, Police Constable the Honourable Mrs Sherman Stonor, her young husband con-veniently away in the war, to be an expert at chantage. Regardless, these vain men continued in their heady sexual immersion and political intoxi-cation.

They found the presence of the Commandant of Women Police, the somewhat earthy Mary Allen, a frequent visitor at Assendon Lodge more than reassuring. Bearing heavily laden saddle bags and habitually uni-formed, Mary Allen arrived at Assendon Lodge astride a powerful motor-cycle, wearing flying goggles and broad, black leather gauntlets. She bore a quite remarkable resemblance to Toad of Toad Hall but nevertheless seemed to lend an atmosphere of endorsement to these Establishment grandees—and conspicuous gangsters. Brown manilla envelopes, heavily sealed, cascaded from twin saddle bags into the ever-ready arms of Jeanne.

Throughout her life, women were irresistibly drawn towards Jeanne. Of this dangerously exciting quality of enticement she was well aware—her earlier conquests had included the playwright Enid Bagnold, wife of her lover Sir Roderick Jones, and, more poignantly, the Poor Little Rich Girl—the gentle, beautiful, vulnerable and doomed heiress Barbara Hutton.

Inevitably the burly Mary Allen was equally susceptible to Jeanne's seductive beauty and exotic, even mesmeric charm. As inevitably there was a jealous rivalry amongst the Guns and Uncles—Jeanne played each one off against the other with consummate skill and largely for her own amuse-ment, in addition to a most considerable lucrative gain. Besides, through-out the Second World War, she supplied all these guests with the added aphrodisiac of sumptuous, sumptuously prepared, exotic cuisine; and an unending supply of fine wines, vintage port, cognac and champagne drawn up from the absentee Sherman's well stocked cellars, deep beneath the

Tudor great hall "up at the Park", to which Jeanne had acquired immediate access in 1939.

Mary Allen was not alone in being titivated at Jeanne's frequent boast that she had been a mistress of Joachim von Ribbentrop during the heady years of the mid-Thirties. Jeanne counted herself equal amongst the entourage of close cousins and successful tycoons, sycophantic courtiers, international aristocrats and selected diplomats, whose largely notorious company she sought and fought for—male and, occasionally, opportunistically, female. And when it came to her own sex, as a matter of course and strategy Jeanne had a preference for the blood royal, habitually wooing susceptible and innocent princesses, at least three royal Infantas of Spain her speciality.

Irresistible to her was the tall, dashing, aristocratic and stylish, Ribbentrop, Hitler's ambassador to Britain (appointed 1936), the blue-eyed, blond-haired diplomat most frequently wore black and silver SS uniform and jack-boots. He was an excellent linguist with bold, graceful script handwriting, an extraordinarily accomplished ballroom dancer; and with a reputation as far as Hungary for the ready seduction of beautiful women, preferably titled. His hapless, long-suffering wife, owner of the Henkle champagne fortune, an eligible but plain woman, was uneasily only too aware of these conquests "in Society". However, the couple shared in common both the Nazi creed, and a most arrogant verbal contempt for their many servants, whether at Dahlem, Schloss Sonnenburg or within the equal grandeur of Carlton House Terrace.

Already a friend of Jeanne's from as early as 1933 meeting her whilst on one of his frequent diplomatic missions to England, prior to his London appointment, Count von Ribbentrop was deeply committed, passionately attached to Hitler. He had swiftly become ambassador following the neatly, coldly, skilfully arranged murder of the anti-Nazi ambassador Leopold von Hoesch—whose little dog still remains buried beneath a poplar tree, alongside the German embassy on Carlton House Terrace. At the head of the Duke of York Steps, the granite headstone, seldom observed, is lovingly engraved: " 'Ciro'—*ein treuer Begleiter. London in Februar 1934. Hoesch.*"

Commandant Mary Allen, Colonel Sir Eric St Johnston, Chief Constable of Oxfordshire, and other Guns and Uncles, Sir Archibald McIndoe, the famous plastic surgeon amongst them, were all too uneasily aware of Jeanne's frequently vaunted boast that she had early been recruited as a highly-paid informer for the substantially funded Ribbentrop Büro, comprised of carefully selected undercover spies from as far afield as Munich, Paris—where there was a branch of the Büro (earlier known as the Ribbentrop Dienstelle)—and London. Its lethal tentacles were everywhere, with much of its sordid but useful information garnered through the dubious tactics of sexual blackmail—the same chantage that Jeanne practised with supreme success throughout her lifetime.

Membership of the Büro brought great power and added prestige for Jeanne. It also ensured that people, great and small, were all the more in awe of her conspicuous power, frightened of her and fearful for their own future. Additionally, Jeanne's conspicuously close relationship with Ribbentrop himself enabled even more doors to be opened into the highest echelons of society, whether close in the wake of the dashing, glamorous, drug-addicted and gay, avowedly pro-Nazi Duke of Kent, Prince Edward, or the set and society clique of the as notorious and wittily worldly gay member of parliament, Sir Henry "Chips" Channon, and his accompanying Guinness entourage. Equally, Jeanne's long-established connection and close relationship with Cecil and Reggie Beaton's set had already brought her into intimate contact at close quarters with the millionaire brothers Sir Osbert and Sir Sacheverell Sitwell, and later their unique sister Dame Edith Sitwell, famous pauper, poet and Catholic convert.

Even more was Jeanne irresistibly drawn to the court, and courtiers, surrounding the Prince of Wales, subsequently the Duke of Windsor, heir to the throne until he abdicated in 1936 upon the death of King George VI. The prince was known to be notoriously anti-Semitic, pro-Nazi, a frequent visitor to, and enthusiastic follower of Hitler and Goering.

As too were many others of the nobility, Lords Londonderry and Lothian, the Earl of Macclesfield, the Marquess of Hamilton, the Marquesses of Burghley, Bute and Zetland, the Dukes of Bedford, Norfolk and Wellington, the purveyor of armaments, the Lords Brabazon and Tara, the Lords Brocket and Weir, the Lords Semphill and Portsmouth amongst a deeply political, deeply self-righteous throng.

Even the near relations of titled families, the Bembridge Bellvilles and Pleydell-Bouveries, first cousins to the Earls of Radnor, the Glasgow racing driver aeronauts the Archibald Kidstons, millionaire founder members of Jardine, Matheson, the titled Stonor brothers, Eddie and Harry of the Camoys dynasty, the son of the Selfridges' tycoon Gordon Selfridge were amongst a more than glittering throng of openly enthusiastic, energetic ever-eager devotees to the Nazi cause. As ever their excuse was a detestation of the mere threat of Socialism and the added terror of Communism. That the former could produce urgently needed social justice nationally, was a matter of sheer indifference. All but a very few of these powerfully prosperous landowners kept their many fearful retainers, farm workers and servants in tied cottages lacking even basic sanitation.

Fascinated by the glamour and glitter of the literary set, Jeanne became alternately mistress to Sir Roderick Jones, owner-director of Reuters, and the close "girlfriend" of his equally Hitler-admiring wife, the renowned playwright Enid Bagnold.

Almost simultaneously, Jeanne also became made intimate conquests of the ageing and distinguished politician Sir Austen Chamberlain (influential half-brother to the prime minister Neville Chamberlain), Sir Richard Sykes (millionaire race-horse breeder and owner of the vast Yorkshire estate of Sledmere Park), the aged Marquess of Carisbrooke and Gordon Selfridge (Chicago millionaire and highly eligible widower, owner of Selfridges). The last was briefly, like Sir Austen, officially designated as "my employer, *olé*!" by Jeanne.

Even more conspicuously, there was the handsome, hot-blooded, virile Brazilian ambassador Raul Regis de Oliveira who had early been drawn deeply into Jeanne's irresistibly honeyed net. The still lively diplomat and bullion merchant conducted a long-term affair with Jeanne. Raul was married to another of her South American cousins, mother of the beautiful Sylvia Regis de Oliveira, later to become not only one of Jeanne's scarlet-gloved bridesmaids but also the second wife of the eligible widower Prince Jean Faucigny-Lusinge following the death of his beautiful wife the Baronne d'Erlanger (whose handsome banker brother Sir Gerald "Pop" d'Erlanger followed in the line of post-war succession of Jeanne's illustrious bedfellows and lovers). Raul was already in his early sixties when first he met Jeanne, then barely nineteen, in 1932. Even after retirement he continued to reside in London well into the Second World War until the mid Forties, his favourite sport being to stay at Assendon Lodge and to shoot his magnificent hand-made Purdey 12-bore guns on the Stonor estates.

Jeanne had become particularly attached to her several South American and Spanish family, several of whom were prestigious, pro-Nazi members of the diplomatic corps in Rome, in Berlin, in Bogotá, in Madrid and subsequently Hendaye. She spoke more than adequate if highly colourful, expletive-spattered Spanish—in "my pure Castillian aristo accent", she proudly exclaimed—and she had a certain if limited command of German as well as a considerable and fruity French vocabulary, though she had a loudly vocalised contempt for "French frogs" and for the "Eyties" as Jeanne loudly declared to peals of laughter. The Vatican was, however, exempt from such censorious comments and held instead by her in a carefully calculated reverence.

Such was Jeanne's strength of character, her emphatic, boastful claims, most of which were substantially true that it was easily believed—at her own word—that she had been, most happily, one of the more than a hundred British guests who attended both the Nuremberg Rally and the Olympic Games in Berlin of 1936.

Here, Jeanne announced grandly she had been one of the British aristocracy attending her beau Ribbentrop's dazzling house party at Schloss Dahlem—where, not for the first time, she came into close contact with Rudolph Hess, Martin Bormann, and two of the dashing, extremely handsome athletes whom Jeanne most admired, Lord Burghley, later 6th Marquess of Exeter, and the Marquess of Clydesdale, later 14th Duke of Hamilton. These two exceptionally gifted young sportsmen were central to the organisation of the British Olympic team in Berlin—and it was on the Duke of Hamilton's Scottish property that Rudolph Hess bailed out of his plane in 1941. He had fallen deeply in love with the duke's ravishing good looks and, in fond delusion, he was persuaded that in combination they could halt the Second World War, bringing with him a personal letter from Hitler to Winston Churchill. This letter the prime minister Winston Churchill emphatically refused ever to read.

Close as ever to "my darlin' beau Joachim—"he has such divine blue eyes, *olé*, and much, much else besides in the vital parts"—Jeanne came into direct contact with Hitler's henchman Heinrich Himmler, his architect Albert Speer and his closest personal assistant Martin Bormann, who held the signature and power of attorney to open the Nazi bank accounts in Switzerland. The need of the British government for this all-powerful signature would become a matter of urgency immediately post-war since the Swiss banking system of the day was obdurate in refusing to release substantial Nazi funds without the authority of Bormann himself.

Their efforts in this respect involved Ian Fleming and his brother Peter from amongst the most prominent in the intelligence corps and British secret service. Rumours abounded for many years that Bormann had escaped from Hitler's bunker—and been smuggled, disguised, across the English Channel under the care of the intelligence officer brothers Ian and Peter. Rumour also had it, just as strongly, that Martin Bormann had then had extensive plastic surgery to his face performed by the expert specialist surgeon Sir Archibald McIndoe at his hospital in East Grinstead. Thereafter, the unrecognisable Bormann had been "hidden" in a couple of safe houses in South Oxfordshire.

Inevitably, enthusiastically throughout the mid-Thirties, Jeanne had become eagerly, increasingly involved in the pro-Nazi preparations for the Spanish Civil War, and, inevitably, together with her grandee brother-in-law, and extremist, the handsome, coldly detached. Marqués del Moral, husband of her hapless half-sister Gytha Stourton. Her husband had no hesitation in taking her to parties and receptions held by colleagues, dealers in international armaments, big business wheeler-dealers and close friends, Lord Illingworth and Ribbentrop were amongst the hand-picked guests at 44 Grosvenor Square. And there were the receptions held under the auspices of Queen Ena of Spain and her courtiers where gathered so many of the important English Catholics and the hierarchy of Westminster Cathedral to further fund and endorse the Spanish Nationalists.

By contrast to her moralistic Gytha to whom these politics were horrifying, dangerous and extreme, Jeanne worked in happy conjunction with her glamorous, unscrupulous Spanish Nationalist contemporaries and cousins.

In 1937 Jeanne travelled to Rome via Paris on the Golden Arrow train, staying at Neuilly-sur-Seine in an elegant apartment belonging to her older and distinguished Colombian diplomat cousins Renée and Carlos Aramayo. They also kept a convenient, chic house in Biarritz which appealed to Jeanne, so adjacent to the French-Spanish border was it. Here her brother-in-law Mon was officially and busily handing out his safe-passage passes to select travellers, agents, arms dealers and journalists.

By June 14, 1937 Jeanne was safely in Rome for the marriage at the Scots College of her cousin Lady Maryel Drummond, daughter of the Earl of Perth, British ambassador to Italy. Escorted by her cousin Andrew Constable Maxwell Jeanne stayed at the British Legation to the Holy See with the Protestant minister, the bachelor Sir D'Arcy Osborne—whom she scornfully described as "a frightful prissy, pussy-cat of an old woman. Simply bores me to tears—BUT, after all, he IS heir to the dukedom of Liverpool, *olé!* And that opens many doors to boot."

Amongst the guests were Mussolini's son-in-law, the foreign minister Ciano, his close friend and confidante Lady Austen Chamberlain, and Ribbentrop—according to Jeanne's oft repeated account of the marriage of the Lady Maryel with the darkly handsome, eligible diplomat from San Remo, Count Alessandro Manassei di Collestatti. All the more significant was Jeanne's first, and deeply consequential meeting with the austerely handsome and distinguished Cardinal Pacelli, con-celebrant at the elegant ceremony. He had been a cardinal since 1929, papal nuncio in Berlin, then secretary of state to Pius XI participating in the signing of the Papal Concordat with Nazi Germany in 1933.

Most significantly to Jeanne, Eugenio Pacelli had been trained in diplomacy by her own great-uncle, the Cardinal Rafael Borja Merry del Val. Meanwhile yet another de Zulueta family member was Spanish ambassador to the Vatican. Jeanne luxuriated in such surrounds.

Intriguingly, she claimed to have had an especial remit to "blow the safe" at the British Embassy—"just a little light gelignite simply did the job," she jokingly explained. "Of course I had to bribe that fearfully borin' decidedly queer butler to give me a hand, ha, ha and *VERDE*!" This colourful boast followed Jeanne throughout her life. It was a clouded and mysterious affair, confirmed by the distinguished career diplomat Sir John Balfour and others, whereby a quantity of official papers and more than a little jewellery was successfully "removed", lifted with considerable dexterity from the vaults of the British Embassy in Rome. The explosion caused by the gelignite was quickly and officially covered up. This was a time when the widowed Lady Austen Chamberlain was busily conveying messages and information directly from Italy's foreign minister Ciano back to the prime minister in London—to the horror of the Foreign Office at such unorthodoxy.

Jeanne found the Civil War in Spain a time of adventure and added excitement. She travelled the lines of colourful Francoist officers, handsome, dedicated, ruthless men. In 1936, on one of many excursions to her innumerable Spanish cousins, Jeanne—in her ever-vivid story-telling—excitedly, colourfully bragged of her participation with Alfonso de Merry del Val in the murder of an unfortunate young woman, a committed socialist. The particularly brutal lynching of Juanita Rico, was a revenge killing organised by an elite group of fanatical Falangists headed by Alfonso.

Several of her Spanish relatives would, upon the outbreak of the Spanish Civil War in 1936, become the dashing, determined officers of the Nationalists, fervent supporters of General Franco.

Meanwhile, Richard Sheepshanks, a handsome, virile Old Etonian and renowned cricketer, former Captain of the POP Club, was a budding young career journalist, graduate of Trinity College, Cambridge. Of considerable ambition and personal courage, habitually known as Dick, he was a protege of the owner-director of Reuters, Sir Roderick Jones—in whose house he too had met the dazzling Jeanne.

Dick had already proved himself professionally in Ethiopia—where he had been a colleague of the prejudiced, irascible Evelyn Waugh. Both had been posted to Addis Ababa during Mussolini's military invasion and brutal gassings and bombings. Now Sir Roderick appointed Dick Sheepshanks for Reuters, accredited, special correspondent to General Franco.

Kim Philby, the brilliant Soviet spy, was masquerading as the pro-Nazi secretary to the Anglo-German Fellowship when, through the auspices and influence of his father, he was also appointed, also by *The Times*, as accredited correspondent to General Franco. Converting in 1933 to the communist cause in Vienna, Philby was somewhat older than Dick—the blood cousin of Anthony Blunt—and had a very different outlook on life from the handsome Old Etonian.

Kim too was a graduate of Trinity College, Cambridge, home of the Apostles—of which his talented colleagues, fellow spies Anthony Blunt and Guy Burgess were members. Early in her membership of the glamorous Anglo-German Fellowship Jeanne had encountered Philby at the grandly formal fashionable dinners where he was in charge of the organisation and vital placement of distinguished guests.

Inevitably the two Trinity graduates became wary of one another. Philby sensed that Dick Sheepshanks was beginning to harbour well-founded suspicions of his correct but cold-hearted reportage, and political motivation, convincing though his, Philby's cover and manners were. It was their shared Cambridge University experiences which would shortly prove to be the calamitous undoing of the intelligent, enthusiastic and deeply conservative, Yorkshire-born Dick.

During the heady months of 1936 and 1937 Jeanne was easily able to make constant visits to Spain, staying with distinguished ambassadorial cousins from Bogotá, the handsome, hook-nosed Carlos Aramayo and his pretty wife Renée. Childless, older than Jeanne, they looked upon her as a loved niece, one who adored to attend the spectacular horse racing, and who added colour, colourful amusement with her spicy, risqué anecdotes in their elegant apartment at Neuilly.

From Paris it was easy for Jeanne to reach Hendaye, where she sought safe-keeping and considerable hospitality once again, in the temporary home of the British Embassy, which "my old beau, darlin' old Henry, olé!", the ambassador Sir Henry Chilton, had hastily removed from Madrid to premises above a grocery store. Here Tom Dupree, future son-in-law to the ambassador, another of Jeanne's "old flames", was First Secretary.

Sometime during the atrocities committed both by Nationalists and Republicans, to Jeanne's oft-repeated excitement, endlessly and racily recounted, the head of the village priest at the prosperous Mugaburu de Zulueta family estate of La Alcaría had been kicked down the village street. This haunted hamlet with its beautiful small castle, lies hidden away high in the cork oak hills between Jérez de la Frontera and Cádiz.

According to her own story, colourfully told, Jeanne was herself in the car following a group of journalists, Dick Sheepshanks—now semi-offi-cially her fiancé—Kim Philby and two American journalists to the front at Teruel on New Year's Eve 1937. Here the territory had twice changed sides in the bitter winter and bitter fighting of that year. It was now set to fall to General Franco and the Nationalists.

Philby gave his own vivid account of the explosion which killed the two Americans outright and mortally wounded Dick. He explained that the two-doored saloon car came under shrapnel fire as the journalists were entering Caude, on the outskirts of Teruel. From his own account he, Philby, had been sitting on the back seat, and had managed to "jump out". He was found the far side of a low stonewall with his head bandaged by local soldiers, and taken to an emergency field hospital for "superficial" wounds. The three corpses were ferried to the British Embassy, two coffins draped in the Stars and Stripes, the third in the Union Jack. From here the bodies of the three murdered journalists were flown, respectively, to America and London.

It was not until 1992 that Tom Dupree put out an official statement con-firming that these hapless journalists had been murdered by Kim Philby. The latter was acutely aware of Dick's suspicions. Nor had he any hesita-tion in sacrificing the two innocent American journalists by hurling a hand-grenade into their saloon car. Philby then inflicted light wounds upon himself, and awaited the arrival of a foot patrol of Nationalist sol-diers. It was a heavy irony that Philby was subsequently decorated by *El Jefe*, who personally pinned an award for gallantry on to his chest.

Wheresoever Jeanne actually was at the time, it is without doubt that she was devastated with shock and acute heartbreak: Dick had become the one true love, and great passion of her life. Throughout her life she never ceased to mourn "my darlin' Dick", whose handsome photograph she kept at her bedside until her own end. In January 1937 Jeanne was treated with due courtesy by his immediate family both at the formal London memorial service and at his Yorkshire burial at Arthrington Hall as the officially acknowledged fiancée of the prestigious young journalist, 28 years old, and much praised in glowing obituaries. But Jeanne was nevertheless dismayed that Dick had left no will, despite the danger of his calling. It would be his mother Olive, who automatically inherited the £16,000 estate of her murdered son.

Back in London the grief-struck Jeanne was acutely aware of her predicament. Unmarried women in their mid-twenties were already considered to be "on the shelf, my dear" by high society of the time. Furthermore Jeanne's prospects, married into the staunchly conservative, prosperous family of sheepfarmers, and to a man whom she truly adored, would have endowed her with deeply needed, necessary respectability—and security. Additionally Jeanne and Dick shared many friends in common, many of them hearty, landed Old Etonians. And there was a suitable Yorkshire family seat not far away from the Stourton cousins, further endorsing respectability.

Their engagement had been a particularly pleasing prospect to Jeanne's poverty-struck mother Fanny, who had never ceased in worried concern for her youngest daughter's activities and deep involvement with the fascist and pro-Nazi factions of the Thirties in England, Germany and Spain. Fanny had, correctly, kindly, accompanied Jeanne to the family burial rites of Dick.

And then, a mere fifteen days after his death, Jeanne was introduced to a millionaire Catholic bachelor, the Hon Sherman Stonor, only son and heir of Lord and Lady Camoys of Stonor Park, a large estate and with its own private chapel hidden away in the secluded Chiltern Hills of South Oxfordshire.

A gentle, fine-boned and slim young man of graceful good looks and sweetness of nature, Sherman was a devoted son to his American mother—his father, Ralph, conspicuously an absentee husband and parent—and a man deeply connected and committed to the English countryside. He was an original, natural ecologist and conservationist, allergic to the application of pesticides, and shocked at the newly-fashionable practice of artificial insemination of his pedigree Channel Island cows.

Conspicuously innocent and still, unusually, a virgin at the age of 24— the same age as Jeanne—Sherman was dazzled by the exotic, glamorous, witty, scent-drenched Jeanne with her deep scarlet finger nails, her cigarette-holder of tortoise shell, her throaty laughter and amusing albeit scatalogical anecdotes.

Previously Sherman had only ever escorted a charming and pretty young woman, Phoebe Houstoun-Boswell, to the various local events, amateur theatricals at the Stonor theatre, dances in Henley town hall, hunt balls, yet grander balls in London and the occasional, chaste motor journey to France in the chaperonage of close friends. Indeed, his mother Mildred, his great-aunt Julia and his Peel and Pereira cousins fondly expected the announcement of Sherman and Phoebe's forthcoming marriage. But this idyll was soon to be destroyed in a brutal and contemptuous manner, causing untold grief to Mildred Camoys, and, before long, to the innocent Sherman.

In the summer of 1937, Sherman's father, the 5th Baron Camoys, owner of the 6,300 acres of the Stonor Estates, was being sued for bankruptcy. Since his marriage to the heiress and millionairess Mildred in New York, in 1911, the indifferent peer had lived off his wife's fortune, paying little if any heed to the husbandry of his estates, the villages, hamlets, farms—and the very many tenants, farmers, servants and retainers for whom the idle Ralph was directly responsible.

Mildred immediately bought her husband out of the court-of-bankruptcy, thus saving Ralph from a very public humiliation which would have entirely ruined the little that was left of his reputation, and reduced this cold-hearted, irresponsible man to an ignominy which even he, the well-known womaniser and absentee husband, would have felt. Besides, having casually run through the Stonor monies, and allowed his lands and London properties to fall into neglect, Ralph Camoys was no longer "land rich" although through the generosity of his neglected wife he had, until 1937, become rather seriously "cash rich".

Much of the time that Ralph spent away from his wife was spent at London clubs, some decidedly louche, with "the little woman round the corner", frequently a hapless seamstress in nearby Wargrave or a terrified maid considered the personal chattel of her all-powerful employer. Sometimes it would be a "lady of greater fire", preferably Continental and thus exotic, whom Ralph would meet through a London connection—such necessities even the better clubs could easily supply, a substantial tip to the hall-porter ensuring due discretion with "ladies of the night". Some of these were frequently and colloquially known as "His Lordship's little bits", were as easily available through the diplomatic dinners to which, though often invited, Ralph only occasionally attended. The effort required to don the requisite white tie and tails caused this supremely lazy, bored man—and a teetotaller to boot—considerable weariness despite the services of a personal man-servant, a valet, as was normal in the wealthy society of Ralph's generation and standing.

Unbeknownst to either Mildred or Sherman, Ralph had met Jeanne Stourton (already beginning to be well known as "the Spanish Adventuress"), at a dinner given by the Brazilian ambassador Raul Regis de Oliveira in 1933.

In the meantime, not only had Mildred bought the 6,300-acre Stonor Estates from her husband, she had also given the majority of it to Sherman as an outright and freehold gift. But Stonor had become an American property after 700 years in the same family, disturbed only by the costly aftermath and fines, of the Reformation. Mildred also gave two daughters separately the estates of Bosmore and Cock's Leas.

In so doing, and because of the emergency of the situation, the legal "entail" (whereby property is passed from the eldest legitimate son to his eldest legitimate son of the blood line, and, occasionally, to the female on the same terms, normally an only child and an heiress-at-law) is terminated, cancelled legally. Thus the Stonor Estates were now all-American. But there had been an inevitable amount of newspaper coverage and publicity regarding the unusual transaction: transfer from husband to wife—and thence by deed of gift, mother to son. London clubs, the illustrious and international St James's Club especially, were awash with rumours of the scandal of the 5th Lord Camoys's near financial ruin.

After the tragedy of her fiancé Dick's murder, Jeanne sought out Carlos Aramayo's handsome, gay and amusing nephew Carlos—always known to her as "dear old Charlie, *olé!*—queer as a Colombian coot to boot! But most frightfully rich. Owns the Charpentier collection of French Impressionists; I'm thinkin', of inheriting them. I'm related to the darlin' boy through those Patiño silver mines. Caramba and *olé!* And no one and nothin' gets past *me*! I'm plannin' to get those paintin's by hook or by crook—no one stands in *my* way."

"Old Charlie" was small, hook-nosed, black-eyed and a remarkably talented pianist and raconteur of amusing, racy tales. He owned a charming house in Alexander Place, minutes only from the cosmopolitan London Oratory, also Jeanne's parish church.

No. 6 Alexander Place was filled with family paintings, French Impressionists, a Cézanne, two Monets and a couple of Renoirs amongst them, a Bechstein grand piano in the heavily-scented, jasmine-filled drawing-room, fashionably on the second-floor. Here Charlie kept an excellent table, a skilled chef providing an exquisite cuisine for the various lovers and the occasional, very smart South American and Spanish guests.

Charlie, the Bogotá millionaire, was a fervent member of the Bachelors' and St James's Club situated conveniently opposite the Ritz at 101 Piccadilly. Noted for its diplomatic membership—Ribbentrop was an honorary member—and the elegant 18th-century house, beautifully furnished, originally the London residence of the French ambassador Talleyrand—this club was, like White's, a great gaming club where the stakes were traditionally very steep amongst the well-heeled members.

On account of his wealth—Colombian, Angolan and Swiss—Charlie had time on his hands between jaunts and sojourns in Bogotá, Geneva, Paris, Montreal and London. Jeanne had made it her business to map out "old Charlie's mysterious jaunts and tristes, ha, ha!"

Now that she was in serious need, Jeanne confided in Charlie. She knew full well that she held considerable power over him, her tone full of nuances relating to the illegality of his homosexual activities, hinting, yet again, at the "unfortunate possibility—possibility only, of course, darlin' boy—of revelations . . ." Jeanne rounded off her request by reminding Charlie of the "most unfortunate fate of my darlin' Reggie—Cecil's brother, you remember, don't you? Beneath that train at Piccadilly Circus just minutes after he and I were together for the very last time . . ."

Charlie had but one thought: to extricate himself from the menacing chantage on the near horizon. In contemplating the richly-endowed membership of the Bachelors' Club he realized the only possible millionaire to buy Jeanne off him had to be the bachelor Catholic and virginal Sherman—who had just become what Jeanne would merrily describe as "most enormously rich, olé!"

Moreover, the gentle and diffident Sherman had travelled very little, other than to his American family in Newport, Rhode Island. And with the exception of two uneventful trips to France, Sherman was a home-loving

countryman, deeply attached to his mother Mildred. That he was also disinterested in politics meant that he was quite unlikely to have heard of
Jeanne's ever-increasing reputation as "the Spanish Adventuress".

Charlie's instincts, finely tuned to Jeanne's insistent demands, quickly
paid off. To the horror of Mildred, who, through the more worldly-wise
Julia d'Hautpoul, had indeed heard wild tales of "the Spanish Adventuress
who also called herself "an aristo Spanish Bastard, *olé!*", Sherman found
himself officially engaged to Pedro de Zulueta's "bastard" daughter Jeanne
Stourton very soon after their first meeting in mid-January 1938.

Shortly before the German Anschluss in late March, their engagement
caused a considerable stir, announced with splendour at the top of the
Court Circular, the couple photographed for *The Tatler & Bystander*,
Jeanne still in full black mourning for Dick Sheepshanks, a corsage of
orchids and several fine diamonds on her ball gown. Sherman wears white
tie and tails, an expression of bewildered surprise on his face. Meanwhile
Jeanne looks in curious combination bitter with grief but triumphant at
her "catch", a prize that would stun not only her several Stourton sisters
and brother, but also cause envy and fear amongst her contemporaries, the
women most of all.

Shortly after the official engagement came a further announcement of
the date and venue for the forthcoming marriage to be solemnized on July
14, 1938 at the London Oratory. That this date coincided with the
anniversary of the blood-drenched Storming of the Bastille did not escape
the horrified Julia d'Hautpoul—who related this back to Mildred, increasingly dismayed at the noose into which Sherman had unwittingly put his
head.

Considerable and costly preparations were now under way for the
"Wedding of the Year". No expense was spared and Jeanne's engagement
ring, a cabuchon ruby intertwined with platinum, was hand-made at
Cartier. As she happily pointed out to her fiancé, her own unfortunate
mother Fanny was penniless, all-but.

Every single expense thus fell immediately to Sherman, whether at
Cartier, Claridge's' Hotel, the Ritz, the Berkeley, the Connaught, the
Savoy or Norman Hartnell's couturier dress emporium. The targeted
bridegroom was completely overwhelmed, compelled to do exactly as he
was told.

Dazzled as Sherman was, nevertheless even he had heard rumours of a
past in Jeanne's life: whereby she had successfully sued the racehorse

owner-trainer and millionaire bachelor Sir Richard Sykes, owner of a large property in Yorkshire, Sledmere Hall, for breach of promise, and with consummate success.

Neither the law relating to breach of promise nor of capital punishment for crimes of murder were abrogated until well after the war. And in English law homosexuality was a crime not rescinded until several more years thereafter—frequently causing dangerous vulnerability, grave cruelty, and deep injustice—and very considerable blackmail, or, as Jeanne termed it gaily, *"chantage"*.

The mere rumour of the threat of a breach of promise action was seriously alarming. There had been several ominous precedents over the course of years. In America there was a much publicised case of John J. Astor's own broken engagement whereby he was forced, in court, to relinquish an immensely valuable solitaire diamond ring to the angry fiancée he had rejected in the Thirties. The last thing a remotely respectable English family wanted was such a scandal, its potential being the all-too public humiliation and ruination of the reputation of the man involved—rather than that of the woman suing.

Jeanne was quite aware of the power she wielded—easily conveyed by a mere but suggestive murmur accompanied by gales of laughter. But it was Mildred Camoys and Julia d'Hautpoul who were initially far more shaken by Sherman's engagement. Ralph, as was habitual, kept a considerable distance from his son—and, for the time being, an uneasy distance from Jeanne.

Handsome photographs of the newly-engaged couple appeared in the popular press. Jeanne had been known as "the non-stop bridesmaid", "the woman about town" and an alarming house-guest at many a smart weekend in the country, in Paris, in Rome, in Madrid and Hendaye. There was widespread speculation and suggestive gossip as to how she had netted quite such an extraordinary catch so close upon the death of her fiancé Dick Sheepshanks. And it was always clear that Sherman was disinterested in politics, quite unlike the landed gentry of South Oxfordshire, and his powerful neighbours, great landowners, members of the House of Lords, members of the Anglo-German Fellowship, Protestant and Catholic alike.

Jeanne hand-picked her seventeen bridal attendants and smaller bridesmaids, her five young pages. Some of the young women were daughters of lovers, "my old beaux", amongst them the beautiful Sylvia Regis de Oliveira, only child of the Brazilian ambassador.

The twelve older attendants all wore blood-red suede gloves up to the elbow, carrying scarlet roses to match, and glorious, wide-brimmed picture hats. No expense had been spared at the Norman Hartnell emporium, where Jeanne's beautiful cream satin dress had also been created, largely to her own design, its long train hand-embroidered with a thousand seed pearls. The small pageboys were tightly encased in satin breeches, chosen, two of them, as sons of "my dear old beaux"—an elaborate warning as to the power which Jeanne now undoubtedly possessed.

Sherman, like his ushers and best man, a half-German, blue-eyed and cheerfully extrovert bachelor, wore a white gardenia in the buttonhole of his bespoke, newly made fine black herring-bone woollen morning coat. On his face is an expression of intense wistfulness as he comes down the aisle of the crowded church, Jeanne upon his arm, her own expression smugly all-triumphant

Two thousand guests had been invited to the marriage ceremony at the Oratory, where Jeanne's uncle, the Archbishop Mostyn of Cardiff officiated alongside fellow priests and Knights of Malta at the magnificent ritual of a nuptial High Mass with its accompanying choir. Sherman's own guests, including villagers from Stonor, Pishill, Maidensgrove and Russells Water, numbered some two hundred. Amongst them were Ruby Heath and Sherman's tutor, the Pishill verger, Phil Hall.

Jeanne's own list was extensive, highly political as evinced by the illustrious names in the usual list of the Court Circular. Amongst them she had included Colonel Sir Eric St Johnston, at that time a senior policeman seconded to the Home Office but shortly to be appointed chief constable of Oxfordshire. And there was another old friend, the substantial, habitually uniformed, bemedalled Commander Mary Allen, founder and head of the Women Police and friend of Adolf Hitler.

Mildred Camoys refused to attend the marriage of her only son to the Spanish Adventuress. She spent the day in bed at Stonor Park weeping her heart out. Meanwhile Jeanne had already vowed, contemptuously, her "perpetual revenge against that American *bitch*, Mildew Camoys", quite openly, and in front of horrified witnesses. From 1938 onwards Jeanne would prove more than true to her word, continuously so, even till after Mildred's death.

She suffered another snub, this time from Queen Ena of Spain—who refused to allow either of her daughters, the Infanta Beatriz and the Infanta Cristina, to attend the wedding. Jeanne swore revenge upon the sisters too—in which curse she would only partially succeed, but at great cost to "Crista", the younger of the two.

Sherman's Aunt Julia, equally appalled, likewise declined to attend the Wedding of the Year. She pleaded her age as an excuse not to undertake the laborious journey to the Oratory. Her brother Harry, equally shocked, and more than a little concerned for his own reputation, let it be known through the Court Circular that "Sir Harry Stonor would be absent abroad in Italy". He was, in fact, on a gay triste with his companion as guests of the Duchess of Simonetta.

Nevertheless the guest list was deeply impressive: ambassadors, diplomats from Germany, South America, and Spain, members of the Anglo-German Fellowship, several members of the Mowbray Segrave and Stourton family, the Crichton-Stuart cousins, amongst them the Hon Mrs Maule Ramsay. Jeanne's more immediate family were well represented by her father Pedro, the Conde and Condesa de Torre Diaz, the Merry del Val dynasty and others of the Mugaburu de Zulueta family. Her own unhappy mother Frances headed the list of social protocol together with Ralph Camoys, self-engrossed, sour and humourless.

By 1938, the 5th Baron Camoys was in actuality a "kept man", entirely at the behest of his wife Mildred, who now supplied her husband with a generous allowance. This generosity would fund Ralph even after Mildred's unexpected death in 1961 until his own demise in Newport, Rhode Island, in 1968.

Sherman's immediate family from Newport included the distinguished cousins Mr and Mrs John Nicholas Brown, his aunt Mrs Lawrence Sherman Gillespie, Sherman's cousins Mr and Mrs John Jermain Slocum, Mrs George Howard, Madame Antoinette Sherman, her son-in-law and daughter Mr Jon and Mrs Dorothée Thoresen. They had all sailed the Atlantic by first-class liner, putting up at Claridge's. Even the idle Ralph knew better than to avoid his wife's millionaire relatives. Besides, he had to answer to his Peel and Stonor relatives, amongst them two of the last remaining grandchildren of Sir Robert Peel as well as Eddie Stonor, married to a wealthy Greek banker's daughter, Christine Ralli.

Significantly Eddie, accompanied by his son Francis (on the eve of departure to Alexandria, to his employ in the secret service), represented the Anti-Communist and Anti-Socialist League, acting as their official, joint secretary and spokesman.

The grandeur of Sherman and Jeanne's marriage was crowned with the

Papal blessing, personally accorded by Pope Pius XI and delivered through the Cardinal Archbishop of Westminster, Arthur Hinsley. This document, its beautiful calligraphy penned on vellum parchment, was a further reminder of the Catholic Sacrament and sacramental value of matrimony, its legality in Canon Law—and a veiled warning against the prospect of any future annulment procedure.

An uncomfortable precedent for this already existed in the Stonor and Clifden family, the cause of a deeply cruel lawsuit in the Chancery Court in 1876 between Ralph Camoys's aunt Harriet Stonor and her harsh husband, the remorseless 5th Viscount Clifden, a dyed in-the-wool, deeply obstinate Protestant of considerable bigotry.

Pius would die the following February of 1938, to be succeeded in March by Jeanne's close friend Cardinal Eugenio Pacelli, Pius XII. It would be Pacelli who created the infamous "Rat-Run" for fleeing Nazi war criminals at the end of the Second World War. And it was through his "Vatican Corridor", another rat-run for ecclesiastical grandees, manipulators of conservative power—the United States chaplain general to the forces Cardinal Frank Spellman amongst them—that Jeanne would, quite brazenly, achieve some of her more unusual ambitions, both during and after the war.

The Vatican Corridor, like Ribbentrop's castle Sonnenburg, Schloss Dahlem, and his London Embassy, possessed a vast, highly organised, efficient and heavily used telephone system. These innumerable telephones were added inspiration for Jeanne's obsession for immediate communication far and wide. Early in the war days, she had swiftly accumulated a battery of field telephones and walkie-talkies with which she issued orders, barked commands over a long-wired "intercom" set of headphones, megaphones, batteries and boxes and army satchels.

On the evening of July 14, 1937, Jeanne took her bridegroom Sherman to Claridge's for a couple of nights. She had a surprise wedding gift for him—two first-class return tickets to Berlin to stay as the guests of "my dear old beau, darlin' Joachim at his simply marvellous castle, Schloss Sonnenburg, *olé!*" Jeanne presented the tickets to Sherman as "a frightfully good bargain, though I do say it myself—only twelve guineas each, there and back!"

All that Sherman knew previously of Ribbentrop was that he had been, for a short time from 1936, Hitler's ambassador to the Court of St James's, holding lavish, well-attended receptions at Carlton House Terrace. Now he was to meet this handsome, sinister member of Hitler's inner cabinet and SS officer in person.

Sherman was bewildered, terrified to find himself in this immense, gloomy, over-stuffed castle at Freienwalde, in the centre of a dank dark forest north-east of Berlin. He was horrified and shocked by the Nazi splendour of it all, the armoured cars, revving roaring motor bicycles, heavily uniformed SS guards, their chests smothered in medals, thigh-high jackboots, metal spurs, guard dogs and an endless stream of "Heil Hitler!" salutes to the accompaniment of heel-clicking and goose-stepping. It was all too much for Sherman. Within a very few days, sickened and quite unmanned, he ran away.

As Jeanne jauntily related over the years to a continuously amused but bemused audience, she was so enraged that she ordered "my old beau, that darlin' boy Joachim to go after Shermie, round him up, olé! and fetch him back immediately". Within a very short space of time Sherman was captured and returned to the over-scented, sinister splendour of Schloss Sonnenburg.

Mocking her husband for "such a God-awful lack of performance in bed", Jeanne had so frightened and humiliated the inexperienced young man that Sherman had almost immediately become impotent—something which both he and Jeanne, independently, later confided to the Infanta Maria Cristina.

Openly scoffing at Sherman's innocence let alone his "performance", Jeanne merrily accepted gifts from her host Joachim: two traditional dirndle dresses, of flower-scattered embroidered cloth, red and blue, silver-buttoned, and a Loden hunting hat of darkest green with a thickly braided crown, its curling brim surmounted by a cock pheasant feather. This trophy Jeanne would confidently sport until the end of her life, frequently dressing it with the regimental bugle of Sherman's regiment—in diamonds.

But as much as Jeanne reviled and spat at Sherman, it was soon apparent that she was pregnant. This was an interruption to social life which intensely irritated Jeanne, though she and Sherman were now well installed in London in a substantial, comfortable family house in Addison Gardens. As a member of Lloyds, a stockbroker and the owner of the Stonor Park Estates, Sherman was comfortably endowed with the funds which so appealed to Jeanne. Besides, he was by nature a generous man.

Arrangements were made for Jeanne's confinement at the fashionable if slightly shady clinic, 27 Welbeck Street. Ironically, she had stayed there for a termination only a couple of years previously, photographed in deep blue sunglasses, accompanied by a black pug and her companion Dickie Sykes. A statement was given out to the popular press that "Miss Jeanne Stourton would be undergoing an operation for appendicitis".

In the spring of 1939 Jeanne and Sherman began to use a pleasant house on the Stonor Estates. Assendon Lodge, just two miles from the Park itself. Mildred Camoys, meanwhile, had decided to re-emigrate to the States, and regain her American nationality—which she had reluctantly been obliged to relinquish upon her marriage in 1911—hastened by ominous signs of the approaching war in Europe on the horizon. Beside, Ralph's continued, callous absence and sheer indifference in addition to his financial ruin had caused Mildred considerable heartbreak that she could tolerate no longer.

To Jeanne's intense rage and chagrin, she now had to watch a possession of pantechnicons, nineteen in all, wind their way down the Stonor Valley, past Assendon Lodge, brimming with the possessions (some of them family heirlooms) which Mildred had bought from her penniless husband to prevent his bankruptcy. Jeanne's rage and frustration knew no bounds and she again swore undying revenge on her hated mother-in-law. In so doing Jeanne entirely ignored the vast inheritance of family heirlooms which Mildred had already gifted to Sherman.

Arms akimbo, the pregnant Jeanne had stood glowering with rage outside the wooden gates of Assendon Lodge at the procession of vehicles conveying antiques and other valuables she angrily described as "looted goods, the whole lot. And all stuffed into that house on Bellevue Avenue, Stonor Lodge no less. Absolutely damnable of Mildew Mildred C. I'll make very sure that she never sees her son again!" Stamping the other foot, Jeanne declared ominously: "And I always keep my word; see if I don't, *olé!*" The grudge that Jeanne held against Mildred now knew no bounds. It would ensue in a terrible revenge in the years to come.

The oncoming war that now would prevent Jeanne from moving into Stonor Park further disconcerted her—but not for long. The house was immediately requisitioned by the National Benzole Company, a subsidiary of British Petroleum, whose vital requisitioning of oil and war supplies was now centred at Stonor. Some forty staff moved in for the duration of the war.

On April 19, 1939, Jeanne gave birth to a girl at the Welbeck Street clinic. She was more than annoyed that the baby was not male. But though she did not herself attend the christening at the London Oratory in early May, Jeanne carefully hand-picked my godparents. Her instinct, as always acute, informed her that she could win back the friendship of Queen Ena's younger daughter Maria Cristina by making the princess godmother of the new baby. Her ruse worked.

Julia Maria Cristina Mildred Stonor was christened the namesake of her aunt Julia Stonor, the Marquise d'Hautpoul, the Infanta Maria Cristina and Mildred Camoys—although the latter would not be permitted even to meet me until 1961.

Jeanne's choice of godfathers, both Catholics, were two of "my old beaux'": the hearty, chubby Alaric, half-Austrian son of ambassador Sir Odo and Lady Russell, and the slim, shy blue-eyed Lebbeus Hordern, an Australian millionaire.

Already, early in 1939, Sherman had enlisted in the Oxfordshire & Buckinghamshire Light Infantry under the command of a near neighbour, Colonel Guy de Pass. He was almost immediately posted away from Assendon Lodge. By the outbreak of war, 5 September, 1939, Sherman was ranked second lieutenant, shortly to be shipped out to the French front and Dunkirk.

Triumphantly, with Sherman safely away in France, Jeanne personally assumed complete command. Together with her father-in-law, Ralph Camoys, who had now moved full-time into the comfort of Assendon Lodge, Jeanne organised more than twice-weekly supervisions of the Park, striding purposefully from room to room in the vast house, some seventy and more rooms (several maids' attics were subsequently stripped out in the late Seventies).

Just as triumphantly Jeanne supervised the French chaplain, Father André Seyres—"that French frog, old Father Cereal!")—and the magnificent contents of the private chapel with its precious antique vestments, in richly embroidered cloths of gold and silver.

Now that the Second World War had broken out, encouraged by her friends Commandant Mary Allen and the newly-appointed Chief of the Oxfordshire constabulary, Jeanne appeared on a daily basis in the uniform of an officer of the Women's Police stationed at Henley-on-Thames. She had swiftly established a household of servants at Assendon Lodge, two nannies, daily maids, scullery attendants and a housekeeper, already an employee of Sherman's, the red-headed Ruby Heath. Ruby bicycled twice daily to and from Stonor Village for her exacting job.

Ralph, in contrast to the First World War, when he had managed to get himself exempted from any military service or duties by the War Board Tribunal, now enlisted in the Air Raid Precaution unit and the Home Guard—where he was appointed captain. He too was now in uniform, and had become Jeanne's frequent evening escort at the weekly dances held at Henley Town Hall—a far cry indeed from the Café de Paris in Jeanne's eyes. But these dances were patronised by another of her old beaux, the diminutive member of parliament Sir Gifford Fox, a tiny baronet married to Lord Eltisley's giraffe-tall daughter Myra, and, with Jeanne, a fellow member of the Anglo-German Fellowship, the January Club, the Link and the New Right.

Jeanne, who had previously confided to Maria Cristina that she was "most frightfully bored in the deadly English countryside", now saw new and exciting prospects on the horizon.

11

'Uncle Fernan
Was a Mere Marquis'

I knew Granny Camoys lived at a house called Stonor Lodge on Bellevue Avenue, from where she sent me presents, clothes and wartime food parcels. And I knew that Bangpa-Pop, who lived with Mama at Assendon Lodge, was married to Granny Mildred, who used to own Stonor Park but had somehow given it to Papa in 1937. And now only seemed to own Bosmore and Cock's Leas.

But my sense of geography was limited in those days. I considered that I knew London where Mama took me on exciting weekly train and taxi trips. Otherwise I had seldom travelled beyond Papa's estates of Bix Bottom, Christmas Common, Maidensgrove, Pishill and Russells Water. I had not even been as far as Reading or Oxford, both of which places my mother had to visit for police duties and wartime emergencies.

The mere mention of both places excited my curiosity but all Mama would say was: "The nearest you're likely to get to Reading is the Caversham Crematorium, ha, ha! And as for Oxford, the knacker's yard at Benson is quite close enough and good enough too for you, child."

But in a way I was lucky since the whole world appeared to come to visit us. Of all my mother's regular callers the most beautiful was Aunt Julia. As Ruby said: "She's the 'Markeys' and a proper lady unlike some." She gave a deeper sigh and a bigger sniff than usual.

Julia Stonor was the Marquise d'Hautpoul. Tall, gentle and blue-eyed, her hair piled high in a silver chignon, she was Papa's widowed great-aunt. Orphaned early in life, she had been bought up on the Isle of Wight at Osborne House by King Edward and Queen Alexandra with their own six children. Now she lived at Turville Heath in a rose-pink brick Queen Anne dower house.

Here she was quite alone, surrounded by the royal memorabilia of her early engagement to the Duke of York, before the Vatican had decided against her marriage to the heir to the throne. She was looked after devotedly by her maid Violet Wickham, her husband the head-gardener, and the chauffeur Ernest Busby. A further maid came in daily, Alice Heath, sister-in-law to Ruby, who bicycled up from Stonor Village.

Unsure what a "Markeys" could be, I suggested the idea to Mama of a magnificent marquee, a vast canvas tent tethered with huge wooden pegs.

"You really are totally absurd, Julia dear. Don't be so absolutely effin' idiotic. Your very dear Aunt Julia was married to an aristocratic French turd, *olé!* Most inconveniently, Fernan d'Hautpoul, from Toulouse you know, died far too soon for my plans. Found mysteriously dead at the Hyde Park Hotel in 1935. And his great friend, that Blue Monkey, the Marqués of Sovéral, bosoms with King Edward VII of course. I knew all about that QUEER scenario. All hushed up, and just in time, ha, ha!"

Mama laughed until she cried, wiping tears of merriment carefully off her mascara with a lace-bordered handkerchief. Opening a gold Cartier powder compact, she looked carefully into it, patted her face and adjusted the rouge on one cheek. "Mirror, mirror, on the wall, and who is the fairest of them all," she hummed cheerfully. Pouting into the mirror she applied a dark scarlet lipstick with a lavish sweeping gesture. "My, oh my," she said crisply. "The fact that Uncle Fernan was a mere marquis from Toulouse simply cuts no ice with me." She opened her mouth wide in a yawn of boredom.

We had other types of neighbours too. One afternoon, my mother drove me to the graveyard at Pishill, precariously perched by a small church on a steep, stark chalk hill looking back deep into the Stonor valley, the Park itself mysteriously enveloped in trees. Here she brought the car to a screeching halt on the brow of the rutted gravel lane. She marched me sharply up a steep bank of long wet grass to gaze at the iron-railed grave of Aunt Julia's stillborn daughter, who had died, nameless, on the same day that she was born, March 9th, 1892.

"Julia's baby brat was born dead, and a jolly good thing too," said Mama, abruptly dropping my hand and clicking her fingers. She suddenly stooped down, a cigarette hanging from the corner of her mouth, and glowered at the grave. "Who, in Gawd's name, has had the affrontry and temerity to put FLOWERS here? I, and I alone, am in charge round here."

Sure enough, someone had placed a brass vase, filled with blue forget-me-nots and pink roses, on the overgrown plot. Standing next to their daughter, Aunt Julia and Uncle Fernan's two-tiered headstone was a gaunt grey stone cross, coarse-hewn, planted in deep weeds and unmown wild oats, barley, grass and groundsel. Further back in the graveyard was a more ornate headstone, marked "Miss Moore, a Devoted Friend".

Mama explained: "Pop's old nanny. His own Ma was most frightfully distant and cold. After all she was only a collateral Carew you know, from a minor, secondary branch in Essex. What would you expect from a county like that? Never showed a drop of emotion, let alone sense of humour." Kicking the gravestone, she continued, "Frightfully Low Church Prot to boot, so what can you expect? Still, *Piss*-hill, such an appropriate name, is one of Sherman's livin's. I must have words with that old sweetie, the Bishop of Oxford as to the financial benefits," said Mama thoughtfully.

Phil Hall, Papa's tutor and the verger, appeared from the church vestry wearing a blue suit, trilby and bicycle clips. His dentures were made from a shiny porcelain in two completely even sets. He raised his hat, laid down his bicycle on the wet grass and smiled timorously at my mother.

"Plenty of room for Pop-goes-the-Weasel Ralph and Sherman in the chapel crypt," she snapped at Phil.

The verger looked rather frightened.

"Other Cartholic grandees other than myself," added Mama mysteriously, "may come up here to this depressin' dreary Prot plot."

Many years later, however, in July 1971, my mother made a special exception for Aunt Esther, Uncle Hugo Stonor's Polish Jewish widow, who had danced "so unsuitably at the Hammersmith Palais de Danse". Though permitted into Mama's hallowed ground, Aunt Esther's body was swiftly consigned to an unmarked pauper's grave the far side of Aunt Julia, adjoining my mother's cremated blonde half-sister Barbara Bellville.

The Chief Rabbi of Reading, despite being bullied and cajoled by Mama, refused to participate at the hapless Esther's burial as (he claimed) she had not been consistent in her practice of Judaism. Yet Esther, a pauper and Stonor-shunned, had remained boundless in her courage, living long years of impoverishment alone and bed-ridden at the Station Hotel in Henley, gaunt and crotched-capped in Uncle Hugo's ragged flannel pyjamas left over from the Thirties. Till her dying day, beneath an iron truckle bed, next to a china chamberpot, Esther kept guard over a yellowing collection of documents and family newspaper cuttings recording the "adventures" of the Camoys and Stonors since the turn of the century.

There would be no gravestone, no headstone for Aunt Esther at Pishill churchyard.

Pausing to scatter ash over Miss Moore's grave before lighting another cigarette, Mama observed: "Aunt Julia of course, is most frightfully rich. So so fortunate she is childless in the circumstances. Dear King George Fifth was her fiancé for quite a while."

"Then of course, dear, dear King Edward Seventh—such a smashin' Freemason to boot, your grandfather Pop Camoys belongs to the very same Lodge—was always so romantic. And most frightfully keen for Julia and Bertie to elope." Mama sighed. "But that was back in the 1880s you know, and our effin' Cartholic Church was more than a bit of a bugger about these mixed marriages. I've had a word or two with the powers that be at the Vatican—my Mostyn cousins and others, you know—but my lips are sealed. Naturally I know absolutely ALL about it, in total confidence of course. As it was, Julia married that dubious Fernan d'Hautpoul, and Bertie married his dead brother's fiancée Princess Mary of Teck, poor woman, handed down like an old shoe." Triumphantly she added: "Divine Queen Alexandra, deaf as a post you know, gave our own dear Aunt Julia those equally divine cast-iron gates and the Grecian urns up at Turville Grange to compensate for all her sufferin's."

Mama turned furiously to Phil Hall, still waiting behind us at the grave-side with his hat in his hand. "And you're totally *de trops* and ridiculous, you old pansy eavesdropper. Fairy lights on your bicycle and in your Bible too, ha, ha!"

Getting back into Granny Camoys' car, she wound down the window and spat back at the hapless verger: "The sooner you're dead and buried and under the sod, the better. Soon won't be soon enough. You look just like one of the homo gnomes from your own cottage garden these days."

Mama revved the engine and tore down the Pishill lane in first gear, a look of grim satisfaction flashing in her eyes.

*

Karen Lancaster, whose husband Osbert drew cartoons for the *Daily Express*, had come to call on Mama. She was sitting, chain-smoking as she waited in the drawing room.

"You, Karen darlin' of all people, should know about royal bastards," laughed my mother. "And you needn't bother to deny to an aristo bastard like me that your grandfather is that divine King Edward VII. Come to think of it you really have inherited his rather stout figure, ha, ha, *olé!*"

Karen turned slowly round to stare at Mama through thick-lensed, heavily rimmed spectacles and lit another cigarette before speaking. "I am far more interested in playing *Les Sylphides* on your gramophone, Jeanne Mary dear. It is my birthday present for Julia . . ."

Thus silenced, my mother looked uneasy. Karen had a similar effect on her as did Hellbags Helen, otherwise known as Lady Dashwood from West Wycombe ("where they make bedroom furniture"). In fact, I noticed, Mama talked far less whenever she saw either of these friends of hers. Nor did she pull my hair in front of Karen or Hellbags Helen.

But Jeanne relished the fact that Karen's husband was a spy in Greece as well as a notorious, viciously entertaining purveyor of gossip. She enjoyed the scandal of Osbert's own affairs, watching Karen's suffering. Though my mother was frightened of the depth of Karen's knowledge about her, she was openly envious of the well-founded rumour that Karen was the illegitimate descendant of Edward the Seventh.

Osbert and my mother later redesigned the colour scheme of the Stonor chapel, together with the artist John Piper, the vulgar, theatrical results of which left Karen deeply unimpressed. She wouldn't otherwise set foot in the chapel where Jeanne held regular court. After the Sunday Mass services and all the way through the war, Mama received the congregation on the chapel steps, sandwiched between two green box hedges outside the heavy black-painted Gothic Revival door. She tripped down from her established place in the gold-and-black painted Gothic Revival style tribune above, her high-heeled shoes clattering on the thick brick steps as she descended, cigarette smoke billowing round the corners of the 16th-century plaster walls heralding my mother's arrival as she coughed mightily on the fumes. These merely added to the heavy scent of the incense, which Father André Seyres' altarboy had swung around his head in a silver thurible shaped like a ship.

Parishioners, including the Lethbridge boys, all four of them, with their father, would gather outside after Mass. Aunt Julia, waiting for her chauffeur, the minute Busby, to open the car door for her, would look carefully down from her considerable height as Mama conversed with the congregation.

"My own dear Sherman's great-grandfather was the prime minister Sir Robert Peel you know, Aunt Julia's own grandfather," explained my mother to an awestruck villager. "Actually he invented the police 'peelers' you know, and I'm quite the best aristo bastard bobby on the beat. Prime minister, of course, for the RIGHT party," she added hastily. "House of Commons and all of that. Although I myself will shortly be sittin' up in the House of Lords."

Perhaps Westminster was beyond my experience but I certainly knew about the powerful little parliament in Henley-on-Thames since both Papa and Mama belonged to the rural district council there. And later, at Oxford too Papa would come home with sheaves of council papers, hand-delivered in pink, scarlet, green, orange, yellow and white. These he tucked into a brown leather briefcase, monogrammed and coroneted in black ink. "But, my dear, Really Important Ministers have red leather dispatch boxes with real gold locks," said Mama once as I watched her stealthily opening Papa's case with a small gold key.

But I was far more interested in the rare pigs from the Barbados estates of great-great-grandfather Sir Robert Peel. Unusually thin and pale pink, with long red hair hanging down over their eyes, these were pedigree Tamworths.

"Your stinkin' rich Peel family, who look so exactly like their pink pigs, made all their other fortune in Lancashire linoleum," my mother told Sherman as he was preparing to leave one day to go to court. "Of course they were already doin' very nicely in the slave trade, along with the rest of your American family and those stinkin' rich Weld-Blundell cousins of Liverpool."

Surreptitiously Mama slipped more homemade stomach medicine into the bottle, which she placed in Papa's briefcase ready for the journey down the Fair Mile to the Magistrate's Court. "It's the same infallible mixture I take for my own delicate nerves. Turns everythin' runny into neat concrete on the spot."

In 1944, after his burst appendix and nervous breakdown, Papa had been invalided out of the army. Mama took him to Claridge's for recuperation in a single green bedroom with cream-coloured blankets bound with watered silk. Papa then sat on the Henley bench, where he judged misdoings and miscreants. As Mama explained again: "My stomach mixture helps steady the nerves when makin' a calculated judgement. Some local unfortunates seem even to have been helpin' themselves in the black market."

Clearing her throat, she inhaled deeply on another of her American contraband Philip Morris cigarettes and blew a thick cloud of blue smoke down her nostrils.

It impressed me that, as Justice of the Peace, Papa was allowed to have a wooden gavel with which to bang the bench once he had come to a verdict. One session, upon glancing down at the charge sheet for the day, he saw with horror that a Mr Affia and a certain Mrs Sherman Stonor were jointly charged with major acts of black-marketeering.

"Case dismissed," he had declared hurriedly, and, as his stomach gave way: "Court adjourned forthwith!" Banging his gavel down, Papa fled the court for the security of the gentlemen's W.C. at Henley Magistrate's Court on the Fair Mile.

Unlike so much else at Stonor, the magistrateship was not an inherited affair. In 1944, Major the Honourable Ralph Robert Watts Sherman Stonor, sole heir to the ancient Barony of Camoys, was 31 years old. The then incumbent, Ralph Francis Julian Stonor, was 62.

"You'd better be more careful how you wield your gavel in future, Sherman dear," said my mother sitting one afternoon on a bench at Assendon Lodge. She winked at Bangpa-Pop. "It appears to have brewer's droop again. Like father, like son, ha, ha, *olé!* But dear old Ralph's quite up to it. Aren't you Ralph dear?" giggled Mama.

Bangpa snorted.

Papa walked slowly away, down the garden path, lost in his own thoughts. Mama laughed and promptly took me off to call on Aunt Julia d'Hautpoul.

Aunt Julia's rose-pink brick and flint house at Turville Heath was magical. Visits there were magical too. I sat as close as possible to my tall, elegant, gentle aunt as she poured tea into paper-thin Meissen cups from the silver tray brought in by her devoted maid Violet.

I loved to look around, spellbound at the charm of the room. Antique cabinets were filled with brightly coloured enamel and gold boxes, diamond-embossed, and with delicate portrait miniatures. Fabergé Russian Easter eggs with ornate decoration and precious stones were carefully laid out on trays of satin and velvet. Most fascinating of all was the ivory set of royal dentures, top and bottom, locked together in the glass cabinet next to Aunt Julia in her stiff-backed, upright chair.

I asked my mother if these belonged to the "Royal Fiancé", King George V. But she hissed back: "Don't you dare ask such effin' impertinent questions, you stupid brat. It might upset the balance of things round here."

It was King Edward VII's Danish wife Queen Alexandra who had herself insisted on installing the new telephone exchange at Turville Heath for Aunt Julia.

"To console her after she lost Bertie York, the Duke you know," explained Mama. "Though we all DO know his older brother, Prince Eddie, the Duke of Clarence you know, was a murky piece of goods, and not beyond knockin' orf a few of those tiresome women on the street."

She turned to the immensely tall Miss Bridges, who had also come to call: "Small wonder Eddie Clarence perished in most peculiar circs. Not adverse to a bit of skirt, and ever so kinky in his habits, ha, ha!"

Aunt Julia's reaction was to bring the tea party to an abrupt end. "I think it is high time for you, Jeanne dear, to leave," she said. "Most inappropriate conversation to have in front of Sherman's small daughter."

Miss Bridges blushed.

Violet in her formal afternoon uniform showed us to the front door, which was opened by Busby, Aunt Julia's chauffeur in his dark-green uniform. Angrily, Mama climbed back into Granny's Chevrolet, banging shut the door.

Once back at Assendon Lodge and comfortably ensconced in her study, Mama laughed and winked in the direction of Bangpa-Pop, who was really Aunt Julia's nephew even though "there is not so much difference in your ages, old boy, only in your performance, and that," she continued, "tends to remind me of somethin' much more sparklin' from Bogotá and Brazil in these lines, olé and caramba!'

She poured herself a Horse's Neck. "I'm just dyin' with thirst after that ridiculous episode up at the Turville Grange," she explained cheerfully. "You're damn lucky, Pop dear, to be in such close competition with my darlin' old ambassador, the divine Raul Regis de Oliveira, and his team of Brazilian sparklers. Plenty of family gold, let alone tin mines, where Raul Regis comes from. Which is more than I can say for the alleys and valleys round this effin' borin' neck-of-the-woods. Give me Claridge's and the Savoy any old day." Langorously my mother yawned. "As Pop knows perfectly well, only too well, the Savoy Hotel is where my darlin old Sir Roderick Jones hangs out. I see him frequently and he certainly doesn't suffer from any form of droop," she sniffed.

Suddenly looking more cheerful, she continued: "After all, darlin' Enid (Bagnold you know), Roderick's saintly wife, and I have always been just as close as THAT." Mama wound her forefingers tightly round one another, pointing them into the air.

Enid Bagnold was Lady Roderick Jones but, as a mere godmother and aunt, she did not qualify for my night prayers. Mama continued: "Darlin' Enid writes such very spiffin' plays. And does a little of this and a little of that. Frightfully pro-Hitler since way back—I know all about that, Anglo-German Fellowship and all of us in it too. We had such cosy times together before this irritatin' war, darlin' Joachim, Enid and I, what with Rottingdean and Carlton House Terrace," she added reflectively. "And my darlin' Bute and Maule Ramsay cousins, *olé!*"

Bangpa-Pop looked round rather uneasily. He spluttered, blowing his mauve nose once again.

"For Gawd's sake put a sock in it and keep quiet. You'll bore me to tears unless, and until, I get my hands on that Bosmore estate. Cock's Leas too come to think of it . . . And just where ARE the vital deeds and entails, I would like to know!" Mama gulped down her brandy and ginger ale before passing the empty glass to Bangpa-Pop. "Fill it up, and *muy pronto*, Pop-goes-the-Weasel, *olé* and heil Hitler!"

As Bangpa-Pop replenished her drink, Mama continued: "After all, we're all most frightfully close to Joachim. Too bad we just had to bump orf that oh-so tedious Ambassador Leopold von Hoesch and his little Pekinese poggins in '36. Such a damn nuisance he wouldn't just take the hint and resign."

With this exasperating thought, she jumped up and went over to play a tune on Tia María's black piano. "Strychnine is just such a bore to get hold of," she said as she played (Mama preferred Gilbert & Sullivan and her father's operettas). "But frightfully easy to lay one's hands on in such dire necessity. You can use it on your wasps, and on yourself, Ralph old boy, come to think of it, if you can't stay in line." She laughed merrily, her spirits revived.

Bangpa guffawed, belched and hitched up the grey worsted trousers, which had fallen again below his stomach.

"When it actually came to the point of bumpin' orf Ambassador Von Hoesch we had to get hold of a bucket, a syringe, yards of black rubber hose. And a stirrup pump in one hell of a hurry to get it all out, just in case," Mama remembered, in between banging out notes on the Steinway. "But, if truth be told, I'm really very much sorrier for that poor little dog havin' to be bumped orf too." She paused to wipe a tear from her rouged cheek. "At least I did the honours for the poor little duck. And arranged his funeral right outside the Bosch embassy on the Duke of York Steps." A yawn. "I'm quite an expert at gravestones and burials you know, what with one thing and another. Ever since I lost my own darlin' fiancé Dickie Sheepshanks in the Spanish Civil War I've specialised in explosives and explosions, ha, ha, *olé!* And *viva el rey de España!* Though, if truth be told, Dick Ovey swears his undyin' love to me," she purred. "Of course, he is Sherman's very best friend, but I never let trifles like that stand in my way."

At that precise moment my Uncle, Royal Navy Commander Dick Ovey, appeared in full uniform at the doorway.

"We're orf to my study, and not to be disturbed on any account," Mama flung over her shoulder as she disappeared hand-in-hand with Uncle Dick.

I was left with my trifle, which Ruby had made for the nursery dining room. Filled with rhubarb and custard it was cooked with my mother's own water-glassed eggs, which both looked and smelt more than horrid. It seemed that Mama's special rations book did not stretch as far as the children's dining room. But I had seen large brown eggs and lavish butter pats sitting on the specially laid breakfast tray that Ruby took up to my mother's bedrooms. Such trays appeared whenever she had a migraine, or an attack of "nerves" and was in "excruciatin' pain". During these black periods, Ruby was sent flying up and downstairs without respite.

The estate in those days was largely self-sufficient. We grew all our own vegetable in the surrounding land and there were orchards and a walled kitchen garden, where I picked mulberries, loganberries, raspberries and strawberries. My father was very much against the use of herbicides, chemical fertilisers and the artificial insemination of stock. Our pedigree herds included Channel Island and Friesian cows, so we had our own milk, cream and butter, which I helped to churn by hand. There were copious quantities of game including dappled fallow deer for venison, pheasant, partridge, rabbit and hare (Mr Dukes and Mr Butler were the head gamekeepers). Behind the vast kitchens, beside the Tudor well house, there were the wonderful Tudor and Victorian outhouses where they hung the game and cured cured the pork for hams and bacon. "Weathered ewe" was a particular favourite of my mother's—she was usually an extraordinarily wonderful cook—and she adored the outhouses and their chilly temperatures and racks of sinister meathooks.

But it was a source of some disappointment to me that there were none of my Peeler policeman great-great-grandfather's red-haired pigs from the Caribbean in the fields round Aunt Julia's walled garden. Nor in the royal arboretum which surrounded Turville Grange, each tree entrancing me with a label naming its donor: Prince and Princesses of Hesse, Prince and Princesses of Saxe-Coburg, Bourbons, Hapsburgs, Battenbergs adorned the grey lead markers.

In fact, the Tamworth pink pigs—"Barbadian Peelers and porkers to boot," Mama called them scornfully—grazed out on the farms nearer to Stonor itself: Balhams, Bix Bottom, Bosmore, Cock's Leas. This strong family connection with Barbados apparently had much to do with the large supplies of sugar and rum that Mama had secretly stored in the tightly closed and tightly locked black-painted cupboards reaching high up on the pantry walls, and along the corridor outside the nursery dining room.

"A touch of the family tar brush comes in most frightfully useful on these tricky occasions," said my mother briskly. "Come to think of it the sun shines very brightly over the Windsors in the West Indies, ha, ha and heil Hitler!"

I said that these islands had to be very near to Granny Camoys' own Rhode Island, where she was surrounded by red chickens.

"Don't be so absurd you idiotic brat," retorted Mama. "The Barbados are just round the corner from the Windsors in Bermuda. Newport, Bellevue Avenue and 'Mildewed' Mildred are thousands of miles away."

All this new information made me think hard. The only Windsors I knew about were a castle I could see on the distant horizon from Bosmore on a fine day, and a thick, dark and glutinous soup which sometimes appeared for nursery lunch ("Far too disgustin' for me to contemplate eatin'," was Mama's reaction). Neither seemed to relate to the exotic Windsors in Bermuda. There was a third contender, the colourful wooden paintbox of Windsor paints in the window of Mr and Mrs Shurvell's intoxicating toy shop in Bell Street. I longed for it.

Mama ignored me when I told her what I thought a "Windsor" might be. "You're a piece of American rubbish just like your tedious, very stupid bitch of a grandmother, old Mildew Lady Cee. Of course," she said, returning to her theme, "Newport and the West Indies are full of people as black as your hat. Just look at Sherman's American family, lookin' just like my own divine chimney sweep, Charlie Creswell. And those angelic coalmen from Henley."

With renewed respect, I remembered the chimney sweep as he struggled up the drawing-room chimney, cap still firmly on his head. Mama had lent a helping hand by pushing him up by his bottom. "So that darlin' boy Charlie doesn't get too stuck up there," she had explained. I also thought of the coalmen arriving in a large flat open wooden truck piled high with hessian sacks of glistening chunks of black coal and rougher, smaller chunks of glazed coke for the boilers. The men were black too, all dusted over with big smiles, flat caps and blue dungarees. They whistled as they worked.

"*Olé* boys and *caramba*!" Mama would call out to them as she whirled her black ebony castanets around her head, flipping a cape in their direction.

When I asked Ruby Heath if she could explain all this, she just raised her red eyebrows and sighed deeply.

"There, there, Miss Julia," was all she said.

12

A Memory of the 'American Heiress'

Mildred Constance Sherman, my American grandmother, was born in Providence, Rhode Island on July 3, 1888, the younger daughter of a respected New York banking tycoon, William Watts Sherman, and his second wife, the heiress Sophia Augusta Brown of Newport and Providence. Mildred was a direct descendant on the maternal side of an early Pilgrim Father, one Chad Brown, who had arrived in Boston, Massachusetts, in 1638, on the ship *Martin*. He settled to live in Providence, the ordained pastor of the First Baptist Church, in 1642.

By 1571, the Brown family had prospered considerably as merchants in trade and commerce. Carefully buying up mansions in nearby Newport, the Browns busily engaged in shipping and whaling. They imported, exported spumaceti, candles, lumber, beef, pork, chocolate, cheese. They traded in molasses, pig iron and Surinam horses. Russian duck were equally profitable, and, in the eighteenth century, tobacco, rum and Negro slaves fetched high prices on the cargo runs to the Caribbean and Surinam, the Dutch colony in South America.

By 1766 Mildred's direct ancestors, the brothers John, Josie, Nick and Mosie, had created a monopoly on their brigs *Sally* and *George*, delving deep into the lucrative markets of coffee, gin, rum, wines. They traded extensively in the British Indies and the French West Caribbean. On several occasions the Brown ships sailed under a carefully contrived flag of convenience, whereby a local agent was commissioned to "buy" the brig concerned, but on a strictly temporary basis, handsomely rewarded with a favourable commission. This cunning ruse was in order that "the Vessel make a French Bottom".

Molasses, in turn, provided the Browns with a lucrative rum distillery.

This distillery, like his chocolate mill, had been the brainchild of Obadiah Brown around 1752. The profitable manufacture of spermaceti candles—conveyed to their destination on the brig *Fairlove* and the ship *Nancy*—coupled with frequent and successful smuggling, was accomplished alongside the more legitimate trading and vital exchange of important Bills of Exchange (these were used in lieu of the contemporary coinage, strivers, shilling, dollars and guilders).

Beef, pork, bricks, onions, chocolate, rum and flour, the Brown dynasty sold them each and all even before the added bounty of the slave trade. Owners of brigs, brigantines, snows, sloops, ships, whalers fancifully named *Dolphin*, *Prudent*, *Freelove*, *Hannah*, *Ranger*, *Britannia*, *Hazard*, *Esther* and *Deborah*, the ever-more powerful Brown family busily plied their trade over the oceans. In 1696 slave trading, the extensive, expansive slave trade, started actively in Newport when fourteen Negro slaves from the Brown brigantine *Seaflower* were sold on the open market.

By 1736, James and Obadiah, the father and uncle respectively of John, Josie, Nick and Mosie, were heavily engaged on the African coast using their ship *The Wheel of Fortune*. Known as "the African Trade", from whence Gold Coast slaves fetched the best prices at £30-£35 per head, on more than one occasion their ship *Speedwell* contained "ten Negroes in a mixed cargo selling at £800 old tenor per head". On another occasion the Brown ship "Sally" carried in her mixed cargo "swivel guns, 40 pairs of handcuffs, 40 legal leg shackles, chains, pistols, blunderbusses, padlocks, cutlasses & c", a cargo to be set against slaves. A mere 48 gallons of rum purchased a girl slave; 52 gallons of the same liquor purchased a boy slave.

In 1800 John Brown, the Democratic representative for Rhode Island, cast his vote firmly against the prohibition of the slave trade. He was "firmly convinced of its socially advantageous, and lucrative necessity", calling it "of Positive Benefit to Mankind". Gradually a spirit of philanthropy filtered its way through the parsimonious house of Brown, well-known for its piety, installed in considerable comfort at its principal mansion, 357 Benefit Street, Providence. Trading as far as St Eustacius, the Barbados and Martinique aboard the brigs and sloops *Hazard*, *Esther* and *Deborah* amongst the many of their extensive fleet of ships and whalers, by 1771 there was a large enough surplus of profit for the Brown brothers to found and fund the Ivy League University of Brown in Providence.

During the American War of Independence, in 1776, funded by this now considerable family fortune, the Browns with habitual expediency swiftly found the means, via the continent of Europe, to continue their lucrative trade with the British. Bills of exchange and the sale of whale oil continued apace whilst there was also a briskly remunerative trade in public securities. Superior quality guns and cannons were manufactured by the family's iron foundry at the Hope furnace. These were then sold at considerable profit to the US Navy.

Substantial manufacturers of cotton, owners of cotton mills, heavily engaged in the profitable China Trade, investing in shrewd family marriages with the prestigious families of Goddard, Ives and Burlingame, the joint family goals were succinctly expressed by John Brown, renowned socialite and prosperous businessman of the 1830s.

"It is my belief that Cash, and Cash alone, give a man Credit and Substantial Consequence in the United States," he stated in 1835, thoughtfully adding: "Mankind and womankind too are inclined to rate an individual according to his rent-roll."

Owners and controllers of the Providence Bank from 1791, and of the Blackstone Canal Bank, the firm of Brown, Ives & Goddard operated an in-house banking and credit system. During the American Civil War of 1861-65 this company dealt most profitably in commodity speculation—as successfully as they had dealt in hard dollars in the China Trade.

The Brown family was single-mindedly determined in achieving the highest profits, both in banking and insurance. In the latter part of the nineteenth century they invested in the acquisition of valuable lands and ranches, trans-Mississippi, in Iowa, Missouri, Kansas and Nebraska, adding to their previous holdings in Pennsylvania, Ohio and Vermont.

Sophia Augusta Brown, Mildred Sherman's mother was the youngest of John Carter Brown's three offspring, born in April, 1867. She was the only sister of the millionaire brothers John Nicholas and Harold Brown. A feisty character of great determination, and known as "the Fiery Duster", Sophia Augusta had met the widower merchant banker William Watts Sherman, of New York and Newport, in 1885. He had only recently lost his beautiful Wetmore wife Anne, mother of his daughters, Sybil and Georgette Wetmore Sherman.

In October the same year, 1885, William Watts and Sophia Augusta were married. Their prolonged honeymoon would be in Europe, the Grand Tour in miniature, travelling by sea and land, purchasing beautiful and rare Canova marbles in Naples, the journey culminating in Paris—

where their elder daughter Irene was born in June 1887. Mildred Constance was born a year later in July, 1888.

William Watts Sherman as a merchant banker, was exceptionally prosperous and successful. First married to Anne, the sister of Senator George Peabody Wetmore, who lived at the magnificent, sumptuously furnished "Chateau Sur Mer" on Bellevue Avenue, Watts's two elder daughters were close to their first cousins, the Misses Maud and Edith Wetmore. These unmarried nieces of Watts ultimately inherited the imposing French-Napoleonic mansion overlooking the Atlantic Ocean—an unhappy cause of internecine strife amongst some of the extended family. Once both sisters were safely dead, warfare broke out over the rich pickings of the vast fortune and priceless antiques

In 1874 Watts Sherman commissioned a very fine house to be built on Shepard Avenue for his first family. The architects were the renowned H. H. Richardson and Stanford White. It was illustrated in the *New York Sketch Book of Architecture*, 1875, with a remit to create a beautiful, gabled, period house. Some five storeys high and with a commanding view, it contained, amongst other formal reception rooms lit by LaFarge windows, an especially handsome library.

With an office at 54 Wall Street, and a brownstone residence on 102 East 25, his brother comfortably installed on Fifth Avenue, and his sister and brother-in-law, the Giraud Fosters, also well placed at 23 Fifth Avenue and in Lenox, Massachusetts, Watts, as a Northerner, could afford to boast of his family connections to the Union General Tecumseh Sherman, notorious during the American Civil War for his scorched-earth tactics.

A rotund, heavily built man with a balding head and a robust walrus moustache, Watts looked every inch the prosperous burgher, the merchant banker and insurance salesman. But he was always a devoted family man, deeply committed to his four daughters and to his two, very different, wives. After the death of his first wife Watts was perceived to be a most eligible, desirable widower. Before very long the determined Sophia Augusta Brown had set her cap successfully at Mr Sherman.

'The Fiery Duster' already showing signs of stoutness of girth—in later life her weight was no less than 240lbs, strictly counterbalanced by the water-lift which mechanically hoisted her from floor to floor—was initially careful to mask her ambitions. A cold young woman of iron will, Sophia Augusta was smug, self-righteous and self-satisfied.

Both John Nicholas and Harold Brown, her younger brothers, born respectively in 1861 and 1863, were handsome and exceptionally eligible millionaires. Sophia Augusta, safely married to Watts Sherman, decided to arrange a match between Harold and her younger and pretty stepdaughter Georgette. She swiftly propelled the eligible, well-born young woman into the arms of her brother. They were married in October 1892 and settled into a large mansion, "Chateau Nooga", 459 Bellevue Avenue, next door to "Stonor Lodge" as Mildred's own house came to be called. In one fell swoop, with customary ruthlessness, the Fiery Duster had achieved a remarkable ambition whereby her own brother became Watts's son-in-law as well as his brother-in-law while Georgette Wetmore Sherman became her sister-in-law at the same time being her stepdaughter.

Sybil Sherman meanwhile had married into the elegant New York-born family of Hoffman. They too maintained a Newport mansion, "Seaweed", on Bellevue Avenue. Even Newport society was somewhat taken by surprise. No doubt a near neighbour, the famous flame red-headed novelist, social commentator, and landscape gardener, Edith Wharton, daughter of Mr and Mrs Edward Jones, paid particular heed to such goings-on.

Watts had become uneasily aware that his new wife had established herself as the power behind the throne in his household. He spent an increasing amount of time at the many clubs of which he was an enthusiastic member. The Knickerbocker, the Metropolitan, of which he was secretary, and the City Club saw him with added frequency. More time was taken up by membership of the Century Club, the Turf and Field, the Suburban Riding and Driving, the Colonial War Club, the American Geographical Society—Watts's interests were many and varied. Last but not least were the Racquet Club and the St Nicholas Skating Club.

Watts had clearly become a compulsive clubman. He particularly relished his position as secretary to the Newport Casino, 194 Bellevue Avenue, the new "social centre" and shopping arcade, architecturally inspired by "the Loire-Chateau style", albeit executed in ornamented wood. Here, and at the elegant Redwood Library, Watts could take refuge from the heavy stuffiness of the Fiery Duster's overbearing ways, for Sophia Augusta had become a compulsive bible reader, possibly even "a bible thumper". At the end of her long life, she bequeathed rare copies of a copious collection of bibles to her father's library in Providence. John Carter Brown's will of 1874 had provided handsomely for this distinguished monument in his memory.

It was into this solid, prosperous and somewhat predictable household that Mildred Constance Sherman was born in July 1888. The youngest of Watts's four daughters, there would be no further issue of the eighth generation, no male heirs, so a great family fortune would ultimately be inherited by the two sisters, the heiresses Irene and Mildred.

Watts's wife, Sophia Augusta, had withdrawn her favours from the marriage bed at the earliest opportunity. So distasteful did she find this aspect of matrimony that upon her death in 1947 a strongly phrased codicil in her will gave instructions for a considerable sum "to be gifted in sympathy to the Providence Lying-In Hospital".

The two girls, Irene and Mildred, were comely, pretty, rather round. They were privately educated, very cloistered, well protected by loving parents and devoted to their elder half-sisters Sybil and Georgette. But the even tenor of the lives of Irene and Mildred was abruptly interrupted in 1900 when, aged thirteen and twelve respectively, their sister Georgette lost her husband, Harold Brown, suddenly on May 10, after barely eight years of marriage and she was left, sadly, childless.

Harold had survived his elder brother by a very few days; John Nicholas died on 1 May, leaving his widow Natalie Bayard Dresser and a baby boy only three months old, also John Nicholas, reputedly "the richest baby in America, born with a golden spoon in his mouth, $85 million".

Sophia Augusta and her family were devastated by the premature deaths of both her younger brothers. Other than the baby John Nicholas Brown, there were now no men left in the immediate family and no guiding spirits for her young daughters Irene and Mildred. Thus there would be no trustworthy younger escorts to show these vulnerable heiresses the ways of the world, nor to protect them from the ruthless scavengers of the predatory British peerage, die-hard members of which had already alighted at New York, and on the wilder shores of Newport's Bellevue Avenue, and illustrious "Bailey's Beach", from the 1890s on.

Several of these scavenger fortune-hunters had ruthlessly struck out for the rich pickings of the Eastern Seaboard, hunting down innocent young American heiresses from among patrician and newly-monied families, so as to replenish their depleted coffers. Among them were the "land-rich, cash-poor" 9th Duke of Marlborough, the 5th Baron Camoys, the 8th Earl Granard and the 5th Baron Decies.

The four buccaneers, John Marlborough, Ralph Camoys, Bernard Arthur Granard and John de la Poer Beresford—two Anglo-Saxons and two Anglo-Irish—were very similar in appearance, each with a fine leg for a hunting-boot, and an absolute hauteur of manner. All four sported thick and bristling moustaches, their small eyes set too close to their noses. But such was their self-possession they strode effortlessly through life with supreme, arrogant confidence. The hunting down and conquest of four young American millionairesses would prove to be their ultimate ambition, their ultimate and ruthless conquest.

Self-satisfied, privileged, plausible, these men set out in considerable style to conquer the United States. Often with their own horses, always with their own valets, they sailed on ships called *La Bourgoyne*, *Aurania*, *Ems*, *La Normandie*, *Britannic*, *La Bretagne* and *Eturia*. Each liner carried a passenger list of distinguished Americans and Europeans. The four buccaneers wined and dined in full evening dress (white tie and tails), with a galaxy of grandees and select millionaires.

A typical passenger list of the First Class included Sir Richard Musgrave, Sir Charles Fairlie-Cunningham, Mrs Ogden Mills, Colonel Jerome Bonaparte, Baron de Struve, Madame Albert Gallantin, Mr George W. Vanderbilt, Mrs Augusta Belmont, Mrs John Carter Brown, Mr John Nicholas Brown, Mr Edward Morgan, Mr Egerton L. Winthrop, Mr Cornelius Vanderbilt, Mr William K. Vanderbilt, the Rt Hon Lord Clifford, Sir Edward Thornton, Mr James A. Roosevelt, Mr Joseph W. Drexel.

First to net a richly endowed bride was the Duke of Marlborough. On 6 November 1895 he married Consuelo, a beautiful, innocent, immensely wealthy, suitable daughter of Mr and Mrs William K. Vanderbilt, residing at 660 Fifth Avenue, New York. The duke had already pointedly told his hapless fiancée that "to live at Blenheim in the pomp and circumstance I consider essential, I need money". The same could be said of the twin philosophies of Ralph Camoys and John Decies in their similar transatlantic quest the better to fund their lifestyles at Stonor Park and Leixlip Castle—not to mention their London and Dublin clubs. Besides, these three men considered their innocent brides-to-be as quite easily disposable assets.

In 1909 the next buccaneer, the 8th Earl Granard, cousin to Ralph Camoys and also a Catholic, married Beatrice Ogden Mills, millionaire daughter of Dutch County tycoon Ogden Mills, in another of old New York's magnificent ceremonies. The elegance once again, the largesse of hospitality, and the magnificent list of presents excelled even the splendour of the Vanderbilt celebrations. And, again, the Court Circular of the

London *Times* breathlessly described in the minutest of detail the lavish and beautiful wedding, the distinguished and international list of guests, some 1,500 at the church and 115 at the wedding breakfast.

The supreme advantage, an added attraction to these grooms, peers of the realm, was the etiquette of such occasions where the bride's parents provided all. No financial contribution was expected of the four bucca-neers. Yet the cost of the Vanderbilt-Marlborough marriage preparations was at least £80,000, the Granard-Mills wedding no less.

The general public of New York seem to have been more than magnan-imous in the face of such ostentatious expenditure—and especially in the snow-bound winter seasons of searing cold. A contemporary reporter was quoted as saying: "I suppose that no American or Anglo-American wed-ding ever excited so much interest among people of all sorts and condi-tions, nor was such a ceremony in this city so splendid and elaborate. If there be any prejudices in this country against wealth, and or against the union of these two, they have on this occasion been suppressed. The mar-riage is extremely popular."

The marriage of the 5th Lord Decies to Florence Gould, daughter of railroad magnate George Jay Gould, on February 7, 1910, was no less lav-ish, a gorgeous extravaganza, outstandingly in style and generosity. The Lord Camoys acted as principal usher to his best friend, John de la Poer Beresford, and it was at this wedding he met the Misses Sherman, and their mother Sophia Augusta. The Fiery Duster, ever ambitious, was captivated by the superficial charm of Ralph.

Yet by 1931 Florence, the beautiful Lady Decies, co-heiress to her recently dead father George Jay Gould and still in her early thirties, would swiftly die. A "mysterious illness" which confined her to the house in London off Curzon Street was diagnosed, bulletins issued through the Court Circular announcing her alarming debilitation. Florence was "cre-mated privately". It was requested that there be no flowers—contrary to traditional English ceremonies. Within very few weeks John Decies had made his way to New York to contest his father-in-law's will. To the hor-ror of Florence's brothers, who contested their brother-in-law's claim to their dead sister's inheritance, he won a very substantial share.

By May 1936, the 5th Baron Decies had remarried Elizabeth Wharton, widow of Henry Lymes Lehr, a daughter of the Philadelphian tycoon and banker Joseph Wilhelm Drexel. The couple retired to live in Paris,

On 25 November 1911, Mildred Constance Sherman became the wife of Ralph Francis Julian Stonor, 5th Baron Camoys of Stonor Park. They were married privately, in a bedroom of the Sherman family house, at the bedside of Watts Sherman, who was dying gradually. Ralph was twenty-seven, his bride four years younger.

Sophia Augusta, habitually parsimonious, had insisted upon this ceremony of utmost simplicity and minimal cost, although she was more than delighted to have acquired an English peer as a son-in-law—as would be reflected in her will in 1947. Despite her pious meanness it is doubtful that even the Fiery Duster could have anticipated the depth of sufferings which this son-in-law would so casually, so cynically, inflict on her romantically-disposed, warm-hearted younger daughter Mildred. Nor could Sophia Augusta have anticipated the expenditure which Mildred would lavish upon the far-away, damp and primitive Oxfordshire mansion of Stonor Park for so many years.

In sweetness of character Mildred took more after her father Watts, her aunt Mrs Giraud Foster and her cousin Antoinette Sherman, married to an Egyptian Copt, George Gabriel Abdel Messih Bey, and their daughter Dorothée. This inheritance, frequently disdained by those around her, Mildred would pass on to her only son Sherman.

Mildred and Ralph were far away in Japan on their round-the-world honeymoon voyage when the news came by telegram, early in 1912, of the death of William Watts Sherman. He had lingered very few weeks beyond the bedside marriage. Certainly his demise caused genuine grief and great heartache to his youngest daughter—and emphasised a new loneliness so many thousands of miles apart from her loving American family.

13

'Nineteen Furniture Vans Sailin' Past My Window'

Two of Papa's magically interesting sisters still lived on the other side of the Atlantic, on Rhode Island and under the same roof as my grandmother Lady Camoys. But they seemed only to annoy my mother.

"Blast those rich gels still livin' with my blasted mother-in-law Mildew Lady Cee. Such close friends of the Windsors—on the American side, of course. And I am in absolutely no doubt that Mildewed Mildred is herself a throwback to the Sophia Augusta Brown family slave tradin' business. No better than bankers those traders. But certainly as rich," said Mama reflectively. "Anyhow, Sherman's descended from Red Indian Baptists just like some of his sisters. They have a lot to answer for and I shall certainly make them pay." She removed her cigarette and spat contemptuously out of the window. "My effin' mother-in-law has stolen all Sherman's antiques, furniture, pictures, silver, porcelain, the lot. Lady Cee has a great deal to answer for. I shall see to it that she pays up. No one jests with this aristo bastard, *olé!*" Mama's eyes had narrowed to slits as she turned to me. "Mark my words, you too, Julia, will effin' well pay for it. You are only equalled by Lady Cee herself. I was forced to watch out of the drawing-room window at Assendon Lodge as nineteen furniture vans went sailin' past my window from the Park to Newport. Can you imagine the agony I felt? I'm in most continuous agony, goddamn them!"

Mystified as I was by Mama's rage, I felt deep concern for Papa who deeply loved his American mother and family. Though I wasn't sure that he was loved back in the same way. But Mama was in evident agony and it made me sad to see her suffer so much.

I asked whether she ought to borrow one of the many medicine bottles

Mama had recently bought to make Papa's health better. Though it might make her feel as dizzy as Papa invariably was after he had been given these medicines.

"Don't talk such absolute bosh," said Mama sharply. "Those are just the inevitable side-effects and your father will soon get over it."

She appeared not to like my suggestion at all, and administered a quick slap and a sharp pinch for my pains.

It upset me that I couldn't make my mother happy and better from her ongoing agony, caused this time by the terrible sight of Papa's disappearing furniture.

"Your wicked grandmother old Mildew stole it all in '38," said Mama furiously. "Nineteen pantechnicons all but broke my heart."

Tears flowed down her rouged cheeks, her mouth tightly pursed as she slammed down her signet ring on the nearest available surface. A marble-topped table cracked from the sheer impact. But she made a speedy recovery after the usual elevenses of a couple of Horse's Necks.

I got to be quite skilled at making Mama's cocktails and thought that these dark brown drinks ("It is most frightfully common and *cursí* to talk about beverages unless you are drinkin' Bovril and Ovaltine!") must have some connection with the underfed, bone-thin horses I saw regularly each Wednesday in the knacker's yard at Benson. They looked dolefully unhappy with matted coats and little flesh, shivering under hemp sacking covers.

The liquid in Mama's rum glass had fiercely bright, sizzling bubbles that fizzed and jumped up and down inside the thick green glass as I carried it carefully to my mother.

"Whoops! Great fun, and a whizzin' wind-banger don't you think, Pop-goes-the-Weasel?" laughed Mama, offering a cocktail to Bangpa-Pop. But, never really fancying such brandy beverages, my grandfather had Kia-Ora squash instead. This simply added to Mama's general exasperation.

"That synthetic muck is made by the Aborigines in New Zealand where they grow oranges," she tutted. "I simply can't abide it myself. Like water I never let such rubbish even pass my lips. For a Cartholic and a teetotaller to boot, Bangpa-Pop, you're quite certainly one of the most crashin' deadly bores I know. You're only ever useful for title deeds, entrails and entails. So just where are the goods?" she demanded sharply blowing smoke rings at her father-in-law.

There were certainly no oranges that came with my ration book as opposed to the cornucopia that was Mama's. "I've been given divine dispensation for my remarkable efforts in this goddamned inconvenient nuisance of a war," she would say sweetly.

She in fact had several ration books and a constant supply of fruit, eggs and butter. She regularly bought cod-liver oil and syrup of figs but did not take these herself, though Papa, the dogs and I were frequently given strong dosages. "Works instant miracles I always say. Straight orf to your pot, Julia. Or are you house-trained by now? I really must ask Nanny."

The cod-liver oil was fishy and strongly nasty suspiciously like the whalemeat steaks and horsemeat that appeared from time to time between the rabbit stews and rubberised, over-cooked pig's liver in the nursery dining room. The texture of the liver reminded me of my mother's mauve-coloured rubber hot-water bottle which I was ordered to place in her bed.

It also reminded me of the solid polish that Ruby used on Papa's antique furniture. This had to be applied with all the elbow grease that poor Ruby could muster.

"Faster, faster, Ruby dear! You're nothin' like quick enough, and this polish must never be allowed to dry even for a moment on MY very own rare possessions," scolded my mother. "Mine I said, MINE, Spanish aristo bastard that I am, *olé!* Everythin' that I now have is absolutely first rank," she continued in a commanding tone.

Mama turned to glower at Bangpa-Pop. "Although I may as well exclude you, Pop-goes-the-Weasel indeed, in fact, as bein' particularly useless at this minute," she snorted. "And quite definitely passé in the 'parts' department. I've had your last useless offerin' shipped orf through the Vatican canal connection."

Trying to hitch his trousers up again, Bangpa-Pop's cheeks and double chin turned a deeper purple.

I was relieved to learn that Mama still had so much furniture left, even if Papa's own mother had stolen her only son's antiques.

"NINETEEN furniture vans. Right beneath my nose!" she repeated.

I supposed these vans to look like the large dark-blue one from Neal's Laundry in Acton. This came twice weekly to Assendon Lodge, and later to the Park, to fetch and carry large and lidded wicker baskets with brown leather straps and brass buckles. This was an exciting event and just like in *Johnny Town Mouse*, which Ruby used to read to me.

But my mother was frequently annoyed because the laundryman had the temerity to want money to pay for all the fine white linen sheets, cotton bath towels and damask tablecloths he took away each week to Acton.

Ruby used to count all the items individually, noting them down in an old-fashioned hand neatly into a thin, blue-bound book with red lines. When the laundryman returned with the sheets, which glistened like snow, the napkins stiff with starch, she would check each item meticulously.

But each time the laundry never failed to leave Mama in an enraged state. "I'm bein' cheated and taken for a ride by these swine, such dirt-common people to boot. I'm payin' over the odds and far too much for this service, which hardly suffices," she sniffed indignantly.

Her outbursts surprised me because Mama appeared to like the laundryman, who was also the van driver. He wore beige overalls and a peaked blue cap and usually came back down to the kitchen for "a nice cuppa char" with Ruby and me after heaving the deep, heavily-laden wicker baskets to the upstairs landing by himself.

"Such a frightfully brave, gallant chap," Mama would announce. "I will go up ahead of him just to make sure he finds the way."

The laundryman from Acton had no name but I was a little disappointed at Mama taking my opportunity to show him where to put the magnificent basket with its flat lid and creaking leather hinges. It bulged with napkins done up in flimsy blue tissue paper, the sheets and towels tied neatly with pink ribbon. Ruby would fold all the paper, wind the ribbon up into a ball and put it all in a kitchen drawer.

"For a rainy day, Doodo darling," she said sadly.

*

Aunt Julia, who looked older than my mother and was much taller, had beautiful silver hair piled high on top of her head.

"That style of your Aunt Julia's is called a chignon. Very French you know. Filthy Frogs, how I hate them. Really quite loathsome, and so different from my own darlin' aristo Spaniards," said Mama complacently.

My own experience with frogs was confined entirely to the yellow-green ones, both fat and thin, which resided in the stagnant ponds in the back garden up at the Park. Mama showed me large and fascinating puddles of thick green frog spawn because, as she said, "it reminds me of that borin' tapioca puddin' your tedious grandmother Mildew Lady Cee insists on includin' in her dreary American food parcels."

I had not yet noticed this tapioca pudding turning into the thousands of tadpoles that leapt their way out of the frog spawn and into the Stonor ponds. They were "well on their way to becomin' French frogs", according to Mama as she peered down into the murky stagnant water across which occasionally flitted a couple of translucent dragonflies. "I do find frog men most frightfully clammy," she said reflectively as she dipped her fingers into the ponds.

I had seen the frogs leaping along the flagstoned terrace behind the Long Gallery, but I could not make the connection between them, Aunt Julia and her dead husband, "that French frog, your dubious Uncle Fernan".

I decided it would be unwise for me to inquire further as I risked another slap round the head from Mama's heavily bejewelled fingers ("Not even when I am in bed do I take my valuables orf!"). Another favourite move of Mama's was to pull my hair, which hurt as much even when she was performing the normal duty of brushing it.

"The child has rats in her hair," she would say scornfully, tugging a tortoise shell comb through my tangles. But strangely she never said this in front of Aunt Julia.

Her own Spanish black hair hung sleekly down in the fashionable pageboy look which the hairdresser Mr John came twice weekly to do. Mama had a special black salon hairdrier installed at Assendon Lodge, beneath which she sat chain-smoking endless contraband cigarette while avidly reading *The Tatler & Bystander*. This my mother alternated with the latest popular novel or detective story.

Sitting bolt upright in her curlers one day, head wrapped in a large hairnet she shouted angrily at the hapless Mr John: "For Gawd's sake, can't you see you're roastin' me alive you effin' fool of a man. You can take a runnin' jump young man, and look sharp!"

So saying Mama took aim with her novel, which she hurled at the hairdresser. Mr John looked quite startled as the book hit him.

"I've been very well taught by my darlin' Joachim at Sonnenburg. He showed me how to aim my thing," Mama declared smugly. "Time for my elevenses after such an ordeal." So saying, she took a quick swig from a silver flask, which she fished out of a capacious black crocodile handbag. "Frightfully soothin' to my shattered nerves," she murmured. "I do have to put up with such very common or garden pansies, ha, ha and *olé!*"

Habitually, Mama had very high standards of attire, ready to be "called upon" at any time of the day—or night—whether by Uncle Eric St Johnston, a king of Greece or Aunt Julia.

Ernest Busby, Aunt Julia's tiny chauffeur, would drive her around in an upright green car, a Morris, wearing a bottle-green uniform and a peaked cap. I couldn't help noting that Busby was even smaller than both Uncle Enrico Marone from Turin and Uncle Carlos from Bogotá—"Darlin' Carlos does somethin' frightfully secret and special for that *mon général* de Gaulle in France," said Mama once again. "And such lucrative tin mines to boot."

All the windows of Aunt Julia's car, which had a small crown discreetly painted on the doors, were of smoked yellow glass. But I could still see my Aunt quite clearly, seated upright and tall on the green leather-covered back seat.

Aunt Julia wore a purple toque on top of her chignon. This was held in place with hatpins, purple stones glistening at their ends. (Said Ruby: "Those are the Family Amethysts, Doodo, darling.") Her long boucle wool cardigan and silk georgette dress were the colour of the mulberries on the gnarled tree behind the potting-shed up at the Park where Mr White, the head-gardener, mysteriously potted up in the straw and the dark. ("Right next door to his very own earth closet," laughed Mama. "Just right for a Plymouth Brethren too.")

On many mid-week days she would be driven over from the Grange up on Turville Heath to call upon my mother at Bosmore or Assendon Lodge some time in the afternoons during those arduous days of the Second World War. Seated always on the back seat, she towered majestically over Busby's minute figure in the front, supervising his speed very strictly as the car wound its way down the Pishill Road, through the Stonor Valley and down the Assendon Road until it swung abruptly to the left at Assendon Lodge, curling round the squalor of Old Mrs Phillip's filthy farmyard and the howling unkempt dogs as the rutted lane became the Fawley Bottom approach to the Bosmore Estate.

Once arrived at her destination, Aunt Julia would descend the step of the Morris to ring emphatically at the front door. Frequently receiving no answer, she would walk round to the kitchen window, pushing her way past the strayed Brussels sprouts and old cabbages as she went, to peer through the glass.

Dragging me with her on hearing the car arrive, Mama would many times hastily hide behind a cupboard door, squeezing me in besides her. This door was full-length but some inches off the ground, and warped. Once squeezed so tightly inside, there was precious little space for the two of us in between the jam jars and Mama's innumerable packets of sugar.

My mother's action seemed quite inexplicable, even most peculiar, because Aunt Julia did such kind things. Not only did I kneel besides her at her special request to have "my niece, Sherman's very dear child, beside me in the chapel for Mass at all times" (my mother herself never left her position of command up in the distant tribune), but I also loved Aunt Julia deeply with the same devotion she showed me.

Whenever Aunt Julia caught Mama hiding in the cupboard, she would rap sharply and even imperiously on the window panes with her long, golden cane, topped with elaborately-carved Fabergé silver-gilt, a simple ferule on its slender tip.

"Come out of there immediately Jeanne Mary!" she called. "I can see your feet sticking out under the door. And I can see poor Julia's feet as well."

Mama would squeeze me still further into the cupboard, jamming the jagged edge of the warped wooden door deeper into my shins. "Aunt Julia can piss orf, the rich bitch," she hissed furiously. "She's an effin' nosey-parker into the bargain. Just you wait till I get my hands on all that Russian Fabergé stuff. That jewellery is to die for. He who hesitates is lorst. Just you wait and see who is in charge and command round here."

*

I knew of other "parkers", though I didn't know if they were particularly "nosey". At the nearby Protestant castle of Shirburn—walled, wild, windy and secretive, hidden on a back road from Watlington Park, near to Christmas Common—we had neighbours from the 15th century called Parker whom Mama seemed not to like at all.

These Parkers had a drawbridge over their moat which the wicked Old Lord Macclesfield with his heavy, walrus moustache ("So much more sex-appeal than Pop-goes-the-Weasel!" shouted my mother excitedly) drew up hastily upon my mother's arrival.

"I'm makin' it perfectly clear to the old boy I'm clad for the assault against the principal Parker," she explained grandly, her Tyrolean hat cocked to the side of her head, a cigarette hanging out of the corner of her deeply scarlet lips as she started to wade in Newmarket boots.

"Loveden, old boy, yoo-hoo, and I'm in up to the knicker-line!" Mama shouted enthusiastically towards the rising drawbridge.

In reply, Loveden, or Old Lord Macclesfield, leant down over the parapet, a 12-bore Purdey shotgun pointed in her direction.

"Darlin' old Loveden is threatenin' to shoot me," Mama laughed back as she scrambled up the bank of the moat. "He means every word, *olé*, *caramba* and heil Hitler!" Mama saluted in the direction of the firmly closed bridge. "Not for nothin' were darlin' Joachim, Loveden and I fellow-members of the Anglo-German Fellowship. All us fellers together if you get my meanin'. Most frightfully jolly stuff one way or another." The white and brown Newmarket boots were soaked while a Molyneux tweed skirt clung tightly to her thighs, moat weeds hanging off it. "But he IS a millionaire!"

Mama finally climbed back into Granny Camoys' Chevrolet. I still could not work out the nosey-parker connection with Aunt Julia. These Parkers had litters of pink and black and large white pigs, in styes of rotting straw, scattered around large acres of undrained muddy fields at Pyrton and Shirburn Castle.

Mama pointed out the pigs to me with glee as she took her newest short cut through the estate to the knacker's yard just round the corner at Benson Aerodrome, "where all those boys look so divine in pale blue". There were now several different routes and short cuts through other people's land which Mama found more convenient even as she drove between Assendon Lodge and Benson to meet the knackers each Wednesday afternoon.

When we called again en route at Shirburn Castle, I was frightened that Old Lord Loveden ("and only a belted Earl, damn it," sniffed my mother) would shoot her as she continued her weekly assault of the drawbridge. Even getting down from the old brake seemed an action fraught with danger and I immediately wet my knickers in fear. But the grass around the rain-bloated moat was long, wet, tangled, and no one noticed my crime until we got home, long after the knacker's yard.

"For Gawd's sake child, and you're not even house-trained," exclaimed Mama mockingly. She advanced towards my terrified backside, her hand held high with her favourite Mason & Pearson's black-and-white hair brush, pink bristled held at the ready for the first, resounding spank.

"Not for the first time you're in a State of Serious Mortal Sin. So," added Mama icily. "Sherman's brat must go at this very minute, and preferably even sooner, straight to bed as a deeply deserved Penance. I'm sendin' immediately for Uncle Alfonso to hear your confession. There will be several acts of contrition outstandin', ha, ha!"

Gleefully Mama clicked her long fingernails together and briskly waving a contemptuous hand. She banished me to a darkened nursery bedroom, tossing forth a torrent of Spanish expletives as I ran out. But I still found space within me to worry that Mama's beautiful, scarlet nails would break, snapping off in the heat and disturbance of the moment. Uncle Joachim was placed even before Banga-Pop in night prayers that night.

*

Pink Parkers were also to be found on the way to Aunt Julia's rose-pink house on the heath at Turville. This was common land and Mama, naturally, had already made her claim to it.

"Personally I always graze my cattle and deer here now that I, and I alone, own the Freedom and Lordship of the Manor. And not before time in my frightfully delicate plans. Thank Gawd for that, and heil Hitler! Nor before time in my own agonisin' poverty and sufferin'," hiccuped my mother through spasmodic sobs. These seem to have increased since she had taken to a double-dose of Horse's Neck elevenses. "I'm in charge and command round here, *olé*!"

One afternoon, Aunt Julia had seemed quite defeated by Mama's hiding-away in the kitchen cupboards of Assendon Lodge and Bosmore, and so she had retreated in frustration back to her Morris. But we finally emerged to find Busby busily polishing the car with a chamois leather and a bright yellow duster.

Yellow was Mama's favourite colour. My own had been pink and I remember spending a particularly happy day painting overblown pink and red roses on thick sheets of grey paper which Mama had supplied me with.

"Strictly only on loan," she had snapped. "I've always regarded pink as a most fearfully common colour myself," she added scornfully.

But I was so convinced that Mama was "always right", as she was the first to say, that I promptly abandoned pink and changed my favourite colour to yellow.

Yellow, after all, was the colour of the newly painted drawing-room at Assendon Lodge, a bright, bitter lemon shade, soon to be followed by the newly-painted drawing-room up at the Park. I thought that Busby must have understood too, to judge from the egg-yolk yellow of his duster that made Aunt Julia's car shine so brightly I could see my own face in the mudguards, which were my height. More interestingly, when I looked between the thick spokes of the wheels, one side to another, and on the same level as the running-board of the dark green Morris, I could catch a glimpse of my mother's silken-encased legs as she climbed onto the back seat with Aunt Julia.

This was one of the very rare occasions when Mama had felt remorse about my aunt.

"I'm orf callin' with the Marquise d'Hautpoul," she called out of the window to all and sundry, even if it was only to Ruby and me. "I'm most frightfully annoyed with myself for mistakin' you, of all people, Aunt Julia dear, as an intruder," Mama carefully explained to my Aunt. "You see I simply had to take refuge until Pop reappeared, Auntie dear. You know how it is with your nephew Ralph these days, when he is so taken up with air-raid precautions. I hardly ever see him out of his gasmask and tin helmet. So I just popped into the cupboard for protection."

Aunt Julia sighed deeply.

"So fortunate your great-niece Julia did not piddle in her knickers this time," laughed my mother.

Catching sight of me out of the window of the stationary car, Mama stuck her tongue out as Busby arranged a woollen rug over Aunt Julia's knees. Mama swiftly wound down the yellowed glass window, hurled a cigarette end in my direction and just as swiftly rewound the window.

I used Mama's discarded cigarette butts for my own experimental smoking in a miniature Woolworth's pipe that I had found in a corner of the carpenter's workshop up at the Park. It was made from plastic and into it I stuffed the ends, combined with pine needles and lit with a stolen match. But Mama's punishments with the Mason & Pearson hairbrush were even direr when I was duly caught, festooned in acrid smoke and covered with smouldering ash.

It was a world in which all the adults smoked, whether their health permitted or not. George Shirfield was one of the Stonor workmen who had just painted the yellow drawing room at Assendon Lodge. The foreman was very tall, a hand-rolled, thin cigarette hanging from the corner of his mouth and a hacking cough, which I could imitate to perfection. As Mama explained, poor dear George could not possibly fight in "this goddamned war" because he was so badly gassed in the first one. "His lungs are hangin' out, and they've gorne quite green inside, just like his complexion, ha, ha!"

I was horrified at hearing this and regarded George with great anxiety. He never took his cap off, inside or out, and I watched him enviously extricating damp, sweet-smelling tobacco from a tin box, hand-rolling the cig-arettes. The box, brightly painted, was much more exciting than the plain-er cardboard cartons of Camel and Philip Morris cigarettes which were delivered to Mama by Papa's American Cousin and Friends in the Navy who came calling at Assendon Lodge.

"I simply have to keep up my American connection," explained Mama. "Quite simply to make sure my vital supplies keep rollin' in on time." She winked again at Bangpa-Pop.

He guffawed and blew his nose hard.

"Quite factually, Pop-goes-the-Weasel, Ralph old boy, I meant, actual-ly, old bore, even your canals, let alone your colonic canal and all of that, are completely bunged up. Can't you just bugger orf for some colonic irri-gation and a damn good sluice-out? I'm givin' you syrup of figs and some of Father Cereal's holy water mix tonight, and that can't fail to trickle-down P.D.Q. And certainly more than high time for your weekly purge, in and as quickly out of André Cereal's confessional as you can make it. I'm timin' you on this new watch from my darlin' Monsieur Louis at Cartier," laughed Mama. She squinted down at her wristwatch, platinum-mounted with diamonds. Snapping her fingers again, she lit another contraband Camel, puffing smoke down her nostrils.

Meanwhile, in the vastness of the kitchen, Ruby was preparing cups of tea for elevenses for the foreman George and his younger cousin Freddie, who helped him and was also my father's great friend. The carpenter and occasional poacher Stanley West would also join us for tea.

The kitchen was mostly Ruby's domain and it was a haven for me. Sometimes I was so fearful that I would run down to hide in her flowery apron there. Later, when I was older, I would run as far as 26 The Terrace, her cottage in the Village.

To distract me from my terrified misery, Ruby would tell me about her beginnings in service. ("Ruby Heath's speech is more than a little quaint," said my mother hastily. "Maybe it's the result of startin' work so young, and for some Maharajah at that.") When she was still but 14, Ruby had started work as a chambermaid in the Rutland Arms at Newmarket.

"That Maharajah had ever-such a beautiful turban, and a lot of jewels," she told me and Mama. "And it was ever-such a hard life, Madam. But I did get to see all those marvellous 'orses 'e owned on the Newmarket Gallops!" Ruby added a small sigh of excited wonderment.

"I'll make quite sure this brat of Sherman's doesn't get away with anything so lightly. Sounds to me that the Rutland Arms would be far too good for the likes of Julia," added Mama scathingly.

Giving me a sharp push, she tweaked my hair from behind. "These god-damned American officers had better ante up, and pretty damn quick. My vital supplies of Camels and Philip Morris are laggin' behind the times," she said crossly. She turned to wink again at Bangpa-Pop. "High time that Sherman's darlin' cousin John Nicholas Brown reappeared on my horizon. Such a divine man in such a divine uniform. "Though I do find his enormous feet rather cumbersome. Still one must keep the bed warm in such very uncertain weather conditions, don't you agree Pop, old boy?"

Bangpa-Pop's colourfully veined cheeks turned a darker mauve in reply.

Mama stamped an elegant foot impatiently. "Really Ralph, for a common or garden baron with only four undersized balls to boot, your flatulence and phletus really irritate me to blazes."

My grandfather looked very uneasy, and attempted to hitch up his trousers again.

Mama continued: "If you don't set about producin' the goodies a damn sight quicker, Pop-goes-the-Weasel, I shall make very sure that bitch Mildew, Lady Cee knows about these THINGS and knows about them pretty damn quick. And by that I mean exactly what I say Ralph. You know me, not a Spanish aristo bastard for nothing, *olé!*"

Bangpa-Pop's chin was now more purple than mauve, and like his slack cheeks, wobbled. He looked like a turkey in crafty old Mrs Phillip's farmyard next to Assendon Lodge. I watched to see if his colour could possibly get any deeper. Unfortunately my interest merely attracted more of Mama's ire.

"For Gawd's sake, eff out of it you borin' brat, and keep your nose out of other people's business. Nosey parkers need to learn," she snarled and hit me above the sock line across the back of my bare knees with her heavily bejewelled hand, with its ruby and diamond rings and the new gold signet ring "from my beloved Monsieur Louis at Cartier, *olé!*" As an afterthought Mama flicked a salute in the direction of Bangpa-Pop. "Heil Hitler, old boy, and yoo-hoo!"

14

Tobacco, Meths
and Tia María

The estate workmen George and his cousin Freddie, who also had the brightest of blue eyes—though George's were rheumy from his gassing—and Stanley, the minute and bent-over estate carpenter, had been brought up with Papa. They were his best friends.

"Oh ah, Miss Julia, and we've known your father ever since he was a boy and he's a fine one," they said in unison, smiling and coughing through their hand-rolled cigarettes. And I understood they truly loved Sherman.

It was Mama, however, who directed them. She had a lot of work to be done at Assendon Lodge during the war years, so the three workmen came down from their cottages in Stonor village and the carpenter's workshop up at the Park, although they were still working there for the men in grey suits from National Benzole while Papa was still away in the war.

My mother supervised busily, with the help of our night prayers for Uncle Eric, Colonel St Johnston, "my blue-eyed beau, *olé!* who looks so exactly like my darlin' Joachim!" exclaimed Mama to no one in particular. When she had no other audience, my mother would simply address Ruby and me. Or even me on my own.

George, Freddie and Stanley brought with them planks and ladders, and old tin buckets filled with mysterious liquids for redecorating as well as thick grey glue, and turps. Big, flat paintbrushes were made of horse's hairs, "straight from my knacker's yard," laughed Mama as she watched warily. The three men also brought boxes of nails, tacks and screws. But, said my mother "their screws are too short, quite useless and not welcome here, goddamn them. Far too common for my own use."

George, Freddie and Stanley, all three chewed tobacco and sniggered behind Mama's back.

"Your mother isn't half a one," giggled Stanley, his twisted and wizened face alight with mirth.

In the now lemon-yellow drawing room, Mama had a newly done-up stiff, upright sofa with sturdy dark brown legs to receive visitors and callers. It had been upholstered in a thick, crumpled, mustard-yellow velvet moquette, a design cut into the material. Its hard buttons protruded into my back, and my feet did not even reach the floor on those rare occasions when I was paraded into and out of the drawing room.

"Sherman's brat is to be seen, but seldom, if at all," laughed Mama. "And certainly not heard. You've already been here at least ten minutes, and that is ten minutes too long. My Gawd and you bore me to tears." So saying she yawned and flashed her fingernails at me. "Out I said, and I mean what I say. Vamoose!"

Ruby served drawing-room tea on a silver tray with a lace cloth. This tray was burdened down with a silver teapot, a silver jug and a silver sugarbowl. She was dressed in her best afternoon uniform, a black dress ("silk crepe, Miss Julia") with an embroidered white cotton apron.

" 'Broderie Anglaise', Madam calls it," explained Ruby in a similar starched white cap. Herself over-burdened by the immense weight of the tea tray, Ruby staggered through the drawing-room door to the obvious irritation of my mother, who was waiting impatiently by a small violet flame beneath a samovar. Into this Ruby poured water.

"The smell of meths does me a power of good," exclaimed Mama, a Philip Morris or maybe a Camel sticking to the corner of her deeply vermilion lips. "Aunt Oinette Esher is here for tea," she continued. "Too terribly rouged to be true. Such a common American habit," she said scathingly. "Rather suitable, come to think of it," she mused, "that the 3rd Viscount Esher, that roly-poly Oliver does practise euthanasia. He knows just when he can start, *olé!*" Mama roared with laughter.

The little old lady, 3rd Viscountess Esher, with her bright cheeks sat high up on the sofa, her rinsed blue hair tightly curled, her hands folded on her knees. Aunt Oinette's fiercely scrubbed fingers wore no nail varnish, and she had a single diamond solitaire ring above her wedding ring.

Mama gazed at her from across the room. "You borin' goddamned New England intellectuals," she said calmly. "Far too rigid and austere for my taste. Totally devoid of a sense of humour, aren't you, Aunt Oinette dear?." Mama paused for a moment's reflection. "Plenty of dosh and cash round here though. I shall really have to speak to Oliver, even if he is as bald as a coot, and comes from that frightfully dreary Bruxelles sprouts suburbia."

The 3rd Viscountess Esher from Watlington Park maintained a dignified silence. I was allowed down to the drawing room, suitably dressed in my best frock of smooth, thick black velvet with a deep cream lace collar.

"King Charles's own," explained Mama grandly. "So fortuitous I just happened to be on the Isle of Wight, passin' by old Carisbrooke's place—the castle you know—when the collar simply slipped into my hands." Mama gazed hard at the chairman of the Euthanasia Society. "Of course you know how it is, old boy," she laughed, winking at the 3rd Viscount Esher of Watlington Park and the Esher Suburbs. Oliver sipped his tea.

His minute wife Oinette had always seemed surprised that I should call her "Aunt", but I had continued to do as Mama had ordered me. One day Oinette told me that her real name was the Viscountess Esher, and as she would shortly be 65 years old, she would prefer it if someone still under five would not call her "*Aunt*-oinette". Mortified with shame and shyness I blushed to the roots of my hair. I had tried so hard to please and I was convinced now that Aunt Oinette did not like me any more. Overhearing the conversation, Mama had laughed until she cried.

Mama's much taller Spanish aunt, Tia María de Zulueta, came frequently to tea. So like my mother in looks, with the same jutting jaw and dark, dewpond eyes. Devoid of make-up other than a heavy white powder, Tia María's lips were mostly pursed in displeasure as she gazed at her niece Jeanne.

"María looks as if she has an early dose of lead poisoning," said Mama hopefully over her shoulder.

But Tia María paid no attention. She had brought with her a black, very shiny Steinway baby grand piano and together with my mother she played duets and sang. Her brother Pedro de Zulueta composed operettas.

"Well María, in the circs and so as there will be no misunderstandin', I'm keepin' this piano," laughed Mama, her fingers nipping up and down the chords.

"Really Jeanne, your fingernails are far too long. Get the nail-clippers immediately," snapped Tia María.

Paying no attention, Mama sang on in a rich, smoky voice that sounded as if it came from far from beneath packet upon packet of contraband Camels.

"Don't imagine for one moment your Tia María is as sweet as the drink of her name," said my mother sourly. "Your Aunt María has gorne back to that sleazy hotel in Queen's Gate, where there's been a very nasty murder, simply made for old cats like her, and that borin' companion Cousin Mónica de Bertodano from Barcelona. Whose spinster face looks like a polished chestnut." She paused for an early evening sip of Horse's Neck. "To say nothing of the dreary Mónica's tree-trunk legs in those Old Cartholic lisle stockin's and cobbled old maid's brown shoes." A light hiccup. "I'm restin' my shattered nerves," she explained to both all and sundry and no one in particular.

Some days Mama amused herself teaching me scales and notes on Tia María's black ebony piano which was now ours. "Frankly child your fingerin' is not up to much," she said witheringly during one such session. She slapped a ruler across the back of my hands and as I tried to work up speed. Taken by surprise I all but fell off the stool, high, black and gaunt, with heavy piles of film music scores tucked beneath the domed lift-up seat. That was strictly forbidden territory, and punishment for lifting the seat of the stool was severe.

Surreptitiously, I tried to look in there on the days when Mama was safely away at Old Windsor with Tia María. Here Aunt and niece visited my Spanish grandfather, Don Pedro de Zulueta y Merry del Val with his black Borja family moustache. He was my mother's real father and María's only brother.

Mama had already carefully explained his business to me. "Dear old Pedro is most frightfully busy lookin' after diplomatic things for *El Jefe*, *el generalísimo* Franco. Things are hottin' up on Gibraltar and *con los Marqueses de Bute* at Algeciras, *olé! Viva el rey de España!* In fact, your Uncle Mon is just flyin' through from the 'Portugoose' via Gib. The Marqués del Moral seems to have mislaid his wife, that crashin' bore Gytha, somewhere along the way. Damn good thing if darlin' old Mon lorst Gytha altogether with those two borin' Spanish brats of hers. Gytha really has more than an overdose of religious mania, permanently intertwined in her rosary beads." Mama sniffed indignantly. "Stuck in a convent at Coimbra and penniless, ha, ha. Serves them right if they starve to death—certainly suits my purpose." She clicked her fingers emphatically.

Uncle Mon del Moral was taller, older and trimmer of figure than Bangpa-Pop. Austerely dressed in a double-breasted navy-blue suit and almost bald he was nevertheless a handsome man though he seldom smiled. He invariably looked a touch unhappy at the ideas that flowed through Mama's conversations.

But Mama was already distracted by another Spanish marqués, Uncle Tío Pepe, who had been at school with Uncle Mon at Stonyhurst, an English Jesuit school that Mama did not think very highly of.

"Such frightful SPANKERS there, almost worse than my favourite Eton," she laughed merrily. "On the other hand, one of my own very favourite Spanish stampin' grounds. Of course darlin' Pepe Manzandeo's surname is exactly the same as my family dry sherry from Jérez, *olé!* And such divine blue eyes. Always reminds me of my darlin' Joachim," she said, wiping away a tear as it rolled down her rouge. "Up and down the lines we all went, Mon, Pepe and I, *olé!* Those were the days, gentlemen," my mother winked coyly at the two marquéses. "No corsets, no stays, only my new two-ways, rubber underclothes you know, quite the latest in fashion," she hummed excitedly. "I always put them out to dry over the Aga these days."

Mama picked up her castanets and whirled them around her head. "I'm dancin' the pasadoble, *olé, caramba!*" she announced loudly and turned up the music on the gramophone, hand-winding it as she leaned over with a cigarette glued to her mouth, ash cascading as she danced on.

Like Uncle Eric St Johnston, Tío Pepe wore suits with a fetching design of blue check and red and black lines when they were in mufti.

"Just like dear old purple-faced Jose Primo de Rivera, *olé!* Pepe always has his Prince of Wales knocked up by a little man in Gib. They've all been doin' it since they were boys together with those sadistic old Jays at Stonyhurst, *olé!* And heil Hitler!" exclaimed Mama.

I could not immediately see how the Prince of Wales and all of Mama's Spanish family interconnected.

"All my Falangist family are heavily titled. *Igual!* And *olé! Viva el rey de España!*" exclaimed my mother enthusiastically. "No one could accuse this aristo Spanish bastard of bein' *cursi* and common. It's only a question of time, and short at that, before I am a contessa in Cádiz and a four-balled baronessa." Mama turned and laughed at Bangpa-Pop and the Spanish Uncles, all of whom were having tea in the yellow drawing room. "We're takin' tea, Ruby dear, so just be sure the door is kept absolutely shut, *fermée*, after the cucumber sandwiches have been served. And make damn certain that brat Julia doesn't come down from the nursery."

It was all most disappointing. By way of compensation, Ruby read me story 14 of *Uncle Wiggly*, Granny Camoys' most recent present from America. " *'Well,'* asked the *Slow Snail of Uncle Wiggly as he met the Old*

Gentleman Rabbit on the beach next day, 'did you get any of your fortune at the Flea's party?' "

I could hear Mama shouting from the drawing room. "Quite out of the question, Mon and Pepe, old boys, that you can catch a glimpse of Julia. The child has got RATS in her hair!"

The Gibraltarian connection also brought its share of consternation. My mother would complain indignantly about her Spanish sister. "That Anne de Zoo, God damn her, is sittin' pretty on that sumptuous pile of an hotel on the Rock. Pretty damn strategic these tedious, dreary days. A smuggler's paradise, filled with black-market goodies. What a dream, *olé*!" She drew in a cloud of blue Camel smoke, puffing it out in the direction of Bangpa-Pop. "I'm a bit low on supplies, so I'm simply goin' to have words with dear old Raul Regis de Oliveira. He's king in Brazil and not just any old doyenne of the diplomatic corps, and don't you forget it Pop."

Slumped across the yellow button-back sofa, Bangpa-Pop looked uncomfortable in his grey worsted trousers and shifted ground.

"Not those old worsted bags again, Ralph? Do you have crabs, fleas, haemorrhoids, piles or WHAT up your parts? I've always recommended flannel for your privates. Whatever it is, you're simply borin' me to tears. You and I simply have to sit down to more entrails and entails, and before it's far too late," said Mama menacingly.

I couldn't help looking from one to the other.

Mama narrowed her eyes, and pursed her mouth into two narrow lines. "For Gawd's sake stop gazin' and starin' at me like that, you stupid brat, Julia. Just wipe that moon-like expression orf your face and beat it child," she scolded. "Sherman's brat that you are you can eff orf, and go and play Happy Families with Ruby." Calling for Ruby, she shouted: "Take the child out of here now and at once. Do you hear me?"

And so I was sent back to bed even though it was still early afternoon, and not so long after Mama's lunchtime Horse's Neck, which she preferred to pudding. "I simply don't eat desserts, I've never even heard of them, come to think of it. Drink up your Kia-Ora, Ralph dear. It will be very good for all that indigestion and high wind you suffer from."

Meal times at any time with Mama were unpredictable to say the least, but meals in the nursery dining room at Assendon Lodge could be particularly hazardous and, later, on our sweet return to Stonor Park in July 1945, ever more dangerous.

"Get that junket down your throat, you stupid little bitch" Mama would say with a passing slap. "Your dumpy figure is so like Mildew Mildred's, and just goes to show you can easily make do with Ruby's puddings: which are not desserts, and you can stuff it up," she mocked, snapping at the elastic round her own waist. "I'm keepin' a close eye on my own exquisite waist-line now that I have my brand-new rubber two-way stretch. Pip and Pop-goes-the-Weasel, you can squeeze your fingers between my divinely flat stomach and my new girdle," she giggled.

Ruby gave a heavy sigh but said nothing as she cleared away the silver pudding plates.

"My best Queen Anne antiques. Everythin' round here is mine, and mine alone," stated Mama emphatically. "And now you, Julia, can bugger orf to bed. Not before time. Get the hell out of here before I count to two," she ordered briskly.

I went as fast as my four-year-old legs could carry me.

*

"Well, Pop, let's get down to it. I've simply got to extricate more than a few farthin's from the Bosmore Estate, let alone Cock's Leas and all that crap, ha, ha!"

I could hear my grandfather's murmuring in weak-voiced reply.

"Too damn bad they're still held by your progeny, Ralph dear," hissed Mama. "I shall see to it, just you mark my words. The very least that terribly tedious solicitor David Drummond can do—son of old Lady Helen D, you know." She cleared her throat and raised her voice. "I will take your progeny, Pop dear, for all they are worth. They'd better watch it from their sham summerhouse in Newport, Rhode Island. I'LL be takin' them to the cleaners, for a change."

Bangpa-Bop hastily blew his nose.

"And as to Old Mildew—that's your wife Pop dear, and don't forget she's been keepin' you Ralph since 1911—she won't know what's hit her by the time you and I are finished."

The smell of Mama's rich, strong French perfume wafted through the air. I could hear her laugh long and loud.

Bangpa-Pop could hardly avoid his daughter-in-law, but he did try his best to avoid other members of Jeanne's family, the Stourton women especially. He did not in particular care to bump into Tia María de

Zulueta and seldom spoke to her. But most of all, he always avoided Sherman.

Although Tia María was kind to me, I was frightened by the severity of her face, so like Mama's, though she wore neither rouge nor lipstick. She for her part certainly disapproved of her niece's maquillage.

"Jeanne-Mary dear, don't you think that particular red is somewhat vulgar," she would ask, gazing down from her greater height. Like Ruby, Tia María too gave a deep sigh.

Silently sharing her views was Cousin Mónica de Bertodano, Tia María's companion and lady's maid, who always accompanied her. Mama had gazed icily at her before passing comment. "Too dreary for words, Gytha's eldest stepdaughter. Why, Mónica was the same age as the bride when dear old Mon del Moral married that deadly bore my demi-semi sister, ha, ha! Both such fervent Cartholics, and crashin' dull to boot," she continued scathingly. "Just by lookin' at those sensible shoes, and that terrible tweed coat you can see it was bought at the Oratory church jumble sale." She laughed.

After our Spanish visitors had returned to London, Mama informed me that: "There's a lot of other Old Bags who frequent that fusty, musty Onslow Court Hotel as well as that divine Oratory. They even hear ejaculatory confessions in Spanish, *olé*, and heil Hitler." She saluted into an oval gilt-framed mirror. "Mirror, mirror on the wall, who is the fairest of them all?" she mused as she gazed dreamily at her image in the dimpled glass. "Far more appropriate if that tiresome Gytha lived with them rather than runnin' round the 'Portugoose' with those two little runny-nosed brats of Mon's in the middle of this goddamned war. I hope to Gawd they stay where they're stuck, on second thoughts. Darlin' Mon is after all frightfully busy runnin' from Spain to Portugal to Gib and back with the Windsors. And my own darlin' Joachim." Mama gave a small sob. "Heil Hitler!"

Bangpa-Pop reappeared.

Mama winked at him. "My very dear Spanish brother-in-law, such a true grandee, Mon del Moral. A frightfully *distingué* Marqués with several strawberry leaves in his crown," she explained. "Works with old Pedro de Zoo, and our friend Franco, *el generalísimo* you know. Both such a help to me up and down those borders," continued Mama, laughingly behind her hand.

15
A Memory of a Dinner Party

Jeanne's description of dinner parties with her patrons and lovers Enid Bagnold (Lady Jones) and her husband Sir Roderick were habitually cheerful. It was at their beautiful London house, 29 Hyde Park Gate, next door to the home of Winston and Clementine Churchill, that Jeanne dined with Hitler's roving ambassador Count Joachim von Ribbentrop on April 8, 1936.

The placement of this sumptuous dinner party was unusual and significant with Ribbentrop placed immediately to the right of the hostess, Lady Jones. The German ambassador, Leopold von Hoesch, by contrast, was seated well below the salt, insignificantly between Mrs Freyberg and the Hon Mrs Bingham.

Jeanne herself was placed between the Comte de Gaillard de la Valdene and the millionaire newspaper owner Lord Camrose. The American ambassador (Mr Bingham) was seated to the left of Lady Jones, whilst the Countess of Carlisle was seated to the left of Ribbentrop.

Conspicuously the only unmarried and very pretty, witty woman present, Jeanne was also the only Catholic invited to this dinner of fifteen, with the exception of the French couple.

Two days later, on April 10, 1936, von Hoesch was found dead, in highly suspicious circumstances, his body hastily removed from the embassy at 9 Carlton House Terrace and returned to Berlin. Von Hoesch was conspicuous in his distaste for and stand against Hitler.

Jeanne's vivid description of this event—accompanied by knowing winks and a drole expression—was of the ambassador's murder by strychnine poisoning, his body then being drained of the chemical with a black rubber pump and hose before he was hastily removed from the British soil.

But there was minimal interest in Britain where many of the main newspapers were owned by the pro-Nazi, pro-Hitler tycoons Lord Rothermere and Lord Camrose. Equally circumspect was Lord Beaverbrook's press empire.

On the fateful evening of the dinner at Hyde Park Gate, Ribbentrop undoubtedly knew he was soon to become Hitler's new ambassador to the Court of St James. The official story is as follows.

On Saturday April 11 came the news that von Hoesch had died the day before of heart seizure at his residence, the German Embassy, 9 Carlton House Terrace. It took a while for the rumours of the circumstances of his to circulate. Meanwhile time was of the essence, especially since it was a weekend.

On that day Ribbentrop left abruptly for Berlin. He had been in London officially since April 1, received by Anthony Eden, visiting Lloyd George, calling upon his friend Lord Londonderry. Back again in London on April 7, Ribbentrop then dined at 28 Hyde Park Gate. On Friday April 10, von Hoesch was found dead in bed by his valet. Ribbentrop was back in Berlin by the time of the announcement the following morning.

Death notices and tributes appeared in *The Times* on April 12, 14 and 15. A state funeral was organized with full military honours from London so that the ambassador's body, horse-drawn, would be taken in solemn procession from Carlton House Terrace to Victoria Station, thence by rail and sea to Germany, passing through Berlin for its final resting place in the family tomb in the Trinity Old Cemetery in Dresden.

A memorial service to take place at the German Church in London was announced for April 24. At this memorial service, where several prominent members of the British government were officially represented, amongst the list of other illustrious mourners were the Countess of Pembroke and Montgomery, next to whom was seated Mrs Terence Maxwell, Miss Jeanne Stourton, Viscount and Viscountess Milne, Viscount and Viscountess Esher, the Duchess of Grafton, and Lord and Lady Kemsley (he being the newspaper proprietor and fellow tycoon brother of Viscount Camrose, one of the dinner guests at the Jones's dinner party only two weeks earlier).

On the same page as this memorial announcement of the many prestigious mourners at the memorial service comes a comment "Complete Boycott of the Jews", a headline article on "Aryan Egg" whereby Hitler's Nüremberg laws banned any Jew from trading in the production of eggs. (Up until this time 90 per cent of those breeding chickens had been Jewish.)

Hitler, meanwhile, and others of his cabinet, had sent messages of condolences to the British government. It is unclear as to whether or not the same sympathy was extended to Leopold's two sisters. Fortunately his dog Cicero had died two years previously, buried beneath a suitable plaque in the garden adjacent to 9 Carlton House Terrace.

In the same month that the Spanish Civil War started, on July 24, 1936, Hitler announced the appointment of Ribbentrop as the new German ambassador in London. The count and former champagne salesman did not, however, take up his post until October 26. During the interim, Ribbentrop took care to replace the embassy counsellor, the popular Otto von Bismark (and his beautiful Swedish wife), with a loyal colleague Ernst Woermann. Most of the embassy staff remained in situ but Ribbentrop arranged to bring to London with him some sixty members of his Büro, known as the *"Dienstelle"*, many of whom had been based in Berlin.

Countess Ribbentrop, meanwhile, had decided on an extensive and fundamental refurbishment of the three houses in Carlton House Terrace. This was a monumental undertaking to the grandiose design of the Nazi architect Albert Speer. Costing five million Reichsmarks it took two hundred German workmen to complete the project in time for the Coronation of Edward VIII scheduled for May 1937.

Meanwhile the Ribbentrops resided at the house of their friend Neville Chamberlain, 18 Eaton Square. They paid frequent visits to their closest friend Lord Londonderry both at Mount Steward and Wynard, the Londonderry estate near Durham Cathedral. It was at the cathedral that Ribbentrop became carried away by a hymn reminiscent in tune to the German national anthem and was seen to give the Nazi salute.

16

'Was Mr Hitler a Gun and Uncle?'

Papa's estate workmen, George, Freddie and Stanley, climbed up on rickety ladders to redecorate Assendon Lodge. Sometimes Mama too climbed up behind a workman, a contraband Camel or Philip Morris hanging out of her mouth.

"I'm just lookin' for a rarity in the bookcase," she explained. But after elevenses one day she wobbled more than usual, and fell off.

Said Ruby as she picked my mother up: " 'Orse's Necks don't help one to keep a balance very well, Madam, do they?"

But Mama was exceedingly cross when she'd finally got up off the floor. "How dare you, how DARE you, Ruby Heath? I can fire you, and fire you right away for such an impertinence. Speakin' strictly out of turn, so you can get the hell out of my sight!"

Though I had heard it often from my mother's lips, I still couldn't work out what an "impertinence" was. It certainly sounded serious, that I knew, and I worried because I so loved Ruby Heath. Perhaps, I wondered to myself, an "impertinence" was related to one of Mama's recurring headaches, which she called "my Migraine".

"I am very prone to My Nerves, you know," my mother would declare, "and I'm in VERY fragile health."

I thought Mama might be ill again and told Ruby that she would need, as usual, the utterly essential remedy of a red rubber hot-water bottle, covered in a hand-embroidered white satin pillow slip, placed in her summer or winter bed. This bed in the summer and winter bedrooms was always covered with the vicuña fur rug, its black-nailed paws sticking over the edge.

"It really is most kind of dear old Uncle Charlie to have bought it so specially for me, in my frail health, from Bogotá," Mama announced from beneath its warmth.

In the ever-growing world map of my imagination, I placed Bogotá somewhere near the mysterious Windsors in the West Indies or Granny Camoys in Rhode Island. Or maybe it was in Brazil, where Uncle Ambassador Raul Regis de Oliveira of my night prayers came from. It gave me lots more to think about.

*

Each and every Sunday Mama took me up to the flint chapel at Stonor, for Mass, driving in Granny Camoy's old Chevrolet up the Assendon Road and through Stonor Village in leaps and jolts as my mother ground through the gears. Abruptly coming to a halt in front of the first pair of gates up at the Park, Mama would imperiously blow her horn for a retainer to spring forth from one of the bungalow-shaped brick lodges.

"Get out this minute, child," she shrieked at me above the noise of the engine.

I rushed to unbolt the locks and flung open the iron gates, trying to avoid being hit by the wide car as my mother gunned recklessly through the narrow gap and sped up the uneven drive to come to a halt at the next gate. Revving the engine, cigarette in mouth, she waited until my short legs had carried me the distance of this drive to unlock and unbar these one too.

"God damn those men at the National Benzole petrol-plannin' unit for lockin' the inside door on me. I'll see to them!" shouted Mama furiously.

She parked loudly outside the chapel and rushed thunderously up the brick stairs to take her place in the tribune. This was a gallery with a balcony at the very back of the small, dungeon-shaped chapel. The tribune was immediately beneath a late Victorian stained-glass window of St Gregory, stern-faced and disapproving in a mitre.

Here Mama held both court and complete command of the chapel congregation. "I'm avoidin' common germs from the lower orders of Sherman's retainers. And all those dreary, third-rate parishioners who simply bore me to tears."

The thickly carpeted tribune had a low, wrought-iron Gothic Revival railing. "Just high enough to stop Sherman's brat from fallin' into the musty congregation beneath" explained Mama to her visitors.

She had her own special chair ("MY pre-DIEU") in the corner nearest to a door leading to the alcove bedrooms at Stonor. This kneeler was heavily embroidered in tapestry, a large rosary festooned along it. Her command of the chapel was absolute. "I simply have to keep an eye on the plate ever since I've been so unjustly accused of takin' the second collection. Of course it always comes to me. I don't take any nonsense from that department. And I can see everyone and everythin', comin' and goin'."

Some years later, in the winter of 1969-70, when Jackie Kennedy and her sister Princess Lee Radziwill ascended the same brick stairs to share a last Christmas with Papa, Mama had already come to the decision that she could better dominate the chapel from the nave of the church. She had therefore descended to take up her throne in the body of the stone building, seated on a pre-dieu draped in heavy white silk damask trimmed with gold braid. Here Mama sat in solitary splendour beneath the tribune and across the doors leading from the chapel porch. (Long before this time, in 1957 Papa had fallen heavily in love with Eartha Kitt, the famous jazz singer, and taken, in his despair, to parachuting indoors from the kitchen table after a further knock-out dose of Mama's stomach medicine.)

Early in the war, lest there was any doubt, Mama had made the loud announcement to the congregation that "I am permanently in command, permanently in charge" as she leant over the tribune railing. This she did from the second of her ceremonial chairs, a spiked Gothic Revival armchair, held a luxuriously soft cushion heavily embroidered with a coat-of-arms, and a second rosary of substantial jet beads on a linked silver chain with a heavily ornate Spanish crucifix hanging off it.

To complete the effect Mama wore a thick black lace veil—"my old Spanish family mantilla from Mexico Bay," she hissed through her teeth. It was held high above her head by an antique tortoise-shell comb ("from the *Feria* in Sevilla, *olé!*").

I had a much smaller, thinner plain net veil. Most of the female servants and retainers from the villages round Stonor wore nylon or woollen scarves to protect them against the running damp. A very few ladies, mostly from Maidensgrove and Russells Water, wore knitted hats. But rarely were there were many in the congregation until after the war, when I returned to Stonor with Papa and Mama in 1945.

"All those terribly tedious, borin' Prots go orf to that Low Church in Henley and Pishill—so *appropriately* named," Mama announced once in a loud overtone that echoed through the chapel. "Rugger-buggers, regatta boys, bishops and archbishops, they're all the same to me." She hiccuped very slightly and took a gulp from the silver hip flask filled to the brim with supplies of Horse' s Neck. This my mother had carried up to the tribune inside a voluminous black crocodile handbag.

"Straight from Cartier, New York, where else," she laughed. "Keepin' up my essential supplies, and simply stuffed full of nylons when it arrived so conveniently with darlin' Cousin John Nicholas Brown. Such a goddamned tiresome wife that borin' giantess Anne Kinsolvin'! Cuts no ice with me that she is the Bishop of Baltimore's daughter." Mama paused reflectively and took another quick sip from her flask. "*Olé* and *viva el rey de España!* No *Juifs* either in my congregation and heil Hitler!" she said smugly

An air of excitement and excited expectancy would mount upon my mother's entrance into the chapel tribune. Throughout the service the door to the house itself opened and slammed continuously. Mama came and went at frequent intervals to answer the telephone, which tinkled and rang shrilly from the main alcove bedroom. Or to take her dogs, which sat with her on their own Gothic Revival chairs, out for a piddle and more.

The congregation beneath sat transfixed by this hive of continuous activity and cacophonous sounds from above their heads. At the same time they were deeply cowed by the majestic appearance of Mama with her royal dogs in attendance.

"I'm exercising my Royal Prerogative you know," said Mama grandly. "My pogginses and I have had the Divine Right since the days of King Charles the Second, of course."

The "piddle of convenience" to which my mother referred usually took place in the long gallery, some rooms further down from the chapel tribune, and on the same floor level as the library, also used for this activity by the King Charles spaniels and occasional labradors that belonged to Mama's entourage. Both these rooms had scatterings of rare silk rugs and Aubusson carpets, but Mama paid these no heed. She would throw open the doors from the tribune time and time again—usually during the sermon—to let her dogs out onto the rugs and carpets.

"My darlin's, like me, are far too fragile for the Great Outside in this frigid weather," she announced in a clear tone over the spiked Gothic Revival rails and into the beige-painted dungeon beneath her. "Furthermore, I'm most frightfully bored by your sermon, Father Cereal!" Mama said loudly, gesticulating towards the French priest at the altar rails beneath her.

Turning round from her pre-dieu, she shouted encouragement to the dogs themselves—"Motions, potions and piddles indoors today, boys!"—as they snarled and barked their way along the alcove passage to relieve themselves.

The organist who succeeded Miss Broslem, Father Seyres' Irish house-keeper, to play the French harmonium tucked away at the back of the trib-une struck up another suitable hymn. "Soul of My Saviour" rang weedily from the instrument, accompanied by Mama in full voice, immunised from the intense cold within both chapel and house by layers of furs, sables, minks and the occasional silver fox.

Beneath her, the walls steamed with damp and mould while the congre-gation shivered with cold and, in many cases, fearful anticipation. Several were only too aware that their tied cottages were now in the control not of the Reasonable and Gentle Sherman, but of Jeanne, self-appointed Camp Commandant, and undoubted Dictator-Empress of Stonor Park and its outlying, far-flung estates.

Mama's heavy gold bracelets, thick gold medals and stout gold charms made a great clanging as they banged cacophonously into one another. The chapel had turned round as one to stare up, gazing entranced at my mother, swathed in pitch-black silks and exquisite cashmeres beneath the furs.

"This is how all us Spanish aristos and grandees dress," she said, swing-ing her bracelets around, and sinking to her knees on the tapestry kneeler. Behind the cover of the railings Mama pinched my cheek hard with long red fingernails. I winced with surprise as they dug in.

"Don't draw any attention to yourself, you silly little bitch," hissed Mama. The ladies from Russells Water and South End Common screwed their heads even further around, looking up at the tribune. Sticking her tongue out, Mama pointed downwards accusingly. "That Mrs Pritchard has got gallopin' gangrene AND she's another of those tedious converts to boot."

Mama's charm bracelet always fascinated me. It was thickly festooned with exotic, mostly unexplained objects. First there was a miniature mon-key, exquisitely crafted with sapphire blue eyes.

Ruby said: "They's diamonds and real sapphires, Doodo darling."

And Mama added: "It comes from the Blue Monkey himself, that mad, bad Marquis of Sovéral, a male 'Portugoose' monkey, all money and balls, ha, ha!" Her fingers played with the charms as she continued. "All balls and money. Queer cards all three of them, the darlin' Prince of Wales, old Fernan d'Hautpoul, and the Blue Monkey. Put them in your night prayers immediately, Julia dear."

And there, further along Mama's heavily laden bracelet, nestling amongst the enamel and gold flags from the Royal Yacht Britannia, was a thick gold swastika. The angular charm looked peculiarly like the coarse steel meathooks that hung in the shadowy outhouses, game larders and kitchen up at the Park.

Ruby made her opinion quite clear: "I don't like that thing at all, Miss Julia, because it is one of those horrid nasty swastikas. And it reminds me of that Mr Joachim and that Mr Hitler. It's very bad news like all the war news these days, and my poor Art away in the RAF and your Papa away in the army. Who knows when we'll see them again? There's a lot gone for good in the village already."

When she was not working at Assendon Lodge and up at the Park, Ruby usually lived with her husband Arthur in Stonor Village at No. 26. Now she gave a big sniff. "Those gone for good are the best ones, too," she said sadly as she wiped her nose on her flowered pinafore.

Being so very young, I couldn't really tell whether "that Mr Hitler" was another Gun and an Uncle. Since Ruby was upset, I didn't want to bother her and turned to ask my mother. But Mama ignored me and only laughed when she saw Ruby's tears.

"This goddamned war has gorne and ruined all my plans," she said crossly. "And I wasted—yes I said WASTED—12 guineas takin' Sherman, your useless father, on my honeymoon to Schloss Sonnenburg. But my darlin' blue-eyed boy Joachim was just so dear, and so understandin'!" Mama laughed uproariously. "Frightfully accommodatin' too in the 'circs'," she continued, giggling. "Jackboots and spurs, all made to order with two divine dirndle frocks at Joachim's very own tailor in Berlin to BOOT. *Olé!* And those were the days, heil Hitler!" Mama clicked her heels together.

She twirled around in a silver-buttoned, blue dirndle dress. I had interrupted her in the middle of giving Bangpa-Pop a dress-show.

"My darlin' Joachim Count Ribbentrop, you remember, Pop dear, from our good old days at the Bosch embassy, and with the Anglo-German Fellowship and all those divine fellows who followed us, dukes, earls, marquises, viscounts, barons and even those borin' baronets." Here Mama paused for a puff on a cigarette before she gave another twirl, clacking castanets above her head as she whirled around. "Don't stare, Pop-goes-the-Weasel. Haven't you ever seen a fandango? *Olé!*"

She slid across the parquet floor to pause at the sideboard to pick up a rummer glass full of fizzing brown liquid. "As I was sayin', my darlin' Ambassador Joachim, always so very thoughtful in his favours towards me once we'd arrived orf the train after we'd passed through the Fatherland, Sherman and I." Indignantly she continued. "Sherman was a bit upset by all those fascinatin' jackboots and spurs, to say nothin' of those uniforms. To die for! I was frightfully excited myself." Mama winked over the top of her bubbling glass at Bangpa-Pop. "After all, goddamn it, I DID pay 12 guineas a ticket for a railway journey with your now-impotent son Sherman. Only got it up a couple of times, and just look at the result in that borin' borin' brat of his, the tedious Julia."

She took a sharp kick at a convenient piece of furniture, and, carefully draining the rummer glass, pitched it at the wall over my grandfather's head as he ducked hastily.

"What a crashin' bore you are, and always have been, ever since I've known you Pop!" Mama said scathingly as her drink dripped down the wall. "All bunged up to the balls and far beyond, I daresay. You can take that brewer's droop with you and bugger orf. You really do bore me silly, just like this tedious brat of Sherman's."

Mama tweaked my hair, causing tears to spring into my eyes.

"One thing I can tell you for sure," she said, puffing concentric smoke circles with concentrated precision, "Shermie has never managed IT since July '38. And when he ran away—imagine what ignominy, what agony to me—from all those glorious jackboots and spurs and medals at Sonnenburg-bei-Berlin, my darlin' Joachim came with me in his private car to hunt him down." Mama thought for a moment, continuing hastily: "By which I mean we just managed to catch Sherman before he boarded the local train." She sighed heavily. "It was most frightfully tiresome, but at least now there is always the regimental colonel and a spare peer or two to hand. One simply must keep the bed warm these days." She winked again at Bangpa-Pop. "Don't look so shifty old boy. You're in it and up to the eyeballs too, *olé!*"

Perhaps, I thought, Mama's "warm bed" was like the rhubarb bed which Mr White the head gardener had so carefully built with thick, damp straw in the kitchen garden. He had also dug trenching for asparagus, which Mama said "is absolutely essential for my Guns' lunches". This made an even deeper bed than the the that of the rhubarb. I found it all very interesting.

There was always a reminder of Mama's "darlin' Joachim" and things Germanic in our lives. Most notable was my mother's Tyrolean hat, dark green with a long cock pheasant's feather sticking out over the turned up brim, and which she wore cocked at an angle. I thought it most exciting though perhaps not quite as dashing as Aunt Marjorie Bryce's hat which had been bought at a St James's Street hatter.

I looked in vain too for jackboots. However, Mama, her hat firmly on even though she was indoors, repeated: "A pity your father was scared orf by those divine boots. Personally I'm mad about them, *olé!*"

I had only ever seen black rubber gumboots on the cowman, old Mr Jenkins, whose son was also a cowman, and Newmarket boots on my mother when she was "wadin' the moat on that assault course against old Loveden Macclesfield" at Shirburn Castle.

What I most wanted to know, however, was what Papa could possibly have been "runnin' away from" when he had, after all, been with Mama on her honeymoon at Castle Sonnenburg. But Mama didn't explain when I asked her why Papa went away.

"You bloody little ignoramus. Sherman continuously continues to upset the apple cart!" was all I got in reply as she clipped me round both ears with the back of her rings.

This was quite an effective deterrent to a small child as the rings were heavy with stones set into platinum prongs and sharp diamond points. Mama banged these rings down just as hard onto the keys of our second and larger grand piano, a golden-brown satinwood Bechstein.

"Mine!" she said firmly as she played duets with Cousin Peter, Lord Derwent, and others of the Uncles and Guns that she had listed in my night prayers. This made her happy, so it made me happy too. I could see her gaiety, and this was magical in my young eyes. On such occasions I would be allowed down to the drawing room to listen to their recital before my bed-time, and before my night prayers, which were always said on my knees at her knees.

There I would pray with all my fervour and fervency for Bangpa-Pop and the Uncles. Mama even included Granny Camoys' in her own list— "May old Mildewed Mildred, Lady Cee, drop orf her perch very soon indeed. Amen." But even I realized that God did not need me to add this particular ejaculatory ejaculation of Mama's.

Now I had a special new prayer to say as Mama stood at the foot of my bed waiting. "Thank you very very much, Mama," I prayed after Bangpa-Pop and all the Uncles. It was an instant success, and my mother patted me lightly on the head with the tips of her scarlet fingernails before she slammed shut the door of my night nursery, flicking off the light as she went with a sharp click.

Even at moments like this, I was transfixed by the beauty of both her rich perfume, which Mr Dior had sent, and the scent of cigarette smoke that trailed behind her. I inhaled deeply. It was all deliciously intoxicating. In the next-door room I could hear the whoosh of Ruby doing up the zip on the back of my mother's little black number, the frock I thought so beautiful. Mama was getting ready for the evening.

Ruby had very many duties because she was Mama's maid when she wasn't the cook, the housekeeper, the scullery maid or my nanny. It all depended on how many dailies my mother had "on hand" or whether she had sacked the nannies, nursery maids and dailies very recently.

For Mama, hired staff was a cross to bear that contributed greatly to her ongoing martyrdom. "I am an essential part of this goddamned war effort," she would say crossly, "and I have a Very Special Dispensation from the Home Office for my essential staff. I am TOP priority with the Ministry— and Stonor too."

In the village there were other stalwart ladies with names like Win and Alice, some of them related to Ruby, who had been maids before the war both at Aunt Julia's house, and up at the Park. At Mama's cajoling, they too came and "did" at Assendon Lodge (". . . and my darlin' police beau, that divine Eric, has seen to it all!"). And together with Ruby, they busily polished the immense hunting cups and canteens of antique silver until I could see my face on the back of the spoons.

Mama once caught me peering spellbound, as children do, at the concave backs of spoons in the pantry. Her comment was brief: "Your foolish face looks exactly like a full-blown moon, you tiresome, borin' brat!"

And so, despite the crisis of the war, there seemed to be an unending supply of servants, though they came and went as Mama chose. "After all I am a total perfectionist," she said sharply. "Never a Spanish aristo bastard for nothing, *olé*!"

17

A Memory of Julia, Mildred and Sherman

My aunt Julia was born in 1860, a granddaughter of the prime minister Sir Robert Peel and his wife Julia, Lady Peel, after whom my aunt was named. "Julie", she of the cornflower-blue eyes, the Marquise d'Hautpoul, was to become my surrogate mother during the Second World War.

Julia's parents, Francis and Elisa Stonor, were a deeply devoted couple who died in 1881 and 1883 respectively. Queen Victoria had appointed the latter a Lady of the Bedchamber to her daughter-in-law Princess Alexandra of Denmark, wife of the heir to the throne, the Prince of Wales. And Francis had been a Clerk at the House of Lords for some forty years. He and Elisa had long been intimates of the royal household.

Upon the premature loss of her parents, the only girl of the family, Julia was taken under the wing of the Princess of Wales, and all but adopted into the royal family, whether at Sandringham, or at their elaborate Italianate palace Osborne House, on the Isle of Wight. Here, from early days, there had always been extra chairs in the nursery dining room for Julia and her three brothers Robert, Harry and Edward.

Julia, known to her intimates as Julie, was a great favourite of both the Prince and Princess of Wales, the latter continuously lavishing her extended family with spontaneous affection and immensity of concern. Princess Alexandra had a strongly cohesive and European sense of family unity, solidarity and, supremely, of loyalty.

The Princess of Wales was devoted to the engagingly pretty, joyous and enthusiastic Julie, who soon became the apple of the eye of her second son, Prince George, the Duke of York. The only drawback was that Julie was a Roman Catholic, and considered "a commoner". Besides, Julie was five years older than her deeply enamoured prince—who nevertheless longed to marry her.

Contemporary letters, diaries, accounts, several of them in George's own handwriting and words, abound as to the depth of friendship between these two young people, whether at Osborne House and Sandringham, or, later on, at Julie's beautiful Queen Anne house, Turville Grange, just two miles from her ancestral home, Stonor Park.

After the mysterious and unexpected demise in 1892 of his elder brother, Prince Eddy, Duke of Clarence (sometimes suspected to be the notorious Jack the Ripper), George became heir to the throne and, eventually, King George V. But even then "Bertie", as he signed himself in letters and photographs to Julie, to the very end remained in love with this beautiful, deeply sympathetic and gracious woman. And he continuously showered her with the most exquisite and delicate of gifts, Fabergé enamelled eggs, precious jewellery, crystal and gold-rigged models of the royal yacht *Britannia*.

That Julie deeply reciprocated his love was widely known and acknowledged within the royal family. At King George V's funeral in 1936, her wreath of crimson roses in his memory bore a black-edged card in her own writing. It was inscribed "from your broken-hearted Julie".

One of the king's many mementoes of his beloved Julie was a spinach-jade, gold-filigree inset Fabergé frame around an especially exquisite early sepia photograph of this gentle woman, her hair arranged in the chignon-style of the day, held in place with her grandmother Julia Peel's amethyst-ended hairpins. This tender memento is still to be seen in the Royal Collection at the Queen's Gallery at Buckingham Palace.

Before the untimely death of the Duke of Clarence, the Prince of Wales had cheerfully, openly encouraged his son Prince George and Julie to elope. He thought this an amusing, romantic prospect, perhaps lacking the knowledge that the Vatican would in no circumstances give permission for a "mixed marriage". Informed rumour has it that, in fact, such permission was sought from Rome—but there would be no papal dispensation since it was obligatory that any children of such a match be bought up in the Catholic persuasion.

Whatever the Vatican's decision may have been, English law still prohibits any Catholic succession to the throne; nor is it permissible for the prime minister to be a Catholic to this day. Since Julie Stonor was, as she remained, an especially devout, obedient daughter of the "Holy Mother

Church", she bowed for her part to the inevitable with her customary dignity and humility.

Amongst the set of European nobility closest to the Prince of Wales, Julie had met an eligible Frenchman from Toulouse, the Marquis Pierre Henri Louis Leopold Fernand d'Hautpoul de Seyre, a mutually close friend both of the prince and of the Marqués de Soveral, a racy Portuguese gambling nobleman, commonly known in sporting circles as the "Blue Monkey". The Marquis d'Hautpoul was known quite simply as Fernan.

The marriage of the Marquis d'Hautpoul with the Hon Julia Stonor, sister of Lord Camoys, was solemnised at St James's, Roman Catholic church, Spanish Place, on Saturday morning, 18 July, 1891. The following Monday, the event was announced together with a list of the most immediate members of the royal family, foreign royalty, ambassadors and many distinguished guests inscribed in several columns of the Court Circular.

The Prince and Princess of Wales attended the wedding at which Archbishop Christopher Stonor officiated and, together with their daughters the Princesses Maud and Victoria, and their nephew Prince George of Greece, they sat down to the wedding breakfast held at the house of Julie's cousin Mrs Pereira in Park Street. Their presence was seen as a great personal tribute to Julie, an added endorsement of the depth of their mutual affection and close friendship.

Not only were the newly-weds given "The Cottage", Sandringham, for their honeymoon, but the press reported that they were also given numerous and magnificent wedding presents: "The Queen (Victoria) presented the bride with a valuable Indian shawl, the Prince and Princess of Wales gave a handsome diamond tiara, the Duke of Clarence and Avondale, a gold bangle with large pearl centre surrounded by diamonds; the Princesses Victoria and Maud, a caduceus encrusted with diamonds, the staff being mounted with a large pearl; the Duke and Duchess of Fife, a large diamond arrow and heart brooch with a ruby in the centre of the heart; Princess Christian, a silver-mounted hand mirror; the Duchess of Teck, silver-stopped toilet bottle; Prince and Princess Wagram, a large silver bowl; and Princess de Sagan, a butterfly hairpin set with diamonds, emeralds, rubies."

It was Princess Mary of Teck that Eddy, Duke of Clarence, had become engaged to shortly before his death in 1892. It was then very quickly arranged for her to become the fiancée of the remaining brother, the more virile and masculine George. Their own marriage took place at the Chapel Royal, St James's Palace, on 6 July, 1893.

However, not only did George keep the Fabergé-framed photograph of Julie in his dressing-room but he also had an exquisite pastel of her hanging on its walls. This was the painting that his widow Queen Mary returned to Julie d'Hautpoul at Turville Grange after the king's death in 1936 with the following note: "My husband always had this portrait in his dressing-room, and I know that he would have wanted you to have it back now."

There was considerable friendship between these two very different yet elegantly discreet women, the queen and the marquise. The queen seems to have understood of the king's frequent visits to Turville Grange. She more than tolerated the dignified, discreet Julie, and her decoratively gay, courtier brother Harry Stonor, the omnipotent "shot" and outstanding "gun" of his generation. Both were frequent companions on the royal yacht *Britannia*—as innumerable contemporary photographs testify.

Above all, Julie remained close to her surrogate mother, Queen Alexandra, widow of King Edward VII. It was she who gave Julie the gift of the elegantly wrought-iron gates for Turville Grange; it was she who arranged for the new telephone exchange of Turville Heath. Stonor Park itself thus became only the area's fifth number, an essential for the many royalty who came to stay and indeed stayed for prolonged, elongated weekends from the 1880s onwards for the conspicuous bagging of game— as the many leather-bound, gold-tooled, gold coroneted game books and guest books testify, with their period photographs of the formal house parties, lists of titled guests, not to mention the quite extraordinary amount of game slaughtered.

Married life for Julie and Fernan began in Paris at 10 Avenue Percier, in the 8th arrondisement near the Faubourg St Honoré, not far from Bernard d'Hautpoul, Fernan's cousin. They also had a London house in Montagu Square but seem to have enjoyed spending more time at Turville Grange.

The tranquil, beautiful, rose-pink Queen Anne manor, once a bakery, is not far from the morose graveyard at Pishill-with-Stonor's Protestant parish church where their only child, a still-born baby girl, is buried in the Catholic plot besides the grim granite cross of her own parents' later grave. Poignantly the child is unnamed but vases of wild flowers were placed regularly in her resting-place all through the twentieth century: snowdrops, violets, daffodils, primroses, hyacinths, bluebells, cowslips, briar roses.

Curiously, this small, lonely and weed-strewn plot, set into the side of a steep hill overlooking the Stonor valley, is predominantly for female members and cousins of the family, especially the non-Catholics. These unfortunate women were not permitted to be buried in the primitive brick crypt beneath the pseudo-marble linoleum floor in the chapel of the Holy Trinity at Stonor Park. Nor even in its as-primitive, ancient and druidical burial yard alongside the flint-walled chapel.

Thus the only male corpse, Fernan d'Hautpoul, is flanked by his American niece-by-marriage, the millionairess Mildred Constance Sherman, Lady Camoys; a distant cousin, Maffra Tatton-Bower, another millionairess; and yet another of Julie's and Fernan's nieces-by-marriage, the tragic and Jewish Esther, the widow of Hugo Stonor, her remains lying cremated in the unmarked grave of a pauper at the end of the row. Mildred's elder daughter Nadine Stonor Pepys was laid to rest there in 2005.

To her great sadness, my aunt Julie would remain childless, a heartbreak to which she seldom referred. Instead, she turned her kindly and observant attention towards her nephew Ralph Camoys—who would succeed to the title of 5th Baron in 1897, aged thirteen. It was six years earlier that the seven-year-old Ralph had been principal page at her wedding.

Fernan, attractive, dashing and a considerable sportsman, seems to have busied himself with very little, though he did become a director of the group that owned the fashionable Hyde Park Hotel. Nevertheless, when he died at the hotel in 1934, he left his entire, considerable fortune to his widow Julie—some £83,321, 13 shillings and 4 pence.

From the time of her eldest brother's premature death in 1897, Julie had watched the progress of his son, her eldest nephew, with mounting concern. Ralph Camoys had inherited outright, under the law of entail to the eldest son, more than 6,300 acres, the estate of Stonor Park, outlying lands, hamlets, villages, farms and common land as well as London properties in Belgravia, Mayfair, and Kensington. Ralph was simultaneously cold-natured (a characteristic inherited from his Carew mother, Jessica) and idle. Educated at the Oratory School, he was too lazy to complete his time at Balliol College, and was rusticated before the end of the academic year at Oxford—a university his ancestors had first attended in the thirteenth century. He then tried his hand as a diplomat and was attached briefly to the British Embassy in Madrid as an "honorary attaché". This, too, Ralph found over-demanding—and the 5th Baron Camoys was "invited" to resign by the British ambassador.

Meanwhile, at Stonor Park, Ralph's uncles Eddie and Harry organised and ran, together with several highly-esteemed game-keepers and under-keepers, highly fashionable formal shooting parties typical of the era. The shoots, much photographed, were held over extended weekends of extensive, generous entertaining on only the grandest scale. Copious, illustrated visitors' books were laboriously compiled in heavy, leather-bound, monogrammed, coroneted, gilded volumes displayed in the drawing room and library for the guests' perusal. Sepia photographs show off the family and its magnificent entourage seated and standing in serried rows—strictly according to rank—on the semi-circular stone steps leading up to the front door of Stonor Park.

These non-stop house parties at Stonor were international, cosmopolitan and regal, with a distinguished assemblage of royalty both English and European, the greater concentration being on the direct descendants of Queen Victoria. Assembled guests brought with them a retinue of servants, valets, lady's maids, loaders for their hand-made, hand-tooled Purdey and Holland & Holland 12-bore, double-barrelled guns, their wooden stocks elaborately decorated, the metal chased. Admittedly, until Ralph Camoys married his American millionairess in 1911, the sanitary arrangements at Stonor Park were in very short supply for the sheer quantity of guests— seldom less than a dozen added to the many family members and ranks of live-in domestics.

Royalty and other male guests, referred to as "the Guns", brought their own dogs, labradors, retrievers, spaniels, to pick up the fallen birds, partridges, pheasants, woodcock, snipe—and deer, rabbits, hares. The scale of the kill was always enormous, and the game-keepers held the utmost importance together with the assortment of village beaters they recruited—for a pittance—from the tenanted cottages to walk up the fields, hedges and woods round Stonor Park and its vast acreage.

Ralph remained idly indifferent to his responsibilities. Tall, dark, handsome, heavily moustached but with eyes set too close to his nose, the Lord Camoys merely continued to delegate to his trustees, to his uncle Eddie Stonor, a brilliant, highly ambitious man, who had married a very rich widow from the Greek banking family of Ralli, the famous firm of East India traders, commerciants of vast fortune and international influence. In 1900 Eddie and his wife Christine produced a son, Francis Edward— named after King Edward VII, whose page he soon would be.

Before long, Julie's attention was drawn away from the deeply unsatisfactory and indifferently irresponsible Ralph towards the new—and very pretty—infant, Francis Edward. She felt herself rebuffed by the coldness of the older nephew, and deeply hurt by Ralph's conspicuous indifference not only to Catholicism, but also to the beauty of the family chapel with its rich tradition and deep spirituality. Besides, Julie had an abiding care and concern for the magnificent antique vestments which she helped care for in the old sacristy, a poorly-built, flimsy, orange brick lean-to which hung precariously off the back of the ancient dressed-flint edifice.

Julie's pride and joy were the remarkably beautiful, historic vestments and finest church linens kept in oak presses and cupboards in the strange room that had been wedged to the right of the Italian green marble altar behind a forbidding Gothic Revival spiked door. The sacristy had been erected in the 1880s simultaneous with the servants' upstairs wing, commonly known as the "Barracks", an ugly, secretive conglomeration of pokey, dark bedrooms slung haphazardly, precariously beyond the library and above the chapel. Both these edifices, built on the cheap, were cold, dark, damp and dank. And haunted.

It was strictly out of bounds to the bewildered non-Catholic Mildred Camoys, as her husband had made it quite plain, explaining callously that it would be seen as "sacrilege" should his wife "interfere with my private chapel". There was no such barrier to Ralph's aunt who made a weekly tour of devoted care for the beautiful vestments.

Cut in the Roman style, austere and magnificent, of the sixteenth and seventeenth centuries, French, Italian, Spanish, they lay neatly folded in long drawers scented with sandalwood in the blond oak French press. Cloth-of-gold, cloth-of-silver, ancient rose-silk damask, deepest violet and deepest black velvet surmounted by heavy gold brocade, embossed with gold crosses, embroidered with exquisite borders of flowers, lilies, roses, columbine, filled the press. And for feast days, great and small, there were scarlet silks, green silks, white silks, watered pink silks, sweeping copes of cloth-of-gold, one and all, were lovingly cared for under the gentle supervision of Julie and her maid. Cassocks, cotters, finest lawn and linen altar cloths, magnificent jewel-studded gold chalices, gold and silver monstrances in the shape of many-rayed suns, came into her remit as sacristan.

Later, much later, upon her marriage to Julie's great-nephew, Sherman, it would be Jeanne Stourton who also glorified in these sacristy "duties", though her style would be markedly different.

From her visits, Julie was becoming only too aware that the

congregation, let alone the entire neighbourhood, was talking about the louche, lax habits of her older nephew—who no longer attended the Sunday Mass at the chapel of the Holy Trinity. Ralph, however, did manage to find ample time to visit his tailor to be fitted for the elegant, dashing, scarlet and maroon, handsomely gadrooned uniform of his neighbour John, Duke of Marlborough's chic regiment, the Oxfordshire Hussars. For this, his brief sojourn "in the regiment", Ralph's thigh-high black leather dress-boots, silver spurs attached, were handmade by the grandest of military boot-makers, Lobb's. Winston Spencer Churchill was as dashing a fellow officer as well as a distant cousin, Herbert Marmaduke Stourton. Both of these considered themselves professional soldiers—an idea of great distaste to Ralph Camoys to whom any, or either, intellectual or physical effort was anathema.

Congenitally idle, Ralph was to find the obligatory military manoeuvres, held on the lawns of Blenheim Palace, and an occasional bivouac under canvas in the palace park, far too demanding. Besides, the 5th Baron decided that the khaki uniform he was forced to don on these tedious occasions was less than photographically flattering. Hurriedly, he resigned his commission—and embarked on a less energetic flying course. But just as hastily, Ralph dropped this new career with the Royal Flying Corps, and then declined an offer from his neighbour Sir John Dashwood to enlist in the Balloon Corps—the manoeuvres of which took place in the skies above the Hell Fire Caves at West Wycombe Park.

Julie watched with ever-deepening horror as Ralph now spent an increasing amount of time at London in clubs and enticing "low dives". His reputation for "laying the little woman round the corner" (common parlance for a hapless maid, dress-maker or milk maid—'droit de Seigneur') was the talk of the neighbourhood. Not only was Julie horrified, she was also deeply disappointed by Ralph's callousness. He did not even have the excuse of drink—unlike his hapless brother Hugo—and remained through his long life a teetotaller, with a supreme disinterest in food, albeit a substantial "doer" once at the dining-table.

On Thursday, November 10, 1910 the following appeared in the London *Times*: "A Peer fined. Lord Camoys was fined £3 and 11s costs at Slough yesterday for running a motor car at over 21 miles per hour in the Slough ten-mile limit. Mr Harrison, solicitor, expressed Lord Camoys's regret for having exceeded the limit, and said that he [Lord Camoys] always endeavoured to comply with the law. As he understood, Lord

Camoys was abroad at present in America. He asked for time for payment. The bench allowed a fortnight".

The solicitor was uneasily aware that Ralph Camoys's grandfather, Francis, 4th Baron was one of the much criticised directors of the Anglo-Australian bank which went into liquidation in 1891. It had paid its creditors only three pence in the pound. When one of the creditors then sued the two directors of this defunct bank, in response to questions over Lord Camoys being "presumed a substantial man merely because of his title", the aggrieved party replied succinctly: "I suppose lords are blackguards, the same as everybody else." Ralph's solicitor Harrison was also unhappily aware that another rogue related to his client, "old Tom" Camoys, had been forced to resign as member of parliament for Oxford after a scant three months, such was the public scandal of "bought votes" in 1833.

But then, in 1910, Ralph's life was set to change irreversibly. Together with magnificent horses, valets and grooms, travelling first class on an ocean liner, he crossed the Atlantic bound for New York, accompanying his closest friend, fellow peer Lord Decies, a considerable Anglo-Irish land-owner. Like the Duke of Marlborough, and the Earl Granard before them, these two men considered themselves to be "land-rich, cash-poor". They were equally determined to net an American heiress apiece, a millionairess, wooing with all the glamour of supreme self-confidence in their own eligibility, their dashing military uniforms, their prowess on horseback.

To the excitement of the prospective brides' fathers—who bore names like Jay Gould, Joseph W. Drexel, William K. Vanderbilt, William Watts Sherman (self-made tycoons, and substantial philanthropists)—the Anglo-Irish, Anglo-Saxon suitors, John de la Poer Beresford, Lord Decies of Leixlip Castle, and Ralph Francis Julian Stonor, Lord Camoys of Stonor Park, members of the House of Lords and peers of the realm, were seen as most desirably, plausibly, part and parcel of the English royal court.

Ruthless and powerful, the American tycoons were nevertheless dazzled, therefore, at the prospects for their daughters, easily convincing themselves of the future happiness of the hapless young women. To this sadly delusory end, the men were supported by their equally ambitious wives. With rare exception these women were deeply flattered by the attentive wooing of the handsome, heavily-moustached peers—who, perforce, paid greater attention to the fathers of their prospective brides, far away from their freezing, insanitary, daunting castles and lonely mansions in England and Ireland.

Ralph's best friend John Decies (formerly in command of the Tribal

Horse Regiment, and South Irish, soon to be appointed Chief Censor of Ireland), wed his millionairess, Jay Gould's daughter, in New York with great and splendid ceremony the year previously, 1910. Following in his footsteps, Ralph Camoys married his own heiress, Mildred Constance Sherman, on 25 November 1911. The brief marriage ceremony swiftly organised by Mildred's ever-ambitious mother, the Fiery Duster, Sophia Augusta Brown, unusually, took place in the bedroom of his new father-in-law, too ill to leave the confines of the New York brownstone family mansion, 108 East 25th Street.

Like the Duke of Marlborough, his cousin the Earl Granard and friend Lord Decies before him, Ralph Camoys had achieved his sole ambition in life. All four musketeers were determined to change their financial circumstances—they had no intention of remaining land-rich, cash-poor.

In due course the legality of Ralph and Mildred's marriage was inevitably questioned and minutely scrutinised by the House of Lords' Committee of Privileges on the death of Ralph, 5th Baron Camoys in August 1968. Their lordships were ever mindful of an earlier precedent, a much-publicised legal tug-of-war of legitimacy and inheritance where the salacious details, which deeply scandalised the monarchy in the Russell case of 1922, involved the Ampthill succession, a notorious society scandal involving an improbable impregnation with a bath sponge.

But it was Ralph's American mother-in-law, a magnificently wealthy, powerful, stout woman of the old and prestigious family, the John Nicholas Browns, long-established bankers and merchants of Newport and Providence, Rhode Island, who had the most encouraged Ralph's courtship of her youngest daughter. She considered him a considerable catch for her highly eligible but extremely naive, innocent, home-loving Mildred Constance. Besides, there were no boys in Sophia Augusta Brown's immediate family, both her brothers having died young at the turn of the twentieth century.

Julie read of her oldest nephew's marriage in the London *Times* where it was announced with a predictable, parsimonious brevity. Ralph had arranged a honeymoon which would take Mildred and him slowly around the world by ship, making a particular point of stopping off in Japan. Here they collected the artefacts and statues, several in terracotta, which were the mode of the day. Here too Mildred took note of the intricate design of Japanese gardens, water gardens, and their delicate use of bamboo which she would translate to her own ornamental gardens at Stonor. Finally, several months into 1912, she and Ralph arrived back in England, and for Mildred's first and stunned sighting of Stonor Park with its conspicuous lack of plumbing, electrical lighting, hygiene and central heating—such necessities to which she had been accustomed both in New York City and Newport, Rhode Island.

Meanwhile, very shortly after the marriage, the ailing William Watts Sherman had died, leaving Sophia Augusta a widow and of even greater substance. To Mildred, so far away, this loss of her father was an immense sadness. But his death meant that she and her sister Irene now became very much richer.

Ralph's conspicuous, quite openly expressed indifference to his innocent, romantic American bride, deeply in love with her husband, was obvious from the earliest days of the marriage. But Mildred's loyalty to her husband and to her marriage vows was staunch. This unfashionable loyalty seldom, if ever, wavered. It outlasted her death in Newport in November, 1961, caring financially for Ralph even beyond the grave until his own death in 1968, specified under the terms of her deeply-contested will—a clause that was not disputed by the challengers in the Providence court in 1962.

This indifference of her nephew towards his newly acquired bride was a further cause of distress to my aunt Julie, and so she took the younger woman under her wing. That Mildred was not a Catholic meant that Julie felt further obliged to care for the chapel at Stonor, and its sacristy and its treasury of vestments and innumerable religious artefacts. Ralph was the absentee "Patron of the Anglican Living" of the nearby Protestant church, Pishill-with-Stonor—absentee since, under a ruling of the Council of Trent in 1562, "English Catholics may not be present at the prayers of heretics without grave sin". It was here that the Protestant Mildred went to worship on Sundays.

From the early days of their marriage it was observed that Ralph spent increasingly more time in London at his innumerable clubs and his Ennismore Gardens house than he did at Stonor Park. Nevertheless in 1913, Mildred was delivered of a son in a London nursing home. Born on 5 July, the baby was christened Ralph Robert Watts Sherman Stonor, heir to the 5th Baron Camoys and to the substantial fortune of his millionairess mother.

Ever optimistic, Mildred undertook a most substantial renovation of the beautiful, but gloomy, darkly decorated and haunted house at Stonor. She installed a sewage system, a new electrical system, fresh running water conveyed in a large pipeline from the Warren, an orange-brick Victorian house high up on the hill above the deer park. Here there was a well even deeper than one in the Stonor carpentry yard behind the mullion-glassed Tudor kitchen and scullery. No less than a dozen bathrooms were installed, plus a comprehensive central-heating system with five new boilers to heat the swingeingly damp rooms, and dark semi-subterranean stone-flagged passages.

Behind the Tudor façade at the back of the house Mildred built an elegant summer house perched on stilts above the walled garden, and on the side of the deer park. Styled as a romantic Japanese-Tudor lodge, a tea-house filled with sunlight, it had a wooden-railed balcony overlooking the length and breadth of the medieval vegetable, fruit and flower gardens still in the original pattern as laid out in the sixteenth century.

Mulberries, medlars, pears, apples, grapes, red currants, black currants, raspberries, strawberries, wild strawberries, raspberries, blackberries and loganberries all poured forth from the heavily netted fruitbeds, and the ancient walled kitchen garden where fruits and fruit trees draped with mistletoe cohabited happily with lettuces, Brussels sprouts, beetroot, carrots, onions, shallots, potatoes, swedes, turnips and deep-dug beds of rhubarb and asparagus in season. Clumps of herbs grew beneath espaliered pears and apples and quinces. Mint, lemon balm, salvia, rosemary, thyme abounded, tomatoes grew sweet in large Victorian greenhouses next to the white and black hothouse grapes. Tended by thirteen gardeners, the rich harvest of produce ensured that "the Park" with its huge complement of retainers was self-sufficient. And Mildred, under the protective wing of Julie, made sure that she too was well supplied with the bounty of this beautiful, organic garden.

Beyond the chapel lies a Tudor barn and the remains of an ancient farm. Here Mildred built several handsomely equipped wooden stables for her ponies and horses in the same gabled style. Names such as "Golden Memory", "Bechamel", "Crimson Conquest", "Heart's Harmony", "Homely Touch", "Road to the Top", "Rattle Along" and "Martha Spanks" identified each animal, brass labels adorning each loose box. Besides the stable yard Mildred built a fives court and a small theatre for amateur theatricals. Within the old barn she installed a fire station with its own axes, hatchets, spanners, thick canvas hoses and an American fire-engine, bright scarlet, with a fireman's helmet, also scarlet, and tin buckets, sand-filled for emergencies.

Inside the house, fire blankets and ropes and rope ladders were also installed as a precaution for any hapless guest staying high up in "attic quarters", especially the deeply haunted Mount Pleasant, the room at the top of the house with its hidden priest holes from the years of the Reformation. No money was spared nor detail ignored in the renovations and restorations of this magnificent but primitive house.

Julie continued to watch over Mildred with affection and to the best of her ability but with increasing concern at the sheer loneliness of this young woman semi-abandoned at the isolated house while Ralph, increasingly absent on London trysts, was more concerned with "little bits of fluff round the corner", whether at diplomatic dinners (where he was accepted as a "grass-widower') or dingy clubs

Although Mildred maintained the Park and its continuous weekend shooting parties—which Ralph always attended—she was unable to take on her husband's duties towards the estate. Ralph, predictably, was utterly indifferent to his obligations, incurred over many generations, which also included the very many retainers and sitting tenants scattered across the village, hamlets and common lands of Bix Bottom, Maidensgrove Common, Nettlebed, Russells Water, Christmas Common, Pishill-with-Stonor, Turville Heath and others as quaintly named.

None of Ralph's tenants' cottages had running water nor did they have lavatories—only outside lean-tos, wood or brick with corrugated-iron roofs, at the back of cottage gardens, sodden with damp and mud, tin buckets filled with Sanilav disinfectant for questionable hygiene. Nevertheless, the 5th Baron collected the rents in cash, all noted down in a red-lined, pale blue accounts book, sometimes by hand, especially during the Second World War. As to vital maintenance and human well being, Ralph was unconcerned. Nor was he ever concerned, once safely married to Mildred the millionairess, with the farms that had always produced, in the past, a most satisfactory income to maintain the Stonor-Camoys family in great comfort.

Quite early in her married life Mildred had acquired the service of remarkably devoted ladies' maids. One especially, Nurse Bradley, would remain with Mildred until her death. Known always as "Buddy", she returned to haunt Stonor and its occupants soon after her own demise.

These personal maids accompanied Mildred on her many journeys to and fro across the Atlantic to "Stonor Lodge" in Newport. Sherman and his younger sisters always travelled with their mother and, since his journey was, of course, paid for, Ralph went too—as innumerable, deeply self-satisfied onboard photographs verify. Sadder images show a downcast Mildred with her children on the porch of her Bellevue Avenue mansion.

Even before the First World War—which Ralph carefully shirked—Julie had been planting a remarkable garden and a unique arboretum at Turville Grange. Several of the close-knit descendants of Queen Victoria, the sisters of Julie's former fiancé George V, and many members of the doomed Russian royal family frequently visited. Here they contributed their gifts of trees and bushes to the beautiful arboretum of the garden with its sweeping view of the deep Oxford valley beneath. Each tree, each bush, was individually marked by a thick lead label bearing the name of its donor: Romanoff, Schleswig-Holstein, Windisch-Graetz, Hesse, Hohenlohe-Langenberg, Saxe-Coburg and Gotha, the royalty and nobility of all Europe.

At the turn of the nineteenth century, Julie had frequently sailed on the royal yacht *Britannia* with George and his doomed first cousin Tsar Nicholas II, Emperor of All the Russians—to whom Queen Victoria had awarded the Order of the Garter in 1893. There were, when I visited my aunt at Turville Grange, many poignant black-and-white and sepia photographs of the trio, sometimes with Harry Stonor in attendance at Cowes, and at Osborne House. These elegant sailors are attired in blue and cream yachting gear, flannels, navy-blue blazers and navy-blue peaked and braided sailors' caps and white buckskin laced shoes. Sporting the royal owner's insignia, brilliant scarlet and blue enamelled and gold yachting pins depicting the royal arms of the Prince of Wales—three white ostrich feathers and his motto "Ich Dien". The first cousins, the Duke of York and the Tsar, look like identical twins.

After the tragedy of the Russian Revolution and the murder of the emperor and empress and most of their family, the tsar's mother, the Dowager Empress, sister of Queen Alexandra, came frequently to visit Julie at Turville Grange. There are many photographs of the two ladies, arm in arm, the Dowager Empress heavily draped in black mourning weeds, gloved, behatted and with a fine black silk veil. She too participated in the planting of Julie's exquisite garden and arboretum.

Deeply disillusioned and dismayed by her nephew's dubious behaviour towards his wife Mildred and to their only son, and by the more disturbing events that were to come to the family, Julia's unique inheritance would be willed in entirety to her half-Greek, greatly-gifted gay nephew Francis Stonor. He had followed in his father Eddie Stonor's footsteps as a most successful spy, subsequently a member of the SOE, active in Egypt and the Balkans. Subsequently Turville Grange was sold by Julie's heir first to Oliver and Antoinette Esher, and thereafter to Jackie Kennedy's sister Princess Lee Radziwill. By then the market value of Turville Grange was in the range of £10,000,000.

Comfortably ensconced at Stonor Park during the First World War, his baby son just a year old, Ralph Camoys presented himself to the War Board pleading his case for "exemption from military service". He gave, as his reasons, the fact that not only was he a most important peer, but also that he was "an expert in cows" and finished his statement with the excuse that "moreover, Lord Camoys is in very poor health"—the implication being that he could expire even before the end of any war.

The following year, in March 1915, Ralph's youngest brother Howard Carew Stonor was killed in the trenches at Givenchy. He was twenty-two. There is no record that Ralph was affected by his tragic death. The young man, unprepared for war, had left no will and thus it was Howard's widowed mother Jessica, Lady Camoys, who claimed the sum left after probate—£8,000 in 1916. A brass plate to Howard's memory was erected in the chapel. *"I have finished the course, I have kept the faith, I have run the good race"* reads the caption in flowing script above the hapless young man's name. His body lies still in a war grave in France.

The situation that Ralph quite callously created at Stonor, including his indifference to the loss of his brother, gave Julie further cause for concern for her great-nephew Sherman—whom his father chose largely to ignore. She felt deeply for Mildred as she busily poured her considerable fortune into the essential costly sewage renovations and refurbishment of the Park. And Julie, herself greatly loved, observed how very much loved Mildred had become by not only the many maids and servants but also Ralph's village retainers and tenants. Moreover, even in the absence of her husband, Mildred continuously, loyally supported local events and local charities with habitual generosity.

She also had considerable enthusiasm for the amateur dramatics, frequently ballet, performed in the Stonor Park theatre she had built. Elegant programmes were printed for the performances. Titles such as *Fan Dance*, *Gavotte*, *Gypsy Dance* and *Harlequin & Columbines* spring off the page with plays quaintly named *Between the Soup and the Savoury*, *The Maker of Dreams* and *Animal Ballet*, combining Frogs, Dragonfly and Grasshopper, Chicks and Rats amongst the youthful performers.

Julie was able to watch Sherman grow up with all the admirable qualities that he had so conspicuously inherited from his mother. He grew into
the sweet-spirited man, deeply loved by all the Stonor villagers who saw
him as a pleasing contrast to Ralph and his parsimonious indifference to
their welfare.

Sherman's deep attachment to Mildred and dependence upon her affection made it difficult for his mother to follow convention in banishing her
young son to the English boarding-school system. For one miserable term,
at the behest of Ralph, Sherman was sent away to the Oratory School. He
cried his heart out and Mildred, horrified at the rigours of an English public school, fetched her son home. Sherman's natural gentleness of character, coupled with a certain timidity, had quickly attracted bullies and mocking intimidation, a pattern which would be repeated many more times in
his life. Philip Hall, the upright verger to the Protestant parish church of
Pishill-with-Stonor, was now appointed Sherman's tutor, and the rest of a
somewhat desultory education took place at Stonor.

Sherman always described himself as self-educated and with a passion
for birds, butterflies, flowers, wild flowers and, especially, the countryside.
He had an abiding love for and great knowledge of architecture and
archaeology and antiques, and loved to explore the English landscape. He
was always an avid reader, ever ready to explore the history of ideas. By
nature always a liberal man, Sherman was likewise a tolerant Christian and
Catholic. Politics interested him little, though for congeniality he joined
the Liberal Club in Henley-on-Thames, contrary to his supremely conservative neighbours and fellow landowners.

Singularly lacking in the pomposity that characterised not only his
father but also his great-uncles Harry and Eddie Stonor—the latter being
officially appointed secretary to the Anti-Communist and Anti-Socialist
Leagues—Sherman was uninterested in the very real class divisions of the
time. He had inherited from Mildred an egalitarian attitude towards those
around him, as evinced too by the deep love which the men of his regiment
showed in their respect for his conspicuous courage in the terrifying days
of Dunkirk in 1940. To the delight of Mildred and Julie, Sherman made no
distinction between a duke and a dustman. In an era of great snobbery,
deep social distinctions, a rigid class structure, quite ruthless in its code,
Sherman stood out as a beacon of enlightenment.

Moreover, Sherman had a profound sense of style and of fun, with a
great enthusiasm for his many friends—invariably from all walks of life—

to enjoy his boundless hospitality. These qualities he shared with Mildred but, as Julie observed, Ralph Camoys became increasingly jealous of his good-looking, sensitive son. He could not even be photographed with Sherman after a time and there are few pictures of father and son together.

Indeed, Ralph was becoming increasingly peevish—and plump from lack of exercise other than occasional bee-keeping with the French parish priest. And, as Julie sadly observed, her nephew had no intention of returning to the fold of her beloved Catholic faith. It would be very many more years before the 5th Baron Camoys made his general confession to the Cardinal Archbishop of New York, Archbishop Frank Spellman, Chaplain General to the US Forces, and an autocratic, religious fundamentalist. Similarly neglectful of the family, Ralph ignored the plight of his brother Hugo and his devoted Jewish wife, a dancer from Poland, Esther Gilbert, who lived in one of Ralph's Bruton Street properties. The childless couple was increasingly poverty-struck—though history does not accurately record the exorbitant rent paid to Ralph.

Inevitably Ralph's attitude would bring about tragic and long-term consequences. He had lived off Mildred's money since their wedding in 1911, making no effort towards the profitability of his large estates, other than to collect rents from the tied tenants, whose cottages and farms he, least of all, maintained. The many and several farms of the 6,300 rich acres drifted towards insolvency, such was his mismanagement, lack of husbandry and sheer neglect. All was far from well with the finances of the 700 year-old estate.

By 1937 the 5th Baron Camoys was in the humiliating position of being personally sued for bankruptcy. For a peer of the realm this would be considered the ultimate of public humiliation. Mildred came to the rescue, confiding in Julie the plan which she and her own family solicitors had devised to save the Stonor Estates—and her unrepentant husband.

To balance the situation, the plan that Mildred and her American financial and legal advisors had now devised to rescue the estates entailed its outright purchase, the title deeds to be in the name of the new—and American—owner, the Lady Camoys. The law relating to bankruptcy meant that the original entailment of the Stonor Estates (whereby automatically the eldest, or only, son inherited upon the death of his father) was immediately null and void. Though, in many of the old Catholic families either the male line had died out (the "tail male" as it was known) or the older title, as with Camoys, of a pre-Reformation barony of writ passed such properties and inheritances to the "female issue of the blood". Thus there were several legitimate such heiresses-at-law in the nineteenth century—certainly no less than a dozen.

Mildred immediately set about giving the majority of the estate to Sherman. He was twenty-four years old. The neighbouring estates of Bosmore and Cock's Leas, Mildred gave to her daughters. Stonor Park was now, in 1937, a freehold property, American-funded, an American purchase.

That he had been rescued seemed not to bother Ralph at all as he continued in his habits, frequently away in London, returning as usual at weekends to shoot. But, by 1937, war was approaching and the impact of Ralph's callous indifference towards his increasingly lonely, semi-abandoned wife, had begun to take its toll on her. The ever protective Julie grew increasingly worried for Mildred's well being as well as for Sherman's.

She was happy, however, to see that her great-nephew enjoyed the companionship of a gentle young woman, Phoebe Houstoun-Boswell, the only child of near neighbours Sir George and Lady Houstoun-Boswell, more usually known as the "Hooster-Boosters". Both Phoebe and Sherman were great innocents, and travelled happily and shyly together, usually in a group of friends, and in their company sometimes to France with family lawyer David Drummond.

Up until the Second World War, and for a few years immediately following, chaperonage was considered an essential for well-born girls and young women, the better to ensure their virginity. Both Sherman and Phoebe were virgins. And, to the pleasure of Mildred and Julie, she shared the same gentle country interests. But this tranquillity was about to be shattered.

On New Year's Eve 1937, a brutal assassination took place in the horrors of the Spanish Civil War during the Nationalists' battle for the control of Teruel. In the nearby village of Caude three journalists—one Englishman, Dick Sheepshanks, a Reuters special correspondent and personally accredited to General Franco by Sir Roderick Jones, and two Americans, one a photographer—were travelling together in a small two-door saloon car with Kim Philby, accredited to *"El Jefe"* by the London *Times*.

On this bitterly cold, freezing day, December 31, there were no witnesses to the explosion. A hand-grenade was reported to have been hurled into the car, horrendously killing the two Americans outright and leaving Dick Sheepshanks so badly injured that he died within hours. The Americans were named as Edward Neil, Associated Press, and Bradish Johnson, *Newsweek* photographer.

Soldiers nearby, Nationalists, found Kim Philby sheltering behind a low wall near to the shattered vehicle, clutching superficial wounds to his head and arm. He explained that "enemy fire" had hit the car, and that he had "managed to jump out just in time". As Philby explained, implausibly, he had been sitting on the back seat of the two-door vehicle. Not only did the conscript soldiers believe his explanation but, with great irony, the carefully-disguised communist spy was subsequently decorated by the fascist General Franco "for conspicuous bravery under enemy fire".

With due pomp and ceremony the three flag-decked coffins were taken to the British Embassy at Hendaye—where Sir Henry Chilton and his staff had taken up official residence above a grocer's shop on the French side of the International Bridge.

At the time much reported and illustrated in *The Times*, the killing of Jeanne Stourton's handsome, eligible young fiancé Dick Sheepshanks was seen as just another consequence and casualty of the brutal civil war in Spain. Its consequences in England, however, would be monumental in many ways.

The beautiful young daughter of the Hon Mrs Herbert Stourton and her grandee Spanish lover Don Pedro de Zulueta y Borja (Borgia) Merry del Val, Jeanne was a distant cousin of Sherman Stonor and was born the same year, 1913, in London barely a mile away from Mildred Camoys's confinement. Her fiancé Dick was a dashing Old Etonian, a member of its famous club "Pop", an outstanding cricketer at school and a renowned player for Yorkshire CC. He was an all-round sportsman of remarkable good looks and immense popularity. Some three or four years older than Jeanne, the couple were deeply in love and had become unofficially engaged. The ambitious Dick came from a substantial, wealthy Yorkshire family with a seat in Arthrington. He was closely related to the spy Anthony Blunt and, after Eton, he had gone like Philby to Trinity College, Cambridge.

While not exact contemporaries at university, they knew each other well enough for Dick to question aspects of Kim's behaviour in Spain, including a barely-concealed contempt that was out of keeping with their shared experiences at Cambridge and quite at odds with the fascist politics of General Franco.

Dick was clearly becoming an acute danger to Philby's cover. He had to dispose of him. That two entirely innocent American journalists would die too seems to have been inconsequential to Dick's assassin. As Tom Dupree, son-in-law of of ambassador Chilton, later revealed, Philby indeed realised that the unfortunate Sheepshanks had seen through his cover and recognized that he was a Russian agent.

In England on New Year's Day, 1938, news of the devastating triple killing had reached the distraught Sheepshanks family and Jeanne. Not only had she been deeply in love with Dick but he had all the essential trappings necessary to an ambitious young woman "of high society" not yet married. At the age of twenty-five such a woman would be considered, sneeringly, "on the shelf, all-but, my dear!", an accusation deeply wounding and frequently damaging to the hapless victim.

Considered an intimate member of the Sheepshanks family, Jeanne, accompanied by her mother, attended first the glittering memorial service held in London in early January. The illustrious list of worshippers was published in *The Times*, as too were the mourners gathered at the funeral itself, just days after, at Arthrington where Jeanne once again had precedence of seating in the front row, the acknowledged fiancée of the dead journalist.

Jeanne was not only bereft but in a complicated position socially. She was also taken by surprise at the fact that her fiancé had left no will—and she had no legal claim to Dick's money. Despite the extreme danger of his calling as an international journalist and his posting to the Spanish Civil War, Dick had surprisingly left no will. Declared intestate, it would be Olive who ultimately inherited her son's estate, valued at £15,000.

Furthermore Dick's Protestant mother Olive did not care overmuch for "the Spanish Adventuress" who would have become her daughter-in-law. Privately, Olive had been displeased by reports of Jeanne's dubious reputation for having been "up and down the lines" during the Spanish Civil War with her many Falangist cousins, most of them glamorous young colonels of great Nationalist, pro-monarchist fervour.

Throughout her life and throughout her marriage to Sherman, Jeanne made no bones about her great and abiding love for Dick. His portrait lived permanently besides her four-poster bed. But now that he was so suddenly dead and in such violent circumstances, Jeanne was swiftly shocked into the reality of the times. She must, and very soon, find herself a suitable husband.

In 1938 her age as an eligible young woman was already beginning to tell against Jeanne, as yet unmarried and with widely acknowledged, questionable, and very expensive tastes. Her position was not helped by rumours that she had blackmailed Cecil Beaton's older gay brother Reggie into plunging to his death beneath an oncoming train at Piccadilly Circus underground station.

She had, however, a huge network to call on of Spanish and South American cousins and friends living in London, Rome, Paris, Hendaye, San Sebastián, Madrid, Berlin and Bogotá. Some of them—her brother-in-law the Marqués del Moral, Ramón de Bertodano, included—were important diplomats, ambassadors or politicians. Several of these men, frequently in London, were members of an international, cosmopolitan and chic gaming club, the renowned Bachelor's and St James's, conveniently near the Ritz Hotel at 106 Piccadilly and not far from the fashionable hotel Claridge's, home to the Spanish and Greek royal families on Brook Street, the heart of Mayfair. Here too, another old friend of Jeanne's, the glamorous Nazi Ribbentrop was an honorary member.

And so, carefully arranged through a mutual friend Carlos Germán-Ribón (the gay "Charlie" was another of Jeanne's many Spanish-Colombian connections), Sherman was skilfully manoeuvred by this fellow-member of the Bachelors' Club into meeting Jeanne. It was the 15th of January, only sixteen days after Dick's brutal murder.

Most of the Catholic, pre-Reformation, Recusant families, reduced though they had become in number, were inextricably, inevitably inter-related by marriage and blood. Many of them had amassed and inherited great fortunes, extensive acres, richly productive lands, castles, mansions, manor houses and villages across Britain.

Inevitably related over and over again through the centuries, it was not difficult for Jeanne to show Sherman their common ancestry in the essential reference books of the day: *Burke's Peerage* and *Debrett's Peerage & Baronetage*. These scarlet-bound leather tomes were essential bedside reading throughout Jeanne's life. And they were to be found in every grand drawing-room, an essential requisite, proof of pedigree and family connection.

Ten days after Dick's interment, Sherman escorted Jeanne to a hunt ball at Burford in Oxfordshire. This was an event to which Mildred Camoys subscribed, buying her son a pair of tickets. There is a glamorous photograph, black-and-white, in *The Tatler & Bystander* of Sherman and Jeanne side-by-side in formal evening dress, he in white tie and tails, she in a magnificent black ball dress with a large corsage of orchids at her waist—

usually supplied by the gentleman escort of the evening—and an amount of elegant, obviously expensive diamonds.

Nevertheless, the expression on Jeanne's face is severely strained, and there is no doubt that she was still in shock from her very recent tragedy. The dramatic black of her ball gown, the traditional colour of both Spanish aristocratic and English Catholic mourning, emphasises a look of bitter grief at the loss of her fiancé.

However, faced with such a considerable personal dilemma as to her future, a serious crisis, Jeanne had lost very little time returning to the social scene. Sherman was overwhelmed. He had never met such an exotic woman, and one so beautifully dressed, a perfume-drenched, sophisticated continental woman sporting long scarlet-painted nails. Jeanne was in stark contrast to his girlfriend, the pretty, gentle-charactered English and Scottish Phoebe Houstoun-Boswell, optimistically considered "so SUITABLE for Sherman" by his mother Mildred, and Aunt Julie.

As Jeanne pointed out eagerly and convincingly to Sherman, she too was a practising Catholic unlike the Protestant Phoebe. The Vatican still did not easily countenance "mixed marriages", making such occasions as dour as possible, disallowing the beauty and drama of a Nuptial Mass, demanding of the non-Catholic party not only "instruction in the Faith", but also a signature on a formidable document requiring that any offspring of such a union "be (automatically) brought-up in the true Faith". The hapless parent involved, he or she, would otherwise incur the extreme punishment of "Mortal Sin", with the consequent "excommunication".

Sherman could not fail to be completely bowled over. Events proceeded with lightning speed not hitherto experienced in the sleepy depths and valleys of Stonor where time all but stood still. This rather melancholic peace was about to be shattered once and for all.

Initially Jeanne brought with her a sense of excitement, even of high drama. But, to the horror of Mildred and Julie, the hapless Phoebe was immediately banned. Sherman was forbidden to communicate with the woman in his life whom Jeanne saw, quite simply, to be her arch-rival in the battle for Sherman's affections—and far, far more.

In those early months of 1938 both Mildred and Julie looked on with growing dismay, powerless in the drama which, like a tidal wave, engulfed and overwhelmed Sherman. Both women were uneasily aware of Jeanne Stourton's appalling reputation and their utter inability to extricate their vulnerable son and great-nephew from the engagement so swiftly announced with such finality in *The Times*.

Julie, more worldlywise than Mildred, was aware that her nephew Ralph had already had an "entanglement" in London with Jeanne. She had also heard the rumours of Jeanne's "entanglement" with Sir Richard Sykes, the Yorkshire baronet and owner of the magnificent estate of Sledmere.

It was said that some of Jeanne's magnificent diamonds came as a result of her breach of promise legal action, publicly naming Sir Richard—which the millionaire race-horse owner had hastened to settle out of court a year or so previously. Simultaneously there had been unfortunate photographs of Jeanne, "very well-known in society", mysteriously entering the notorious clinic at, 27 Welbeck Street for her "emergency appendix operation". She was accompanied by a black pug, which she merrily described to the waiting photographers as "a recent gift from my dear, dear Sir Richard Sykes".

Jeanne's ambition was swiftly achieved. In the month of March 1938, around the time of the Anschluss, Hitler's annexation of Austria, the formal engagement of "Miss Mary Jeanne Stourton to the Hon Ralph Watts Sherman Stonor, only son of Lord and Lady Camoys of Stonor Park" was announced in the London *Times*. Such an announcement was further distinguished by being at the head of the engagements column of the Court Circular. It denoted a match of great social consequence and of serious money, if not a most considerable, desirable fortune.

The instrument of their match, "Charlie, dear old boy Charlie" Germán-Ribón, as he was known to Jeanne, had already filled her in with the minutiae as to the generosity the previous year of Mildred's gift of the Stonor Park Estates and the majority of its priceless contents. Always scrupulous in her own research into other people's wealth and potential, Jeanne had immediately, in that eventful month of January, established Sherman's background and considerable fortune, confirming him a highly desirable catch. His rich acreage, 6,300 and more, was usefully printed in *Who's Who*, another favoured book of reference.

The ugly rumours of Jeanne's reputation as a "Spanish adventuress", a woman who did not hesitate to announce herself as a "Spanish bastard to boot", finally reached the ears of the horrified and heart-broken Mildred. Even she had now heard of the various "old beaux" with whom Jeanne had involved herself: the aged Gordon Selfridge and Sir Austen Chamberlain, Sir Richard Sykes, Prince Aly Khan, the Hon William W. Astor (always known as "Bill" and the eldest living son of Nancy, Lady Astor), plus a string of others including peers of the realm, foreign diplomats such as Ribbentrop, all regarded as highly dubious, including that particularly flash English conductor of music, Malcolm Sargent. It was rumoured too that Jeanne shared a great liking for the fashionable uniform sported by Sir Oswald Mosley's British-Fascist party, which can hardly have reassured either Mildred or Julie.

It was Charlie, the Colombian-Indian principal heir to the Patiño-Charpentier tin and silver mines dynasty, famous collectors of unique French Impressionists, who told Jeanne that the young man was apolitical, disinterested in the high politics of the far right, British fascists or neo-Nazis, with which Charlie was as obsessed as Jeanne in the heady hedonism of the Thirties whether in the worldly glamour of London or in hot pursuit of the erotic temptations of Berlin or Bogotá. Sherman was all but unique in this amongst his land-owning neighbours—the owners of great estates like the Earl of Macclesfield, Viscount Esher, Viscount Bertie of Thame, the Duke of Marlborough, the Lord Rathcreedan, Commander Richard Ovey and the Fleming banking dynasty among them. Certainly as the great-nephew of Eddie Stonor, the ever-active secretary of the Anti-Communist League and the Anti-Socialist League, and his own quiet membership of the Liberal Party and its club in Henley, the young man was unique in his circle.

Sherman's main interests were those related in the first instance to the countrysides, the cultivation of indigenous plants and flowers, the farming of fine herds of Guernsey and Jersey cows producing the finest quality milk, cream, butter churned out of golden oak casks. He protected his pedigree cows with the same care that he endeavoured to protect his three-hundred strong herd of dappled fallow deer which roamed the park and woodlands round Stonor. He deplored the increasing use of chemicals on his well-husbanded land, and felt uneasy about the newly-popular artificial insemination of the pedigree cows. He always ensured that his animals grazed lush pastures, that they were given only the purest cattle food, the best of hay and straw, drinking from deep troughs of clean water. He was universally known as "Sherman" to his men, retainers, tenant farmers and villagers.

Like all gentleman of his time, Sherman shot, and shot excellently. This meant that any bird—pheasant, partridge, pigeon, woodcock—was cleanly and decently killed. The same applied to the killing of game such as rabbits, hares and occasionally buck deer. Several of his contemporaries shot far less cleanly, causally announcing with a hearty shout "casserole bird, casserole bird!" as a peppered, mortally wounded pheasant careered wildly overhead before crashing heavily to the ground, wings still thrashing.

But Sherman never liked the so-called sport, despite his beautifully made pairs of Purdey & Purdey handcrafted 12-bore guns. Nevertheless, it would take him until after the Second World War—and the trauma of his experiences at Dunkirk—to announce his profound shame that he had participated in this chilling, killing field, an act of considerable courage on his part for which he was merely despised. Sherman never shot again.

Long before the legalisation of homosexuality, the gay Charlie's reputation, scandalous and salacious as it was, rested and relied on Jeanne's discretion, notorious as her betrayals had become. Her animated, frequently quick-witted conversation was laced with suggestive nuances, thinly veiled threats in Spanish or French of chantage, blackmail, extortion and enticement. Charlie had hastened to encourage her engagement to Sherman and suggested to the shy young man that he should accompany his fiancée to Cartier, the famous Bond Street jeweller much patronised by Jeanne's former employer, Barbara Hutton, the glamorous American millionairess known as the "Poor Little Rich Girl".

Before the end of March, Jeanne sported a magnificent ruby and diamond, cabuchon-cut engagement ring commissioned at Cartier. As usual she wore equally magnificent trophies from Barbara Hutton: diamond and ruby double clips, a hand-carved diamond, ruby, sapphire and emerald watch, its bejewelled strap shaped like a garland of flowers. Triumphantly she swept down to Stonor with Sherman in newly acquired couturier clothes, scent-drenched, her nails a gleaming scarlet enamel.

Mildred regarded Jeanne with ever-growing suspicion and the deepest of gloom. So too did Julie. As did her brother, the gay, debonair Sir Harry Stonor. He felt an instant distaste for Sherman's flamboyant, bossy wife-to-be and he had already made up his mind that he would certainly not attend the forthcoming marriage.

Mildred had observed the direction of Jeanne's eyes as she inspected the beauty and the immensity of Stonor Park. She seemed curiously overwhelmed by the 17th-century carriage, painted canary yellow and midnight blue in the family colours, wood-shafted and ready to be pulled by four horses. And by a colourful, *naif* painting of Stonor in 1690, its many windows still mullioned, the family carriage carrying a portly ducal ancestor of Sherman's portrayed in the foreground.

Furthermore, there was an exciting array both of servants, and of seemingly endless formal rooms: magnificent Gothic hallways decorated with stained-glass windows of great antiquity; dining-rooms, study and farm office, book-room, boudoir, an immense and barrelled, concave ceilinged Tudor library, a long, long gallery, even a somewhat drab but ancient private chapel, all giving onto a glorious series of walled rose gardens, walled kitchen gardens, Victorian glasshouses, shrubberies, Japanese water gardens delicately sculpted into the exquisite landscape of gently undulating Chiltern Hills. And Jeanne saw, as she gazed towards the park, Sherman's herd of dappled fallow deer and the several Guernsey and Jersey cows grazing the luscious green pastures behind the copper beech trees, beyond a long, neatly trimmed beech hedge and a clump of lilac bushes.

Jeanne was initially overwhelmed by the sheer size of Stonor. By contrast to the London flat perched over a butcher's shop which she had shared with her mother, this estate was a prize beyond even Jeanne's wilder dreams and ambition. Quite overcome with excitement, and with her habitual audacity she asked indelicate questions of Mildred as to "the usage of all those sixty-four rooms at Stonor Park", a remark that caused as much offence to Julie as to Mildred for its sheer impertinence and high-handed flippancy. To them, Jeanne's intentions were blindingly obvious.

They were forced to observe with horror Jeanne's sudden passion for Sherman's antique Georgian silver cutlery. Engraved with the Stonor crest of a Roman skylark pecking at a druidical worshipping stone, Jeanne was transfixed by the velvet texture of the silver, and found it irresistible to stroke the pistol-shaped knives, forks and spoons. Overcome with excitement, she turned the cutlery over to examine the hallmarks. Jeanne then did the same with the porcelain plates—to the equal horror of the butler waiting at the dining table. She up-ended the cut-glass wine and water glasses, explaining merrily, that she was "most frightfully interested in antiques, ha! ha!'

Sherman remained transfixed. He chose to ignore Jeanne's tendency to highly colourful stories, frequently scatological, which could reduce her audience to gales of laughter. But the reaction of the scandalised women of his family, Julie and Mildred, was at a distinct variance: they considered the prospective bride as a dangerous, capricious exhibitionist and "show-off", with a decided mania for name-dropping. Like the butler, they found the scarlet lipstick marks left on the table linen somewhat offensive and derisive of their hospitality.

From the onset of the engagement Jeanne was in a considerable hurry, and she had no time, let alone patience, to convince her future mother-in-law and her aunt-to-be of her sincerity. Besides Jeanne really did not care much—if at all—for the company of any other women unless they were both rich and beautiful, and with a famous name. Thus Barbara Hutton, the "poor, little, rich girl", the tragic Woolworth heiress, gullible, sensitive, habitually generous, had already been an easy target for Jeanne—who was expensively covered with Barbara's gifts of diamonds, rubies, sapphires, emeralds. There were also the two Spanish royal princesses, the eligible, gullible and attractive Infantas Beatriz and Maria Cristina de Borbón, and Sylvia, the renowned Brazilian beauty and heiress, daughter of the tycoon ambassador Raul Regis de Oliveira, a keen guest shot on grand estates, and doyenne of the Diplomatic Corps in London. Sylvia would soon after Sherman and Jeanne's spectacular marriage (at which she was a principal scarlet-gloved bridesmaid) become second wife to another of Jeanne's "darlin' old beaux", Prince Jean Faucigny-Lusinge, not long widowed from the French banker and beauty Baronne d'Erlanger.

A further Court Circular announcement, handcrafted again by Jeanne, now appeared in *The Times*: "The forthcoming marriage of Miss Mary Jeanne Stourton with the Hon Ralph Watts Sherman Stonor will be solemnised in a Nuptial Mass on Thursday, 14 July, 1938, at the London Oratory". It was Julie who pointed out to Mildred that this date was the anniversary of the Storming of the Bastille, the celebrated blood-drenched Bastille Day of the French Revolution.

Preparations for the "marriage of the season" proceeded at breakneck speed. Two thousand guests were invited by Jeanne to London's grandest wedding. The protocol of the day meant that invitations, hand-engraved onto heavy, stiff-folded white card at Cartier, or the fashionable printer Smythson's were sent out in the name of the bride's parents.

Sherman paid for everything. His fiancée's widowed mother Frances was penniless, all-but, existing on the pittance of an allowance meted out to her on a monthly basis by the parsimonious head of the Mowbray, Segrave and Stourton dynasty, William, 23rd Baron, premier baron of England. Feckless Fanny's husband, the indifferent Herbert, was temporarily a fellow officer of Ralph Camoys in the Oxfordshire Hussars. Herbert had quite casually galloped through his wife's fortune inherited from her father Viscount Southwell. This had become the cause of embarrassment and, even more, of inconvenience to the pompous, insular, highly political Mowbray, Segrave and Stourton family of the day, constantly aware of their image, and position in high Catholic society despite some well-publicised episodes of heavy violence in the early Thirties. The police charges of grievous bodily harm against the brothers William Marmaduke, 23rd Baron, and the Hon John Joseph Stourton, MP, ardent admirers of the Nazis, had been most hastily swept under the carpet.

The day of the wedding, 14 July, Mildred Camoys refused to attend. She stayed at home at Stonor, confined to her bedroom, weeping copiously. In front of startled witnesses Jeanne promptly announced her "campaign of revenge". Julie also declined, pleading her age and the difficulty of travelling to London from Turville Grange. Jeanne again swore revenge—but of a different sort. Besides, unlike her mother-in-law, Julie would shortly be of great and useful consequence to Jeanne's well-laid plans.

Julie's brother Sir Harry placed an announcement in the Court Circular to the effect that he would "be abroad, in Rome, on the continent, unable to attend forthcoming nuptials". He stayed away on a gay triste at the palace of the Duchess of Simonetta, relieved not to participate in the fate of his great-nephew's precipitate marriage. Besides, Harry was already fearful of joining Jeanne's well-known blackmail list of homosexuals.

According to the official list in the Court Circular of Friday, July 15, Ralph Camoys did attend his son's wedding. Despite his manifest jealousy and disdain for Sherman, it would have been difficult for Ralph to explain his absence in front of several of his American in-laws and cousins who had travelled by liner from Bailey's Beach, Newport and New York for the occasion. Besides, two of his daughters were amongst the seven "grown-up bridesmaids" included with the three pages and the five little girl attendants, all hand-picked nieces and cousins from as far afield as Brazil, Paris and Bogotá.

Contemporary newspapers in New York and Rhode Island announced that "Mrs Nicholas Brown's gardens were open for the Newport civic league. Mrs Brown with her nieces, the Hon Nadine Stonor and Miss Natalie Bayard Merril, sailed from New York today on the *Queen Mary* to attend the marriage of the Hon Sherman Stonor, son of Lord and Lady Camoys, to Miss Mary Jeanne Stourton. Mrs Brown plans to stay abroad two months." The papers continue: "Two dead, one shot was the record to-day of violence in London, Kentucky, during the Harlem labor conspiracy trial now in its eighth week."

Meanwhile, in London's Bow Street court, Countess Barbara Hutton

Haugwitz-Reventlow's battery of legal talent accused her titled Danish husband of demanding $5 million and their two-year old son Lance in return for a divorce. In two and a half hours of sensational testimony, he was further accused of threatening to shoot an unnamed Mayfair society man "like a dog". The golden-haired, black-clad Woolworth heiress kept her sad, childlike eyes on the back of her husband's head as her attorneys declared that he had threatened to "put her on the spot" and give her "three years of hell and headlines".

In another Court Circular announcement the same week as the marriage, the London arrangements of the Queen of Spain and her daughters, Beatriz and Maria Cristina were announced. To the never-forgiven, never forgotten rage of Jeanne, both these handsome young princesses of the blood royal, daughters of King Alfonso XIII and his "English Queen" Ena, were expressly forbidden from attending the marriage of their "beautiful and very dangerous" friend. The queen had, with reason, delivered a most royal snub, leaving Jeanne further smarting with fury and self-righteous indignation.

Nor did Ralph's disapproving first cousin Gwendolyn Sladen or her long-time companion the actress Marjorie Bryce attend the celebrations. Their sympathy lay entirely with the sorrowing Mildred, left weeping at Stonor. And also with Sherman, his fate already decided so summarily. A great many rumours had reached the two lovers at their Cherry Orchard cottage in the hamlet of Pishill-with-Stonor. They especially disapproved of the unfaithful Ralph's shabby behaviour and besides, because Gwendolyn, daughter of a general, and Marjorie, whose Anglo-Irish family owned the garden Island of Garnish, had met as landgirls in the First World War, they both shared a deep distaste for Ralph's cynicism in shirking wartime duty so shortly before Howard Stonor was killed in the trenches. But these kindly, caring women felt powerless to pull Sherman out of the deftly-set, deeply alluring trap. Like Julie they could only look on with increasing horrified concern.

Sherman was dazzled by Jeanne's quite extraordinary quick-witted repartee and lively knowledge of Spain and the Spanish language. The grandeur of her family—the Marqués of Merry del Val y Borja, brother to a famous Cardinal Rafael Borja Merry del Val, her own father, Don Pedro de Zulueta y Merry del Val—was daily impressed upon Sherman together with Jeanne's other impeccable connections with the Vatican via her Mostyn baronet cousins, bishops, monsignors and Knights of Malta.

Sherman was literally swamped, initially unable to see beyond all Jeanne's astonishing, amusingly-recounted and endless stories, many of them relating to her most recent experiences "up and down the lines on El Jefe's side in this damn nuisance civil war, *olé!*"

Even before they were married, Jeanne had amply demonstrated to her fiancé her snapping, flashing castanets, a heavy black lace mantilla mounted on an ornate tortoiseshell comb high on her head, as she whirled and twirled, pausing only to remove a long cigarette holder from her scarlet-painted lips. And at the piano where she was inclined to play her father's operettas, and to sing Gilbert & Sullivan and lively extracts from nightclub songs. In accompaniment Jeanne's heavily-laden gold bracelets, hung with 18-carat madonnas of the Macarena and occasional stump-like golden swastikas, crashed and clattered in unison to the music-making.

Sherman was completely bewitched, and since he was disinterested in gossip, he heard nothing of the rumours flying around. In fact he felt great pity for Jeanne's story as she related it herself so convincingly. And, completely inexperienced sexually, he was further bewildered by Jeanne's intoxicating, scent-drenched style and seductive flippancy. He was only later to understand that her conversation was, in fact, deeply barbed, deeply unkind and deeply, convincingly calculated. Further and further the hapless young man was sucked into a vortex from which escape would swiftly become all but impossible.

Despite such indignations and embarrassing setbacks for Jeanne, the marriage solemnized at the London Oratory in a nuptial Mass with her uncle the Archbishop of Cardiff, officiating was nothing less than magnificent, an extraordinary spectacle of equally extraordinary international chic, style and glamour, the very height of fashion—and social achievement. The waiting crowd, assembled in the forecourt and inner courtyard, and on the Brompton Road outside the grand church, gasped with excitement overcome with astonished amazement at the beauty of the bride and her many attendants exquisitely arrayed, carrying exotic bunches of gardenias, lily-of-the-valley, ruby red roses and deep crimson roses—and blood-red suede gloves to the elbow.

Jeanne had chosen a gown designed by her close friend Norman Hartnell, a famous couturier employed by the royal family. Made out of heavy ivory-white satin, the dress and its long train, cut in one, was hand-embroidered with a thousand seed pearls, her lace veil, draped with tulle, held in place with a head-dress of orange blossom. All seven of her bridesmaids wore pale pink picture hats trimmed with ruby-red roses matching their red suede gloves.

The Times and *The Tatler & Bystander* carried telling photographs of the "Wedding of the Year". Sherman, slim, elegant, wistful, slightly mournful, somewhat pensive, wears an elegant bespoke morning coat, a gardenia in his buttonhole. Jeanne, on his arm, descends the aisle triumphantly, very sure of herself, pausing for frequent photographs as she went.

Sparing no attention to the minutest of detail in the wedding preparations Jeanne had excluded any invitation to Sherman's once girlfriend, Phoebe. Though there were other women rivals in the assembled congregation now quite subdued by Jeanne's conspicuous social victory. Moreover, most of her highly political friends, many of them closely related, attended with great alacrity such a sumptuous afternoon reception.

Standing in the side aisles, Sherman's staff, retainers, tenants, farmers and their wives gazed in wonder. They had been carefully organised into coaches for the day-trip from the villages around Stonor—as Ruby Heath, the under housekeeper, vividly described. Some of them are to be seen in the photographs, the wives in felt hats, some with long cloth mackintoshes, others in tweed overcoats, looking slightly bewildered.

Though Mildred in the acuteness of her misery was aware that Sherman and his new bride would be spending their honeymoon on the Continent; she was unaware that at the invitation of Jeanne's "old beau" Ribbentrop they would be on the continental train via Berlin to Schloss Sonnenburg. "Such a surprise honeymoon for darlin' Shermie," she explained at large upon her return to England.

The large, magnificently furnished, pretentious and gloomy 18th-century castle complete with golf course, Hitler's minister had acquired at Bad Freienwalde with his wife's Henkel champagne fortune. This estate was purchased in 1934, two years before Ribbentrop became Hitler's ambassador in London. Like the German embassy at 7, 8 and 9 Carlton House Terrace, Sonnenburg was remodelled to the design of Albert Speer in a grandiose classical manner, over-furnished, flamboyant, slightly louche

Ribbentrop invariably, with military discipline, made sure always to have his castle filled with exotic bowls of heavily scented hothouse lilies and musk roses. The one modern incongruity was a quite obsessively excessive number of telephones; in London no less than eighty-two were installed in Albert Speer's renovation of the German Embassy's three large houses on Carlton House Terrace. Later on Jeanne would emulate Joachim's extravagance with an equally excessive number of telephones and extensions in her conquest of Stonor Park; where she would shout down the black Bakelite receiver: "Turville Heath THREE HUNDRED here, and who the HELL are YOU?"

After the triumphant success of the Bastille wedding day Jeanne had arranged one, possibly two nights at Claridge's. Here Sherman finally lost his virginity to the highly experienced, ever-enticing Jeanne. A few days later on 18 July, the couple had arrived at the gloomy, oppressive grandeur of Schloss Sonnenburg, greeted by their host resplendent in the black and silver uniform of the SS, booted, spurred, heavily bemedalled, and surrounded by guards in similar livery. The very air around them was dense with the frequency of the Nazi salute, hand and arm shot stiffly forwards and upwards to the sharply barked sound of "Heil Hitler!"—something that Ribbentrop had already openly practised both around London, in Durham Cathedral, at Lord Londonderry's country house parties.

Sherman was horrified—and deeply fearful. So fearful indeed, that he could no longer perform the sexual act of intercourse. He had been married no more than five days.

Jeanne, on the other hand, was overcome with excitement, she was quite literally enthralled. The grandeur in which Jeanne now found herself so comfortably installed she casually accepted as "my absolute due . . . I've always done so much for the darlin" boy Joachim!" as she later exclaimed incessantly, merrily to captive audiences. Intoxicated by the headiness of the atmosphere, triumphantly, Jeanne did not hesitate to wrap her arm through Ribbentrop's.

But Jeanne had miscalculated her new husband's reaction to the atmosphere in the castle. Sherman was horrified. He was also very frightened and shocked by the realisation that his new wife was so conspicuously an admirer of Hitler and the Nazi regime. Slowly it dawned on the hapless Sherman that he had been irreversibly trapped and the object of shrewdly calculated seduction. He now took a momentous decision. Taking to his feet he ran away from Schloss Sonnenburg, from Ribbentrop, from Jeanne, from the stormtroopers. Within hours the young man had been "recaptured" and returned to the schloss. Motor bicycles mounted by soldiers had been sent put in hot pursuit, and Sherman was unable to flee the nightmare in which he had been unknowingly engulfed.

Even more triumphantly, Jeanne returned with Sherman to their London house in Kensington. She discovered that she was pregnant, a baby due in April 1939. And she boasted to her circle of admirers of "Shermie's runnin' away durin' OUR honeymoon, God dammit, and I quickly got him back, ha! ha! He wont be doin' that again in a hurry, I'm makin' pretty damn sure, frightfully amusin' as it was at the time." Jeanne sighed as she sniffed delicately into the finest of linen handkerchiefs, heavily bordered with antique lace.

In April 1939 a baby girl, Julia Maria Cristina Mildred Stonor was born in the same clinic, 27 Welbeck Street, which Jeanne had attended some two years previously for quite another operation. Some two weeks later, carried in the arms of a newly-acquired nanny—"Flicky", the *sage-femme* Sister Gertrude Flick, "would not arrive from Loch Ness until 1940—Julia was taken by Sherman to the London Oratory to be christened. Jeanne declined to be present—"It is simply, quite simply NOT DONE in upper-class Cartholic circles!" she had announced grandly to her husband. But Jeanne could afford to be triumphant as she had used all the powers of her habitually seductive flattery, to persuade Maria Cristina to be my god-mother.

The following day, christening photographs of the baby in Maria Cristina's arms appeared in *The Times*. Handsome commanding, statuesquely tall, the sapphire-blue-eyed Infanta's hat, the height of fashion, is of a blue bird ascending from a cloud of tulle perched on top of her very blonde hair.

But Jeanne's triumph in stage-managing this proved to be a serious miscalculation. It simply never occurred to her that Maria Cristina (to whom Jeanne always insisted on curtsying, even when at the height of her blackmail campaign against the princess) took her duties as Julia's godmother extremely seriously and throughout her own long life. To Jeanne's horror, Maria Cristina also insisted on giving me proper gifts of attractive, and antique jewellery, which she had personally chosen and taken from her own collection.

Less of a problem were the quiescent godfathers whom Jeanne had hand-picked from her unique collection of "my darlin" old beaux, ole!", although the delicately-boned and gentle Australian millionaire and Fleet Air Arm fighter pilot, Lebbeus Hordern, persisted in loyalty to his new godchild. However, he was in marked contrast to the half-Austrian, Alaric Russell, an Old Etonian with a raucous laugh, the rumbustious son of Sir Odo Russell, the colourful British ambassador.

Aunt Julie, driven as usual by the minuscule Busby in her antique

Morris, attended the christening of Sherman's new daughter in the font of the London Oratory. She was less than amused by the seeming array of Jeanne's former lovers acting as godfathers, she was distressed too for Sherman, outflanked already by the many imperious decisions taken over his head by Jeanne—she most conspicuous by her absence from the baptism.

Mildred was not in England to see the first of her grandchildren. She had already moved to America after deciding finally that living any longer by herself in England, at Stonor Park, was far too lonely, too sad-making. Jeanne's much-vaunted threat of revenge had already become a reality and now she determined that Sherman would seldom, if ever, see his mother.

Mildred had left Ralph installed dangerously close to Assendon Lodge on her estate of Bosmore—a fact of considerable convenience, unbeknownst to Mildred, to Jeanne in the early days of 1939. Sherman's new wife bided her time, now raging that Stonor Park itself was about to be war-requisitioned by the prestigious petrol company, National Benzole. This firm would occupy the still handsomely furnished, fully modernised, well-equipped house, stables and grounds until July 1945, some forty of the senior executive officers living in. "MY very own petrol blokes! Such darlin's—well, most of them that is," as Jeanne would come to exclaim happily.

But now installed in what Jeanne scathingly described as a "country cottage", the spacious Assendon Lodge, she turned her attention to Sherman's aunt Julie. As the elegant and perceptive old lady had feared, Jeanne needed her. Indeed, according to the protocol of the time, Jeanne needed the chaperonage of Julie in order to present her at the various country estates and outlying manors as the new and respectable wife of the Hon Sherman Stonor, son and heir to the 5th Lord Camoys. Without this vital escort Jeanne would not be able to achieve this social acceptability and vital status in the county.

Julie had no option but to show loyalty to her newly acquired family member. And she now had to make a conscious decision to ignore the rumours which continued as to Jeanne's murky past. But, unable to overlook Ralph's role in that past, Julie deeply mistrusted him and was concerned by the consequences of his actions since Ralph was entirely devoid of a moral conscience. That Mildred had allowed him to stay a stone's throw from Assendon Lodge also concerned Julie deeply.

By 1938 Sherman had already enlisted in the Territorial Army, commissioned as a Second Lieutenant in the Oxfordshire & Buckinghamshire Light Infantry, commonly known as the Green Jackets, their badge a silver trumpet. He was then posted away from Assendon and Stonor to Devon. On and off he would thus be away almost continuously through the tragic combat and evacuation of Dunkirk until 1944 when he was invalided out. He was just thirty-one.

Meanwhile, chauffeur-driven by the immaculate Busby, his silver buttons engraved with the d'Hautpoul cypher and coronet from Toulouse. Jeanne sat triumphant on the back seat next to the ramrod-tall, straight-backed Julie, acutely aware of how much she now needed the support of the old lady known throughout the neighbourhood as "the Markeys".

Aunt Julie's silver chignon was surmounted by a purple toque, her elegant clothes mulberry, mauve, or purple—the colours of mid-mourning with occasional touches of lavender—long, soft, suede gloves, champagne in colour, gently rolled to the elbow. Her toque was pinned with the jewels she had inherited from her grandmother, Julia, Lady Peel, the deep purple amethysts being an especial favourite. A Georgian-cut deep blue sapphire ring, the stone mounted in bright, white diamonds on a yellow gold band, matched the old lady's eyes. She carried a long, narrow blond-wood cane of spotted maplewood, the silver-gilt chased mount and plain ferule of great and simple elegance, designed by Fabergé and one of very many gifts from her beloved George.

Julie herself was acutely aware of the protocol which now had to be accorded her nephew's wife. Jeanne was also as acutely aware of the protection socially which this would bring her. The need was acute indeed: the whispers of Jeanne's "colourful, dangerous past" continued to travel. Furthermore, there was a newer, more ominous rumour as to Jeanne's fascination for the renewed orgies and sacrilegious "black masses" at the Hell Fire Club at the estate of close neighbours and old friends of Jeanne's, Sir John and Lady Helen Dashwood. Only a few miles from Assendon Lodge and Stonor, West Wycombe Park in all its conspicuous Palladian grandeur, considerably enhanced by Hell-Bags Helen and her vast Canadian grocery fortune, held great appeal for Jeanne. Besides, Johnny was quite an easy catch for another brief fling—whilst Hell-Bags, herself a great beauty and socialite, much photographed by Cecil Beaton, was heavily involved in her own tristes.

Remarkably undaunted by the scandal of these new rumours, Jeanne continued to hone her new strategy. Besides, she was in awe of Julie for, like her nephew Sherman, Julia's unassuming attitude to the servants, retainers and villagers brought her considerable respect and trust.

Jeanne observed all of this but with a dawning impatience. Carefully she calculated the advanced age of her newly-acquired aunt. Born in 1860, by 1939 Julie was a remarkably healthy seventy-nine years old, shrewd, serene, reserved, elegantly austere and highly observant. Additionally, as Jeanne quickly noticed, Julie was the soul of discretion with formal, old-fashioned manners. For the briefest of moments Jeanne contemplated emulating the old lady. But the sheer boredom of such a prospect overcame her. Anyhow, as Jeanne confided to her new daughter's royal godmother, Maria Cristina, she already found the countryside "most profoundly borin'. I'm simply bored to tears at Assendon Lodge"—Jeanne laughing pronounced this as "*Arse*nden"—let alone those other borin" bits of Shermie's estate, *Piss*-hill, Russells Water, Maidensgove and Christmas Common. Who in God's name ever invented such places?" But, as Julie had already noted with dismay, Jeanne excluded the Bosmore Estate from her litany of "bein' most frightfully BORED, goddamn it".

During this period Sherman was largely away from home on military duties. The virile grass-widower Ralph lived less than three miles away from Assendon Lodge, up a long, narrow road, bordered by beech woods leading to Fawley Bottom, and thence up a steep, loosely gravelled drive to the isolated, unkempt orange farmhouse of Bosmore. He had no hobbies other than the lightest of interests in carpentry, and an occasional foray with the puce-complexioned, heavily perspiring parish priest Father Seyres to the beehives kept in the wilderness of the gardens.

Jeanne was now the proud possessor of Mildred's eight-seater Chevrolet, in which she roared around the Stonor estate, driving in excited fits and starts. Over the summer and autumn of 1939, the car was continuously observed parked precariously outside the old barn at Bosmore. Julie could do nothing to prevent her nephew's coarse, casual sexual antics with Jeanne. She could do even less to forestall his exceptionally disagreeable jealousy of Sherman. For the lazy and egotistical Ralph had quite a capacity for spite—and revenge. He was never able to acknowledge, for example, his own good fortune at Mildred's generosity in rescuing him from bankruptcy, and now he realised that Jeanne was—and not for the last time—offering him a perfect path to vengeance.

Besides it was he, Ralph, who held the key to the title of Camoys so highly desired by Jeanne. Curiously revived at the very considerable cost of £15,000 in 1839, through the female entail, still known and recognised legally as a barony of writ, the title of Camoys (its meaning is "crooked nose" and was used by Chaucer to describe the Miller's daughter— *"with camoys nose and eyghen gray as glas"*) had been in abeyance for five hundred years. It was inherited through a female of the blood of the original Sir Thomas de Camoys, standard bearer to the English King Henry V at the Battle of Agincourt in 1415. And, as Jeanne subsequently discovered, after the birth of her first baby, Julia, in 1939, the same laws of inheritance were still applicable for a girl to inherit the renewed title of Camoys.

Ambition overriding discretion, as was her usual way, the exotically glamorously dressed, scent-drenched Jeanne ostentatiously threw herself into the welcoming arms of her father-in-law Ralph. Even the local paper, the *Henley Standard*, took note of the dances held at the town hall where "the Hon Mrs Sherman Stonor was escorted by her father-in-law, Lord Camoys". These *thé dansants* were the height of the Henley social scene, once coupled with extravagant celebration of the Henley Royal Regatta both in the exclusive Stewards' Enclosure and at the charming Phyllis Court Club on the far side of the Thames.

Julie's closest friends locally were the giraffe-tall Miss Bridges, the scarlet-haired sisters and owners of the best solicitors in Henley the Misses Cooper, her near cousins Gwendolyn and Marjorie, their actress neighbour Gladys Cooper (mother of the actor Robert Morley and grandmother of the critic Sheridan), the Pishill verger Phil Hall, even the florid-faced Father Seyres. They could do nothing but gaze on powerless while a certain Colonel "Bob" Lethbridge, another of Jeanne's dancing partners and another of "my darlin' OLD beaux", was swiftly relegated to what she always described scornfully as "the lower ranks, rank and file, quite redundant to my needs, *olé*!"

Her overwhelming ambition was for a title. To this end she adopted an ever-increasing ruthlessness. And the Second World War, despite her openly expressed admiration for *"El Jefe"* General Franco, and for Hitler's policies, played straight into her hands. In her instinctual, usually immediate grasp of circumstances, Jeanne habitually showed great versatility and a deeply cunning strategy, but she was never able to resist the compulsion to be the centre of attention, a dire need to boast, to name-drop, the cynosure of all eyes. Quite blatantly, once the essential social necessity of the neighbourhood calling with Aunt Julie was safely accomplished—all those heavily engraved cards left upon grand hallway silver plates—Jeanne dropped her guard. Inextricably involved with the cavalier 5th Baron Camoys, she slowly, very slowly, changed her attitude, taking it upon herself to call on the old aunt at her own home at Turville Grange. Jeanne made it clear that she now no longer required such a frequency of calls at Assendon Lodge from Julie.

Julie was shocked at the speed of Jeanne's ever-increasing avarice and the manner in which she successfully wrested estate deeds and entails from the Ralph, still idle yet shortly to become a uniformed captain of the Home Guard and a member of the ARP representing Assendon and Bosmore. More shockingly to her, Julie now heard Jeanne increasingly refer flippantly to Ralph as "Pop-goes-the-Weasel". She called him this to his face even in front of servants. For once Ralph had the grace if not to blush, then to flush an extreme mauve at this blatantly sexual epithet as he clumsily cleared his throat in acute agitation. His reaction only caused gales of throaty laughter from his daughter-in-law, her long cigarette-holder spinning around with merriment.

Not only did Jeanne have well-laid plans for Ralph Camoys, she also had a new plan for "the Markeys", but she would have a further ten years to wait before its successful execution. Meanwhile, with consummate ease of strategy, she merely bided her time. There were, after all, many another ruse to accomplish meantime. After all, Jeanne was a highly spirited woman of quite remarkable energy, tirelessly driven by ruthless, pitiless ambition, and a consummate greed for the immediate acquisition of beautiful, priceless gems, and glitteringly expensive jewellery.

At Turville Grange, Jeanne had early on set her sights with a magpie intensity not only on the old lady's own unique and inherited collection, but even more upon the acquisition, by any means, of her magnificent diamond tiara, the 1891 wedding gift of the Prince and Princess of Wales. She further coveted Julie's unique collection of Fabergé eggs.

Entirely to Jeanne's own convenience, the Marquise d'Hautpoul would, conveniently, die at home at the grange in February 1950. There would be no autopsy, nor inquest—only a royal funeral and Requiem Mass of considerable grandeur within the cold, sweating beige plaster walls of the chapel of the Holy Trinity at Stonor Park.

A relatively small sum, extra to the administrators of the dead person's estate, was discreetly requested for an inexpensive, morose granite headstone duly supplied at the behest of the deeply sorrowing the Hon Mrs

Sherman Stonor. Even the undertakers were quite undone by her over-whelming charm, finding themselves semi-drowned in the instant intoxication of her expensive, alluring French perfume.

*

In 1839, there had been great celebrations at Stonor over Queen Victoria's revival of the title of Camoys. Quite unaware of its huge cost, an innocent tenant had composed a paean of praise in the form of a whimsy poem:

> *Let all the tenants of my Lord Camoys*
> *On this day tune their hearts to mirth and joys,*
> *Rejoicing that to him, a man of merit,*
> *Descends the title he does now inherit.*
> *Come, friends of freedom, hail this joyous day*
> *And join with me in wishing that he may*
> *Make all that envy him his present honour*
> *Opposition find from all the house of Stonor*
> *Yes, may his tenants 'midst their other joys*
> *Say: "Bless the Queen which made him Lord Camoys!"*

From 1938 onwards Jeanne habitually hummed this ditty to herself as she gazed, with increasing frequently into her long wall mirror. She was filled with complacently at her singular perfection of figure, her perfection of complexion, her perfection of pedigree reflected so flatteringly in the glass of the gilded mirror.

Humming happily, reflectively Jeanne transposed the "Lord" of the Camoys ditty to that of the "Lady". Not only did she have vivid images of herself in Julie d'Hautpoul's diamond tiara but, very early on in marriage to Sherman, she awarded the title of "Lady Camoys" to her person, quite oblivious to the embarrassment that other persons in smart hotels heard this announcement more than clearly. That both Lord and Lady Camoys—Mildred and Ralph—were alive and would live on until the Sixties, phased Jeanne not in the slightest.

Jeanne saw herself quite simply, as another deeply wronged Jeanne, the 15th-century illegitimate daughter of William de la Pole, Duke of Suffolk, and the beautiful Jacqueline, Countess of Hainault, Holland and Zealand, an early ancestor of Sherman's. Though, as it later transpired, unlike

Jeanne Stonor's own parents, the Duke and his Countess were secretly married—despite the Duke's subsequent cruel repudiation of his daughter. Nevertheless, after her mother's premature death in 1436, the earlier Jeanne came to live with her ducal father at Ewelme from the age of seven. It was the highly influential, deeply political and powerful Duke of Suffolk, a significant powerbroker who gave his daughter in marriage to Sir Thomas Stonor in the year 1445. Jeanne Stonor, herself the illegitimate daughter of aristocratic grandees saw an exact parallel to her own situation.

The bastard daughter of Frances Stourton and Don Pedro de Zulueta y Mugaburu finally became Baroness Camoys, but not until 1968 after the death of Ralph, 5th Baron Camoys, in Newport. Until the last year of her life, 1986-1987, Jeanne had come to believe, using all the power of Sherman's money, that she was invincible and that she had taken her revenge on one and all of her enemies. The most delusory, the most vivid vanity finally overwhelmed this highly intelligent, most convincing, most scheming of beautiful women. *"Mirror, mirror on the wall—who is the fairest of them all . . . ?"*

Society Girl As Secretary

By Our Secret Reporter

MISS JEANNE STOURTON, one of Society's loveliest girls, has been appointed social secretary to ex-Barbara Hutton, now the Countess Reventlow.

She once worked in a London store selling cosmetics, and confessed she enjoyed the long hours.

Further exclusive news by the Secret Reporter on Page 13.

ON THE STEPS OF THE RITZ

The Hon. Mrs. Sherman Stonor, formerly Miss Jeanne Stourton, married Lord Camoys' son and heir in 1938. She is the youngest daughter of the Hon. Mrs. Herbert Stourton, a daughter of Viscount Southwell. She is seen leaving the Ritz after lunch with Mrs. Lebbeus Hordern, who, before her marriage in May, was Miss Ursula Gibbons, daughter of the late Sir Walter Gibbons, and of Doris, Lady Orr-Lewis

Jeanne enters London's high society in the 1930s.

THE COMMITTEE OF THE QUEEN MARY'S HOSPITAL MATINEE

... ... Committee took place at Lady Hambleden's town house in Belgrave Square. ... ... Lady Patricia Herbert. In this group are Mrs. Raymond Massey, Lady ... Mrs. John Gordenough, Miss Jan Stourton, Miss Denise Behar, Miss Bathivala, and Lady Hambleden (seated). Lady Hambleden is acting as chief programme seller

LIFE ON THE LIDO AND
BIARRITZ SUN BATHERS

IN THE VENETIAN SUNSHINE

A group taken on the Excelsior Palace Hotel's private beach at the Lido. Included here are: Mr. Henry Channon, Lord Rosse, Sir Richard Sykes, Lord Weymouth, Mr. Hubert Duggan, Mr. Colin Davidson, and Lady Weymouth. Lord Rosse called in at this Venetian sun-trap after visiting Salzburg. Sir Richard Sykes owns Sledmere, where so many aristocrats of the equine world are born, and Mr. Duggan is Lady Curzon of Kedleston's son. Lady Weymouth always looks ravishingly pretty, whether sunburnt, as at present, or not

ANOTHER LIDOITE: THE HON. MRS. FITZGERALD

MR. ERIC HATRY, MISS JEANNE STOURTON, AND LADY ILLINGWORTH

THE TATLER

THE HON. RALPH STONOR AND MISS JEANNE STOURTON

THE TATLER

Arthur Owen

MISS JEANNE STOURTON, MISS KATHERINE HORLICK, AND LADY BRIDGET POULETT AT A RECENT COCKTAIL PARTY

It was at the one given by Mrs. Sieff and Mrs. Dudley Ward at Sussex Place last week as a little "thank you" to all those who helped to make the recent Midnight Ballet a success. Lady Bridgett Poulett is Lord Poulett's sister, and Miss Katherine Horlick is a daughter of Colonel and Mrs. Jimmy Horlick

MISS ELIZABETH BURBURY AND MISS JEANNE STOURTON

At the Children's Ball at the Hyde Park Hotel, which was in aid of the Waifs and Strays Society. Miss Jeanne Stourton, who represented a Gainsborough picture, won the first prize for the best costume

Miss Stourton's New Film Job

MISS JEANNE STOURTON has been given a year's contract on the executive side of British Unity Pictures "I hope to go with the company to Pa in the New Year," she said to-day. "Recently I did several days' work an extra at Denham, but I could not stand

THE HON. DAVID RHYS AND MISS
JEANNE STOURTON

At the Eton Ball at the Dorchester in Eton and Harrow match week. The Hon. David Rhys is a son of Lord Dynevor and married Lady Anne Wellesley last March

A SOCIETY SITTING IN SCOTLAND

Lord Southwell's niece, Miss Jeanne Stourton, having her head sculpted by Miss Ursula Constable-Maxwell, the Hon. Bernard and Mrs. Constable-Maxwell's clever daughter, who has her own studio at their Inverness-shire home, Fairlie House, Beanly. The resemblance between Miss Jeanne Stourton and Mrs. Charles Sweeny has often been noted. There is no blood relationship, but there is now a special link between them, for the Hon. Mrs. Stourton's daughter is one of little Miss Frances Helen Sweeny's godparents

MISS JEANNE STOURTON

MISS VIVIEN ST. GEORGE

Major and the Hon. Mrs. Stourton is generally to be seen about with and Lady Baskett Prosett. Energy and enterprise are characteristics of Miss Vivien St. George, whose portrait by Doris Zinkeisen hangs in this married on June 7 to Mr. A. F. Stanley-Clarke, Captain and Mrs. right has an original mind and likes to think things out needs no introduction as author, lyric writer, and super-humorist

Edith Bagnold.

Dorothy Wilding

EDITH BAGNOLD (LADY JONES)

Edith Bagnold, the author of "National Velvet," is, in private life, the wife of Sir Roderick Jones. Her new book, "Family Life," will appear at the end of this year

Richard Sykes and companions.

SIR RICHARD SYKES (ON LEFT) AND LADY LETTICE COTTERELL

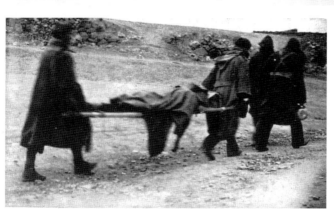

(Left) Picture from The Times showing the body of Dick Sheepshanks being carried away in Spain, New Year's Eve, 1937.

(Below left) Seating plan for dinner at Sir Roderick Jones's home.

(Below) Hitler's foreign minister and ambassador to London, Count Joachim von Ribbentrop.

29 HYDE PARK GATE, S.W.7.

April 8, 1920.

WINDOW.

Lady Jones.

Herr von Ribbentrop.	The American Ambassador.
The Countess of Carlisle.	Lady Camrose.
Comte de Gaillard de la Valdène.	General Freyberg.
Miss Jeanne Stourton.	Count Durkheim.
Lord Camrose.	Mrs. Freyberg.
Comtesse de Gaillard de la Valdène.	The German Ambassador.
	The Hon. Mrs. Bingham.

Sir Roderick Jones.

ENTRANCE.   **FIREPLACE.**

En route for America, 1920s, Ralph and Mildred with (L-R) Noreen, Nadine & Sherman.

*(Above) Passenger list for the S. S.
Leviathan including Mildred, Ralph
and their children and servants.*

*(Right) Mildred with her children
Nadine, Sherman & Noreen,
Newport, Rhode Island, c. 1925.*

The young Jeanne Stourton.

MAYFAIR AT THE COCOANUT GROVE

Above, from right to left, are : Mlle. Sylvia Régis de Oliveira, daughter of the Brazilian Ambassador ; Sir Austen Chamberlain's recently married daughter, Mrs. Terence Maxwell ; Mr. Angus Malcolm, Mlle. German-Ribon, whose father is Bolivian Minister ; Miss Jeanne Stourton, Sir R. Sykes and Mr. Eric Harry. Also at the Cocoanut Grove, London's new " bottle-party " rendezvous, were Mr. Whitney Straight and his fiancée. Mr. Straight is related to Golden Miller's owner

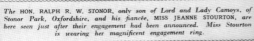

The HON. RALPH R. W. STONOR, only son of Lord and Lady Camoys, of Stonor Park, Oxfordshire, and his fiancée, MISS JEANNE STOURTON, are here seen just after their engagement had been announced. Miss Stourton is wearing her magnificent engagement ring.

The engagement of MISS JEANNE STOURTON, daughter of the late Major Herbert Stourton, and of the Hon. Mrs. Stourton, to the Hon. Ralph Stonor has been announced. Miss Stourton is very well known in society.

TUNBRIDGE.

Three of the little trainbearers who helped to carry the train of ivory satin heavily embroidered in pearls and diamanté.

Sherman and Jeanne on their wedding day
at the London Oratory, July 14, 1938.

Capt. Lord Camoys
Sixty-one-year-old peer of the realm is the
administrative officer of "E" Coy.

Ralph Stonor.

*Julia Stonor with her husband "Fernan",
Marquis d'Hautpoul,
at Turville Grange, 1891.*

*Julia Stonor, the Marquise d'Hautpoul,
formerly the fiancée of King George V
when Duke of York, 1880s.*

The Infanta Maria Cristina.

Picture feature in The Tatler on Jeanne at Assendon Lodge, 1939.

(Top) Sir Harry Stonor; (above) Sir "Jock" Balfour; (right) Archbishop David Mathew, former Chaplain General to the British Forces, with his brother Gervaise, Dominican monk and Byzantine expert; (far right) Francis Stonor.

Jeanne with Julia in a pram, with nanny and dogs, one called Ruby, 1940.

Ruby Heath, housekeeper at Assendon Lodge and Stonor Park.

Nanny Kathleen Cooper at Assendon Lodge with Julia, 1942.

Sherman with Julia in an American cart, a present from Mildred, 1942.

A typical shooting party at Stonor (L-R): tycoon Lord Balfour of Inchyra, Sherman (who had given up shooting), Colonel "Jack" Rutherford (Master Vintner and wine merchant), David Colville (senior director of Rothschilds), Jeanne, Sir Miles Thomas (MD BOAC), Major Eddie Tyler (cousin and MD of stockbrokers), Freddie Cockburn (of Cockburn's Port).

Stonor on the cover of a Catholic history by Evelyn Waugh – the Jesuit Edmund Campion had his illicit printing press at the house where he printed his 'Ten Reasons for Being a Catholic' in 1581 which he distributed around the Oxford churches and colleges.

Views of Stonor Chapel: (left) the interior, reconstructed around 1800; (right) a pagan stone set in the foundations testifies to the chapel's Saxon origins

Views of the house and gardens of Stonor.

Jeanne in the uniform of commandant in the St John's Ambulance Brigade with war medals.

18

'Gothic is In, Roman is Quite Out'

All through the war Aunt Julia came every Sunday to Mass at the chapel at Stonor and on the special feasts of the Madonna, martyrs and saints. Since her chauffeur Busby was a Protestant, he was made to wait outside on the gravel standing by the two round, clipped box bushes. This hour of visit from my aunt was a weekly treat that made my heart beat with happy expectation.

Once inside the damp chapel, Aunt Julia would turn around from the well of the linoleum-covered floor to gaze up at the tribune. Slowly, leaning slightly on a tall, elegant, gold-topped rosewood cane, she beckoned me down from my perch up at Mama's side to kneel beside her. I would bound down the steep brick stairs and through the gaunt porch to join Julia where she knelt, sternly upright, in the high elm-wood bench to the right-hand side of the green marble altar.

Catching my breath in the freezing cold I marvelled at God's Great Table and the drab colour scheme of beige and kitchen-green set against a darker brown background, with huge patches of damp that made the chapel ceiling and walls glisten with condensation and moisture. A cracked, rusting iron radiator slowly dripped rusted cold droplets of water onto the floor near Aunt Julia's feet. A romantically solemn Sacred Heart of Jesus, his long pageboy locks remarkably like Mama's, peered down at the congregation from a painted glass window above the high altar. The white-draped robes of this Sacred Heart were as magical to me as were the family vestments for the various Feasts.

These were kept carefully in long drawers in the sacristy which my great-grandfather, Bangpa-Pop's pop "Old Tome Camoys", had "banged onto the back of the chapel". They were made from rich damasks, silks, silk moiré, velvet and cloths of gold and silver. They were all richly embroidered, with embossed gold crosses, and thick satin linings. The most dramatic vestment, a dashing scarlet silk moiré, was used for feasts of the martyrs—and "Slaughtered Virgins" as my mother would add firmly.

"All these Virgins are almost as much of a crashin' bore as your Aunt Gytha with her 'stigma' thing," she continued. "That martyrs' Coliseum in Rome reminds me of the knacker's yard at Benson. Serves all those virgins right if they did get butchered by the *Romanos*. Cuts no ice with me," she chortled. "I've exempted myself at the Vaticano, *olé!*"

But she never said this in front of Aunt Julia.

The plaster angels, their chipped gold paint flaking off, hung onto the ceiling joists above the Sacred Heart and the stern-faced St Gregory in the tribune window. They looked peculiarly cold, if not frozen.

Aunt Julia had a high fur collar to her long overcoat, and long cream suede gloves tightly buttoned over her narrow hands and wrists. I could see my breath condensing in the frost of the chapel as she removed her right glove and held my hand in hers.

Father Seyres raised both his hands high into the air, standing with his back to the congregation. Aunt Julia leant down towards me to share her prayer book. At the altar, it seemed to me that Father Seyres—or "Old André Cereal" as Mama preferred to call her confessor—was holding an outsize spoon-and-fork, as this was exactly how the coloured illustration in my tribune prayer book looked. I wondered whether my mother had lent them to him from the servants' hall up at the Park.

Aunt Julia's own leather prayer book was bound in gold-tooled brown morocco, black printed with scarlet capitals on thin, cream India paper, with six scarlet silk markers. Out of her bag also came a volume of Additional Devotions, half-bound in blue cloth, with an ivory spine. These were prayers to be said after communion. Young as I was, I knew this was when she prayed for the baby girl who had died the day that she was born: March 9, 1892.

Dutifully, I returned to Mama's side in the tribune when Mass ended and the congregation started filing out. I told her about the baby.

"And a damn good thing too," Mama said sharply when she was sure Aunt Julia was out of earshot. "I don't need anyone else, yet another body, interferin' with my rights." She took a quick sip from the silver hip flask buried deep inside her black crocodile Cartier bag.

It was at moments like these that the Sacred Heart, who had a greenish halo, looked sadder. And St Gregory looked even crosser at the back of the tribune. But his bishop's robes were that much brighter than those of the Sacred Heart of Jesus, and he carried a small gold temple in his hands.

I looked at Mama in surprise at her outburst over an innocent life extinguished so early.

Crisply she commanded: "Make an immediate Act of Contrition to make amends for all your impure thoughts and sheer rudeness to your mother." So saying she gave me a sharp pinch, and tweaked the elastic of the Spanish black veil beneath my chin. "You're nothin' more than a soundin' brass, and piece of nonsense to boot."

Mama saw the tears welling in my eyes and took a well-aimed kick at my shins. Too late I tried to avoid her well-shod foot.

"You can get goin' down on your knees, child, once that Busby has removed your Aunt Julia," hissed Mama. "And I'm waitin' to hear your prayers of penance and ejaculation. You can stop when I tell you," commanded Mama again, locking me firmly into the now empty chapel. "I'm orf to see the foreman of the National Benzole Petroleum Company to make sure he and his minions clean all those sordid, squalid ink spots orf the Long Gallery floor pretty pronto, *olé!*"

She immediately drove off in the company of Uncle Eric St Johnston, now out of police uniform and dressed in his mufti Prince of Wales check knickerbockers. I was left alone, praying as hard as I could in the shivering cold of the silent chapel. I wrapped my fingers around the red coral rosary with its silver crucifix which Aunt Julia had given to me. I clutched onto it hard for relief from the fear I felt at being left entirely on my own. My breath made wreaths of steam in the air above the bench where I had knelt with my Aunt. I plunged into the Sorrowful Mysteries, and made endless Acts of Contrition, but it failed to bring Mama back very soon.

When she finally returned from her expedition to see the Benzole foreman (who'd "spilt the ink, and practically spilt the beans too, goddamn it") Mama gave me a stinging slap for wetting my knickers when courage ultimately and completely failed me.

"Such a miserable little cowardly custard," she said scathingly. "You're to pay absolutely no attention to the brat, Eric dear," she ordered my Uncle. Mama did not approve of her beau showing kindness towards me.

I had eagerly watched the only light in the chapel, pink paraffin spluttering in what looked to me like a silver-gilt kettle. It hung just in front of the green and white marble altar embossed with the Lamb of God, while

I waited and prayed for hope. Now Mama lowered the kettle on its three wires and lit another cigarette from its sacred eternal flame.

"Hold on hard, Eric darlin' boy," she suddenly shouted, forcing him to steady the holy kettle. "That's the sanctuary lamp, far too heavy for my delicate hands. That light is ever so precious, quite sacrosanct. Guardin' the Blessed Sacrament you know, and must be kept lit day and night." But Mama's own contraband cigarettes seemed the more sacrosanct, taking immediate precedence.

Uncle Eric was a little perplexed by this behaviour.

"Don't you dare say a word to anyone," Mama hissed as she snatched me by the shoulder, jerking me down the chapel aisle and marching me out of the thick black door and down the stone steps onto the gravel.

My teeth chattered with the cold, and fear made me sweat through my Viyella vest. I longed for Sundays and the special church feast days known as holidays of obligation so that I could kneel besides Aunt Julia and feel her warm hand in mine in comforting proximity. Occasionally she would turn in her stately way to gaze up at the tribune whenever Mama produced her usual roster of extraordinary noises. Others in the congregation would take quick peeps with trepidation.

One particular Sunday, this noise accompanied by the jangling of gold bracelets hung with medals and dangling charms, became all the louder as Mama contrived to trip down the steep crumbling, old brick stairs. She descended from the tribune into the porch with a huge clatter and a cascade of Spanish expletives.

Picking herself up from the hard flagstones, Mama glared at the congregation on either side of the chapel as she swept majestically up the aisle. No a soul stirred as she ensured that she, and she alone, arrived first at the altar rails to receive communion.

"I'm just gettin' rid of some old phlegm," my mother announced, coughing deeply as she knelt down at the Gothic Revival altar gates. "Catarrah as well," she added.

Two altar boys in white lace cotters and black cassocks over their scuffed shoes and grey shorts tinkled a small bell. One was from the Thomas family of eleven (who lived crammed into a dingy cottage up Maidensgrove Lane), the other a twin son of night prayers Uncle Bob Lethbridge, a retired colonel from the Army Catering Corps.

Father Seyres, mauve-faced, advanced down the marble altar steps to the railings, a large gold chalice set with the Stonor rubies in his hands. As

Mama walked away, first in line as always, the congregation one by one meekly followed the upright figure of Aunt Julia to kneel in front of priest and the server boy holding a silver paten beneath their chins. In the distance, on the strict orders of Mama, the organist struck up *Jerusalem* on the harmonium.

Bangpa-Pop would seldom come to Mass as he was far too busy bee-keeping. "Really poor old Pop-goes-the-Weasel is hardly up to it these tedious days. He is quite done in by our hop at Henley Town Hall!" explained Mama.

"You know how it is these days with such frightfully exactin' duties fire-fightin' for the ARP, and supervisin' the Home Guard on manoeuvres at Bix Bottom. What's more all those hives have given the Old Boy a bee in his bonnet, and where else I wonder," she laughed merrily. "Too damn bad what the congregation thinks. As if I am in the slightest bit interested. Too effin' annoyin' if it does get back to that divine Cardinal Spellman, sittin' pretty in New York," she added as she wound the first two forefingers of her bejewelled hands around one another, pointing them sharply towards the sky. " 'Frankly-Frank', old Spellman you know, and I are just like that," she explained, twisting two fingers extravagantly. "God bless His Eminence," she added, making another genuflection, dropping to the floor on one knee, and kissing the air in lieu of the Cardinal's hand. " We're frequently on the blower to one another, and I've made it perfectly clear as to how the field stands here." She sniffed with contempt. "The 5th Baron Camoys has Special Interests to look after in this neck of the woods. All those parts and particles have got to be kept well-oiled durin' the Emergency. I've seen to that," she ended triumphantly. "Mortal Sin is absolutely out, unless it comes to the monstrous behaviour of that brat of Sherman's, the abominable Julia," said Mama as an afterthought, narrowing her eyes at me.

Bangpa-Pop kept himself very busy indeed on Sundays with his bees and beehive activities until lunchtime came round at Assendon Lodge. As usual with most of his family, he didn't seem to enjoy seeing Aunt Julia and avoided her as much as possible. But Aunt Julia made me feel full of happiness and warmth. Her cornflower blue eyes were filled with kindness while Mama's eyes were even blacker than the grapes Mr White the Plymouth Brethren gardener grew in the Stonor greenhouses. Bangpa-Pop's own pink-rimmed eyes were dark brown, like deep puddles of muddy water and the stagnant dew-pond sulking up the back drive hidden behind the house at Stonor. And Father Seyres' eyes were a kindly, rheumy blue, bobbing above his florid cheeks.

"André Cereal looks most frightfully constipaggers to me," snorted Mama after one of her quick confessions held behind closed doors in the Yellow Drawing Room at Assendon Lodge. "Penance and an Act of Contrition indeed," she said furiously, drawing deeply on the cigarette which had accompanied her. "Never heard such rubbish. Father Cereal can certainly stuff all of that up. Does he forget who and what I am?"

Making a beeline for the telephone, Mama shouted over her shoulder: "And I'm callin' my Ordinary. That darlin' Cardinal Hinsley. He'll sort him out and all the other Sacred Heart boys to boot." Tears of rage started down her rouged cheeks, dragging smudges of mascara with them. "Excommunication is hardly good enough for such friggin' farts, French frogs, beekeeper or no beekeeper and just what does André Cereal think he is up to with that fusty, musty, dusty house-keeper of his, Miss Broslem?" she demanded menacingly in between hurling instructions down the telephone. "Of course, darlin' boy, I do have my own *très distingué* aristo French blood from that divine Château Serrant, just hangin' over the edge of the Loire—you must come and stay after this damn nuisance war has gorne before. And gorne OUR way," she continued silkily.

Mama persuaded Bangpa-Pop to accompany her to the sacristy, the ugly brick outhouse which had been slung onto the back of the chapel immediately behind two khaki painted Gothic Revival doors which led nowhere in particular, one on either side of the over-high green marble altar.

"Bloody-awful taste in paint my mother-in-law had," said Mama scornfully. "The colour of ripe shit, just like old Mildew Mildred herself, ha, ha!" she hissed mockingly. "Wartime camouflage, warpaint and all that other tommy-rot of hers," she continued mockingly, poking a sharp red nail into Bangpa-Pop's well-padded ribs.

He wriggled and guffawed uneasily.

"Not that your grandfather is much of a practisin' Cartholic these days," my mother giggled to me as she showed him how to lay out the vestments for the next service. "Good practice habits for our next Requiem," she explained. "Which, all things considered, should be quite soon," she added thoughtfully as she folded the satin-lined black moiré silk vestment back onto the sacristy table. "Take another lesson from me, Julia Stonor, and make sure all the points of this cassock meet as they should so you get on with it by yourself next time, you idle borin' brat of Sherman's!" Mama winked at Bangpa-Pop as she pinched my thigh beneath the long table-cloth. "As it is, you're only here under sufferance and strictly incognito, child," Mama reminded me sharply. "And kindly keep all that wind, phletus and flatulence to yourself for a change, Pop old boy," she continued as Bangpa-Pop belched while leaning over to see what she was doing deep in the folds of the vestments. "And kindly desist from borin' me to tears again with tales of darlin' Frank Spellman and his St Patrick's Cathedral in New York. I'm not in the slightest bit interested in the Irish-American connection, let alone the Irish themselves. Common as muck," she scoffed. "Not a drop of Irish blood myself, come to think of it."

But, I immediately piped up, what about Mama's connection with Castle Mattress and Tipperary, and her own mother, Granny "Feckless Fanny" Stourton?

"Don't you dare speak out of turn!" came the cross reply accompanied by a stinging slap and a chunk of hair pulled for good measure.

The sumptuous vestments up at the Park always amazed me. Neatly arranged and layered, they lay in a long narrow oak clothes press, drawers filled with antique French, Italian and Spanish cloths of silver, cloths of gold, roses and garlands of flowers embroidered over them. The more ordinary white silks interspersed these best vestments, and silk damasks, and drawer upon drawer revealed yet more in a rainbow of velvets and silks.

Aunt Julia had explained them all very carefully to me. "Roman styled are these precious vestments, Julia dear. The white is for Virgins and Saints, the scarlet is for Martyrs—all Saints you know," she said gently in answer to my eager questions.

I knew Mama was one of the latter because she had always told me—"I am, of course, an Absolute Saint myself"—and I believed everything that my mother so magically, sometimes rather mysteriously, said. Most especially when it referred to herself. Aunt Julia did not seem quite as certain about this as I was. She gave a small sigh, like Ruby.

"Gothic," said Mama firmly, reviewing the vestments. "Gothic is IN, and Roman is quite OUT. Mind you, the Vatican is IN too, ha, ha!" She pushed her fingers firmly into Bangpa-Pop's ribs again.

I was a little worried at this pronouncement of Mama's and ventured that I so much preferred the more beautiful Roman vestments. The fashionable Gothic ones reminded me of the ghosts which I heard and sometimes saw in the night. But Mama's tastes were cast-iron. Even her chapel kneeler, her pre-dieu, was Gothic Revival.

"Very valuable to boot," she stated firmly. "Your own taste is exactly as I would have expected Julia dear, really rubbish. Roman, indeed!" She sighed. "Anyhow, in my own appallin' poverty I have to realise these valuable assets. I'm changin' the borin' old, dowdy Roman vestments to new Gothic NYLON in the nearest future. My absurd demi-sister Gytha, the old Marquesa herself, has got a little nun up the sleeve of her dowdy old cardigan who can run these things up in a nice synthetic in a matter of minutes." She reflected a minute, puffing smoke circles in front of her towards Bangpa-Pop. "That is, when they are orf their knees from rosary beads and religious mania," she scoffed and sniffed back the smoke rings as they hovered in the cold haze of the Sacristy.

Aunt Julia had explained that the purple and black vestments were for mourning. I knew this already because my mother had so many Requiem Masses said. On these most frequent of occasions, the vestments were of blackest velvet, embroidered and picked out with large crosses in cloth-of-gold braid. Arranged round the head and foot of the coffin, peched on a curious arrangement of trestles, were tall catafalque candles of thick orange tallow. The coffin itself was sometimes, in the case of "aristo grandees, *olé*!" covered with a purple cloth and sometimes not.

"Just had the box run up for the occasion by our head carpenter Stanley West in his less randy moments," explained Mama, laughingly. "Saves a bob or two durin' all the rationin'," she continued with a knowing wink. "I'm most frightfully keen on our divine undertakers. They do me quite a bargain price, Special Offer too!' my mother winked again. "We're most frightfully close, and all of that. So very essential these delicate days." Once again Mama wound her forefingers around one another, and gesticulated towards the sky.

"But all these candles at least should be made of precious beeswax, Jeanne Mary dear," exclaimed Aunt Julia.

But Mama only laughed uproariously. "I've got a job lot, and somewhat more than my usual bargain from Mr Affia. Anyhow, damn it, I'm savin' up out of the First Collection. There's not much comin' in from the Second Collection these tedious war days, *olé!*"

One of the most important days in the Catholic Calendar, the Feast of the Sacred Heart merited a very special vestment: white silk damask with a fat red heart in raised stump-work on a brilliant background of scarlet satin, rays of lightning in bright yellow gold, spinning out in a Catherine wheel cascade of fireworks. It was quite my favourite, and matched an equally magnificent, flowing cope used for Benediction while the orange-haired Miss Broslem sang down from the tribune as she thumped laboriously and triumphantly away at the harmonium. Even more did I like the intoxicating sandalwood incense which one of the village boy servers, dressed in white cotter and starched lace, swung violently around in a vessel shaped like a silver ship.

Inhaling the thick smoke one time, I suddenly felt as if I had a religious experience high in the tribune. Knowing this would please Mama, I whispered this in her ear.

"Don't talk such damn ridiculous rubbish, you stupid child," she snorted with indignation. "A few more of my ejaculations won't go amiss. High time you were down on your knees again and into the Litanies of the Saints. They could teach you a thing or two about your own Mortal, Deadly Sins. Now repeat after me the Ten Commandments, *muy pronto, olé!*"

The blue fumes of incense gave me a vision of Mama magically beautiful, perfume-drenched in a shining gold halo, her mouth bright scarlet, tinkling, coughing laughter pouring out in a constant stream of merriment. But, as Ruby Heath pointed out later: "All you've 'ad is an 'allucination, Doodo darling. Ever so nasty."

Aside from her duties on the harmonium, Miss Broslem was appointed the official sacristan who laid out all the vestments according to a special pattern in the sacristy.

"To save time gettin' in and out of the house," explained my mother, who was bored by her own sacristy chores with my grandfather. "Anyhow, it is high time Miss Broslem was laid out too," she laughed, winking again. "Fusty, musty and dusty Miss Broslem is much too close to Father André Cereal. And she smells of Irish stew."

I wondered what Mama could mean. Neither she nor Father Seyres seemed to like my mother. But they quite obviously liked Aunt Julia. And Papa, who sometimes came back from the war on leave.

After 1944, Papa also knelt upstairs in the tribune. He would be completely silent while Mama busily created her ceaseless chatter and clatter, banging all three of the communicating doors into the tribune, the alcove bedrooms and at the top of the brick stairs leading steeply up to the bell tower and down into the well of the chapel foyer. The small French pottery statue of St Anne, robed in blue and yellow, standing in her niche beneath a 14th-century blue-glass window with the Stonor coat of arms, shook worryingly to the door slams. Ancient dead bees in yet more ancient cobwebs lay at the saint's feet.

"Mother of Mary indeed and such a sweetie, but they can damn well stay there," said Mama, poking at a dead bee. "I've absolutely no time for dustin'," she announced, slamming the doors more vigorously. Brass handles and locks vibrated musically to Mama's ferocity.

Papa jumped in his seat and sighed heavily.

Though no one was allowed to talk during the service held at 9.30am each Sunday morning, Mama was clearly different. She talked all the way through Mass whenever she was inside the tribune, and not outside, and in the big alcove bedroom answering the telephone, or calling the visitors to get up in time for lunch. "The darlin' boys have a habit of sleepin' late, and I'm worried they might miss Sunday luncheon," explained my mother hurriedly.

The telephone tinkled and shrilled and rang without stopping. Mama found that her silver hip-flask fortified her from "these agonisin' draughts which bring on my migraines", as she further explained—and took a quick sip of Horse's Neck to renew her circulation as she sat sumptuously arrayed in sable or mink. Sometimes a family labrador wandered casually through the open door in the porch, making his way languidly up the aisle to the sanctuary itself. Then Father Seyres would turn around completely, looking up at Mama, an expression of crossness creasing his red face.

Halting the service mid-sentence, the priest would wait in indignant silence until my mother strolled down from her seat and fetched her "poggins". Much her favourites were the King Charles spaniels, which slept in chintz-lined wicker baskets in her summer and winter bedrooms.

"They have the Divine Right of Kings," declared Mama firmly as she sat one on her knees. Standing up, she leant over the tribune railings to make this pronouncement loudly to the astonished congregation, mid-Mass, crashing her gold bracelets together for greater emphasis.

*

Mama's royal dogs sat with Royalty and other glamorous guests on stiff Gothic Revival or Chippendale chairs for meals, mostly in the big dining-room and, more occasionally, with out-of-favour Guns and Uncles and sundry tutors in the nursery dining room. I was a little wary of the spikey shapes of the angular, upright, black-painted, gold-sprayed chairs. They looked angry, not unlike my mother with the spikey chin that stuck out like a spire whenever she was "put-out".

"I'm more wounded Julia, than crorss," said Mama, sighing. "And your best is certainly not good enough, you totally yawn-makin' tedious brat and bore." She yawned. "High time you said your night prayers again, even if it is only elevenses." She poured more golden liquid into a thick green glass.

Even with additional night prayers I couldn't succeed, try as hard as I might, in pleasing my mother. She invariably seemed less than satisfied with my efforts.

Yanking my hair as she spoke, my mother said again: "You, my child, should make far more use of the time which you already use so uselessly. Down on your knees in Perpetual Penance, makin' ejaculatory prayers in amends to me for all the agonisin' sufferin's you cause without ceasin'." Mama's voice rose. "Mortal Sin AGAIN! And, furthermore, you can begin with Commandment Number Three: Honour your Poor, Penniless Mother, who has Suffered such Agonies. My Gawd, and just look at what I have done for you, tiresome brat, so like your grandmother Mildew Mildred in character and looks. Just like your father too. *I* can hardly bear to look at you."

I was left bewildered. But then later Mama had said that I could have one of her dogs could be mine. I was very excited. And so, outside Assendon Lodge, in the kennels of the backyard, lived my beloved blonde labrador puppy, Flora.

Ruby gave me a small book, which she had bought at WH Smith in Henley on her day off. "It's from Crufts, Doodo darling, and it tells you all about dog training," she said, showing me the pictures.

Eagerly I started learning the commands of dog discipline and house-training. It all seemed quite like my own nursery training. The commands were quite peremptory and abrupt, and reminded me of Mama. I spent a lot of time with my puppy, soft, cuddly and kind.

Then, one terrible day, the wooden front gate at Assendon Lodge was left open for Old Mrs Selwyn to "come callin' " in her pony trap. Nan Selwyn came spanking up the road from the Lower Assendon Sewage Works, her cheeks highly rouged, her feet neatly clad in black-and-white brogues—"Co-respondents, just like the dear Prince of Wales and my own, darlin' Primo de Rivera," said Mama brightly afterwards. "Heil Hitler, Nan old girl!"

Old Nan Selwyn held a small, curling brown leather whip in her right hand, flicking the back of her brown-and-white horse's neck. Her driving gloves were of cream pigskin.

"The one piebald, the other skewbald!" shrieked Mama. "I'll skewer the Selwyns silly, all those borin' Prots, married bishops, effin' Old Etonian wet-bobs, all bald as a coot to boot." She roared with laughter. "Intellectuals indeed! I'll show them just who is intellectual round here in this hotbed of regatta rugger-buggers and incest, *olé*!"

And so round the corner Nan Selwyn span, in her black bowler hat and black veil. As she did so, the wheels of the pony trap crushed the soft body of my divine Flora as the skewbald horse rounded the corner, and cantered through the gateway. I could not believe my eyes and I started to cry.

"Yes, yes, and well, maybe I am sorry, but this is all too much, and most frightfully sissy of you, Julia Stonor. Stop makin' such a Gawd-awful public scene and issue. Snap out of it and pull yourself together!" ordered Mama sharply. "You absolutely bore me to tears, I'll just give dear Fred Machin, my vet, a quick tinkle at his surgery. He can bugger up the Fair Mile in that smart black car of his and see to things."

So saying my mother turned sharply on her heel to accompany Old Nan Selwyn, who was Uncle Dr Alan Hartley's mother-in-law, into the Drawing Room for afternoon tea. But my tears for Flora would not stop.

"Oh, for Gawd's sake stop makin' such a public exhibition," said Mama crossly; and poured herself an early afternoon Horse's Neck straight into a Meissen cup. "So soothin' in these troubled times," she explained to Mrs Selwyn as they sat down together on the button-backed yellow velvet brocaded sofa.

Even in my grief, I couldn't help noticing that Mama was wearing new shoes and new blond silk stockings. Old Nan Selwyn's stockings were of thick black wool. Giving a quick sharp tug to the elastic beneath my flannel hat, my mother slammed the drawing-room door on my shins before sinking hastily back onto the sofa.

My bare legs were suddenly frozen. So too were my hands. I was cold all over from the sorrow of losing my lovely, loving, happy-spirited dog: Flora, my beloved puppy who had a long pink tongue with which she had covered me in kisses as we sat together and played, hidden and undisturbed in the garden. My heart stood still but there was only Ruby to comfort me in my grief.

19

'Tinker, Tailor, Knackerman, Thief'

Before Flora was killed at Assendon Lodge, she was frequently examined by Mr Machin, the fat black-eyed black-haired vet, bursting out of a double-breasted navy-blue suit, each time he came to give Mama's dogs their "potions for motions".

"All frightfully constipaggers again," laughed Mama, who was as enthusiastic for "motions and potions" for people other than the dogs. "Of course I'm a firm believer in enemas myself," she said, glaring at Bangpa-Pop. "Frightfully efficacious for all that wind, old boy. Nothin' like some colonic lavage, ha, ha!"

Mama had several bottles of special potions. Some were labelled "Syrup of Figs", others "Milk of Magnesia". Yet others, in dark-blue ribbed glass bottles with whitetops and dark-brown glass bottles with tin tops had no labels. They stood in rows in Papa's bathroom, neatly arranged on top of a chest of drawers covered with a white linen cloth, Mama's own speciality were "My Little Brown Pills" which she gave in quantities to both Papa and me.

Sometimes she alternated these drably coloured pills with capsules of a bright red, orange and brown stripes. These my mother frequently produced from the copious depths of her black crocodile handbag, where they lurked in smaller, screwtop bottles. They had a curious smell, and labels "from those darlin' boys who run such a frightfully convenient chemist in Wigmore Street. Just round the corner from darlin' Sir Stuart Duke Elder," Mama explained. She blinked through the blue-glassed sun spectacles which the Duke had prescribed "for my blindin' headaches and splittin' migraines that I inherited from darlin' Sir Dickie Sykes up at

Sledmere—1937 you know, such an adventure that most unfortunate car crash—I cant think how, but I landed up in 27 Welbeck Street havin' a premature appendix op," Mama reflected laughingly. "It certainly cost Richard Sykes very dear. The greater the libel, the greater the truth I always say. A breach of promise case of course." She fingered a bright solitaire diamond ring lovingly.

My mother had a habit of stroking her jewellery and fingering the silver cutlery in other people's houses, turning knives, forks, spoons upside-down to check the hallmarks. "I simply can't abide fish-knives, aristo Spanish bastard that I am. So common, so nouveau and *cursí*, most frightfully Continental and pretentious you know. Don't you agree, Fred dear?" said Mama turning to the dumbstruck vet who had driven over after Nan Selwyn had run over poor Flora.

Mr Machin agreed hastily.

Mama had appeared for a moment from the yellow Drawing Room. Do stop that brat Julia mopin', Nanny dear," she said briskly. "Take her for a good sharp walk to the Lower Assendon Sewage, and she'll snap out of all this sentimental nonsense." She beckoned the vet towards her. "Be an angel Fred dear, and just remove the corpse for me," she said, turning up her nose and sniffing into a lace handkerchief.

Mr Machin obligingly carried Flora's limp body to his car and laid her in the boot. I sniffed as I said goodbye. Mama promptly gave me one of her little brown pills.

Even before Daddy was renamed Papa, Mama had provided him with many bottles of medicine. These stood in a neat line next to a bottle of Trumpers' hair-oil, lime-scented and colourless in the green glass, the stopper a silver crown surmounting the cork, elegantly labelled with the Royal Warrant.

"One can't do without all of this, absolutely vital to the constitution all these medications you know. Your dear father has a very nervous constitution these days. Most frightfully susceptible to nervous breakdowns," she said.

Breakdowns always made me think more of Granny Camoys' old Chevrolet, immobile on the Assendon to Stonor road when my mother had "run out of gas, goddamn it" on her way to the petrol pump hidden in the darkness of the Tudor coach house up at the Park.

Here the men in grey overalls from the National Benzole Petroleum Company would usually wait on Mama. One of them pumped petrol while another went over the car engine with a can of thick oil. Yet another, dressed in a boiler suit, lay beneath the brake to test out the air in the tyres.

Sometimes Mama ordered the garage staff to jack up the Chevrolet. I remained on the back seat, terrified as the car was suspended in the air for what seemed eternity, giddy and fearful that I would receive a spanking if I wet my knickers in mid-air. "This goddamned child is not even house-trained!" Mama declared triumphantly to the petrol-pump man as the car was winched back to earth.

Back at home, the blue and brown medicine bottles, filled with mysterious white liquids, and arranged by Mama in Papa's bathroom, looked like a battalion of soldiers I had seen in nearby fields of Bix Bottom.

"The Boys are doin' their exercises!" shouted Mama excitedly. She promptly jumped into her police uniform and rushed out of the house. "I'm just makin' sure they are properly supervised in these dangerous days," she shouted but Bangpa, who was also in uniform, was told to go down to the cellar with his gas mask and tin helmet to wait until my mother returned. "You can eff orf out of it. Don't you dare to interfere, Pop-goes-the-Weasel. Sometimes you're such a crashin' fart of a bore and a very big blight in my life. Ruby can bring you down a pot of Indian tea on a tray. Maybe that will do somethin' to your brewer's droop. And as for you, Julia, you're to keep sittin' on your pot until you have BEEN!"

On her return from the Bix Bottom field manoeuvres, she burst in shouting as before: "Have you done your utters today, child? And what about you, Pop dear?' She glared at my grandfather "You're quite purple, and obviously constipaggers again."

Bangpa-Pop guffawed and hiccuped.

When the answer to my mother's daily questions regarding the movement of bowels displeased her, there would be many more doses from the medicine bottles and her "little brown pills". Nanny would also serve a bowl of stewed prunes adrift in a puddle of watery juice for nursery tea. A further session of pot-sitting there ensued, my small fat bottom well sunk beneath the china rim. From this angle I could see the length and breadth of the nursery floor covered in brown linoleum but very little else. Being so low down it was cold and draughty, and I felt rather lonely.

Occasionally Ruby would be sent to relieve me from my misery. Otherwise my orders were to wait until it was convenient for Mama to arrive. I was none too clear as to whether this was another punishment as

I seemed to attract so many. Which was ever more puzzling because I adored my mother and only ever wanted to be close to her.

*

Whenever the American Uncles arrived at Assendon Lodge in their dashing, sand-coloured uniforms and officers' caps, Mama sent me immediately to bed for my afternoon rest. Uselessly I tried to explain that I was not tired, but the only response was a hiss of rage, a quick slap, and a fierce sharp kick on the shin.

"Get out of my sight, and make it quick!" snapped Mama gazing towards the front door.

It was a considerable blow to me as I could only see the officers, their arms filled with cartons of cigarettes and packets of silk and nylon stockings, by surreptitiously lifting the corner of the blue-black air-raid blind and peering out of the nursery window. The blind was supposed to keep the light hidden so that, as Mama explained, "the Huns can't see enough to bomb Assendon Lodge in this damn inconvenient war that is puttin' all my plans out. *Olé* and heil Hitler!"

Shortly before Mummy became Mama, she had become quite overexcited when our neighbour Wing Commander Waghorne had "gorne up in his Spitfire, and good gracious, he's come down a mighty cropper. And that is the end of him," she concluded in a tone of relish and pleasure. "I think I'll just pop down to the Fair Mile to give comfort and consolation to his frightfully tedious widow. All alone with two tiresome small brats."

So saying Mama fastened the buttons of her uniform and draped a silver whistle on a white cord over the epaulettes on her shoulder. "I've had a few subtle alterations added by the Bell Street family tailor. Just a bit more froggin' adds to my glamorous appearance."

I remembered Wing-Commander Waghorne as handsome, smiling in his blue RAF uniform, which matched his eyes. I felt sadder than Mama seemed and I couldn't understand why. His widow Olive came a few times to Assendon Lodge but she finally went away quickly and didn't come back after she overheard my mother saying, with a big yawn: "Really, that morose woman bores me to tears. Too, too tedious, and I simply can't stand the sight of Olive nippin' around in widow's weeds. Just like that borin' widow Anne Phillimore."

Olive Waghorne looked as if she had been crying continuously. And she did have two small children, who Mama said were now orphans. I felt sad for the Waghornes. Their house was all white plaster with dark green wooden slatted shutters and was set in a large, mournful garden planted with cypress trees behind a tall evergreen hedge. It stood alone beneath the Lower Assendon sewage works at the top of the Fair Mile, the straight road that led directly into Henley. "So totally appropriate," had said my mother silkily, "just opposite the local loony bin and the cemetery."

The garden of the Waghorne house was secret and sad, and I was sometimes taken there to play. But, Mama said, "for what was a decent Queen Anne house, Olive has really gorne and buggered up all the architectural details. Such terrible, predictable taste. Frightfully middle-class."

Mama never told me whether Queen Anne was alive or dead, which was strange since she was so taken up by royalty. After all, as Mama declared: "I can only ever move in royal circles with my aristo Spanish blood, even if I am a bastard, ha, ha. *Viva el rey de España!*"

There were always various Guns and Uncles that Mama called "My Royals". They came to shoot and eat, and sometimes to stay, at Assendon Lodge. Chauffeur-driven in stiff upright cars, each Gun and Uncle brought with them one or two other men who, Ruby said, were "the loaders".

The Royal Guns and other Uncles each carried a brace of shotguns with polished barrels and ornately carved wooden stocks. Bright orange cartridges in neat rows were packed into leather bags with wide canvas shoulder-straps, and slung over tweed jackets. The rest were tightly loaded into sturdy cartridge belts worn round capacious waists.

I was enraptured by it all, the stately cars, and the rich smell of cigars. And by the contagious merriment of laughter as Mama poured wine and port. "Straight from my own family cellars in Oporto, *olé!*" she laughed, filling Waterford cut glass to the brim.

I never knew where the loaders ate. The chauffeurs had to eat in the kitchen, but perhaps the loaders were only allowed to eat their homemade sandwich packs and drink the dark-brown Indian tea they called "char" from thermos flasks with the beaters, who had to sit outside on the wet grass.

Mama, who was still Mummy when first the Royals started coming to shoot and eat at Assendon Lodge and sometimes to stay, explained: "It is most frightfully important for my staff, just as it is for the convent at Ascot, to realise there are upstairs servants and nuns, and downstairs servants and nuns. The servants' hall is the only place suitable. None of that rubbish about democracy—it's all rubbish, balls and pills. Servants are all completely disposable in my most certain view."

But at Assendon Lodge there was not enough room for a servants' hall and Mama impatiently waited to be installed and back at Stonor—up at the Park—where there was a great big dark brown room with mullioned windows, filled with brown sofas that Ruby Heath called "settees", which Mama said was "most frightfully common". There was also dark brown linoleum, perhaps left over from the chapel floor. I first remember seeing this room on inspection tours that my mother took me on with Uncle Eric St Johnston. I thought it would be a dry place for loaders and beaters to eat their rations, wrapped up in cotton handkerchiefs and sometimes the grease-proof paper which Ruby supplied from the kitchen and her duties there.

"I'm bidin' my time," said Mama smoothly. "After all, it can only be a matter of time until Sherman comes back from this goddamned inconvenient war that is ruinin' all my plans."

She gazed at Bangpa-Pop, bundled up in sloppy-fitting, porridge colour tweed shooting bags. He wore a crotched scarf which Mama did not seem to care for.

"Where, in Gawd's name, did you get that piece of tasteless tat from Pop?" she asked witheringly. "I can only presume you've been frequentin' parts of the Women's Institute I've not yet penetrated? Or did you get that old pussycat of a cousin, Gwennie Sladen, to knit it for you in her spare time between those monstrous Manx cats and doin' Aunt Marjorie?"

Bangpa-Pop looked uneasy and gave his habitual guffaw, clearing what Mama said was his "usual 'guitar' and phlegm" into an unclean handkerchief.

"On second thoughts I'm not so convinced that crotched *número* does not come from that airy-fairy wispy-haired maid of yours, Mary. She's just as likely to give you crabs, and so on and so forth." Mama roared with laughter. "The sooner we get those entrails and entails together, the better Ralph dear. I'm askin' that darlin' David Drummond to see to it there are no more cock-ups when I give specific instructions. He of all oversexed ferrets well understands how to fix up a few deeds on Bosmore and that other property belonging to your oldest nuisance at Cock's Leas." Slowly she advanced towards Bangpa-Pop, flicking the air round his head with a kitchen fly whisk. "The sooner we get this little matter of power of attorney fixed, the better," Mama added menacingly.

Flinging open the door of the Chevrolet, she shouted from the driveway back into the house: "You'd better come up to the Cock and Comfort with me, Pop. I'm in dire need of supplies, runnin' quite dry on ginger ale and no brandy, *olé!* You can shift it up the Bix Bottom road to our hide-away at Maidensgrove in Mildew Mildred's old car, all wind and whinge." My mother took a deep breath, breathed in her cigarette fumes, and continued in her loudest voice: "And Gawd only knows how you ever got a leg-up to sire those four *tedioso* girls. They all, one and all, bore me to tears, just like their stud father. A bit of inbreedin' round here so watch it, Pop-goes-the-Weasel, that I don't let on to Mildew Lady Cee, my horrendous mother-in-law, about the latest duo of Camoys-coloured chamois-leather textured bastards. *Olé!* And I'm an aristo Spanish bastard too!' Mama winked, hic-cuped and whirled a flywhisk round Bangpa's head as he got into the car.

"Tinker, tailor, sailor, knackerman, vet or thief. Look what I've got in this Camoys' conker. Coach, carriage, wheelbarrow or dung-cart, prefer-ably the latter, old cock," she mocked. "How many cherry stones do we have round here? Darlin' Joachim always put on a better performance than you can muster the 5th Baron Camoys. To say nothing of Raul Regis de Oliveira, the king of Brazil—where the nuts come from but not the ones you know, Pop-goes-the-Weasel. Your eyes are far too close together, and you can wipe the snot orf the end of your nose. Lady Cee WILL know all about this. I will make very sure about that. The lawyers have my absolute instructions to get the goods and goodies at Bosmore and Cock's Leas handed over *muy pronto*, or you'll catch it Ralph old boy, ultimate sponger that you are."

Such outbursts were master classes in family trees. My mother had a very strict sense of precedence, studiously studying her scarlet-bound books of etiquette, genealogy and forms of address. From a very early age I knew all about rights of way and rights of precedence because Mama habitually trumpeted at anyone standing on the grounds and parklands, which she owned.

"Get orf immediately, did you hear me? Eff orf out of it before I call my colleagues in the police. You can beat it!" Turning to anyone else in the vicinity, she would painstaking explain: "I'm an absolute stickler for Protocol and Precedence. And I know all about my rights, and the rights, very dubious as those are, of others. No one could accuse me otherwise. Rights of way indeed! So much stuff and rubbish, like the rats in your hair, Julia, my girl." Stamping her foot, Mama would shout out again at the hapless interlopers: "Do you know WHO and WHAT I am? If not, why not, and you can eff orf out of it! Happy Christmas even if it is July. I'm not an aristo Spanish bastard for nothing, *olé!*"

But I, at least, knew that Christmas usually came in December when Bangpa-Pop dressed up in red velvet and a nightcap, a white bobble hanging off it over his pyjamas. The hessian sack slung over his shoulders, filled with gifts for my mother which she had herself handpicked, was invariably lent to him by Mama from the knacker's yard.

20

'Simply Not Done South of the Border'

My mother liked to curtsy deeply to her royal guests whether indoors or outdoors, and in all weathers. She had taught me to do the same to all the grown-ups, starting with herself and especially the Guns and Uncles, followed by occasional duchesses. The foreign Guns would bow back to Mama as she extended her hand with the long red fingernails. So I was surprised that she didn't allow the tiny count to kiss her hand as others had done and did.

"Enrico Marone Cinzano is just an effin' Eytie, and I'll knock his dentures in," said my mother furiously between clenched teeth. "Furthermore he has held on to most of that gold and cash, damn it."

From the look on her face, I thought that Mama might possibly have contracted lockjaw. One of the great danes, the blonde Ruby, had recently died being unable to open her mouth, and even Mr Machin's potions could not save her.

I watched Count Enrico Marone Cinzano almost fell backwards in surprise when Mama raised her hand so suddenly and sharply that she all but knocked his new Swiss dentures in with her heavy Cartier rings, sapphires, rubies, emeralds and diamonds. "Protocol and soft talk be damned, Enrico dear," said my mother silkily. "You'd better find that money and hand over the goods we arranged." Mama's habitual Philip Morris contraband clung to the side of her shining scarlet lips.

She wore a favourite mustard-yellow checked shooting suit, and strong brown brogue shooting shoes, heavily spiked in metal, with leather tongues. The same colour as the seat of her shooting stick, this sporting ensemble was the bounty from one of her pre-war expeditions to Inverness and Beaufort Castle at Beauly in the company of Ribbentrop.

"Of course Joachim and I had just such a heavenly time at Beaufort with divine Sheemie Lovat, my cousin the 17th Baron, with that Fraser tartan in all the colours of marmalade jam. Just so chic. But Sheemie is out in India with his scouts in this goddamned nuisance of a war," recalled Mama merrily.

She herself frequently wore tartan. "My dress tartan," she would say, explaining the shrill orange plaid. "Vegetable dyes, for huntin' only you know," she added, laughingly referring to the softer russets, greens and blues of her day kilt. "Sporrans and kilt-pins are absolutely my thing. My darlin' Andrew Constable Maxwell, who could so easily have been the Duke of Norfolk, never wears underpants north or south of the Borders. It's simply not done with our family kilt, *olé*!"

She had several of her study chairs covered in the orange Fraser dress-cloth. Later, this vital room was renamed first the "Boudoir" and then the "Book Room" as it filled an ever more vital role in the collation and filing of deeds, entails and entrails of the estates that my mother was kept so busily, frantically occupied in plundering.

"Such a frightfully excitin' colour," exclaimed Mama as she twirled around in an orange tartan dressing-gown which matched the newly acquired study carpet and chair covers. "A pity it's machine-dyed these days," she reflected.

None of the Guns were allowed to wear their kilts for shooting parties at Assendon Lodge or up at the Park. "Simply not done south of the Border, and I'm tellin' all those darlin' old boys, Cameron, Lovat, Perth and assorted others."

Mama was very impressed by her Scottish ancestry and direct descendancy from the notorious 11th Baron Lovat. "Simon Lovat, that first-class murderer was most frightfully glamorous. Hung on a silken halter by his fellow peers, *olé!* Too, too chic for words . . ."

I thought deeply about this information as Papa's prize Jersey cow was led on a beige rope which the senior cowman Mr Jenkins had told me was a halter. There must be some connection, which I could not entirely see. Mr Jenkins dressed in a long white coarse cotton overall and high black rubber gumboots, an old tweed hat on the back of his head.

Said Mama: "My hat is the very best from my darlin' Joachim. So very much smarter with this cock pheasant feather shot at Castello Sonnenburg no less. Not too many heirs round there, thank Gawd. But plenty of jack-boots and spurs. A damn sight smarter than black rubber galoshes and gumboots. Pity they put the fear of Gawd into Sherman. Quite did for his privates and parts, ha, ha! But I've made up for all that lorst time. Heil Hitler!" Mama saluted towards Bangpa-Pop mockingly. "Lily-livered Mildew Mildred Lady Cee sittin' pretty in Rhode Island. Like mother, like son. To say nothin' of you Pop-goes-the-Weasel sittin' pretty under your bee-hives at Bosmore. Deserves a medal for gallantry," she continued winking at my grandfather, who had been practising Home Guard manoeuvres in his gas mask with the rubber nozzle and his tin helmet.

Bangpa-Pop looked rather uneasy as Mama smoothly switched the topic of her conversation to murder. "And we'll avoid the unfortunate topic of Madrid '36, if it is all the same to you Ralph Camoys. That woman was a goddamned Socialist, and she was for the chop anyhow. So don't you dare bore me stiff with recriminations. The boys, *mis primos* and I, made quite sure in a little light-hearted lynchin'." My mother paused for a moment. "I have to say it quite did the trick," she finished smugly, "revenge or no revenge, *olé!* and I think it could have been the former."

Mama moved on to other murders but this time in Teruel rather than Madrid. "I was just decampin' from one of our excitin' train journeys with darlin' Dickie Sheepshanks, the only man I've ever loved," she said dreamily, wiping away a tear from behind her blue spectacles before it could trickle down into her rouge. "Simply divine, such a dashin' Old Etonian and a Cambridge man to boot," she sighed. "There was another old pal from the Anglo-German Fellowship, that damn nuisance Philby, jumped into the same car as Dick and that thunderin' bore of an American pressman. Reuters and *The Times* altogether, jam in a Spanish sandwich, I suppose, and dear old Sir Roderick Jones (such a sweetie-pie) cocked it all up," said my mother fretfully. "In front of my eyes there was a frightful explosion, and my darlin' Dickie was blown into the air. My heart is still broken in pieces." Mama sobbed into a delicate lace-edged handkerchief. "Such treachery. To think that turncoat shit Philby was a Trinity College fellow with my divine Sheepshanks," she added furiously. "And when the hell did Kim learn how to throw hand-grenades around?"

The photograph of Dick Sheepshanks that stood on the table beside Mama's beds in her summer and winter bedrooms would later be flanked by signed photographs of Lord Brabazon of Tara, Sir Malcolm Sargent and Graham Greene, accompanied by Sir Austen Chamberlain.

As she wept, Mama clutched the cream lace handkerchief that Ruby had so recently ironed for her. It had a very small silk centre and it was, Mama said, "far too *delicato* to be sent to those effin' butchers Neal's laundry. All my lace comes from King Charles I as it is, like the collar of your black velvet party frock from that divine old Carisbrooke himself," she sighed. Hers scarlet fingernails poked through the lace-bordered handkerchief as she dabbed away another tear. "Those effin' bastards Reuters, rotters and bastards, and how I loathe the lot of them," Mama picked up a green rummer glass filled with bubbling liquid and shouted, "*Verde! Arriba el rey de España!* And God damn those shits for bumpin' orf Dick."

Aunt Gytha, who had come to call after her precarious return from Portugal, was standing nearby. She tried, like Ruby, to calm my mother down. But Mama turned quickly and shouted even more loudly at her. "You really are quite the most tedious of my demi-semi-sisters!"

Aunt Gytha, Uncle Mon del Moral's second wife, left as quickly as she could. Mama hissed at her departing back: "Darlin' Mon, dear old boy and beau as he is, a frightfully important spy, and I can't have him put out by anyone as goddamned borin' as Gytha."

As the front door closed, she continued in a voice that carried far beyond the building: "Not only is your Aunt Gytha a colossal bore, a religious freak, and as poor as a church mouse—I've made sure of that—but she knows FAR too much. Good riddance to a sackful of bad rubbish," Mama finished triumphantly. "And her figure's quite had it, unlike my own exquisite shape. Such a nuisance she made it back from Portugal with those two brats."

Unlike my mother's other two demi-semi-sisters, Barbara and Magda, Aunt Gytha was kind by nature. Gently pretty with Plantagenet fair skin, blue eyes and blonde hair she was in sharp contrast to the other women. They were equally blonde, but haughty with hooked disdainful noses and aloof expressions.

Magda and Barbara sat grandly in the drawing room and sneered in their beautiful clothes and smart shoes, contraband American cigarettes hanging out of their mouths like Mama. Both had what Ruby explained were "shingled hair-dos", cut very short into shimmering layers. Mama's own hair was beautifully arranged in the pageboy look, "which my little woman round the corner in Wargrave arranges for me," she said hastily, smoothing the sharply pointed widow's peak at the top of her high white forehead. It reminded me of one of her angrily spiked Gothic Revival chains.

Displeased and dismayed, Magda and Barbara still could not keep away from the allure of Stonor Park. Furthermore, Jeanne knew too much about them. They now returned hastily to the considerable comfort of Lowndes Square and Sunningdale (both sisters were now remarried to magnates: one from Detroit, the other from Bembridge, on the Isle of Wight).

Though Magda never gave way to Jeanne, it was Barbara who ultimately became beholden to her sister. After her third husband had died and she lost her house in Carlyle Square, she was seduced into renting the Stonor dower house after its occupancy by Professor Bruce MacFarlane and Dame Helena Wright—he a gay Oxford don of history, she a birth control expert—whom Jeanne had evicted summarily. Barbara's "compromise" with her half-sister inevitably turned to disaster and she too was evicted in 1975.

*

Mama was very displeased I had seen her quite real tears over Uncle Dick Sheepshanks' murder. Especially as I was easily confused between him and the other Uncle Dick, our burly neighbour at Assendon Lodge, old Lady Ovey's son, handsome and stout as a barrel in naval uniform.

When I told her my thoughts the reaction was combustible. "Get the hell out of here in my hour of grief, you bloody little fool! You're so god-damned stupid and entirely useless Julia Stonor, quite redundant to my plans. Get out, get out, and make it quick!" Mama commanded.

She landed a quick slap round my head and a sharp kick on the bottom as I tried to oblige as fast as possible. This latest commandment of hers meant that I was banished to the garden and locked out there, since it was before lunchtime. If it was afternoon, I ran the equal risk of banishment to the nursery upstairs "for my rest".

"And more Mortal Sin!" Mama would shout after me.

On one of these punishment days, Mama forgot she had locked me out into the garden. I was standing up to my waist in the wet grass beneath the drawing-room window, sheltering from drizzling rain when I heard a tinkling laugh from my mother followed by a yet deeper one from one of the American Uncle officers.

Usually there were two of them, the brother officers from Grosvenor Square who came assiduously to call on Mama. The smaller one was called Teddy MacCaulay and the taller one was John Nicholas Brown, who, Mama said, "is the quite divine first cousin of my bitch of a mother-in-law,

Mildew Lady Camoys. So, so special, such a darlin', John Nicholas. Born with a golden spoon in his mouth, but not quite posthumously," she added thoughtfully.

But her reaction to Cousin John Nicholas Brown's short-statured fellow officer was very different. "Really that Teddy is most frightfully bog-Irish. And I should know because my own mother was an aristo heiress from that divine Castle Mattress. Direct descendant as I am too of that saintly Cartholic martyr Robert Southwell. Hung, drawn and quartered actually. Frightfully bloody times in that stinkin' Prot Reformation. After all it was only about Henry VIII and his BALL games," laughed Mama.

The American Uncles laughed with her, but I could hear Cousin John Nicholas murmur: "Really, Jeanne Mary dear, don't you think you are going a little too far?"

There was more laughter, and my mother's gold charm bracelets clanked against a glass. "Give that Gilbey's gin a slap of Angostura bitters," she cried.

Above, the window shot up suddenly, and a cascade of bright pink ice descended over me, scattering into the long grass. I was enthralled at this magically coloured ice, quite certain my mother could create such a miracle. I kept the wondrous lumps of ice in my hands as it melted into a small, pink puddle. So excited was I by this miraculous manifestation that I made another puddle in my knickers once again.

Ruby let me in by the kitchen door, trying to hide my mistake from Mama. But Mama noticed everything.

"If you must make pee-pee in your pants every time you're over-excited we'll just have to see to it," laughed my Mother with her tinkling laugh. "I cannot possibly afford any more knickers for you as it is. Have you quite forgotten about wartime rationin', you dreary brat? My coupons are sorely stretched as it is," she explained briskly. "High time for proper penance for your Mortal Sins of the day against me. I shall have to teach you the Catechism all over again. And we shall have to have an emergency session with your darlin' Uncle old Alfonso de Zoo."

Uncle Alfonso de Zulueta y Borja Merry del Val had a Chelsea parish but could only use a bicycle because of his poor sight. "Myopia from our aristo Spanish blood, inherited of course," explained Mama emphatically. "*Olé!* Explains my own blindin' migraines and double-vision to boot. Makes absolution in my drawin'-room confessions so much easier since old André Cereal can see far too much. Too too tedious."

I was returned for an early afternoon rest, and meals quite alone in my nursery bedroom, the black-out blinds fully down to block out the daylight. There was a mighty crash as Mama slammed and locked the door

"Use the china pot under your bed," she called as she went away.

But I was frightened by the dark below the bed and tried to hold onto my bladder for as long as possible, wriggling around in the sheets.

*

Bangpa-Pop, with his funny, abrupt "haw-haw" laugh and deep snort sounded, like Ned, one of the old donkeys up at the Park who Mama did not terribly care for. My grandfather was back after a brief expedition for beekeeping and butterfly hunting up at the orange house of Bosmore in order to take Mama "orf for my evenin' hop at Henley Town Hall". She had changed from police uniform into "my little black number" and very high-heeled black shoes. Thus attired, Mama shot off into the night with the 5th Lord Camoys.

Ruby would have to stay on for the night and put me to bed if Nanny had been sacked again. Ruby's red brick cottage, which she shared with her husband Art when he was not away in the war, was a couple of miles of bicycle-ride away. But the road was lonely, tree-lined and unlit, full of unexpected ditches and even a hidden stream. If she had to go home late at night, Ruby would hang an oblong black tin lamp on the handle-bars of her solid, upright black bike outside a square wicker basket. Battery-powered, the lamp glowed a very faint arc ahead of her, a small dim round red light on the rear mudguard casting the faintest glimmer along the lonely route.

My mother was a marvellous dancer, consumed with energy, forever performing in the kitchen, whether at Assendon Lodge or up at the Park. She was, as she put it, "showin' that brat Julia my Spanish numbers" and teaching me to use her castanets. But I was slow to learn, which caused considerable annoyance.

Mama's lessons involved a good deal of clicking of fingers, clapping and clacking, with fervent shouts of "*olé, ola!*" and "*verde!*" She would shriek with laughter as she explained "that means '*viva el rey de España*' and 'green as my hat', *olé!*" I simply could not see the connection, but Mama persisted: "I'm rootin' for the King of Spain you fool. *Arriba* Don Juan! *Arriba* Joachim, Adolf and Carisbrooke, *olé!*"

This was quite a while before Mama had taken me to Carisbrooke Castle and I still did not quite know who any of these mysterious people could be. But I always loved the deep-throated way with which Mama pronounced their names in her mounting excitement and all those exotic expressions such as "*cursi*" and "*racée*" interspersed with shouts of "heil Hitler", "*basta*" and "you can eff orf out of it!"

The dizzy swirl of black castanets held high over her head and the cacophonous banging together of Papa's copper saucepans from Boston, Massachusetts all made what Mama called her "percussion" as she whirled ever faster across the kitchen floor.

"*Olé* and *caramba*! I'm doin' a pasadoble!" she screamed and hurled her castanets over a passing servant.

*

During the military exercises and manoeuvres in the fields round Assendon Lodge, soldiers in khaki were running up and down the hill behind the Rainbow Inn.

"A bomb has gorne and fallen at Holland Ridge," exclaimed Mama. "Such a frightful nuisance. It has gorne and blown up some of Sherman's bunny rabbits," she added with a laugh.

There was indeed a large crater at the bottom of a field not far from Pishill, and Mama donned a tin helmet with her uniform before she left in a great hurry with Uncle Eric St Johnston, who had arrived in a police car.

"We're orf to have a good look before anyone else appears on the scene," she announced grandly. "For security's sake I've got to make sure no one else has gorne west and been killed. Just possible one of my game-keeper's in the vicinity, and if Mr Dukes hasn't gorne west himself, and even if he has, darlin' Eric, I can bring back the bits and just pop them into the rabbit stew or stuff them in the stockpot, ha, ha!"

I asked whether Peter Rabbit had also "gorne west" since I was reading about him and the scarecrow Worzel Gummage, who I saw standing in the midst of nearby fields, stuck into a pile of rotten straw, surrounded by large white turnips and rotting Brussels sprouts.

"It all makes our first-rate manure that much riper, and all the more choice. I can add it to the pigswill for old Mrs Phillips' Parkers," said Mama enthusiastically. "I'll talk to my farmer Albert Hunt and Mr White about the new plan."

Mr White was just as fierce as Mr MacGregor, Peter Rabbit's head gardener, while Albert Hunt was a small, rotund farmer from Stonor Village. He was a fervent Freemason with a portly stomach and a heavy gold watch chain stretched over his tight tweed waistcoat. Mr Hunt simply smiled at Mama as Mr White scowled.

"Stand to attention when I speak to you!" she shouted commandingly. "Orf with your hats this minute."

The two men hastily removed their caps even though they were still outside in the backyard.

"And don't forget who pays the wages round here," said Mama with a click of her fingers.

Mama paid the weekly wages in brown envelopes laid out alphabetically on the immense pine kitchen table, whether at Assendon or Stonor Park. Secretaries, tenant farmers, agents, tutors, nannies, maids, governesses, gardeners, knackers, butlers, dailies, foremen, carpenters, beaters and keepers were all paid in the same manner—though sometimes some of the envelopes were mysteriously "missing". The rents of the sitting tenants Mama collected weekly on foot in the village of Stonor and by fierce visitations to the outlying hamlets in Granny Camoys's old Chevrolet.

Frequently, until his return to America in 1947, Jeanne was accompanied by her father-in-law Ralph, carrying the rent books, blue-covered and red-lined. Pleas for proper sanitation would be noted but ignored completely until the Fifties. There was no running water in Stonor village nor in the surrounding hamlets before 1952; even then not every cottage was modernised. Until that date, only John Stracey at White Pond farm and the Freemason farmer Albert Hunt had inside lavatories and running water.

In addition to this guaranteed supply of revenue, Jeanne also had a signature from Sherman to obtain both from his account at the Barclays bank in Henley and via his solicitor an endless supply of ready cash.

21

'A Most Frightfully Devout Cartholic'

Whenever the air-raid siren went off, Ruby Heath would take me down to the cellar at Assendon Lodge. I was frightened of the mice down there but she always reassured me. Sometimes "Papa who had been Daddy" would be back from the war, and he too came down wearing a white towelling dressing gown. "Mama who had been Mummy" was invariably rushed away in a police car into the dangerous darkness of night. Papa explained that Mama had very important duties to attend to in Henley town hall with the member of parliament. And that we must learn to be patient with her.

When Mama returned one night from her "Air Raid Practice and Practical" as she described it, she explained that "dear Old Sir Gifford and I had to crawl under the council meetin' table on all fours because there was a bit of a false alarm after the smoke bomb set one of the curtains alight. We simply had to take refuge, the two of us. So hard to see what was goin' on under the green baize cloth . . ."

Papa sighed.

"Don't be such a crashin' bore Sherman," retorted my mother indignantly. "YOU'VE got nothin' much to write home about."

Sir Gifford Fox, member for Henley-on-Thames, was a mere five feet tall. With his bristling red moustache he reminded me of my Spanish grandfather, old Pedro de Zoo. But I never saw my Zoo grandfather dressed up in the big gold chains, medals and scraps of fur that Sir Gifford wore.

Mama would announce: "Gifford will be Lord Mayor soon if I have anything to do with it. From a very long line."

I knew that my English grandfather, Bangpa-Pop, who also had a

238

moustache, was an important landed lord too, because Mama said so. "Pop-goes-the-Weasel's line is much, much longer," she said, "like his plumbin', hundreds of years old. Poor dear Ralph, with his effin' nuisance of a wife, that Mildew Cee sittin' tight in Newport. I'll see about all of that in due course. Pop-goes-the-Weasel indeed but never EVER without me," she said firmly and poured a new Horse's Neck, tossing it down her throat with a flourish.

I wondered whether Bangpa-Pop ever went fishing with a line in the murky dew-pond halfway up the crumbling back drive at the Park, or held a line over the gold fishponds in the back garden. Maybe my grandfather further idled his time away sitting on the banks of the Thames at Hambleden or in Henley on the regatta course at the Leander Club. But the only fish to appear on the nursery dining room table were tinned sardines and carp full of bones from Mama's own fishing trips.

"I've just been out on darlin' Jerry Wellington's moat for a spin in his boat," she explained. "Such an old beau but even now that he's the Duke of Wellington he still can't make up his mind if he's for the boys. All those sea scouts!"

Uncle Jerry Wellington too had a moustache, a white one.

"My dear, he shoots like the angel he is," declared Mama triumphantly as the duke drove an elderly pheasant across the lawn at Assendon Lodge.

I never did see Bangpa-Pop with a fishing-line or rod. The nearest he had to that was a long stick to poke at the Bosmore beehives when he and sometimes Father Seyres donned a green hair-net before visiting the bees.

"Pop's takin' vital precautions for his parts," laughed Mama.

I thought this must have something to do with Air Raid Precautions, and the Home Guard uniform beret, which my Camoys grandfather wore jauntily on the side of his head when he wasn't wearing a tin helmet and a gas mask. He frequently carried a beautiful and gleaming gun.

"A hand-made Purdey 12-bore—and those double barrels can tell a story or two," said Mama, laughing.

A loader always took this gun and its identical pair away to oil and clean after Bangpa-Pop had shot a pheasant or two and finished off a few rabbits and hares for the stew. Mama too would "finish orf any unfortunate animal not quite dead which I find lyin' around, *olé!*" with a good sharp crack of a stick to the head.

"I'm teachin' that damn nuisance Julia how to get on with life and face reality," she said sternly. Taking aim again with the head of her stick she clubbed the remains of a rabbit still quivering life on the ground. Taking me firmly by the wrist she placed a short, thick stick in my hand. Lifting my arm with hers, Mama continued to beat the dying animal round the head.

My Camoys grandfather was considerably taller than Sir Gifford Fox, whose wife, Lady Myra, seemed as tall as the yellow giraffe I had seen illustrated in *Babar the Elephant*.

Lady Myra, who used a great quantity of orange rouge and who wore seven rows of perfectly matched pearls, seemed perpetually annoyed with my exquisite mother. Precisely why was a mystery to me. Mama stared at the seven rows of perfect pearls, lightly dusted with Lady Myra's pink face powder, held together with a perfect Georgian clasp of sapphires and diamonds.

"Myra is really just like a horse," mused Mama, narrowing her eyes so she could focus her gaze more easily on the magnificent antique setting. "Frightfully rich of course, and someone to know' keepin' all those stallions just rearin' to go on her Newmarket stud, *olé!* Such breedin' commands a toppin' fee just for the mountin' and sirin'." She pealed with laughter "And those family jewels I could kill for."

I was still in the dark as to why Lady Myra did not like my mother even when Lady Myra found her minute baronet husband in bed upstairs at Assendon Lodge. She picked him up by the collar, frogmarching him out to the chauffeured car. The bedroom window was flung wide open and Mama's head leaned out.

"Gifford, you old fox fool!" she shouted indignantly. "I'll make quite sure you're thoroughly unseated before I'm finished."

Below her, the giraffe-tall Lady Myra towered over the quivering, diminutive figure of Sir Gifford seated besides her on the leather-covered back seat as the car sped off towards the Fair Mile and the safety of Newmarket Gallops.

My mother shot out of the front door still shouting: "And he won't be a member of parliament for very much longer, ha, ha, *olé!*" She stamped a Delman shoe into the wallflower bed. "I'll make very sure of that," she finished, clicking her fingers sharply. She stood outside in defiance, dressed in her orange-dyed Fraser dress-tartan dressing-gown, the slippers made to match in a peep-toe pattern, showing brilliantly enamelled scarlet nails.

Easily as tiny as Sir Gifford was Aunt Oinette Esher, the American wife of Oliver, 3rd Viscount and president of the Euthanasia Society. "Of course she does come from a frightfully rich family in Boston. August Hecksure is her darlin' brother, such an absurd name," Mama laughed.

But my mother was as nervous of Aunt Oinette as she was of Old Lady Rathcreedan from Ulster and Sister Gertrude Flick from Loch Ness. Together with Hellbags Helen, Lady Dashwood and Karen Lancaster, they all seemed to unnerve Mama.

"Though, of course, I'm frightened of absolutely nothin' and NOBODY," she would insist scornfully.

Sister Gertrude Flick came south from the mysterious Loch Ness once a year. "Flicky" dressed in a starched green uniform with a white linen cap.

"*Ma sage-femme*," announced Mama grandly. "And absolutely no more questions and none of your nosey-parker behaviour Julia," she remarked sharply. "Sherman's brat is only ever to be seen, and as seldom as possible. Never, ever to be heard," continued my mother briskly.

I loved Flicky and immediately inserted her into my night prayers, squeezing her in amongst the Guns and Uncles. Aunt Julia, Flicky and Ruby were very close to one another at Assendon Lodge, and up at the Park. Mama made rude faces behind their backs but said almost nothing at all.

Mama made even ruder faces in front of Aunt Oinette but behind the back of her small round husband, Oliver, 3rd Viscount Esher. He had an unusually large, shiny, rotund head, a high domed forehead and was completely bald. He habitually wore a thick worsted City suit, a heavy gold Albert chain across his waistcoat, a full-hunter gold watch sticking out of a pocket.

"Oliver Esher's suits look just like the suburb of his name," sniffed Mama scornfully. "He might as well run a Belgian pawnbroker's. Furthermore, Oliver Esher runs a society to dispose of people before they're even dead." My mother's voice rose indignantly as she shifted a cigarette from one side of her mouth to the other. "I'm a most frightfully devout Cartholic and I'm tellin' the third Viscount just where he can put it." Turning round Mama narrowed her eyes and spat: "Euthanasia indeed! You can get started with yourself. So eff orf, Oliver Esher, and take your Sarawak son-in-law with you too."

Aunt Oinette and Oliver's daughter, Sylvia, was married to His Highness the Rajah of Sarawak.

Mama and I had bumped into Oliver one day walking down Hay Hill in Mayfair as we went up the street on one of my mother's exciting train expeditions to London. Getting as close as she could, Mama grabbed the 3rd Viscount Esher by his striped braces. She hissed angrily at him: "Piss ORF, Brussels sprouts and all, and don't forget to start on yourself!"

So saying, Mama walked firmly on from Berkeley Square to her favourite rendezvous at Cartier in Bond Street, her fingernails dug firmly into the back of my shoulders.

As we went, I asked Mama why there was neither hay nor straw on Hay Hill, but explanation came there none as I had to canter to keep up with my mother's brisk pace towards her assignation with Monsieur Louis at the emporium filled with beautiful jewels, gold boxes, clocks and photograph frames and enamels all colours of the rainbow. I sat swinging my neatly ankle-socked legs from a chair while Mama disappeared into a back room with Mr Louis.

"I have to have absolute privacy for these frightfully delicate negotiations," she explained. "You're to sit exactly where you are my child. And don't move an inch until I return under pain of death."

So saying, Mama swept away in her fox furs with the silver-haired, silver-suited Mr Louis. A heavy door in the corner of the shop, well behind the counter, closed silently behind them.

Mr Louis had silver socks, and black shoes with silver buckles. His wristwatch was a slim gold oblong with Roman numerals on a narrow brown crocodile strap like Papa's. But Mr Louis's French wrists were not as narrow as my father's, and his fingers were shorter and fatter. "Of course, my beloved Louis is a Frog," said Mama merrily.

But he didn't appear to be the right colour to me. Count Marone Cinzano, Uncle Enrico, was far more like a frog in colour, but he was, according to my mother "just a common-or-garden Eytie from Torino". She used the same language to describe the innumerable maids and gardeners later who Mama found to work for her up at the Park, giving them an uncertain rescue from the digging of cabbages, Brussels sprouts and swedes at Littlemore lunatic asylum and the Huntercombe golf club, all of them prisoners of war.

The wartime weekly train journey to London with Mama was exciting. My mother specialised in black taxis, paying regular visits to Bond Street, calling in at Claridge's on the way there and on the way back ("I simply have to empty my tanks"). Cartier, J. Arthur Rowe and Tessier, where Papa's family silver was buffed up and polished, were favourite shops.

"And everythin' must shine until I can see my own face in my own coat-of-arms," Mama would order at Tessier. "My heraldic lions are absolutely RAMPANT and I need to see them at all times very clearly."

Back in Oxfordshire, Ruby ceaselessly polished the Stonor silver with her bare hands, dipping her thickened but agile fingers deep into a well of pink paste mixed in a scallop shell.

Mama fetched out a case of gadrooned, frilly-bordered antique silver plates wrapped in tissue paper and green baize cloth. "Darlin' Queen Adelaide's very own," she murmured, stroking the silver softly.

These plates Ruby tied neatly into green baize bags ready for Mama's London train journey. Mr Livingston, a local poet and the stationmaster, lifted his peaked cap, and gently placed the bags of silver on the seat besides my mother in the first-class compartment of the Henley to London Great Western Train. Once arrived at Paddington a taxi-man was ordered to carry it because, as Mama said, "the weight is far too great for my frail health, and frightfully delicato aristo wrists".

That the weight might break my mother's bright-red finger nails was a far greater cause of worry, though her hands were neatly, safely encased in soft black suede gloves, embroidered by hand, and short enough on the wrists for me to see the gold charm bracelets that came flying my way to cuff me at inopportune moments.

Calling her taxi imperiously to a halt, Mama's first port of call that day after visiting Mr Louis at Cartier, was invariably Claridge's in Brook Street. Here stayed Mama's friends, the Greek royal family, King George of the Hellenes, who reminded me in looks of Ruby's husband Art, and George's younger brother and heir-apparent to the throne of Greece, Prince Paul, a taller, darker edition of his brother. Above the main entrance to Claridge's, the Greek flag swung precariously from its pole.

Enraptured, I was left in the immensity of the black-and-white marble foyer, in the care of the Hungarian String Quartet. These four men from the Mile End Road encased in tightly-cut green hussar uniforms trimmed and frogged in yellow cording, obligingly played and replayed *The Teddy Bear's Picnic* for me while Mama was away "callin' on a delicate invalid friend, who must not be disturbed".

As she disappeared up a flight of elegant stairs, Mama turned round and hissed over her shoulder: "You're my alibi, and you're to stay put until I return."

Ensconced in a deep, velvet-covered armchair I listened avidly to the musicians. The quartet winked knowingly at one another when I asked anxiously how long Mama would be away. Strangely only one of the quartet seemed to have a Hungarian accent.

But they all four bowed low to Mama when she at last reappeared, and handed them a tip. "M'Lady," they murmured in appreciative undertones.

My mother smiled graciously, and bought me a fat millefeuilles from the sweets trolley. I did not dare tell her just how horrid I found this cloying cake with which I had been rewarded as her "alibi".

"For once child you've managed to make yourself useful," sighed my mother as she gazed at her reflection in the mirror of the lid of a gold Cartier powder compact. Thoughtfully she smoothed back her eyebrows, plucked far back on her forehead, with a wettened finger and traced the outline of her mouth in a dark scarlet lipstick.

Sinking back into the cushions my mother beckoned a waiter with an imperious forefinger. "A Horse's Neck," she ordered, "and make it snappy."

On the way to Claridge's from Paddington Station we always stopped to call on Aunt Nellie Soames in her grand brick town house, No 33 Upper Brook Street. She lay recumbent in bed wearing a bright red wig, and I knew she had to be very old because, as my mother said, "darlin' old Nellie is Sir Robert Peel's other granddaughter. And she's still quite a catch, bein' that borin' old bastard Gilstrap Soames' rich widow from Sheffield Park. Even if the darlin' gel was born in 1876 cuts no ice with me. Got Gilstrap to change his will in the nick of time too, to boot, before he kicked the bucket. The old gel inherited it all, lock, stock and barrel, ha, ha!"

Aunt Nellie gazed long and hard at my mother from the bed where she lay propped up on cushions, fully clothed. A maid had let us in to the semi-darkened room. Sometimes a little confused because of her deafness and age, Aunt Nellie strained to hear what Mama was saying from behind her hand.

"She's got pots of money and NO HEIRS," whispered my mother excitedly, ignoring the fact that Aunt Nellie had a Dutch son by an earlier marriage. Swiftly she turned the family photographs round with their faces to the wall, and smiled beguilingly towards the contents of the four-poster bed. The uniformed butler showed us out while Aunt Nellie's maid hovered anxiously by the door.

Aunt Nellie, when not confused as to who my mother actually was, would sit upright on her bed asking about Aunt Julia, and my father Sherman.

"And just how is that naughty boy my nephew Francis Stonor doin' in Alexandria?" she asked. "Once a spy, always a spy!"

Aunt Nellie was happy to explain the Greek connection to Mama. "All those rich Rallis you know. Quite useful to have a Greek mother from the bankin' world these days. And Francis's mother Christina was always quite a gel. Caught Eddie Stonor the second time round," she mused, falling back on her cushions. "Or did Eddie Stonor catch Christina Ralli? Both frightfully political you know . . ."

Mama looked thoroughly put out. She had come especially to Upper Brook Street to explain how eligible she, Jeanne, was for the Soames' inheritance. "I do rather fancy this frightfully convenient London house as my steppin'-orf point, Aunt Nellie, dear," she explained. But she had a hard time keeping the attention of the old lady for long. "Such a damn nuisance I can't put any more pressure on darlin' Winston to get all my rightful inheritances immediately. He is most frightfully busy sortin' out this goddamned war. Even more of a pity my own darlin' Austen Chamberlain isn't still around to see to my best interests," sighed Mama crossly. "Rather a hasty death, come to think of it. Most frightfully sudden and most frightfully inconvenient," she continued, "ruined some of my best-laid plans come to think of it." She stroked Aunt Nellie's silver photograph frames lovingly. "And we all had such fun together, Enid, Roderick, Austen and I. And my own darlin' Joachim in the thick of it all too."

Despite the war my mother had no difficulties finding London taxis. She kept them waiting, leaving me alone as a frightened hostage on the back seat while she stopped off at different ports of call between Paddington and Claridge's and back. Nervously I would pray and pray for her return.

Journeys from Henley to Paddington were eventful as we frequently had to change trains at Twyford. This interruption would cause my mother the greatest pain and frequently entailed immediate help willingly proffered by gallant males to hand.

Several particularly painful occasions were eased by three males neatly attired in dark blue or black City suits, bowler hatted and with red carnations in their buttonholes. Enthusiastically the Colonels Cockburn, Lambert and Rutherford escorted Mama across the windy platform to transfer from one first-class compartment to another.

The same pattern was followed religiously on the return journey from to Henley with a furious scrabbling to change back to the branch line at Twyford and my mother with each arm intertwined with the alternating, ageing colonels who jostled for her favours. They too were Guns and Uncles.

It was so much easier for Mama to cope at Henley station where Alec Livingston was the station master and a great friend of my father. Like Papa, who sometimes came back from the war before his nervous breakdown, he loved expeditions searching out rare plants and orchids and wild flowers, birds and butterflies. But he never killed them as Bangpa-Pop did or pinned the chloroformed moths and butterflies onto specimen trays.

"I absolutely have to travel first class in case of germs and more common *cursí* people," said Mama faintly. Her hands swept the horizon dismissively. "Just in case—and I don't want anyone forgettin' I'm a most frightfully important Spanish aristo policewoman, bastard as I may be, ha, ha, *olé!*"

She would tap her gloved hands impatiently as Alec Livingston hastily wrote out her first-class ticket for London. A red carpet led from beneath her feet to the first-class compartment, thickly upholstered in cut velvet. The express train at Twyford had replicas of the same style for the continuation of Mama's weekly expedition. There was seldom more than one other person in her carriage, usually a close friend "doin' somethin' most frightfully important in the City for the war effort and not quite up to the actual fightin'," offered Mama by way of explanation as she pushed me firmly back into a middle seat. "You're to be seen but certainly not heard," she hissed as a scarlet-nailed hand adjusted the elastic band of my hat more tightly beneath my chin.

The wartime exemption which had exonerated her three colonels from fighting on the front had also been given to certain of the local doctors round Assendon Lodge, Turville Heath and Henley. As my mother explained: "Those darlin' boys Alan, Kenneth and Norm are forbidden active combat because there is so much else, and far more important, to take care of right here and now."

This meant that the doctors could help out with "my emergencies and walkin' up the birds", as Mama described the garden shoots she organised through nearby fields of rotting vegetables, mostly Brussels sprouts which had run to a great height, and low-lying water-logged cabbages. Old root turnips and orange swedes had run to seed and been left behind in the mud for bullocks and heifers to graze in the Stonor fields.

"Old Albert Hunt's husbandry is not up to much," Mama had laughed brightly, stamping briskly through the mud in her Newmarket boots, swinging a shooting-stick, the pheasant feather in her Tyrolean hat cheerfully cocked as she followed her troupe of Guns.

Now she turned her attention to the minute and uniformed figure of the station master as he smoothed the red carpet before her. "Quite frankly I'm not into geldin's," she said with a sniff.

Mr Livingston bowed and doffed his deeply peaked cap.

"His ridiculous over-ornate uniform looks most frightfully Frog to me," continued Mama as she graciously picked her way towards the waiting train. "I'm quite allergic to gettin' my feet dirty as I'm in such frightfully delicate health bein' a Spanish aristo grandee," she continued, casting a disparaging glance at Mr Livingston's bow-tie and at his equally minute wife Edith who hovered close behind him.

Edith Livingston had thin wisps of white hair, which floated quite gently round her pink scalp and over her thick pink plastic spectacles. She had an air of perpetual anxiety.

"Another absolutely crashin' bore," Mama announced in her loudest voice. "Just like a governess, and I'm not invitin' her around with Alec to lunch at Assendon Lodge."

As Mama carefully explained to me, "all those very dear boys, the doctors, and darlin' old Fred, my vet, are 'Uncles' . They must go immediately into your night prayers." But she exempted poor Mr Livingston. "Simply not my class, Julia dear. Somethin' you're far too stupid and dim to understand now, God help me from your quite frightful stupidity—inherited no doubt from your God-awful grandmother that *tedioso* millionaire Mildew Mildred sittin' pretty in Newport."

Picking up her silver hip-flask Mama gave a deep sigh, and took a gulp of Horse's Neck, dipping deep into the new black crocodile bag recently "picked up from my darlin' Mr Louis, such a saint of a man".

"But at least I have the comfort of seein' the flicks at the Regal cinema when the boys are orf duty from their medical chores," said Mama reflectively. Of course, with my own medical trainin' now I'm in the police, administerin' motions, potions and medications, mixin' medicines and doin' operations are my very first love, all very much in my line of country," she continued happily. "I may have missed out on my vocation, but I'm certainly makin' up for lorst time."

Back in the comfort of her bedroom, Mama carefully turned over the page of her latest purchase, another Angela Thirkell novel. "I do rather fancy myself as the Lady Pomphret. But certainly not before I am THE

Baroness Camoys," she said, puffing on a cigarette as she flipped over another page. "My Gawd, and that frightful bore of a woman Lady Hoosters-Boosters gets her nose in everywhere. To think," she continued indignantly, "the old gel damn nearly bagged Sherman. I soon put a stop to that, even if he did run away from me in '38. That was a frightfully close shave, what with my own darlin' Joachim and all those divine jackboots marchin' up and down at Castello Sonnenburg-bei-Berlin."

Mama placed a hand across her bosom. "Too bad it made Sherman so squeamish, positively sea-sick, let alone impotent. To say nothin' of what it did to me, back-firin' in every way," yawned my Mother "I had to make pretty quick resource to my darlin' old Ambassador Raul Regis de Oliveira to deliver the essential goods again. Just in the nick of time, ha, ha, *olé!* All that brass and bauxite in Brazil, heil Hitler!" Drawing herself to her feet Mama shouted merrily: "*Cojones* to them all, and some with, and several without! *Olé, olé!*"

Mama stretched her feet out beneath the vicuña skin now laid over a chaise-longue on which she was resting. She yawned again. "I'm most frightfully bored," she stated, "which is the only reason why I can even tolerate the sight of you, Julia."

She had allowed me to remain with her for much longer than usual, and I was happy as I drank in the rich fumes of her perfume and cigarette smoke, and caught an occasional heavy whiff from the top of a green rummer glass filled with a bubbling Horse's Neck. But I knew it couldn't last.

"On second thoughts I'll stick to Camoys," said Mama reflectively. "That old Pomphret title is a frightfully new creation, round 1889, and most tiresomely post-Reformation." She winked at Bangpa-Pop, who reappeared after our train journeys. "How come Pop-goes-the-Weasel that it has taken all that time, from 1283 until 1943 to get to only the 5th Baron Camoys? If my division is right, that means you must be about 110, ha, ha! Did you have a sex change by any chance? Your title actually descends down only through the female line through dear old Chaucer himself. I shall be THE Baroness Camoys, just you watch me old boy. Quite my thing too and 6,000 acres to boot." Mama appeared lost in delight at her contemplations. She turned again to my grandfather "How's your Thing today, by the bye? Do we have yet more brewer's droop? Or are you up to it? I've got a very nifty number in aphrodisiacs, Ralph old boy. Picked it up with my vital prescriptions at my favourite chemist. Wigmore Street is so frightfully convenient and no ridiculous questions asked."

Bangpa-Pop looked uneasy again, and guffawed. He cleared his throat, blowing noisily onto a grey handkerchief.

"Don't murmur Ralph, you colossal old bore. I've already told Frank Spellman all about you in New York, effin' inconvenience that you are. Your sole and doubtful use is for the production of bastards, entails and entrails, and all those other wind-producin' *cojones*, *olé* and heil Hitler!"

Mama saluted my grandfather, and then turned sharply on her heel, two fingers stuck in the air in a V-sign. "No one mucks me or my darlin' Joachim Ribbentrop around without payin' the price for it, so watch your step, you old fart the Fifth Baron Windbag!"

22

'To Catch a
Millionaire or Two'

Wing-Commander "Dead-in-Full-Flight-Ha-Ha!" Waghorne
only lasted a week in my night prayers. There was such a waiting list for the living as Mama said. "The dead simply bore me
to tears. With the one exception of my own darlin' Dickie Sheepshanks."
A tear rolled down her rouged cheek as my mother clutched the silver-
framed sepia photograph of the Spanish Civil War correspondent.

"God damn that bastard Kim Philby," she said furiously in the kitchen.
"Murderers cut no ice with me, *olé*!" Mama stubbed out a cigarette. "I'm
all in favour of the death penalty; hangin' would be far too good for the
likes of Philby," she snorted in the direction of Bangpa-Pop—who took
refuge behind a cupboard door.

With a quick sip of an early elevenses and the support of Uncle Eric St
Johnston, who today had appeared in mufti, Mama balanced on a ladder to
climb up to inspect the sugar-hoard cupboards.

"Eric darlin' boy just be an angel and hold onto the bottom rung,"
shouted my mother hanging onto the top step and the opened cupboard
door. "I really have no head for heights. Hold on for all your might, Eric
sweetie-pie. And just you stop gapin', Julia Stonor, we may have a blockade," shouted Mama as she counted the lines of sugar packages.
"Frightfully hush-hush, and special permission from the War Office," she
explained as she clambered down into the outstretched arms of the chief
constable of Oxfordshire.

Ruby was reading *Held Fast for Gibraltar* to me and she straightaway
explained that this was the sort of blockade meant by Mama. "Gib", as
Mama called it, was a rock sticking up out of the water off the side of Spain
where several of my Uncles kept their tailor and where several of Mama's

family lived, trading with Tangiers and Algeciras and their own cousins there.

"Just a touch of the Moorish tar brush," said Mama happily. "Such a frightfully lucrative smugglin' pitch," she continued merrily swaying a little on the ladder which Uncle Eric held on to as she recounted the sugar packets.

She locked up the cupboards again. "Against marauders. My chatelaine is pure silver, of course," She swung a big bunch of keys from a long silver chain attached somewhere round her waist. "My darlin' old colonel, that divine Jack Rutherford gave it to me in my hour of need, *olé!*" So saying Mama wobbled carefully back down to the floor, this time with a cigarette end dripping ash as she aimed a playful kick at my shins. "All ready for the next blockade from the bottom rung of the ladder, not to mention BLOCKAGES, *olé!*" she laughed as she lit up another contraband American cigarette.

By now I was getting the hang of these blockades and blockages, but I was already extremely familiar with the "motions, utters and actin'-pains for when nothin' gets through those maddenin' blockades and blockages". And, of course, there were Mama's remedies which she applied to Papa and me, or more of Fred Machin's medicines and potions-for-motions.

"What's good enough for the dogs is certainly good enough for you both, Sherman and Julia," said Mama firmly. "And I'm experimentin' with these divine little brown pills," she exclaimed excitedly, holding them up to the light as she shook them into a dark-brown bottle full of bright orange capsules. Then she carefully poured thick white liquid into yet another of the regimented glass bottles which stood on Papa's dressing table.

The effect of Mama's potions-for-motions was instantaneous and produced what she described as "the Good Mornin' Squitters, ha, ha!" These were so painfully awful that I wondered, from the depths of the china pot to which I was glued, whether Ruby the great dane had died of this total misery as well as lockjaw.

Ruby, still a young dog, had looked so well, gentle, beautiful. "Such impeccable breedin'," my mother had said when old Mr Swaebe, the court photographer, had been brought down from London to take the yellow drawing room conversation piece before the sudden tragedy of Ruby's death. Mama had had the photograph taken wearing her best rubies.

"That darlin' gel Barbara Hutton, and my own darlin' Sir Orsten

Chamberlain gave these to me," she explained to the startled Mr Swaebe. "Long before you came out of hidin' in the Austrian ghettos," she sneered, knocking the cigar out of the photographer's hand. "There are certain conditions to this game, old boy, and even mentionin' the payment of a bill is simply not one of them. So watch it, *olé* and heil Hitler."

Throwing her head back, Mama roared with laughter as she fingered a large ruby-and-diamond brooch and lightly touched her matching earrings before shaking heavily bejewelled fingers in Mr Swaebe's face. "Those darlin's Barbara Hutton and old Orsten certainly knew my hour of need." Ruby and her companion great dane sat on either side of Mama as she posed for photographs for *The Tatler & Bystander*. I sat on the floor, well beneath my mother, in a white party frock recently arrived from Granny Camoys in Newport. The Uncles and Guns all said how beautiful Mama looked. And Ruby Heath gave the once-finished pictures, black and white in a thick velvet texture, a long hard gaze. And sighed again.

*

One of Mama's routes to the knacker's yard at Benson lay via Russells Water and Maidensgrove. We returned through Pishill, and I was convinced there was a connection linked to what my mother described as "essential pot-trainin' habits, and toilet needs for that tedious brat of Sherman's constipated bowel movements". But she did not explain. "Piss-orf you fool. Never explain, never complain is my motto," snapped Mama. "Just continue to do as I say, and not as I do. Mrs Do-As-You-Would-Be-Done-By indeed! Never heard such balls, nonsense and absolute pills," she finished briskly, revving up the engine.

Mama's words puzzled me a lot, and I thought hard during my afternoon rests as to how I could find a way to please her. Most of my efforts somehow displeased my mother, and frequently my "rests" turned into the punishment of early bed. This "punishment" was deeply disappointing, and furthermore I could not always see exactly what was happening downstairs at Assendon Lodge, and later, up at the Park.

Supper, which was high tea with toast ("horse drippin' is such an economy," commented Mama) was brought up to the night nursery by Ruby Heath or Nanny-of-the-Day—who seldom, if ever, had a first name, and only occasionally a surname. When I managed not to finish my lunch, or other meal, it was carefully put to one side at Mama's orders. And produced again and again for me to eat until it was completely finished. This was especially difficult with our Parker neighbours' pig's liver, which was cooked hard enough to bounce off the plate. I could barely swallow it without choking. By pushing it surreptitiously down into the hot-water system of my Peter Rabbit china bowl I disposed of the liver until the awful day when the bowl broke, revealing the chewed remains of the previous week's ration.

Mama's vengeful glee knew no bounds. There followed an instant spanking with the black Mason & Pearson's hairbrush, white bristles stuck onto a convex pink base. "My gold hairbrush is far too good for you Julia, you tedious little bitch," shouted Mama between spanks. "Straight orf up to early bed, and no argument, *olé!* "

I decided that picking bunches of flowers would make my mother feel better about me. Whenever Papa came home from the war he picked armfuls of lilacs, purple and white and deepest pink, and bunches of copper beech leaves, flowers from the herbaceous borders, wild cowslips, daffodils and narcissuses. I started with primroses and some pretty white flowers which I thought might be like crocuses. Lovingly I arranged them in a vase which I had just managed to reach down from a shelf in the pantry. I placed my gift in Mama's best bedroom.

"Where in Gawd's name did you find the WILD GARLIC, you bloody little fool?" screamed my mother, her eyes even blacker than usual. Flinging open a window, she hurled the pungent contents of the vase out onto the drive beneath. "How dare you, how DARE you," she screamed. "And into the bargain you've stolen one of the chapel vases. You're nothin' more than a common thief, just like your tiresome American grandmother Mildew Lady Cee. It's more than high time you learned the Third Commandment, you disobedient brat." Mama commanded in her most withering tone: "Honour your father and, most especially, your MOTH-ER!"

She yanked my hair as she went past. Tears sprang to my eyes and I hoped she would not see. "You're such a cowardly-custard and Sherman's sissypants daughter," said my mother scornfully, puffing cigarette rings towards me.

I was disconsolate that I could not come up with anything that I could give Mama to make her happy. My next idea was to make up to her with the chocolates Colonel Micklem gave me every year as a Christmas gift. Embedded in a sumptuous red and green velvet box from a shop in

Piccadilly which Uncle Henry Micklem called "Fortnum's", the chocolates were exclusively hand-made. Uncles Tio Pepe Manzanedo and Pepe Primo de Rivera called it *"Forrtoon ee Masón"* when they came down to Assendon Lodge or up to Stonor Park as Christmas Guns, each with a pair of soft black suede gloves for my mother wrapped in the same Fortnum paper, a gold bow on the ribbon.

Mama glared down at my lovingly wrapped present. "Go away Julia, you damn nuisance!" was all she could say. "Go away, and get the hell out of my sight. I don't want your damnable second-hand presents. Always in the wrong place at the wrong time, and what a crashin' bore you are," she shouted.

I plucked up the courage to stand my ground, my present still extended in my shaking hand to this beautiful vision who, as always, was smartly dressed this time in handmade mustard-yellow tweeds and brown brogues equipped for that week's "shootin' party".

But Mama was merely enraged further and cuffed my ears as she shouted again. "Keep right out of my sight, and just learn *muy pronto* to take a back seat in my life! You're completely redundant, and the sooner you learn that fact of life the better you idiotic little bitch. And don't for one moment think that your best is ever good enough Julia," she continued icily, turning away. "You are Julia and you will pay the price for bein' Sherman's brat. I guarantee you that, if nothin' else," she scoffed. "Ruination of my honeymoon at my darlin' Joachim Ribbentrop's divine Castello that you and Sherman are. But revenge is mine!"

Revenge was a regular subject whenever my mother was around. One day, I found myself squashing an enormous bright mustard-yellow wasp on the nursery window sill with my shoe after it had stung me. From behind, Mama had crept up quietly and now gave me one of her fiercest pinches, thumb and middle finger biting sharply into my upper arm.

"Retribution is mine, and mine alone, Miss Do-As-You-Would-Be-Done-By!" she laughed. "And THIS is what it feels like to be squashed onto a plane of glass."

*

Mama had a friend who looked her twin.

"This is your Auntie Margaret Sweeny, my goddaughter and your third godmother," said Mama brightly. "Of course," she turned to our visitor, "I gave Sherman's brat two more for the christenin', and the Royal One is vastly superior to you, Margaret, AND to darlin' Contessa Angela Antrim, *olé!* A Spanish Princess and Infanta of the blood royal to boot. Borbóns and Habsburgs and Battenbergs and all that sort of thing. We've always been as close as that," said my mother happily, curling her fingers around one another. "*Olé! Viva el rey de España* and heil Hitler!" Mama saluted Aunt Margaret gleefully.

Auntie Margaret Sweeny, who was waiting to be a duchess, came to tea at Assendon Lodge with my mother's semi-demi-sisters, the blonde aunts Magda Stourton and Barbara Bellville.

Mama regarded the semi-demi-sisters with amusement. "My dear, they're both so frightfully much married, and so many times I can hardly remember which husband is which, let alone quite when, or quite which we've got to," she laughed to Flicky, who stood sternly in the kitchen down from Loch Ness on her annual visit. "Such truly admirable behaviour for Cartholics you know. Gawd only knows what my darlin' Uncle Archbishop Mostyn would've made of it all. As it is his darlin' brother the Monsignor Joseph is buried alive at the Vatican. He is, of course, just occasionally dispensin' dispensations and handin' out incentives for this and that. He and I are most frightfully close to my darlin' old beau Sir D'Arcy Osborne at the British Legation, borin' old pansy Prot though he is." Mama sighed with pleasure, gazing over her cigarette at the three aunts. "Such a useful corridor, the Vaticano. Such a humdinger for baby smugglin', and a little of this, and a little of that," she laughed. "A brat too many, and all of that goddamned nuisance wartime inconvenience." She clicked her fingers suddenly, stubbing out the cigarette on the parquet floor beneath her heel. "And Gawd knows I know all about that."

The semi-demi-aunts sat stiffly upright on the yellow button-backed sofa, Magda shorter than Barbara but their voices very similar. Their lips pursed thinly, the two women looked down hooked, bony Plantagenet noses, gazing, sometimes staring at Mama while Ruby all but staggered into the yellow drawing room, bowed down by the weight of a heavily ornate silver tray, engraved with coronets and a coat-of-arms. On the tray balanced an equally ornate silver teapot, cream jug and sugar bowl and tea strainer. The fine porcelain teacups, saucers and plates were painted with flowers.

I thought it all magical. Ruby herself wore her best "afternoon" uniform of black wool crepe, with a starched apron and frilly cap, perched like a crown stiff with starch high on her red curls.

My mother sat behind a large silver kettle pouring the hot water. "My family samovar," she explained grandly to Magda and Barbara. "Russian, you know, like the late dear tsar and that divine dowager, the tsarina—such a very dear friend of Aunt Julia, the Markeys you know." Mama continued to pour scalding water from a great height into the teapot, then out down its beak-like spout through the silver tea-strainer that Ruby held over the cups. I was entranced by the bright blue flame flickering in a silver bowl of purple liquid beneath the samovar.

"Meths, you know," said Mama brightly. "I always find methylated spirits such a frightfully good substitute for cognac when the worst comes to the worst."

Magda and Barbara sniffed, and drew deeply on their own contraband American cigarettes. They exhaled thin blue circles in the direction of my Mother. But she paid no attention and continued to pour the scalding water from a great height. "*Olé* and *caramba* and *cojones* to one and all," she laughed mockingly.

The demi-semi-sisters regarded my mother indignantly. They continued to smoke from long tortoise-shell holders, mounted in silver, clenched between lips of deep scarlet. Their eyes narrowed.

Aunt Margaret said she aimed at being a duchess before very long. Mama's response was instant: "Don't be so damn ridiculous, Margaret! And you can't because you're still effin' well married to Charlie Sweeney. Damn it all. And don't forget that I'm your godmother for your Conversion of Convenience to Cartholicism. All of that effort just so that you could have that glitter and glamour and hoo-ha for your weddin' at the Oratory church in '37 to boot. So much codswallop and *cojones* to that sham. More than a pity you didn't have to go in for Total Immersion in Holy Water."

It was around this time that Ruby Heath was reading *Alice's Adventures in Wonderland* aloud to me. Being so identical in looks, as beautiful as one another, I thought Aunt Margaret and Mama could easily be twin Red Queens and shout "orf with your head!" to one another.

Instead they continued sipping cups of tea.

"This tea," announced Mama, "was made in China for my great beau Earl Grey himself, dear old Charlie you know, from the prime minister's family." She turned towards my grandfather, who had looked round the drawing room door. "But I can't say there was much up top in that peer's head. And only a most frightfully third-grade major in a Guards regiment in the last war. Not that YOU were up to much in your own hot-air balloon at the time, Ralph dear," continued Mama. She flicked her hand dismissively. "Beat it, and beat it quick, Pop-goes-the-Weasel," she hissed. "You're most strictly out of bounds, and with as much tact as that proverbial rhinoceros. Quite simply nothin' but a bull in a china shop. Get goin'!"

My junior godmother Aunt Margaret Sweeny, and my two semi-demi-aunts continued eating the slim sandwiches, cut elegantly into four, crustless and filled with the cucumbers which Mr White grew in the cold frames up at the Park.

Ruby had filled brown bread sandwiches with Gentlemen's Relish, which Mama had unlocked deep from a store cupboard. I was not sure what this was but thought hard if it had anything to do with Mama's Gentlemen Guns or, indeed, with the dead relics and rations that my mother always talked so much about. I envied the adults in the drawing-room as they ate their crustless sandwiches because in the nursery dining room thick crusts were left on.

"My orders is that they're good for you, Miss Julia," Ruby would always assure me. "But it's all upstairs for some," she said, wiping my mouth.

*

"I feel quite undressed without my jewellery. Quite naked in fact," announced my mother grandly. She fingered the several rows of pearls round her neck and throat. Down her front she wore a long, finely linked silver chain, which she called "my chatelaine—strictly NOT my chastity belt, ha, ha and *olé!* Just such a thoughtful gift from that darlin' boy Jack Rutherford. French of course, straight from Bordeaux—no problems there this time of the war what with one thing and another, heil Hitler." The chain lived deep in a pocket in the vicinity of my mother's waistline, a heavy, jangling bunch of keys dangling from its end. "I simply have to take it orf at night. Gets most frightfully in the way of things and anyone could hear me comin' a mile orf," she laughed.

Puzzled by this, I asked Mama as she brushed my hair what else she could possibly be doing in bed when she was asleep.

"You're just too damned stupid and ignorant for any words. Just remember the Third Commandment!" she snapped and gave me a sharp slap around the head as she pulled the large tortoise-shell comb through my hair, wrenching out a chunk of tangles. "For good measure I'm just removin' all the rats and rat's tails while I'm about it, you silly brat," said Mama, triumphantly holding up the hair matted into the teeth of the comb.

More tears sprang to my eyes as I felt a lump of pain rising in my throat.

"Dry up you sissy-pants brat of Sherman's. No more of that rubbish and nonsense. You can pump them up and squeeze them out, but it cuts absolutely no ice with a Spanish aristo bastard like me, my girl. Early bed is the only suitable place for you, Julia Stonor," said Mama firmly. Inhaling deeply on her cigarette she turned on her heel. "Ruby, you can draw the black-out blinds down immediately. If not sooner!"

All the Assendon Lodge wartime cupboards were tightly under lock and key. Those in the pantry and larder especially were bursting full.

"Quite like one's own bladder, really," declared Mama. "Burstin' full, and ready for immediate evacuation and ejaculation, *olé!*"

The taller of the cupboards were full of Barbados sugar. I was not sure what the other items, piled equally high, were. There were things other than supplies of Wheatena, cream-of-wheat and tapioca, which Granny Camoys sent by sea from Newport on a cargo ship.

"I'm damned if I am goin' to starve and fade away in this damnably in convenient war," said Mama indignantly. "My darlin' Joachim has already made sure of that for me." Leaning down from the top of a stepladder she saluted Uncle Eric St Johnston merrily. "Heil Hitler and *cojones* and pills to everythin' else, *olé!*"

But water glass and preserved eggs, and nasty foul-smelling things were never locked up. Nor was the dog meat.

"My dogs absolutely thrive on entrails and entails," said Mama, confusing me greatly since she talked about the latter incessantly in so many other areas of her conversation.

The "entails", I supposed, might have something significantly in common with the overwhelming smell of horse entrails that my mother invariably brought back from the knacker's yard every Wednesday. Bangpa-Pop was clearly as interested as Mama in these "entails" and discussed them with her incessantly, often sequestered in the seclusion of the study at Assendon, and at Bosmore, shuffling through piles of documents on the big brown desk, and later at Stonor. I had watched my mother's silver and red fountain pen working away at furious speed, a cigarette hanging from the corner of her mouth, a green rummer glass at her elbow. Bangpa-Pop would have a glass of Kia-Ora fruit squash at his elbow, next to a large bot-tle of medicine against acid stomach and wind attacks.

Mama's Regency rosewood desk always held sheaves and sheaves of papers, deeds, letters and mysterious brown envelopes. Some of the larger envelopes were very stiff and came hand-delivered by motorbike. These Mama put to one side. The small, floppy brown envelopes she immediate-ly tossed away.

"Straight into the bin," she said imperiously. "I always make it a rule sel-dom, if ever, to pay small tradesmen's bills. They can all jump for it, and stuff it up as far as I am concerned."

Bangpa-Pop explained that he always called the waste paper basket a "trash-can".

"Somethin' you no doubt learnt durin' your courtship in New York, Ralph dear," replied Mama. "From all accounts, and all things considered, quite a successful period of your life, old boy," she giggled. "At least you came back with the goods in the shape of Mildred Mildew's millions." Tossing back the contents of her glass, Mama winked at my grandfather "And don't suppose I don't know all about your little game of flattery and seduction, Pop-goes-the-Weasel. All that sentimental bosh and bunkum you served up to Mildred Constance Sherman just when her father old William Watts Sherman was about to kick the bucket into the bargain. Very quick thinkin' if I may say so in catchin' a millionaire or two in your butterfly net, olé!" said Mama reflectively.

She blew smoke rings into Bangpa-Pop's face until even his double chins were wreathed in blue smoke. "Quite some hot sell of your four-balled coronet. The 5th Baron Camoys of the Four Balls, ha, ha! Tell THAT to the Marines old boy." Mama gestured emphatically with two fingers in his direction.

My grandfather looked increasingly uneasy. He guffawed, hiccuped and blew his nose.

But Mama was just starting . . . "Not even a hand's turn have you done since your marriage in a brownstone bedroom in 1911, Ralph. Don't think I don't know that you left your father-in-law to pop orf the very next week, so determined were you to get your squalid hands on all that filthy lucre. Yanked Mildew Mildred right orf to Japan *muy pronto* so that old Watts Sherman wouldn't guess just what sordid activities you were up to, old boy." Mama took a step closer to Bangpa, placing her hands on his shoulders. "You just buggered orf out of New York as fast as your new galoshes would take you, old fart of a fraud that you are." She laughed her deep throaty perfumed laugh and blew another smoke circle. "With the ripe exception of certain bedwork—and don't I know all about that— you've done precisely fart-eff all ever since, tedious old windbag that you are." She paused for a moment. "And don't think I can't and won't tell Mildew herself. I'm keepin' Sherman at arms length from his mother, and all that sentimentality about lovin' one another, frightfully dangerous to my cause. I'll make certain they both eff orf out of it. Stuff, nonsense, pills and *cojones*. And where's the MONEY, Ralph Camoys?" She slammed the study door so hard it reopened with the ricochet. "Tycoons indeed they may be, and certainly are, and richer than Croesus into the bargain, but common as muck all these American Wasps from Newport and Philadelphia, by my own Spanish aristo standards, *olé!* Most frightfully recent."

Bangpa-Pop nodded, his white head and white moustache shaking over his loose purple double chin. He reminded me exactly of old Mrs Hughes' turkey cocks in the scruffy yard at Pishill Bottom farm. He said it was quite a pity that the entrails and entails had all been broken up. It had happened rather inadvertently when he was forced to sell up the Stonor Estate and his London properties to his wife Mildred in 1937 because he'd had a "frightfully near miss with bankruptcy and all that sort of thing".

But Mama was very indignant that it had all happened while her back was turned, and she was still away in the Spanish Civil War. "And then that BITCH Mildew Mildred Camoys got her hot sticky paws on the Cock's Leas and Bosmore estates too. I'll make quite sure Lady Cee comes unstuck pretty damn quick, and that won't be quick enough at the speed I work, *caramba* and *olé!*"

My grandfather ventured uneasily that he had power of attorney.

"Power of attorney indeed! And over WHOM?" shrieked Mama. "Just another spoilt brat. Get my tame solicitor, that rat, my darlin' David Drummond on the telephone, Pop-goes-the-Weasel. And move it. I want him right here, now and immediately. And nothin'—NOTHIN', did you hear me clearly?—is goin' to thwart me."

Mama stamped her foot furiously when Bangpa-Pop tried to explain that David Drummond was otherwise involved in the war effort.

"And get me darlin' WINSTON on the blower immediately. Don't stand around with that ridiculous expression on your face, Pop. After all, he is half-American and actually runnin' this absolutely absurd war which has gorne and ruined all my plans." Mama gazed intently at Bangpa-Pop. "Perhaps it's your brewer's droop and recessive genes which make you so wet. I could wring you out like an old flannel, ha, ha! Heil Hitler too, come to think of it." She saluted Bangpa-Pop.

Mama still seemed to prefer Papa's second sister to Granny Camoys because she was even richer and married to a whole institute in Philadelphia. "Banks and those divine bankers, *olé!* have always rather taken my fancy, startin' of course with my darlin' old ambassador in Brazil, Raul Regis de Oliveira and his steelworks," she reflected thoughtfully. "Bankers over the water, components and *cojones*, *olé!* I'm most frightfully cosmopolitan after all." She rattled off a list of surnames. "I'm not a Spanish aristo bastard for nothin'. There's my old beau the prince acrorss the water in Parigi. And Carlos Aramayo and Raul Regis. I used to nip acrorss on the *Flèche d'Or*—first class all the way natch—and catch up with darlin' Jean-Louis Faucigny before pickin' up a divine little number from that sweetie-pie Gabrielle Chanel. Such a duck."

Mama winked a dewpond black eye at my grandfather. "Well, duckie, Mildew Lady Cee is a bitch. How DARE she break the Stonor estate entail right over your head, Pop-goes-the-Weasel. And now that it all belongs to Sherman outright if course it belongs to ME. Shall we call it 'My Very Own Freehold', Pop dear?" she winked again, cheerfully. " 'MY VERY OWN FREEHOLD'," she repeated, giving a tinkling laugh and a deep, smoky cough that cleared her throat and nose in one movement.

23

A Memory of Stonor,

1940-1950

Jeanne remained vociferously anti-Semitic. She was also anti anyone of any other religion, aside from Catholicism, or for that matter, skin colour (she had eagerly supported D'Arcy Osborne in his request to Pius XII not to allow American "Coloured troops" into Rome). There had been rumours in Sherman's American heritage of racially "tainted" blood, put around by Jeanne from the early days of her marriage.

"Rhode Island Reds,and Red Indians in under Someone's bed not so long ago," she hinted darkly to her Oxfordshire neighbours when out calling. Miss Bridges, old Mrs Whitaker from Marsala, and pink-nosed Major Ellison, an army physiotherapist practising at nearby Caversham were transfixed by Jeanne's intimate revelations of communism and Red Indian antics beneath her mother-in-law's Bellevue Avenue bed. "Furthermore, Sherman's Baptist blood is most frightfully black," Jeanne announced with glee.

By this time she was calling on Viscount and Viscountess Esher, the latter Aunt Oinette (one of the few women Mama permitted to enter my night prayers), a millionaire Heckscher of New York—incredulous with horror at such steamy revelations about the illustrious families of the John Nicholas Browns and the William Watts Shermans, old stock from Providence, Newport and New York with formerly impeccable credentials.

Oliver Esher, the 3rd Viscount, once Secretary to the Secretary of State to India, Viscount Morley, like many of Jeanne's beaux had been in Military Intelligence. He was also president of the Euthanasia Society, a fact that enraged the superstitious Spanish Catholicism of Jeanne.

"Common Belgian from the suburbs. Practise euthanasia on yourself. And you can start right now," shouted Jeanne by way of greeting, at the bald, rotund and squat Oliver. "Bein' 3rd Viscount cuts absolutely no ice with me. Personally speakin' my own Castilian ancestry is hundreds of years older. Pre-Inquisition you know. And I'm heir to that divine castle in Cádiz, La Alcaría, *olé!* Contessa Jeanne de Torre Diaz, Borja de Zulueta no less."

Jeanne had begun early on in the war years to punctuate her speech with sharp claps from the castanets which she whirled around her head, her black mantilla held in place with its high tortoiseshell comb. Her high heels clicked against the parquet floor as she whirled around. Both Aunt Oinette and Jeanne's Aunt Tia María pursed their lips and sniffed.

"Self-exterminative 'euphanasia' for you, Oliver, old boy," said Jeanne brightly. "And you're quite deleted from night prayers."

Food parcels arrived weekly from Mildred Camoys, posted from Newport, and filled with Cream of Wheat, Wheatena, sugar, maple sugar sweets and rice. Clothes also arrived for Julia from Cabbages and Kings on Bellevue Avenue, smocked dresses, white socks, brown and white shoes, infuriating Jeanne. Her own American silk stockings, cigarettes and scent arrived by courier, tall American officers in uniform like John Nicholas Brown, Mildred's first cousin, and his shorter ADC.

Jeanne paid considerable attention to the revenues for her shooting par-ties, and to nursery dining-room food as distinct from the adult dining-room. She took personal charge of dog food, lights, offal, stomachs and gizzards. On more than one occasion a dog would die mysteriously after Jeanne had "mixed the dog food myself, ha, ha!"

Mr Machin the vet looked perplexed at the symptoms displayed. When he questioned whether or not the labrador that had died could possibly have had access to "rat poison", Jeanne laughed mockingly at him, snap-ping her fingers in derision.

Mr Machin's concerns continued to grow when a bright yellow canary abruptly stopped its singing and died in hideous contortions. Jeanne had examined its cage with a cigarette hanging from her mouth before she consigned it to the dustbin, ordering Ruby to get rid of the rubbish immediately.

"None of this flotsam and jetsam in my cuisine," laughed Mama. "And I'm gettin' rid of a maid or two. They dared to contradict me." So saying she would sack servants briskly. "You can leave within the hour. Come to think of it that is far too long. I'm givin' you ten minutes. And don't you dare to ask for references. WHAT references?"

With a series of swift kicks Mama would frogmarch the maids through the back door carrying their paltry belongings, more often than not in floods of tears. "I'm very important in this goddamn war, and there are plenty more where you came from," she shouted as they fled through the garden gate.

Over the road from Assendon Lodge, behind the Rainbow Inn, Jeanne supervised uniformed men on war manoeuvres, issuing instructions through a loudhailer, blowing furiously on the silver whistle which she kept on a lanyard over her shoulder. Sometimes Uncle Eric would join her in uniform or Father Seyres came down to hear her confession at Assendon Lodge.

During the sacrament, the devoutly Protestant Ruby was given orders to "keep that brat of Sherman's, that tedious Julia, out of the way. And His Lordship can keep his mauve complexion at a distance too," said Jeanne waving wildly at her father-in-law. "I want him flagged down before the old boy makes it to the drawin' room."

Here she incarcerated herself with "my chaplain Father Cereal." But Father Cereal was not included in night prayers as he had continuously made himself unpopular with Jeanne. From the drawing-room could be heard indignant cries of "since when did playin' the black market to a fine profit become Mortal Sin? You know what you can do with it and all your Vichy scum, Father Cereal!" Jeanne's voice descended to a whisper but rose again in a crescendo as the door burst open, the hapless priest leading the way, shaking his head.

Between flying visits to London on the train, stopping for long sessions at Cartier in Bond Street and eating at Claridge's, accompanied by me as an alibi, seated upright on the back seat of the taxi that habitually met us at Paddington, time was found for us to make journeys to visit Sherman's lesbian cousin Gwennie Sladen, and aunt Marjorie Bryce in their secluded, hidden-away cottage at Pishill-with-Stonor.

Here the two ladies lived their lives in reclusion surrounded by fine English furniture, money, seventeen Manz cats and kittens without any tails. Jeanne bolted up the long grass-grown drive in fits and starts in Mildred's Chevrolet, swearing at every pot-hole and bump in the lane, stopping abruptly outside Cherry Orchard.

Cousin Gwennie and Aunt Marjorie had been land girls together in the First World War. They were now very high up in the Women's Royal Voluntary Service, and keen members of the Women's Institute. Aunt Marjorie especially had very fine medals and decorations on her uniform, of which Jeanne was envious.

"Damn it Marjorie, old gel, you've got more than me," she said furiously.

"Well, Jeanne dear," said Aunt Marjorie reflectively, "you could always become an expert in the diggin' of portable latrines, like me."

"I'm doin' a very special excavation in the Stonor cricket field for starters," Jeanne retorted brightly.

In January 1944 Jeanne's friend Ciano, Mussolini's son-in-law and foreign minister, was executed. Later on in the year Sherman was forced to relinquish his Commission in the Oxfordshire and Buckingham Light Infantry and invalided out of the army with the combination of a nervous breakdown and a burst appendix. Jeanne arranged for his convalescence in a single room at Claridge's. She was, at this time, very taken up with King George of Greece and his brother Prince, later King, Paul. She had also continued her liaisons with the Brazilian ambassador and doyenne of the diplomatic corps Raul Regis de Oliveira (until his death in 1942 in London) and Enid Bagnold's husband Sir Roderick Jones.

During the early and mid-Forties, Duncan Sandys, the red-headed, handsome son-in-law of Winston Churchill had become a frequent visitor to Assendon Lodge together with the Australian millionaire Lebbeus Hordern, now a squadron-leader in the RAF. Despite his tuberculosis, it was Hordern who lead the successful attack on the German battleship *Tirpitz*, sinking it on November 12, 1944.

Jeanne's activities in black marketing with Mr Affia, the carpet salesman from Friday Street in Henley, finally caught up with her. She was jointly summonsed to the magistrates' court on the Reading Road, unbeknownst to Sherman, the newly appointed magistrate, who was forced to cancel the hearing which now appeared unannounced on the list in front of him. The case was dismissed, unheard. But not far away Sherman's cousin Lady Peel was tried and heavily fined for a similar offence.

By May 7, 1945, Germany had surrendered unconditionally. Jeanne now became determined to move immediately back to Stonor Park, and ordered the National Benzole Petroleum Company to remove themselves forthwith. Sherman was deeply unhappy and adamant that he wished to remain at Assendon Lodge. Ralph, his father, had already been returned to the Bosmore Estate, where he was to stay before emigrating to New York and Tennessee in 1947.

Reluctantly Sherman followed the grand removal of Jeanne from the Lodge to the Park, accompanied by her dogs and Julia, packed into the Chevrolet. Ruby Heath followed on her bicycle.

Jeanne set about refurbishing Stonor, immediately stripping out any sign of her mother-in-law. She set about the removal of the wood and coke-fuelled central-heating boilers, destroying them with a vengeance. The house heaved with cold and damp, and began to leak prodigiously. This caused Jeanne considerable mirth, in which the various male guests joined. Women guests left within very few hours, unable to cope with temperatures frequently sub-zero. Their passageway was complicated by the physical isolation of Stonor Park. Exit could only be effected either on foot and by an infrequent bus. Or by use of an expensive and infrequent taxi service from Henley with a one-eyed driver.

Jeanne's friends Ian and Peter Fleming and many other officers, including the sons of Lady Cynthia Colville, were back from the war. Many of them were busily occupied with their nearby estates: Merrimoles for the Fleming brothers, Harpsden for Guy de Pass, Binfield for Lord Rathereedan.

Jeanne was immediately able to hire cheap labour from the German prisoner-of-war camp nearby. There was an Italian prisoner-of-war camp at Nuffield, and "my Eyeties", as Jeanne put it to her neighbours, were employed "diggin, out my spuds and swedes, turnip-shaped sods the whole lot".

The servants' hall at Stonor was again in full occupancy, with Italian cooks and maids, and meridionale southern Italian labourers. A stabbing or two took place, bottles were broken to make weapons to slash the women domestics. Jeanne carefully concealed these events from the police. She also filled the larder next to the servants with great quantities of rancid horse meat, supplied by knacker friends in Benson for the Stonor dogs, one of them a ferocious Pyrenean called Mary.

Jeanne ruled her staff, always referred to as "my retainers", with a rod of iron, and with all the manners of her ancestors from the Spanish Inquisition. Otilda, one of the Italian cooks, from Udine, was set to work in her spare time to spin the wool from Mary's coat on an old spinning frame left behind "by my bitch of a mother-in-law". The white wool was then knitted by another servant into a blanket for Jeanne's King Charles spaniel, the neurotic Periwinkle. Jeanne trained her dogs to sit on Georgian chairs, and to bite all and sundry.

Sherman protested in vain at the accounts now set up at all the grocers in Henley. Jeanne also had a series of accounts at Fortnum & Mason, Robert Jackson & Co, Harrods, Debenham & Freebody and at the jewellers Cartier and Tessier.

These were shops that she had frequented during the war and to which she now travelled with greater frequency, departing from Henley station with the red carpet out and Alec Livingston, the station master, doffing his cap as Jeanne grandly ascended the steps of a first-class carriage accompanied by the new owner of Assendon Lodge, silver-haired, suavely spoken, champagne salesman and master vintner Colonel Jack Rutherford, another Gun and Uncle in Julia's night prayers. "So like my Joachim," commented Jeanne.

Rationing, ration books, clothing coupons were still in force for some years immediately after the war. But not at Stonor Park. Nor, indeed, at Assendon Lodge during the war itself. Jeanne continued to have her clothes tailor-made, whether her uniform at the tailor in Bell Street which had supplied the liveries for the footmen and butlers in her mother-in-law's time, or her couturier frocks, coats and skirts, sporting jackets— "Absolutely *de rigueur* for shootin' parties', Jeanne explained to Sherman's dowdily dressed cousin, Lady Agnes Eyston, her nose and hands blue with the shivering cold at East Hendred house and the even damper Mapledurham House, with all the exigencies of wartime coupons, rationing and widowhood. Jeanne sniffed contemptuously at Cousin Agnes's RC piety.

Increasingly sumptuous meals were prepared and heavily supervised by Jeanne, herself no mean cook, with a remarkable addiction to experimentation with only the finest of victuals, delivered daily in vans from Henley and Wargrave. Mysterious medicines appeared on a motor-cycle commissioned to call at Cartwrights, a chemist on the fashionable Bell Street.

"Essential supplies," explained Jeanne briskly to the kitchen staff and new governess. "Frightfully necessary ever since I dropped my coil in front of Pop-Goes-the-Weasel. Silly old Ralph simply couldn't cope, ha, ha! Jeanne poured from one bottle to another, shook the mixtures into a cloud raised the bottles to gaze with satisfaction at the contents, giving orders to Julia to immediately place them in her father's bathroom. "Now then my girl, you may as well be useful for something, brat that you are. Take Papa's stomach medicine up immediately. And immediately is not quick enough—do you hear me?"

Outside of the houses it was just as frenetic, Sammy Marvel the head-gardener had been replaced by Mr White, the stout Plymouth Brethren expert in the growing of grapes in the several greenhouses at Stonor Park. Mr White and Jeanne did not care for one another. She took her revenge by spying on him in the garden privy, an earth closet built on a mound that could be minutely observed from the ground.

When Mr White died in the Bottom Lodge it would be several days before Jeanne would allow for his body to be collected by his Brethren. But he was a marvellous provider and the post-war table groaned with beautiful produce from Granny Mildred's old orchards and fruit-beds, the medieval walled kitchen garden and the green houses filled with tomatoes and grapes.

Geraniums were cultivated in Jeanne's summer house—she had two, one within the walls and the other without, hanging over the furthest wall of the walled garden, a handsome mock Tudor cottage with ornate balustrade. And there was an electric bell to summons servants from the faraway kitchen. A further bell summonsed either Sherman or his farm secretary.

A separate telephone was installed to the outside world, an extension of Turville Heath 300, the line installed for the benefit of Aunt Julia by Queen Alexandra.

"Turville Heath 424 and 300 combined," Jeanne would shout merrily down the line. "Who's speakin'? Make it quick, I haven't got all day to waste. I'm deep into my essential research," she said sharply, flicking the pages of *Mrs Beeton's Household Management With a Special Supplement on Poisons*.

In October 1946 Jeanne's former lover Ribbentrop was hanged at Nüremberg together with other Nazi war criminals. Also condemned to death was Martin Bormann, who conveniently, however could not be found to face judgement. Despite all the pleas from Ribbentrop that his many former friends in Britain, London especially, would testify on his behalf and as to his good intentions for the harmony of relations between the British government, British Establishment and the Nazi government, no one was forthcoming. Not even Lord Beaverbrook, the Canadian press baron and close friend of Winston Churchill, who had stayed with Ribbentrop when he was German ambassador to Britain, at Schloss Dahlem together with a further hundred English and American guests for the house parties of the Olympic Games held in Berlin, 1936.

"The Beaver", as Beaverbrook was known, was also a close friend and constant companion of Mama's, frequently visiting for the wartime shooting parties at Assendon Lodge. He enjoyed the magnificent, lavish hospitality provided by Jeanne at Sherman's ancestral home, where no expense was spared (other than on the central heating).

Lights blazed throughout the house as Harry Clack, gassed in the Great War, trundled his iron wheel-barrow through the long passages, assuaging the remaining hot-water boilers with coke and damp wood from the park. Even damper logs, green wood, wheezed and spat their way in the hall and dining-room fires that hissed and sighed a dim heat.

In the kitchen there was an old iron stove, kept constantly alight, alternating between the fiercest and the dimmest and unpredictable heat. On the top of this stove simmered a pot of steaming fat, mostly composed of cow or pig lights and offal, being rendered. Above this Jeanne had a wooden laundry line upon which one of the maid's dried Sherman's clothes wrung out of a washing machine, newly acquired from Jeanne's bachelor friend, John Foster, QC. "He's my favourite don at All Souls," Jeanne explained eagerly to Sherman's inquiry.

Tall, slightly slouched, sallow of colour and with a hooked nose, Foster had recently returned from Czechoslovakia bringing with him the author and journalist Marcia Davenport, the lively American mistress of the Czech president Jan Masaryk.

Mysteriously the washing-machine had also arrived with them, to be installed in the nether regions of the pantry, where it danced on its hind legs whenever plugged into the electricity. Jeanne was in awe both of machine and of Marcia, the handsome Jewish daughter of Lena Horne, a famous Romanian opera star.

"Jan's just fallen most conveniently out of an upstairs window in Prague," laughed Jeanne. "I don't think he'd had much practice in fallin' before," she added nervously to Marcia's enraged face. The prime minister of Czechoslovakia had just been murdered by the Communists.

Jeanne embarked on a lifelong spending spree for antiques. Dragging Sherman with her, accompanied by his cheque book, she frequented only the best, whether Blairmans of Mount Street or Malletts of Bond Street. Nothing was too good for Jeanne. Aided by Sherman's own impeccable taste and discerning eye, Jeanne swiftly built up a formidable collection of the finest antiques, porcelain, objets d'art, sporting paintings and, predominately, jewellery, with a concentration on Cartier, building on the extensive collection she had accrued from her former lover and employer Barbara Hutton. Meanwhile I had no new knickers—Jeanne economised by buying me second-hand clothes and shoes.

When Don Bradman arrived as the mysterious German tutor, Sherman avoided him but Jeanne had already banished her husband both to a single bedroom after his return from the war, and to his study in between meals.

"I do find the old boy a most frightful bore, after all my excitin' days in Madrid and Teruel," she would explain soulfully to Uncle Dick Ovey—who was Sherman's best friend from childhood.

He and Sherman were the same age, thirty-two in 1945. Dick was built like a hulk whilst Sherman was slender, slim boned with fine, aquiline features and long aristocratic hands which tapered away. Dick's hands always reminded me of ham bones such as those I had seen them in the larders where Jeanne cured her pigs and hung the venison which Alfred Butler and Dick Dewkes shot up the back drive at Stonor.

Don the tutor did not participate in the increasingly frequent shoots which had become even more glamorous since the war had ended. But he accompanied Jeanne as an extra beater, and went with her to the Merrimoles estate at Nettlebed, land which Ralph Camoys had sold to the Fleming family at the turn of the century. Here the Fleming brothers themselves ran an extensive shoot.

As with all such men who had been in uniform, she regarded officers as her own unique property, whether on active service or, as with her father-in-law, Ralph Camoys, merely a captain in the local Home Guard and ARP.

Even after the war food and clothes parcels continued to arrive during the rationing period from Mildred Camoys. Semolina, tapioca and various forms of rice products alternated with maple sugar sweets and smocked frocks for me. Jeanne was deeply contemptuous of these "paltry" offerings. And so, after the war's end, she decided "to see for myself", and booked to leave for New York and Newport in the dreadful winter of 1947.

This trip coincided with the death of Sherman's millionairess grand-mother, Sophia Augusta Wetmore Brown, widow of William Watts Sherman of Bellevue Avenue and the brownstone 102 East 25th Street, New York. Jeanne's beau from Middle Assendon and the Hernes estate, Commander Dick Ovey was left in charge. I was left with my seven-year-old cousin Robin Phillimore ("soon-to-be the lord," added Mama), his governess Miss Lynes, and their cocker spaniel Winkle. Sherman had left his best friend Uncle Dick to supervise the Stonor estate, the cowman Jenkins looking after his prize herd of Jersey cows and heifers.

But reluctantly, Sherman, an early ecologist, had finally given in to the artificial insemination of his herd. His concerns were trashed by Jeanne, who stormed: "Stuff and rubbish Sherman, you're just an impotent fool! And don't forget I've known all about this since my honeymoon of '38."

Jeanne threw such remarks about with abandon whether in front of the cowman, or his son, the second cowman, or visiting Guns such as the Flemings and Sir Archibald McIndoe—the famous plastic surgeon who was said to have completely rebuilt Martin Bormann's face at the end of the war.

Jeanne explained that: "My old friend, a great boyfriend you know, dear old Martin, is livin' just round the corner now. We needed his signature to those Swiss bank accounts. Frightfully important, just as dear old boy Duncan Sandys and that crashin' bore Evelyn Shuckburgh from the Foreign Office always told me. Plays his cello on the train between Henley and Twyford. Sticks it between his legs you know, ha, ha!" Drawing deeply on her cigarette, Jeanne would reminisce, tears welling to her yes. "If only THEY had plea-bargained for my darlin' Joachim. After all he was a blue-blooded count—Graf von Ribbentrop don't you know, and worth six of that borin' Bormann. Aptly named, don't you think?"

Jeanne's wintery trip to America was momentous in many ways. Sherman had only been allowed to see his mother Mildred once after she had moved back to the East Coast. During the war he had accompanied a member of Sir Walter Monckton's family on a mission to New York on the Cunard liner *Queen Mary*. Jeanne had expressed her deep displeasure. "You impotent arse to return empty-handed from your bitch of a mother, old Mildew!" she exclaimed contemptuously.

Jeanne was determined therefore that the 1947 expedition would succeed for her at least. Sherman's grandmother Sophia had left a vast inheritance and bequeathed more than a million dollars to a hospital for the lying-in of women, so deeply did she mistrust the medical profession, male doctors and gynaecologists most of all. She had given birth to only two daughters in great travail during the 1880s and found the whole idea abhorrent and deeply distasteful—as she pointed out in her last will and testament bequeathing many more millions to Mildred.

"The boot is on the other foot this time," declared Jeanne firmly to Uncle Dick before she set sail.

Freddie Shirfield, Sherman's foreman and best friend since childhood did most of the maintenance work, overseen yet again by the general agent Major Holt, a handsome man with smooth black hair and red hands. Miss Lynes, the governess with hand-knitted waistcoats of a pink boucle wool strengthened with shiny nylon, took charge of lessons and nursery arrangements.

Robust and stern-buttocked she had a low opinion of Jeanne, and sniffed disdainfully at the continuous flow of orders which Mama invariably gave. But she was in charge of Lord Robin, and Jeanne was acutely aware that this semi-orphaned young cousin of Sherman's owned the Phillimore Estates in London, Shiplake Hall and Coppid Hall not far from Stonor. He was already several times a millionaire, ward of his uncles, the colonels Claude and Robert.

"My dear," said Jeanne, gazing at Miss Lynes, "I am sure you know dear Claude has eloped with his butler again. I am so sorry for his dear wife. Of course they've hopped it for that Malcontenta *palazzo* in the suburbs of Venice. Quite a fetchin' piece of Palladium architecture on a frightfully smelly canal."

Sherman and Jeanne sailed to New York the month the great storm broke over England in 1947. The snow and wind caused the fall of many trees, cutting the water supply that Mildred Camoys had laid on from a well in the park in the days when she was busily installing electricity, bathrooms, and central heating at Stonor. After the snow and gales came the big flood, further isolating the big house. With Otile in the kitchen boiling kettles, Miss Lynes ruled supreme with her charges Lord Robin and myself, and Winkle the cocker spaniel.

Jeanne returned triumphant from her visit to Stonor Lodge, Bellevue Avenue, where she had stayed with Sherman's mother Mildred and a daughter whom Jeanne referred to disparagingly as "a Philadephian pretzel-nut".

"I've got more of the Sherman fortune, and about time too!" she declared happily at her tea parties. Ladies like Helen Lady Dashwood, Antoinette, Viscountess Esher, old Mrs Whitaker from Marsala with the yacht that trumped the Kaiser, Aunt Tia María de Zulueta and Miss Bridges still came to call, together with Mrs Charles Sweeny, soon to be a notorious Duchess of Argyll.

Even Jeanne's hook-nosed, blonde half-sisters Magda Stourton and Barbara Bellville now found it irresistible to be at Stonor Park. Their poverty-struck aunts Nora and Trix came too, down for the day from their reduced circumstances in Stanhope Gardens (later to become a well-known male brothel), dressed in English Roman Catholic black—Stourtons both—listless, heavy lisle stockings hanging down their legs, cascading over black lace-up, sensible walking shoes. Heavy jet rosaries with silver crosses came tumbling from capacious handbags. Aunt Trix triumphantly produced spare knickers from the depths of hers, as she had suffered from extremes of cold along with her cousin Lord William Mowbray, Segrave and Stourton.

"Stuffed away in the servants' wing, those two old Cartholic crows," Jeanne explained in a loud whisper to a Protestant neighbour. "Quite unmarriageable you know. Most original of my virgin cousins to boot."

She laughed merrily, ringing a Georgian silver bell to indicate that her tea party was at an end.

24

'Tinker, Tailor, Tutor, Traitor'

Frankfurt: The American Ambassador in Germany announced at
2.45am that von Ribbentrop and the ten other Nazi war leaders
sentenced to death by the Allied War Crimes Tribunal were hanged this
morning in Nüremberg prison. The executions were completed in one
and a quarter hours, beginning at 1am and ending at 2.15am.
(The Times, October 16, 1946)

Mama, who had once been Mummy, stood in the vastness of the black and white beamed Tudor kitchen at Stonor. The twice-weekly supply of dog meat had just arrived in a battered grey Austin van from the knacker's yard at Benson.

The van came to an abrupt stop at the back door of the gated yard, with a shrill screech of brakes and a sharp skid. Two young men appeared, caps to one side of their heads, the meat slung over their shoulders in loose-woven hessian sacks, lightly knotted with string. Horse's lights, lumps of purple offal and sweating glistening slabs of rancid flesh were tossed swiftly onto white marble-slabbed tables in the dank, darkened and humid game larder next to the servants' hall.

My mother's brittle laughter tinkled down the long passageway between a series of wooden doors painted *eau-de-nil* green. Briskly ordering the knackers to unload the horse meat, she shouted at them, "God damn it, my men, can't you get a move on? Stop dawdlin' about."

Simultaneously shoving the knackers sideways Mama slammed the door shut, catching their heels with the sharp edge of the massive door. "Piss orf, and stop complainin'," she hissed.

The cavernous, gloomy servants' hall had a flooring of dark brown linoleum, flaking, cracked and split. There was a scattering of heavy, shabby, sad Edwardian furniture, old brown sofas of torn, worn leather, and chairs with sunken, reeded seats. In a corner sat some of Mania's "Eyetie" servants, and Michele, a Neapolitan prisoner-of-war, very short of stature with thick stumpy bow legs. Michele dug potatoes at the local lunatic asylum in the village of Littlemore, where Cardinal Newman was buried.

"Quite a randy little Meridionale, my bow-legged boy Michele. All things considered, that is. Ha, ha, ha!" Mama laughed triumphantly, and inhaled mightily on her cigarette. She exploded into an excited bout of coughing, overcome with merriment. "All that spud diggin' really is most frightfully appropriate," she said with relish. "With any luck, Michele will bump straight into that dear old bore Cardinal Newman's bones. Come to think of it, he's buried with his boyfriend. Such an amusing gaiety gang." Mama exhaled a cloud of smoke and coughed up some more catarrh. "So Michele might disinter the boyfriend, too. No worse than my best rabbit ragoût!" She laughed merrily, then paused to take a long sip from her glass of brandy and ginger ale.

Next to the servants' hall came a stinking, ammoniated water-closet, thinly divided from the dank larder. These malodorous rooms were separated from the kitchen by a flagged stone passage leading right around the vastness of Stonor, a perfect track for my tricycle, and for Mr Clack, the boilerman, pushing coke and illicit coal in a rusting steel wheelbarrow.

Stonor kitchen was a hive of activity, the main focal point of many focal points scattered round the house, of the highest possible drama, a huge and spectacular theatre for my mother.

It was handsomely furnished with a magnificent pine kitchen table, three quarters the length of the room. The black enamel and cream painted iron kitchen range was permanently lit. Lavishly equipped with a long and high oak dresser, a high and deep cupboard with a black-pitch door, and sundry new electrical stoves, the kitchen had the great advantage of three exterior doors.

Thus one could enter, or, more likely, exit to the boiler-room down the back stairs, and the Japanese Room (so called as a souvenir of Bangpa-Pop's honeymoon there with Granny Cee in 1911), or one could run alongside the old brick bread ovens and up a step into the passage opposite the larder with the fermenting horse meat. The third door was by far the stoutest, and more effectively noisy when slammed shut by my mother.

The kitchen was the hub of activity from early morning when the dogs started to stretch and whine in their wicker baskets before lifting a leg against the corner of the scullery. Governesses, game keepers, butlers, maids and sundry of Mama's retainers scuttled in and out.

My mother, meanwhile, started early morning supervision in her night-gown and Delman slippers, a cigarette dangling from her mouth already painted a brilliant scarlet. "I always have my face on from earliest dawn," she declared triumphantly as she issued a series of shouted commands to the maids. "Heil Hitler, I said! Jump to it or you're sacked on the spot. Get a goddamned move on. Move it, I said!" she bellowed as she belted one of the Italian maids across the back of her ankles with a broomstick.

Otilda scuttled into the scullery crying, wiping her chapped and thick-ened red hands down her soiled pinafore as she shuffled in clumsy carpet slippers to the sink.

The largest of the three kitchen doors lead directly onto a roofed court-yard where a heavily blackened oak stanchion propped up the beamed plaster ceiling. A long thick bell rope of woven hemp hung slackly down the wall, a knotted noose hanging loosely from its end. The floor beneath was of old red bricks, irregular in pattern, crudely pointed, rough-textured and uneven. Down this floor swilled the gutter water during the frequent winter storms and summer thunder, causing a flurry of tin buckets, Italian maids and screams from Mama, who habitually supervised all servants and retainers in this manner. Not least Ruby Heath who was the constant butt of my mother's finger-snapping wrath. But Ruby was my heroine. I adored her.

Inside the courtyard and behind the stanchion stood a tall, firmly locked steel fridge filled with sides of salmon, steaks, and mysterious medicine bottles full of curious liquids. I watched Mama unlock it with one of the innumerable keys she kept firmly at her side on the end of a silver shining chatelaine chain—a gift, as she said, "from that darlin' old boy, Jack Rutherford. His colonel's uniform is to die for up at the Warren. And as to his shootin' . . . well!"

Uncle Jack, who was sometimes married to Aunt Joan, or so Mama said, was one of her favourite guns at our wartime home, Assendon Lodge, Papa's house that Mama sold to Uncle Jack when she took over at Stonor itself.

"Get to it, and pretty damn quick," yelled Mama. She aimed a random slap, and a quick kick at my ankles and bottom, pushing me through the heavy, black nail-studded wooden door towards the bell. "Hangman's noose, indeed," she said sneeringly, and paused for a moment to look at her gold watch, her second-best Cartier. "My own darlin' Joachim's finally had it, God damn it. As for you, Doodo, you tedious, tiresome reminder of my time at dear Joachim's Schloss Sonnenburg, you'd better get crackin' and ring out the Angelus." So saying, Mama thrust the knotted rope end into my hands. "Start swingin'," she commanded. "You're in mortal sin as usual. To hell with you, Sherman's only solitary brat to boot. Ha, ha, ha!"

I swung hard on the rope. The knot scalded my hands as I rang.

"One, two, three, one, two, three, one, two, three, one, two, three, four, five, six, seven, eight, nine!" Mama stamped in time as she counted. "The angel of the Lord declared unto Mary. And she conceived by the Holy Ghost," she said firmly, taking a pull on her Philip Morris cigarette. "There goes all the evidence. They've done away with him. How dare they get rid of my beloved Joachim? God damn them! God damn them! God damn them all!" she shouted.

The bronze bell rang out dully into the park and woodlands of the Stonor valley, mournful in its message. The plaster wall behind the bell rope sweated fat white flakes of sodden plaster. My heart lurched with fear.

Taking a quick pull of my hair, Mama incanted another stanza of the Angelus: "*Be it done unto me according to Thy Word* . . . What a lot of bosh, Bosch, and bunkum!" she shouted. Swinging sharply around in her Delman slippers, she pulled my hair more fiercely as I swung on the rope. "Be it done unto me only according to my word, indeed," she hissed. And spat straight over my shoulder, missing the small iron grill of the floor drain.

Around the corner of one of the courtyard doors appeared Papa, dressed in a tweed jacket and cavalry twill sand-coloured trousers hung on scarlet braces. His socks were a deeper scarlet cashmere, cable-stitched, his shoes thick plain brown leather, sturdily soled. In those days he still wore a gold signet ring on the same hand which sported an oblong, gold Cartier watch on a fine, narrow brown leather strap. I could smell his hair oil, Mr Trumper's Best, as he came carefully, quietly round the door from the two dining rooms, walking cautiously towards Mama.

He cleared his throat and began to speak. "I must implore you, Jeanne . . . ," he began.

Mama glowered at him through her blue-tinted spectacles, tortoise-shell framed in the shape of butterfly wings. Raising her glass she threw the remainder of the contents in his face. "You, Sherman, are just an impotent fool," she hissed furiously. "Don't think you distinguished yourself so marvellously on that goddamned honeymoon at Castle Sonnenburg, my very own Joachim's proper place. Your shabby Stonor Park full of taste as common as dirt, just like that bitch of an American mother of yours, is not even a patch on Joachim's Castello." She gave a sniff and heavy gulp.

Papa tried vainly to ignore her. He cleared his throat again. "Your dog meat is beyond control, completely unhygienic. It must be removed immediately. I do beg this of you, Jeanne."

Mania marched behind him as he progressed to the game larder and threw open the door. The dim light, seeping through a clouded glass fanlight high up the sweating wall, revealed a mass of heaving rancid flesh, thickly covered with a busy crowd of heaving, fat white maggots, rising and falling on a large white marble slap atop a grey slate table.

She laughed uproariously. "Oh for God's sake fuck orf, Sherman. That is, if you CAN!"

Pushing Papa vigorously in the stomach with her long, sharp scarlet painted fingernails, she shoved him backwards as she slammed shut the larder door, her cigarette still hanging precariously from the side of her mouth.

"For God Almighty's sake, stop that damned bell tollin'!" she then shouted at me, looking round wildly.

Mama started back towards the kitchen. There, she grabbed the black Bakelite telephone standing on the corner of the oak dresser. Jerking at the machine, yanking the coiled cord, she held the receiver tightly in her hand, close up to her mouth.

"Get me Nettlebed 304," she said angrily to the operator, ejecting "they've hung my very own Joachim!" over her shoulder at nobody in particular.

The operator put her through.

"Heil Hitler!" she exclaimed, to whoever it was at the other end of the line. Then she said something in German which I didn't understand, before replacing the receiver.

Don Bradman, the recently arrived German tutor, had appeared in front of me at another of the kitchen doors. His lightly curling dark brown hair was parted in the middle and, like my mother, his teeth divided down the centre. Don blushed and grinned sheepishly as Mama deftly entwined her arm in his.

"Your divine new tweeds are most frightfully prickly," she murmured,

278

nestling deeply into the arm of Don Bradman's russet brown speckled Donegal suit. His tight-laced Oxford brogues gleamed, and the high rounded collar of his white linen shirt was stiffly starched. A thick-lined Albert chain lay across the last two buttons of his waistcoat, a gold hunter watch tucked neatly into a small pocket.

After about a year with us, Don disappeared from Stonor. Neither his arrival nor his sudden departure were ever explained. I never knew what the German tutor taught—Mama already spoke some German, as well as Spanish and rather heavily accented French, mostly punctuated with vivid Spanish curses and vivid expletives (to the continuous horror of her aunt Tia María de Zulueta, who made constant novenas on her rosary for Mama).

Most of Don's tutoring took place behind the solidly closed and locked doors of my mother's duck-egg blue boudoir—and sometimes in the inner recesses of the stark white book room, which Mama had recently draped in bales of scarlet Fraser cloth. This strident tartan she had especially ordered from "our family shop at old Sheemie Lovat's place, Beaufort Castle. My cousin the 15th Baron, you know." This was a refrain that Mama repeated frequently. "But not quite the same sort of bastard as I am," she would add for good measure. "Pretty good hell, all the same."

Mama entertained in the book room in a green tartan dressing-gown, with high-heeled slippers to match. "I've had it all run up by my little man in Bruton Street, dear old Charles Creed," she told me. "I so much prefer the dress tartan Fraser clorth. Vegetable dyes, of course. Such a divine contrast to the murderous scarlet of my exciting ancestors. Murderous bastards, the whole lot of them. God damn it, old grandfather Simon Lovat was hung on a silken rope by his fellow peers. All goes to show what happens when you're only a baron with four balls."

In between the tutoring and teaching, and meals with the grown-ups in the big dining room, Don wandered the vastness of Stonor, habitually clad in brown. Crisp, clean, the handsome German tutor.

This well-fed, pink-cheeked man was certainly in stark contrast to my "Yiddish governess", as Mama referred to Mademoiselle Priess. As she said: "Madame Pee-Pee is merely a tiresome, inconsequential fly in my ointment, a deplorable Jewish problem shipped out from Vienna. It all just causes maximum aggro for me and my boyfriends." Mama sighed heavily. "How I sympathise with that dear old Hermann Goering. God damn them all, those bastard judges at Nüremberg. I don't care a tuppenny damn for

Yids and Jews. Cuts no ice with me and my boys. We'll make them glad to go away, Central European scum. You can quote Joachim, Hermann, Martin and me any old time," she continued, drawing deeply on her cigarette before exhaling a billowing cloud of smoke. For good measure, she took a random swipe at my bottom with the shiny black and white-bristled Mason & Pearson hairbrush. This she retrieved from the inner depths of a large black crocodile handbag. The hairbrush, which filled me with alarm, lived at the bottom of this capacious square bag, intertwined with a rosary made out of jet beads threaded onto a silver link chain. An ornate crucifix dangled from its knotted end.

Mademoiselle Priess, a senior school teacher, had arrived in England after Hitler's Anschluss and the Austrian pogrom of March 1938. With the aid of a Jewish charity she was established as a domestic servant in Aldershot.

Already in her late fifties, the refugee was a bulky, heavy woman entirely dressed in beige and brown serge and worn strips of torn silk. Her legs were swollen with varicose veins, frequently wrapped in thick bandages beneath lisle stockings of a dark coffee colour.

By the time she arrived at Stonor in 1946 poor Mademoiselle Priess was a physical wreck, wracked with stomach troubles, frequently doubled up with pain. Her thin, frizzy hair strayed wildly out of a small tightly-screwed bun, spilling out with innumerable steel hairpins. Her blue eyes were rheumy, her complexion leaden-grey and sweaty. And her rimless spectacles were frequently clouded with scalding tears. My mother had no mercy for "Mademoiselle Pee-Pee".

"She looks just like another large load of squitters, ha, ha, ha!" Mama would roar with laughter, picking her nose and examining the contents with interest before she flicked the pickings off the end of sharpened scarlet nails.

My governess was one of 3,000 "B-Class" women refugees who were rounded up in Great Britain for interrogation and internment late in the night of Monday May 27, 1940. Seven thousand men were also interned at Huyten Camp at Liverpool and on the Isle of Man before June of that year. None of the refugee organisations in Britain had been consulted, despite their detailed knowledge of the status of each person. Some 82 per cent of those interned were Jewish.

On June 11, 1940, Osbert Peake, MP, carefully explained to the House of Commons that to publish a list of their names was "impractical" as "waste of paper is a consideration at the present time, and it would involve considerable expenditure."

Deportation orders were issued indiscriminately, and several innocent refugees—"enemy aliens"—were drowned on overcrowded ships and liners torpedoed by the enemy. When even the local papers echoed the crude, cruel anti-foreign propaganda put out by Lord Beaverbrook in *The Sunday Express* and Viscount Kemsley in *The Times*, the general public was easily convinced that refugees, rather than the original members of the Anglo-German Friendship and their cohorts in the House of Commons and the Lords, were fifth columnists and traitors. That Count von Ribbentrop, above all, had commanded such a devoted enthusiastic following amongst the aristocracy thus conveniently faded into the background.

Mademoiselle Priess's release from internment brought her employment as my governess. My mother found her at an employment agency in Reading. My teacher's time at Stonor Park can only have added considerably to her six-year nightmare in England. Jeanne installed her in a small back bedroom above one the few remaining boilers of "that bitch Mildew, Lady Cee", where on a windy day the coke fumes oozed through the floorboards.

"Hope it reminds the old dear of the gas ovens she escaped," ruminated Jeanne. "And as to her waterworks," she sniffed, "the old gel's got the most frightful squitters. All those damn Yids totally responsible for the Crucifixion—and it is in the Catechism to boot . . . Repeat after me," she added turning to me for her night prayers. "New additions tonight," she said gaily. "That damn nuisance agent Major Holt is out, and that divine Colonel Jack Rutherford is in. So's that old soak Freddie Cockburn, purple in the face from his own brand of port. But what a shot, ha ha!"

Mademoiselle Priess's bedroom was riddled with mice in the nursery wing down the passage from mine, far too near to six shallow stairs from the top of which Mama declaimed the orders of the day early in the morning. Snapping her fingers, stamping, swearing, my mother shouted instructions at the poor Austrian each morning from the top of the stairs, to which the latter paid very little heed, having become conveniently deaf to shouts.

Once downstairs in the kitchen, this early morning drama was swiftly heightened as Mama started bowling corrugated-iron dustbin lids with considerable accuracy towards anyone who might have crossed her, or, whom she anticipated might cross her in the course of the day.

Mademoiselle Priess would take swift avoiding action, peering cautiously round the corner of the thin black door dividing the kitchen from the boiler-room, before slamming it against the onslaught of my mother's dustbin lid hurtling noisily towards her across the flagged floor. I watched with horror and alarm.

"For God's sake, get out of my way, you tiresome nuisance!" yelled Mama, flailing out with her fists. "You're spoiling my aim!"

Then she broke into shouts of rage, heavily punctuated with shouts of "Olé!" and a stream of Spanish swear words. "Damn it, I'm not a de Zulueta bastard for nothing. And don't forget my Borgia blood to boot," she shouted, crashing a couple of copper saucepans together in cacophonous unison. "Fetch me my black castanets, you tiresome brat," she ordered, pausing to bend down and stroke one of the dogs in the wicker baskets, a blond labrador who had just returned from a piddle in the back passage. "There, there, darlin' Trigger," she murmured soothingly. She straightened up abruptly, and picked up some of Papa's second-best Mason's stoneware, pausing briefly to examine the china mark before she threw them at Otilda in the scullery.

Mademoiselle Priess became a firm friend of Sherman's. She did not hide her displeasure at the illnesses which struck him after doses of Jeanne's "special medications" and "potions". She also grew bolder in some ways, taking avoiding action in the kitchen at Stonor Park when Jeanne in her fury took potshots at "that Yiddish bitch" by bowling yet another corrugated dustbin lid at her, pointedly snatched from the top of the pig swill which bubbled and fermented in a corner of the vast room.

One day Mademoiselle Priess disappeared without any explanation. The last I saw of her was a gaunt, wind-swept figure in a large green mackintosh, her hood drawn-up round her head, running as fast as her lame feet could take her down the drive in the twilight. No one divulged where she had gone to, nor why.

Undaunted, undismayed, Mama quickly appointed another governess for me. Miss Stollery arrived from Henley, dressed entirely in brown from head to foot. She had previously lived with her ancient father near the RC church in St Mark's Road. Her hair was frizzy, streaked with white, her clothes, her shoes, her stockings and her bag were brown.

"Wire wool, as far as I can tell," were my mother's first words, said while she peered closely at Miss Stollery and sniffed contemptuously. "I do think Miss Stollery is most frightfully mud-coloured and mousy," she added with contempt.

The day after her arrival, Miss Stollery announced that she was cold in the bedroom designated to her, high in the large attic roof, heavily haunted and full of bat droppings and mice. Bravely she peered closely at my mother from behind her thick tin-framed spectacles.

Mama gazed back, slowly drawing on her cigarette. "Quite frankly, Miss Stollery dear, you'll have to make do. I simply cannot afford more blankets. Stuff your bed—and I mean stuff it—old girl, with *The Express* and *The Sunday Sketch*."

Miss Stollery also vanished one day, once again without explanation, leaving on the orange twice-daily Watlington-Pishill with-Stonor bus to the toilets at the town hall in Henley.

"I've appointed Miss Lynes as your new governess," announced Mama. "Now let us see what we shall see. Oh for labernum, deadly nightshade and stomach pumps," she added, mysteriously.

My mother spent an hour or two a day studying cookery books. One, sent from New York, was entitled *The Way To A Man's Heart*. The second, Mama's favourite, was *Mrs Beeton's Household Management Together With A Special Supplement On Poisons*. This hobby was an important part of her daily routine.

"Fuck orf, you tiresome brat," she snapped one afternoon.

As I turned to leave the kitchen, I saw her turn a page of *Mrs Beeton* and jab a scarlet fingernail at a passage which had caught her attention. Concentrating hard, she began to read aloud: "Arsenic: Mostly seen under the form of white arsenic, or fly-powder and yellow arsenic, or king's yellow. Symptoms produced in those who have swallowed it. These vary very much, according to the form and dose in which the poison has been taken. There is faintness, depression, and sickness, with an intense burning pain in the region of the stomach, which gets worse and worse, and is increased by pressure. There is also vomiting of dark brown matter, sometimes mixed with blood . . ."

25

'I'm All for Formaldehyde'

At my tender age, no one had yet told me the difference between the sexes. Mama, however, did constantly call Granny Camoys a "bitch", and that this was meant unkindly I did realise. But, despite the war, my kindly grandmother was constantly sending large parcels from Newport. Like the clothes parcels which she also sent for me, they came wrapped in thick yellow paper, wax-sealed, tied with string. Declarations of content and large customs labels were plastered over the paper and proclaimed Wheatena, cream-of-wheat, maple sugar and tapioca, while the clothes ones announced smocked seersucker and new shoes.

"Size triple-A for Sherman's tiresome brat's impossible American foot!" said Mama indignantly, wrenching out the linen, the seersucker and striped linen frocks from a shop next to Cabbages & Kings not far down Bellevue Avenue from Stonor Lodge.

Mama was incensed by the white boxes of Vermont maple sugar candies. These came shaped in the forms of rabbits, four-leaf clovers and maple leaves. Sometimes they arrived together with packets of dark brown West Indian sugar, and bars of soap, White Ivory by name.

"Really, candies are most frightfully common in the aristo circles where I come from," Mama stated firmly.

It seemed to me that she was more cross than pleased by Granny Camoys' parcels yet impatient at the fact that they came by sea.

"I can lay in my essentials and supplies a damn sight quicker than any old packet ship, effin' Cunard or otherwise," announced Mama, dropping cigarette ash into the paper as she tore open the latest arrival. "Goddamn it, and somethin' else for that brat Julia. I'm puttin' a stop to this, see if I don't, Pop-goes-the-Weasel." Indignantly Mama shook out the parcel contents. "Where the hell are the Camel cigarettes I asked for? So damned inconsiderate of my effin' mother-in-law!"

Papa came back from the war on leave to Assendon Lodge after he had sailed on a military liner to America. In those days he was still "Daddy" and I could hear him explaining to Mama, who was still "Mummy", how he had accompanied his cousin, the First Lord Monckton, on a "secret mission".

"So you and darlin' Walter and all his strawberry leaves and viscount's balls—such a divine coronet—went to see your effin' bitch of a mother, Mildew Lady Cee TOGETHER!" she screamed. "Not for the first time I'm warnin' you, Sherman dear, there's NO smoke without fire. Got yourself burnt at the stake at Castello Sonnenburg, and don't you forget it. And I don't mean Shiplake or Sonning-on-the-Thames." Snapping her fingers at Papa, Mama shouted again. "You'd better watch it, I warn you Sherman. Or you and your mother Mildred are for the high jump. Heil Hitler, *olé!*"

From the expression on Papa's face I could see he was most unhappy.

Ruby just gave one of her sighs. "There, there, Doodo darling."

Later, my my father came and told me about the port at New York where he and cousin Lord Walter Monckton had disembarked from an enormous troop ship called "the *Queen Mary*". Since I had only before ever seen pictures of Queen Mary wearing a magnificent diamond crown in Aunt Julia's house, Turville Grange, I was quite confused.

Granny Camoys had given Papa a thick brown fur hat with earflaps in Newport. It was smooth, dark and exciting, and kept snow and icy winds away from my father's head. I thought the hat beautiful. Granny had also sent my mother the gift of a toffee-colour sheepskin overcoat with a deep reefer collar and horn buttons. Mama's arms stuck out in a straight line, so thick and stiff was the coat. She looked remarkably like Worzel Gummage.

But Mama was not amused. "Where, in Gawd's name is the mink?" she shouted. "I'm exceedin' crorse that my essential police duties and vital war efforts are keepin' me tied to the spot. But this is the VERY last time you'll be seein' Her LADYSHIT without me, Sherman Stonor. And you can stuff that one up and lump it—that is, if you can even begin to remember *how!*"

Laughing, Mama reached up for a copper saucepan. She took aim and hurled it at Papa. Hastily he ducked as it hit the wall behind me instead.

Stuffed or otherwise, I wanted badly to know how far away Rhode Island was. And whether it was filled with iced igloos like the one that Papa made out of the snow at Assendon. Obviously, I was still convinced, Rhode Island would at least be filled with the same chickens as those that wandered round the back door at Assendon and the dusty farmyards up at the Park and at Bosmore. Though they were called Rhode Island Reds I was disappointed their eggs were only brown or white. But it was exciting to find them laid in peculiar places such as forgotten and derelict prams and the interior of an ancient four-wheel family carriage.

I had always been fascinated by the carriage's yellow and blue paint cracked and faded, flaking with age from this high-sprung vehicle which was liberally festooned with cobweb strands. It stood, still proud, but slightly slumped to one side, mournfully rotting away inside a tall mock-Tudor barn in the farmyard up the back drive at Stonor, a level above the fading squash court, the mysterious garage with its greasy pit and hidden, illicit petrol pump up at the Park. Field mice nibbled busily at the silk and velvet lining, while the Rhode Island Reds busied themselves laying eggs on the horsehair stuffed carriage seats. An orange marmalade cat stretched out asleep on the cracked blue leather hood.

Papa explained that it needed four strong horses to pull his family carriage. He showed me an oil painting which had hung over the fireplace in the big dining-room at Stonor since 1690 with the very same carriage going up the drive towards the front door. In it I could just see two small men in velvet coats and three-cornered hats.

"A most important duke from Shrewsbury," announced Mama grandly. "If it weren't for our darlin' ancestor, Dukie Shrewsbury himself, we grandee Catholics would still be goin' round in a donkey and cart," she laughed. "Though certainly not a Spanish aristo like me," she added scornfully.

My father explained that the royal family and the British government of the day considered Catholics to be so politically dangerous and ambitious that they were forbidden any kind of wheeled transport.

"All my own divine ancestors, nobility one and all of course, had simply to foot it in their knee-breeches and codpieces," added Mama happily. "Then along came that darlin' man the Duke of Shrewsbury—Lord Chamber Pot to the Royals at Buck House and St James's Palace, frightfully onerous work—so divinely handsome and full of swarthy sex appeal. He got concessions for us carriage folk so we could, at least, at last, travel further than Pishill in a dung-cart, *olé!*"

My mother paused for a brief sip from her silver hip flask. "Early elevenses always keep the cold at bay. Maidensgrove Common and Russells Water on horseback must have been frightfully excitin' in those days what with the highwaymen and all. Personally I would have gorne side-saddle myself of course," she laughed. "And cantered up and down the branch line to that tedious Twyford station to boot."

I thought of Mama's terrible experience experimenting with a bicycle, and asked whether mounting a horse would unbalance her again.

"Quite frankly I've always gorne in for stallions myself," she said, gazing up at an oil painting of a large brown horse. "Rather a nuisance that your father does not have as many pictures by Stubbs as those nosey-Parkers next door," continued Mama pensively. "They're so frightfully lucrative even in this goddamned tedious days." She sighed heavily. "No more geldin's for me since that saga at Sonnenburg," she hissed at Papa, turning on her heel, and stubbing out a cigarette end at his feet. "Those darlin' boys Ralph, Raul and Guy de Pass have seen to that in all respects, ha, ha!"

The *naïf* picture of Stonor hung over the fire in the big dining room at Assendon, the one for the use of grown-ups only. The medieval house was painted bright red, narrow Tudor bricks standing out between a multitude of mullioned windows, 41 in all, white-painted beneath the pointed eaves of the roof. Papa pointed to an avenue of young sycamore trees, just 20 years old in 1690. Two of them still stood besides the flint chapel up at the Park, alongside yew trees and mournful pines guarding mysterious graves beneath unkempt mounds of soil, flint-strewn, where the blue periwinkles sometimes strayed. Broad-boled, thickly foliaged and bent over with a certain nobility. I had swung from the branches of those very sycamores surreptitiously while my mother strode imperiously round the gardens up at the Park. She was "most frightfully busy inspectin' " the ravishes and ravages of the National Benzole Petroleum boys, ha, ha, *olé!*"

I recognised the original layout of the kitchen gardens from Papa's painting. Nothing there had been altered since. But the mullioned gatehouse in front of the Park itself had been torn down by my grandfather

"The 5th Baron Camoys and his four balls have gorne and buggered up the architecture," explained my mother scornfully. "I can't quite see Pop in a full-skirted velvet coat like the darlin' Duke," she sighed. "Ralph's taste in clothes is pretty third-rate if you ask me. Only ever seen in worsted and some frightfully second-rate, probably secondhand up-yours knickerbockers. Not to mention His Lordshit's pants and knickers," sniffed Mama derisively. "Remarkably baggily cut, ha, ha!"

Trying to make sense of this new flood of information was a hard task. I tried without success to make the connection between the branch line at Twyford and the Duke of Shrewsbury, who appeared to be a peer of the Chamberpots at Buckingham Palace. I concluded he was obviously closely related to my great-uncle Sir Harry Stonor, a Gentleman Usher of the Bedchamber, and to Cousin Bernard, Duke of Norfolk, who announced himself as the Chief Butler of England and, as my mother explained, "takin' considerable precedence over our own butler Windy Wingrove".

Mama gazed appraisingly at the huge ornate frame of the Stonor painting. "Carved by that darlin' old master of the art, Grinling Gibbons," she said. "Vastly more valuable that that rather common *naif* picture of the Park."

The bright white carved wooden frame, with its scrolls of acanthus leaves, and the dark green of the sycamore trees against the red of the bricks reminded me of the doll's house which Uncle Dick Ovey had recently made for me so hastily after I had chanced upon him and Mama together. They were deep down in a sofa in her unlocked study at Assendon Lodge and, later, in the long gallery sofa at Stonor.

The doll's house was on a much smaller scale than the house in the painting: square and white-painted on two floors with five windows, a bright-green roof and a postbox-red front door. The whole of the façade opened out sideways on a hinge, folding back magically so that I could see all four rooms and the staircase, and imagine the furniture it would contain.

"A thoroughly modern design," explained my mother, "and it'll make you forget all about flies and zippers . . ."

It seemed that Uncle Dick Ovey had got his idea from the new houses built down by the Lower Assendon Sewage Works, where I was taken by Nanny for my afternoon walk. The sewage works were still on Papa's own land but ran alongside the Ovey plot at Middle Assendon Sawmill—which had been sold off inadvertently by Bangpa-Pop at the turn of the century. It had somehow been squeezed out of the Bosmore and Cock's Leas entrails and entails.

Rumour was rife locally, especially in the Middle Assendon pub The Rainbow, of Jeanne's "carry-on" with the burly naval commander, the handsome blue-eyed bon viveur Dick. Owner of the nearby 3,000-acre Hearnes estate, he temporarily abandoned his pretty, well-born American wife and frequently popped over the Fawley Bottom Road to Assendon

Lodge from the Sawmill where his mother, Lady Ovey, was installed. This affair was a cause of intense scandal for the elderly woman.

Lady Ovey and Mama spent many hours in the yellow drawing-room at Assendon Lodge screaming at one another. This appeared to make them both remarkably happy, though there were cascades of words, angrily repeated over and over again, which I did not understand.

Uncle Dick had a brother-in-law whom Mama called "that blue-eyed old soak and war shirker from Orstralia, Cuthbert Sheldon".

Uncle Cuthbert too came to call on my Mother. "Frightfully handsome even if he is short in the arse with those shapeless flannel bags and baggy tweeds," she declared.

He was yet another of my mother's old flirts: a dour, Benedictine-educated "fellow Cartholic" totally unlike Uncle Dick, who resembled a jolly barrel of beer stoutly swathed in naval uniform. Uncle Cuthbert was extremely vain and thought himself in competition with his more virile brother-in-law. But he was, as Jeanne explained, "an idle Orstralian millionaire, frightfully well-born like his ancestors who made the Sheldon tapestries with all those huntin' scenes".

*

I always wanted Ruby to come on my afternoon walks with me. Invariably, however, she was kept too busy cleaning the silver for my Mother She polished innumerable crested knives forks, spoons with her bare hands. Every piece of silver was heavily engraved with an elongated Roman skylark pecking at a squat, prehistoric pudding stone.

"Gloves just ruin my silver," said Mama firmly. So Ruby rubbed up the teapots, cream jugs and sugar bowls, the hunting trophies and cups, and all the heavy silver plates with gadrooned borders, without gloves. Even the Royal coat-of-arms on the biggest silver dish had to be buffed up with only her bare hands, pink paste and spit.

"Quite a privilege for you Ruby dear," said Mama acidly.

Once again Ruby mixed pink paste into a well of water in the centre of a pale pink scallop shell. Patiently she polished and buffed the Queen Anne silver hunting-cups, wine coolers and all the other antique Stonor trophies until they all shone like mirrors.

I gazed at my face in the plainer silver; and admired the horses rampant on the bigger, more ornate prize cups, seemingly springing off the engraved surface beneath dragon-shaped handles. They reminded me of the rowing trophies of Henley Royal Regatta which Mama so loved to gaze at in the afternoons at Leander Club.

"I'm just makin' sure that Ruby has got down right inside," explained my mother, opening and shutting the lids of silver urns and cigarette boxes with a tinny slam. There she inspected the underside of her shoes, which Ruby had just polished, "to make sure she got down there properly too. Soles and souls, and which are which! No matter what, polish just has to go on the underside," she added firmly, flicking ash over the top of a pair of shoes she was inspecting. "Frightfully good for the Aubusson. Polish and labrador pee-pee are a must for the weave," she continued, peering over the top of her indoor spectacles made of blond tortoise-shell.

She stamped and ground the ash into the large red cabbage roses woven and festooned into the centre of the deep brown Aubusson carpet at her feet. It stretched out in front of the four-poster bed in her Summer Bedroom.

Mama took enormous trouble over the interior decoration at Stonor after her wartime experiments at Assendon Lodge. She saw this excitedly as a part of her calling: "My vocation IS Stonor. I AM Stonor!"

And once all the smartest of the interior decorators had been called in at vast expense (their accounts not always paid), assisted by tame architects of Jeanne's handpicked choice (preferably "bachelors"), she took a perverse delight in assaulting her antique possessions. After all, with Sherman's millions she could so easily replace the Aubusson carpets, antique Persian silk rugs, Regency furniture and historic portraits from John Evelyn's loaned family collection. The actual arrangement of the Stonor antiques transfixed Jeanne as she had a military eye for each and every detail for each and every room in every passageway of this 64-room mansion.

Outside the nursery dining-room was Bangpa-Pop's unique collection of butterflies and moths in a many-shelved cherrywood cabinet into which Jeanne frequently gazed though her fashionable spectacles. Shaped like one of the Death's Head moths which Bangpa-Pop had chloroformed and pinned onto a specimen tray, my mother's spectacles ("never EVER to be called 'glasses', Julia dear, most frightfully common and *cursi*") were handmade to the specifications of Uncle Stewart Duke Elder at a shop in Wigmore Street which supplied the thick, blue-rimmed, blue-framed plastic glasses that Mama ordered for me.

This emporium was owned by another wealthy Uncle Theodore, who now based his design for Mama's glasses on the Death's Head Moth once he had heard of my grandfather's long-time hobby.

As my mother had explained to him sweetly: "The 5th Baron Camoys is most frightfully busy with his 'ornithology' and all his 'bee-keepin' ' for the war efforts while he is Captain of the Home Guard for Middle Assendon, Bix Bottom and Bosmore."

As always, Bangpa-Pop was at his happiest when capturing innumerable butterflies and moths in a large loosely woven green net attached to a long pole. Dressed in equally loose worn grey worsted trousers and a baggy jacket, he waved the net purposely around in the grounds of Bosmore and the garden at Assendon, and very occasionally up the Back Drive at Stonor, carefully skirting the edges of dark, murky woods and the stagnant dew-pond.

But Bangpa-Pop didn't like to make too much effort, invariably provoking Mama's comments.

"It's most frightfully bad for your brewer's droop, Pop, old boy, to be wavin' things around in such an abandoned fashion, ha, ha." She eyed a bottle he was carrying. "But I'm all for formaldehyde myself. Frightfully good smell of ether. Just the thing for gassin' dear little corpses. I've always had a penchant for poison gas!"

Carefully Bangpa-Pop dipped the bodies of the butterflies and moths into this mixture. Just as carefully, using Mama's eyebrow tweezers (the ones she used mostly for extraction of blackheads), he pinned the dead butterflies and moths in rows onto glass-inset trays in a tall narrow-shelved slender specimen chest of drawers. It stood outside the nursery dining room and caused me a fearful fascination.

This, then, was the source of Mama's inspiration for the Death's Head Moth shape of her tortoise-shell glasses. "Such a very distinctive shape for my very own most distinguished Spanish aristo features, *olé!* It always says something special to me whenever I have one of my blinders." And, as she explained to a group of Uncles who had come to shoot: "In my semi-invalid state I simply must not be disturbed when I'm forced into a lyin'-down position in my Best Bedrooms." Turning towards me she snapped, "I've one of my migraines comin' on you ridiculous brat, so just keep out of my way and steer clear. Did you hear me? Jump to it, and jump to it quick!"

It depended on the season as to whether Mama was ensconced in her summer or winter bedroom. And Ruby Heath, even sometimes the grumbling Otilda, had to be on hand to carry all the silks and satins, cushions and covers from one wing of the house to another for the Change of Season. Wicker dog baskets lined with Colefax & Fowler chintz, at least three of them, had to be transported from one wing to another. Georgian sidetables, silken rugs, Aubusson carpets, silver and gold dressing sets, Paul Lamarie silver gilt mirrors, hampers of finest towels, rose geranium bath essences, silk dressing gowns with satin lapels, matching satin slippers, Mama's vicuña rug and a quantity of detective stories and the latest novels together with Jeanne's capacious haute-couture wardrobe and innumerable handmade shows were transported from winter bedroom to summer bedroom and vice-versa. Once the Henley Royal Regatta resumed in 1946, these bedrooms, each with their three external doors, were busily occupied. A swift trade of suitors toing and froing.

Papa's bedroom, into which he was frequently locked, remained the same throughout the year. The room was next to one of Mama's busy boudoirs (the connecting door heavily locked from her side). Sherman's "bachelor room" had a dark green carpet and a high single bed with a mahogany headboard, white linen sheets, green blankets and a cover of cotton damask. Between the two windows stood a military chest of drawers, the top layer containing elegant silk foulard ties, bow-ties, hand-rolled linen handkerchiefs and an 19th-century embroidered yellow waistcoat. Lower down, beneath an array of fine linen shirts—Papa changed twice a day—were pairs of cashmere socks in yellow and red. Atop the chest and in his bathroom were silver-backed hairbrushes and serried rows of Mama's frequently administered medications in ribbed glass bottles.

And so Jeanne subtly set the stage for her New Order in the post-war years to come.

*

"Jump to it Ruby, up and orf on your bicycle this minute!" shouted Mama cheerfully.

Obediently, Ruby mounted her black, upright bicycle with its sturdy wicker basket and red night lights, and, following as best she could, came after Mama, the dogs and me, all packed tightly into the immensity of Granny Camoys's long Chevrolet brake,.

Ruby's red curls flew in the breeze as she pedalled frantically to keep up with the convoy—followed by Papa, ever reluctant to return at all to the Park, in his own two-seater motor car.

Up the Stonor Valley, along the Upper Assendon Road, past the Assendon Spring, we sped in leaps and lurches as Mama revved up the engine in a series of hiccups, blue smoke belching from the exhaust.

Past Mrs Cannon, aged 100, in her black crochet hat, black overcoat, black cobbled shoes, crab-apple colour cheeks withered and sunk, leaning precariously on her garden gate, wooden-paled, we sped. Mama always blew her horn even louder outside the ramshackle almshouses.

"I am the king of the castle!" she shouted over the roar of the revving engine, through a thick cloud of cigarette smoke.

"*Olé, olé!*" My mother put her foot down on the accelerator as we swung abruptly round the corner at right angles towards the iron gates of the bottom lodges, two late-Victorian orange brick and flint-dressed bungalows with lean-to "lavvies"—as Ruby Heath always described the outdoor sanitation in Stonor Village—outside the their kitchen doors, water dripping mournfully off corrugated iron sheeting which served as roofs.

Simultaneously Mama slammed on the brakes as she noisily disengaged gears, and leant heavily on the horn of the belching Chevrolet. her green hunting hat with its triumphantly cocked cock pheasant's feather tilted over the brim as she rolled down the window, imperiously summoning Mr White, the elderly head gardener.

"Open these gates *muy pronto*, and immediately! Don't you know who and what I am old boy?" Excitedly Mama leant down on the horn again. "And just WHO pays the wages round here?" she laughed.

Slowly, very slowly, Mr White came towards the tall iron gates. His cap was worn well-down over his low forehead, and he looked less than amused by the barrage of commands coming from my mother, now busily fingering the walkie-talkie set which was besides her on the front seat.

"Roger, over and out—do you hear me?!" she shouted.

Mama edged impatiently ever closer to the spear-shaped railings and bolted gates, pausing perilously near to Mr White's carpet slippers as he bent down to release the latch. Through the widening gap shot the car with a dramatic jolt. The dogs and I, and a copious bundles of linen fell to the floor, napkins, tablecloths cascading over us.

"Ha, ha! *Olé, caramba and verde!*" shouted Mama merrily as she skidded the length of the old brake this way and that through the thinly gravelled, deeply rutted driveway up to the second pair of spear-shaped gates, much lower in height.

"Get out, get out child immediately!" she commanded, a new cigarette hanging from the corner of her scarlet lips. She paused, as was her way, to contemplate her make-up in a gold compact as I got out to unlatch the gates.

But Mama did not have time to wait for me to climb back again up to the circular stone steps, in a flurry of gravel flying this way and that she skidded Granny Camoys's car, coming to an abrupt halt between the front door and the chapel door, one painted pitch-black, the other vermillion.

Throwing open the Chevrolet driver's door, Mama slid excitedly to the gravel. She stood a moment to compose herself before she ascended the steps of her regained prize, her castle, Stonor Park itself. Its conquest had taken Jeanne seven long years.

And now, for the next thirty-one years, there would be no retreat. On the near horizon lay the prospect of endless trophies, not least the title that Jeanne craved, indeed, would not hesitate to kill for. But all this was a prize that would exact its price.

* *
*

Afterword

*O*ur *friend was Jeanne Camoys, the dowager, the avenger, the endlessly quarrelsome, whose abundance of malice made her excellent company. She was a small, pale, dark-haired woman who had been a great beauty in the Thirties, with the exotic habit of painting her fingernails green. At some time a dose of Spanish blood had been pumped into her, making her liable to take instant offence and she was singularly unforgiving. Her features were small, but her jaw was strong and could set like an iron trap . . .*

I liked her because she carried the strange art of being herself to unbelievable lengths. When she first invited us to lunch and we suggested we should ask her back, she said, "No need to swap cutlets." She regularly visited the King of Nepal, whom her son had tutored, and on her return would immediately ask for an obtain an audience with Mrs Thatcher to discuss the affairs of that remote kingdom. When a rat appeared on her garden wall she rang up Michael Heseltine, then Minister for the Environment, and told him to do something about it at once. When he failed she vowed undying enmity to Heseltine and said she was voting Labour . . . She was extremely well read and had worked in some capacity for Edith Sitwell. She hinted at a distant, passionate relationship with Graham Greene, but I noticed that he was nervous of visiting England when he heard she was in the country.

Jeanne was the only character I put directly into a work of fiction. One day she came to lunch, loud-mouthed, fragile and beautifully dressed. As I was sitting on the sofa beside her, she asked me to admire her shoes. I did so obediently and told her that she had very pretty legs, if I might say so. "You already have said so, I think. IN YOUR BOOK." I apologised for the use of her, and she smiled tightly. "Better to be lampooned than ignored," she said.

So wrote John Mortimer in his memoir *Murderers and Other Friends*—and I too found myself inspired to tell the story of Jeanne Camoys, my mother, according to her pungently boastful and scatologically witty account and—as I have researched it—using my childhood diaries. Part biography, part social history, part detective story, this is the chronicle of an extraordinary life shot through with intrigue, politics, high society blackmail and power-driven greed.

Set largely in the years of the Second World War, this book recalls Jeanne's vigorous campaigns to achieve the power, wealth and noble title she lusted after. These were the decisive years of my mother's "other war" while the narrative lashes backwards and forwards to cover her early career as a dashing and dangerous debutante to her later life as the avenging dowager.

But I did not originally set out to write a book about my mother. Rather, following my father's death in the spring of 1976, I decided to write a biography of Sherman Camoys.

Almost immediately I was side-tracked. As soon as I reached the point where Sherman met my mother, Jeanne Stourton, she took over the narrative. It quickly became apparent to me that it was my mother on whom I should concentrate my research, and whose story I should tell. She was the real subject. She was not only irresistible in herself, it was clear that in a number of ways I needed not only to record her life but to exorcise her memory. So the present book is partly a work of historical happenings, and partly the biography of a remarkable woman. It is also an act of exorcism.

How much of what I have written can be authenticated? One of the early titles for this memoir was *Too Bad to be True*, as I realised that, set down on paper, the details of my mother's life often strain credulity. Would any one who had not met Jeanne Stonor believe all that she had said and done? I therefore set about finding original sources to verify material which she, always boastful, ever-talkative, ever-vivid, had communicated to me at close quarters since my earliest years.

Much of what I have written comes from my direct testimony. I was born in 1939, when my mother was 26, so I knew her for two-thirds of her life. The early years can be verified against known facts to a degree; thereafter, I can only say that I have faithfully recorded what she told me, what I have learned from contemporaries or what I myself personally experienced.

Astonishingly, my mother seems to have kept very few secrets from me, and she would recount even the darkest acts of her life with gusto and satisfaction. Her main stories were repeated to me constantly, Mama seldom lied—she had no need. That she sometimes embellished but exaggerated seldom was part of her personal magnetism. I was not her confessor, I was her audience.

Sadly, most of those who knew my mother best and spoke to me of her, are no longer alive. I have used their testimony but appreciate that they are no longer around to confirm directly the veracity of what they told me. Again I have endeavoured to find supporting evidence for everything that appears in the book, though it has sometimes not been possible and access to vital source material denied. And so I leave it to others to judge the truths Jeanne trumpeted far and wide.

*

I had always known that Sherman was far more than the dimly-lit, minimalised shadow of my compelling mother. Yet in his lifetime, Jeanne had always referred to Sherman in tones of deep contempt—she wheedled and needled, mocking and trashing him incessantly, quite openly and in front of estate workers, servants, guests, retainers, tradesmen regardless. I was deeply puzzled by this contrast between my parents from early childhood. My experience of my father was that of a warm, kindly, enthusiastic person, deeply attached to me and to his far-away American mother, deeply attached too to his land and devoted to all the people who worked for him.

Conspicuously, Sherman was a natural ecologist, dedicated to his estate workers and the humane husbandry of his farms. He was fascinated by trees, wild flowers, birds and butterflies, increasingly allergic to the slaughter of the weekly shoots, so well attended from the earliest days of war by foreign royalty that included Prince Bernhardt of the Netherlands, the Kings George and Paul of Greece, South American ambassadors, peers of the realm, industrialists, chief constables, lawyers, doctors and aspiring tycoons. Instead Sherman made and flew his own kites, the red, blue, yellow coarse cottons framed in flimsy balsa wood high above the commons of Maidensgrove and Russells Water. His many tenants, one and all, loved him dearly, cheerfully called him by his Christian name or referred to him just as affectionately as "the Major".

Conversely Mama insisted upon deep formality with a lofty, patronising distance of manner. Furthermore she talked incessantly, mostly at the top of her voice, her rapid conversation punctuated by a simultaneous performance of staccato commands and orders delivered down her many telephones.

One of my earliest memories of my mother was the glamour of her black military uniforms. Her obsession with the colour black harks back to the fascist uniforms of the Thirties, both of Oswald Mosley's infamous Blackshirts, and of the uniforms which Joachim von Ribbentrop himself designed for the SS, the "Black Guards". There was frequent mention to "My Little Black Number", whether a couturier uniform, an outfit for a funeral of "one of my old beaux, *olé*!" or for a much favoured Requiem Mass, a grand ballgown, or merely a cocktail party dress: with the rare exception of mustard-hued "shootin'" tweeds. My mother was always steeped in the most expensive black: furs, silks, satins and cashmere, occasionally high-lighted by a white silk blouse. "Nothin' common and orf the peg for ME!" she announced, smoothing long black suede gloves over jewellery laden wrists. "Made to measure in that borin', burstin'-fat Sunny Marlborough's village. We're not on speaks actually!"

Yet, despite Mama's mania for black, she had exquisite decorative taste at Assendon Lodge, Stonor Park in its immensity, the Dower House and lastly, at a deeply improbable, unsuitable workman's cottage on Maidensgrove Common. And she always employed only the best: Syrie Maugham, Nancy Lancaster, Colefax & Fowler, Cole's of Mortimer Street (hand-made wallpapers), Blairman's, Mallet's, the White House. Innumerable male architects came—and swiftly went when Jeanne failed to pay their fees.

Whistles, silver buttons, cockades, cockaded hats and military medals adorned Jeanne's tailor-made uniforms—and Mama was quite likely to appear fully uniformed at the crack-of-dawn since her activities seldom started later than 6 a.m., the cavernous kitchen and squalid scullery at Stonor being the setting for the first act of the day. Her energy was truly prodigious, and her acting needed support actors—mainly supplied by poverty-struck Italian domestics (in considerable supply immediately after the war) .

Further to emphasize the distance Mama expected me to keep from her, I was obliged to curtsy on a daily basis—a habit which remained largely unbroken into my thirties. Nevertheless I remained spellbound and bewildered, totally unable to comprehend this dizzy-making, magnificent theatre, superbly set upon such an immense stage. I was evermore eager to be at my mother's side, as close as close could be.

In 1957, Mama summarily dismissed and banished me from the home where I had grown up from mid 1945. I had had earlier, harshly surprising episodes of being "thrown out"—when I was only fourteen—and sent packing on the train to London to beg for mercy from kindly Acton cousins in Wilton Place, terrified, penniless and bewildered, armed only with a third-class train ticket on the Great Western Railway and the price of a taxi.

In 1957 I was barely eighteen, ill-educated, exceptionally obedient, naive in every respect. Fatally I was deeply in love with, seduced by, Mama and her magic. In my eyes she was a towering figure, beautiful, scent-drenched, dynamic, a heroine (frequently self-acclaimed). I believed in her absolutely. Though, from very early days of the Second World War, my mother was already deeply steeped in an extreme of the harshest Spanish Catholicism which seldom accorded mercy, forgiveness or compassion. Like a frightened rabbit in my timidity and blind adoration I was completely mesmerised by Mama. She was, quite simply, spellbinding. Even her laughter, whilst seldom kind, spelt magic to me.

Looking back at Sherman's life, the gentleness of this sweet-natured, generous-hearted and humble man began to contrast ever more vividly with my mother's forthright, magnetic personality, and overpowering ambition. Furthermore she was a dragnet to innumerable male companions, and Papa, once invalided out of the war in 1944, receded ever further down the immensity of the dining-room table, almost totally silent and completely alone.

I had expected to find reasons for Jeanne's imperious, assertive behaviour in her own background which would go some way to exonerate the more profound extremes of her behaviour, the harsh manifestations of rage and revenge which, quite literally, roared and reverberated around Stonor Park from early dawn until dead of night, and with such dramatic consequences.

Jeanne skilfully wove all around her an endless cat's cradle of intrigues, and well-rewarded, spying intriguants, a finely spun skein of silken, silky threads. These schemes were based upon her undiminished pre-war commitment to the profoundly pro-Nazi cause in London "high society" with its emphatically anti-Semitic views, and headily intoxicating dedication to all the exciting worldliness of hedonistic, exclusive, expensive glamour and elite, international grandeur.

From the late Twenties, and early Thirties, Jeanne, emulating her innumerable men friends, was a "Boiled-Shirt Fascist". As too, her immediate family, the Stourtons, the Butes and the Crichton-Stuarts, the Norfolks, the Perths and the Constable Maxwells, the Semphills and Stirlings. Others within their powerful, secretive cabal included Colonel Sir Eric

St Johnston, Lord Londonderry, Ambassador Raul Regis de Oliveira, Commandant Mary Allen. "Boiled-Shirt Fascism" was most expeditious of expedients.

This group of money and power brokers—exclusive, arrogant individuals, women as well as men—were highly ambitious for political, and nationalistic dominance, They were, expeditiously, nominally right-wing Conservative, but with a strong allegiance first to Mussolini's Fascism, quickly followed by Hitler's Nazi regime. The deadly policy of Appeasement was deeply intertwined in these movements. Several were inextricably involved with Franco, and the clandestine, secretive, lucrative funding and arming of the Nationalists in the savage Spanish Civil War. They frequently worked in combination with unscrupulous, rich adventurers like Rupert Bellville—and millionaires like Gordon Selfridge supplying guns and fighter planes.

This heady, exotic deadly atmosphere of the Thirties, its ever-present potential, for social and political power, absolute power absolutely, regardless of cost, Jeanne would carry with her throughout her life. Above all, she could not, would not, accept failure and all its consequences. Thus she would ignore, and with total contempt, anyone whose life, for whatsoever reason, had what she would scathingly describe as "taken a nasty turn, *olé*!"

This merciless approach would apply even to Jeanne's own hapless mother, "Feckless Fanny" Stourton, originally reduced to grinding poverty by her far more than feckless, estranged husband, Herbert—who, quite literally, devoured Fanny's fortune inherited as a minor from her Irish father, Viscount Southwell of Castle Mattress, County Limerick. Jeanne, who considered herself personally stigmatized by such shame, shameful, shabby poverty, and social humiliation, never forgave her mother.

Fanny Stourton died in 1950 alone in a shoddy, unheated hotel room on a gaunt terrace in South Kensington. Her youngest child, Jeanne, was conspicuously absent from the Requiem Mass and burial at a faraway London cemetery.

My mother's strategy, it became increasingly obvious to me, was based on an extraordinary grasp of the deeply lucrative potential of bribery and blackmail, the latter based upon a technique well honed by Jeanne's mentor Ribbentrop, an expert in sexual blackmail—and with devastating consequences. His Büro with its tendrils everywhere could not possibly have kept out of politics. With its sophisticated propaganda, powers of infiltration and blackmail, these Nazis, Nazi sympathisers, knew everything about

their opponents. Their techniques enabled the organisation to keep comprehensive black lists. With such unscrupulous power its members were
able to reduce political (and other) opponents to "Utter Ruin". Thus the
Nazi Party Leadership through its system funded the most powerful and
all-embracing police and spy organisation the world has ever known. From
these rubrics Jeanne took her example, fervently adhering to her own
proven and honed capacity for the Utter Ruin of anyone, or anything,
which stood in her way.

Throughout her life—my mother died in 1987—Jeanne was obsessively political, addicted to highly fashionable fascism of the Thirties and
Forties, and thereafter, keeping closely in touch with "all my Old Beaux",
as she continuously referred to persons like "Nol" Lymington, the Earl of
Portsmouth (treating his second wife "Bricky" with a condescending contempt and a *"who* was she born, dear?"), frequently calling-upon, entertaining a nearby duke—"Dear old Gerry, woofter-poofter though he tends
to be, rather too keen on the boys you know. But then, just LOOK at his
wife Lady Dorothy—boot is on the other foot, *olé*! The Other Persuasion
indeed! Never mind, he IS the 7th Duke of Wellington!"

Important government ministers, Lord Brabazon of Tara, another of the
"Guns", had, as Alan Lennox-Boyd, and Duncan Sandys—later Lord
Duncan-Sandys, red-headed son-in-law of Winston Churchill—long been
Jeanne's frequent companions, frequent guests both during and after the
war. Their names and nicknames were constantly on her lips—a mantra of
the aristocracy of power and wealth. Amongst their ranks were the Lords
Semphill, Kemsley, Beaverbrook—'that darlin' boy the Beaver, ole!'—
Rothermere, Buccleuch, Willoughby de Broke, Perth, Pembroke, and
Malmesbury.

Like a Litany of the Saints this non-ending, continuously paraded list of
"my Conquests, ha, ha!" was poured over Sherman's head on a daily basis.
He sighed heavily—and escaped to the offices of the Henley District
Council, or to the bar of the local Liberal Club. And when he could bear
no more, drive his distinctive E-type Jaguar, DBW 999, to the safer shores
of the St James's Club on Piccadilly.

But even here Sherman was at the mercy of Jeanne's imperious summons to "return home IMMEDIATELY". delivered by me, still a very
small child, to the hapless, terrified hall-porter, as I stood, trembling with
terror, on the stone steps leading up to the club, my mother barking orders
from a taxi parked beneath.

By this time Mama had established herself in a permanent suite at the Connaught Hotel, close to her essential shopping needs at Cartier, Tessiers, the White House—and the chic book shop, Haywood Hill on Curzon Street. In between lay her hairdresser, a certain "Mr John"—and the antique carpet emporium of Mr C. C. Johns, a famous Jewish dealer, the Henley branch of which shop had had its plate glass window stoned and shattered in an anti-Semitic attack in 1947. The Jesuit church of Farm Street stood opposite the Connaught—Jeanne had many friends of importance here.

From the outbreak of the Second World War several of this elite group of men, all connected with the Anglo-German Fellowship, many also members of the notorious Right Club, the English Mystery Club, the Nordic League, the Link, habitués of the Carlton Club, shot eagerly over the Stonor Estates, their hostess the seductive, vividly dressed and beautiful Jeanne, whilst Sherman was away with his regiment the Oxfordshire & Buckinghamshire Light Infantry.

Its commander, Colonel Guy de Pass, a wealthy local landowner, extremely short of stature, briskly moustached, was considered too old to fight abroad, and was quickly recruited to join the Uncles and Guns. Besides, his conspicuous wealth allowed Jeanne to forgive Guy's Sephardic Jewish ancestry, so lucrative was his banking and stockbroking firm, so prosperous his farms at Harpsden, where the armorial glass in its ancient flint church denotes former Stonor ownership.

That Guy de Pass had no male heirs, only a trio of daughters, was a further sexual incentive—and became an irresistible temptation. Furthermore, to Jeanne's faultless calculation, it made this accessible local millionaire easily open to blackmail—as Guy's cuckolded South African Boer wife Anne was to testify, the hapless, powerless witness in the dark of many a night of sinister menace in the remoteness of Huntswood Park. Here, at 3 a.m. Jeanne would appear, heavily veiled in a black lace mantilla, chauffeured in a bottle-green Jaguar by her younger son, Robert, to accompany the pyjamaed, diminutive figure of Guy de Pass to the safes in the cellar.

Guy too, had been recruited to the ranks of the glamorous, highly prestigious, Anglo-German Fellowship in the mid-Thirties, its elegant white tie-and-tails attired dinners at the Dorchester or Savoy hotels, serried ranks of bemedalled grandees, peers, politicians, bankers, power brokers, their wives and the female guests in long evening dresses and tiaras. Held in splendour under the august auspice of the Nazi Duke of Brunswick these were glittering events, frequently photographed, hugely prized social occasions.

The rich prize of Stonor, gifted to Sherman by his mother Mildred in 1937, was rich indeed. Jeanne assumed its command in the early years of the Second World War, 1939. She was still only 26 and quite determined that she would never relinquish such a prize. From that moment onwards Jeanne's ambitions knew no bounds as she aimed towards the hereditary peerage of Camoys by fair means or foul. To that end, and to the acquisition of a diamond tiara she bent all the rules until, finally, in 1968, Ralph Camoys, Jeanne's father-in-law, died in Newport, Rhode Island.

But even the peerage did not satisfy Jeanne's insatiable ambitions, and she set about the disposal of Stonor Park and Stonor Village. When Sherman inherited in 1937 he had some three hundred dependents many of whom were sitting tenants in the various villages, hamlets and estate cottages to whom he had, at very least, a moral obligation.

By 1947 Jeanne had quickly over-ridden these tiresome constraints—and sold the Bosmore and Cock's Leas Estates to the benefit of her game and personal bank account, usurping the power-of-attorney granted by Mildred Camoys to the family lawyer, and old friend of Sherman's, David Drummond ("my old beau with that foxy face, such a frightfully sexy, bristlin' red moustache, ole!"). Now Jeanne threatened the startled solicitor (with whom she had had a quick fling) with exposure. David hastily capitulated, explaining to the lawful inheritors, of Bosmore and Cock's Leas, Sherman's sisters Nadine and Noreen, that they would be "wiser" to give way to Jeanne's demands for the proceeds. The perceived threat to Mildred Camoys—that she would be informed of Jeanne's four-year affair with Ralph Camoys—was barely veiled in Jeanne's extortion and simple blackmail.

Spurred on by her easy success and now assisted by David, Jeanne gradually laid waste to Sherman's beautiful estate, insisting on the sale of farms, fields, houses, to fuel her insatiable appetite for jewellery, yet more diamonds, yet more furs, yet more fine paintings and antiques, a four-poster Tudor bed, a Daimler car. Another legal beau, a red-headed neighbour, George Bellord, swiftly arrived on the scene, enlisted by Jeanne to "organise the Deeds, old boy". The Stonor Estates, still intact after 700 years, now faced the gradually whittling away of 6,300 acres of land and history.

From 1945 onwards Jeanne consolidated her power, concentrating her overwhelming ambition on the acquisition of all that Sherman had, and had inherited through the generosity of his American mother. There was much for Jeanne to do in this demolishment, focusing in detail on the intricacies of the vast estate and its many tied cottages.

That there was no longer an entail—the bankruptcy of Ralph Camoys had meant that there were no remaining legal fetters to the sale of lands and houses—gave Jeanne limitless powers. And over dependents, sitting tenants, estate workers, parish priests, servants. She had never hesitated to hire and fire, reducing any opposition to "utter ruin".

Simultaneously Jeanne entertained in great style, on a magnificent scale, with access to all the best butchers, fishmongers, grocers and green grocers which abounded in Henley and Wargrave. Sherman's cellar was well-stocked with vintage wines; the greenhouses yielded remarkable grapes and vine tomatoes, geraniums, pelagoniums and jasmine. Jeanne's reputation as a glamorous, lavish and exciting hostess grew the greater. So too her reputation for temper tantrums, and dramatic scenes with the staff.

Immediately upon the return to Stonor itself from Assendon Lodge in 1945, Jeanne had stripped out all the central heating boilers installed by her mother-in-law, leaving hapless guests to shiver in their overcoats round a heavily laden table, Her main target was women guests, whether wives or mistresses, who were discouraged from overstaying their leave or staying at all. It was not unusual for wives of peers and Anglican bishops to be banished on the spot. Thus Jeanne's usual coterie of pre-war men friends continued to frequent Stonor, accepting Sherman's lavish hospitality with scarcely a thought for their all-but silent host seated the furthest end of a vast mahogany dining-table.

Tutors came and went, governesses came and went, butlers came and went. One old retainer "Windy" Wingrove, departed to the American family in New York in high dudgeon with Mama's autocratic behaviour. The mysterious Hitler admirer, our German tutor "Don Bradman", disappeared to the nearby estate of Peter Fleming, while the aged Austrian Jewish Mademoiselle Priess, the tragic intellectual refugee released from Huyten internment camp, ran away down the drive in drenching rain never to be seen again. Priests came and went in similar manner—Sherman's gentle monk cousin Julian Stonor also ran away down the drive his black robe flapping in the wind.

Jeanne had begun to put it around "the county" and in London society, that "Sherman is very far from well". Yet he had recovered from the peritonitis and subsequent nervous breakdown of 1944. Convincingly, with a maximum of pathos and drama, Jeanne painted the hapless Sherman as "a near invalid to whom I'm absolutely devoted, night and day, *olé*!" She had begun, quite slowly, systematically, to administer "motions and potions all prescribed by our darlin' chemist". Row upon row of ribbed glass medicine bottles were laid out in Sherman's bathroom.

Shortly after the war's end Jeanne had transferred from the Women Police to the St John's Ambulance Brigade, rising rapidly to the position of the local county commandant. To this end she had ordered another bespoke uniform—which she took to wearing at meals, astounding the startled guests. Jeanne vouchsafed them no explanation.

The year 1947 was the last time Sherman would ever be allowed to see his mother. All through the war, and for the austere years thereafter, Mildred had continued to send food parcels and clothes from Newport; to which generosity Jeanne was completely indifferent.

Sherman was still only 34 in this, the year of the Big Freeze in England, coinciding with Jeanne and Sherman's sea voyage, first class, to New York to claim the inheritance from his grandmother Sophia's considerable estate and fortune. A war-widowed cousin, Anne Phillimore, her two children, and a governess were left in residence at Stonor—with Sherman's best friend Commander Dick Ovey and another of Jeanne's old beau, the conductor Sir Malcolm Sargent, to oversee the estate.

Sherman's maternal grandmother, Sophia Augusta, known as the "Fiery Duster", was a formidable, pompous woman of huge girth and vast weight, a millionairess—and a snob. Amongst other handsome bequests the old lady left a legacy to her feckless, bankrupt son-in-law, Ralph.

The idle Ralph Camoys, absentee husband, had been comfortably installed in a bachelor apartment in New York City by Mildred. He had been forced to bolt from Bosmore after Jeanne had pocketed the proceeds of its sale, and Mildred had funded his return to the States.

Arrived in New York, Jeanne had a vital mission to call upon her wartime friend, Frank Spellman, the Cardinal Archbishop of New York.

Formally uniformed, Chaplain General to the American Forces, Archbishop Frank Spellman had been entertained by Jeanne at Assendon Lodge, together with Ralph Camoys and Sherman's cousin John Nicholas Brown in the early Forties. The powerful prelate had significant links with the famous Vatican Corridor, Pope Pius XII, and with Jeanne's pro-Franco

Spanish family. Like her uncle and early mentor, Cardinal Borja Merry del Val, Cardinal Spellman was anti-Modernist, a strict, unyielding traditionalist. To him Jeanne had decided to delegate Ralph's spiritual welfare, a lapsed, utterly indifferent, Catholic.

After his return from America in 1947, Sherman's health became strangely fragile Increasingly he became isolated, and his formerly reasonable physical health began to deteriorate in an alarming manner. His hitherto slimness of figure gradually disappeared. He had strange symptoms, profuse sweating and considerable giddiness complicated by sharp stomach cramps for which Jeanne had a ready supply of medication.

Marcia Davenport, famous American journalist and novelist, had been bought to nearby Wargrave in 1948 from Prague by another old beau of my mother, Sir John Foster, QC, MP. She had been the mistress of the tragic, murdered prime minister of Czechoslovakia, Jan Masaryk. My mother was transfixed by this handsome, powerful woman. A frequent visitor to Stonor, Marcia became quickly fond of Sherman—and increasingly concerned for his health. Inevitably this led to fierce confrontation with the resentful Jeanne. But not before Marcia had given the very first model of an animated, American-made dishwasher to the Pantry at the Park. And it was Marcia rather than Jeanne, who decided that "enough is enough" of their increasingly raucous relationship.

Increasingly Sherman suffered physical collapse, turning night into day, sleeping heavily through the day itself, frequently locked into his bedroom, trays of over-cooked food left outside. On the occasions in 1948, and in the Fifties, when the Hugh D. Auchclincloss family, Sherman's aunt Irene Gillespie and his Slocum cousins came to call, he was locked into his bedroom, unable to arouse himself from a semi-coma despite all pleas from the American family. In strident mood Jeanne stood guard and they were forced to depart the house, perplexed and suspicious since Sherman's behaviour was completely out of character.

Jeanne still needed Sherman—at least in name—as a steward of the Henley Royal Regatta. Here, and at Stonor she could, and did, entertain grandees—the Churchill family, Anglican bishops, Etonian beaks, American oarsmen, peers and "Regatta Buggers" in ever-increasing splendour, day and night, throwing glamorous house-parties well staffed by maids, dailies and butlers. In the background were Jeanne's Spanish dressmaker Consuelo Juantorena, and an eccentric millionaire, Sherman's bachelor cousin Charles, an anthropologist infatuated by Jeanne.

Nominally Sherman was a necessity as Jeanne's host for the talented inventors of 1951's Festival of Britain: John Betjeman, Osbert Lancaster, Kenneth Clarke, Johnny Cranko and John Piper were frequent guests although Jeanne stipulated, as at the Regatta, that neither wives nor mistresses were welcome.

Sherman's closest friends Graham Greene, Archbishop David Mathew and the artist John Piper, gave him as much loyal friendship and moral support as Jeanne's personal cronies were indifferent. These three men cared deeply for Sherman, trying, without success, to remonstrate with his wife—they were powerless to influence her. In revenge Jeanne initially increased David's rent from £65 per week to £67—and then banished her principal lodger, ejecting him from the house forcibly.

Graham was of significant importance to Jeanne. "HE had an affair with ME," she habitually insisted, and widely broadcast, despite all Graham's remonstrations and denials. Nevertheless not only did Graham give some £2,000 to help the maintenance of Stonor, but Mama continued to go to the theatre, to the cinema and to Brighton to meet Terence Rattigan in his company. And Graham came frequently to Stonor to seek out the ghosts, and to sit with the isolated Sherman.

A greatly favoured guest, Prince William of Gloucester, put his efforts into protecting Sherman—but to no avail. Jeanne merely laughed mockingly as Sherman became increasingly isolated.

During the years away at boarding school from 1951 to '55, continuously homesick, I began to keep a diary. On going-out days, infrequent as these were, I habitually received the heart-breaking telephone message, relayed by Mother Perpetua from my mother: "Your father is most unwell. Goin'-out arrangements cancelled." Bewildered I clung all the closer to a small collection of postcards from my mother—in Madrid, in Paris, in Jérez de la Frontera.

After the debacle of my banishment in 1957 my only ambition was to be able, somehow, to return home. I should have known better. Only a year earlier I had had an emergency operation for appendicitis while working for Mama's glamorous friend, the actor Richard Todd, who joined the parties at Stonor Park. My mother arrived at my bedside at the Henley War Memorial Hospital to demand the "outstandin' rent for livin' at Stonor. And that will be another £2 for the telephone too." I was obliged to pay her in full from the NHS sickness benefit.

Retrospectively, I believe my mother realized that I had seen her, all too frequently, in compromising positions with some of her innumerable beaux, including Dick Ovey, Colonel "Jack" Rutherford, Sir Malcolm Sargent and sundry others, many of whom she entertained in the heated Japanese summer house perched along the top of the walled garden. But that I failed remotely to understand the implications, let alone meaning of these encounters, only made Mama all the more furious. Possibly, to the smallest degree, she was frightened.

She was, however, truly fearful of my immediate reaction to her plundering of Aunt Julia d'Hautpoul's tiara and Fabergé jewellery in February 1950. Early that month the old lady had died at Turville Grange in the presence of my mother and a local doctor. In Julia's will there was no mention of Jeanne's name. The entire fortune was left to Julia's nephew Francis Stonor, with generous legacies to her servants.

During that first weekend of February 1950, Jeanne acted with haste, removing quantities of valuable jewellery, silver and gold "royalty" photograph frames and precious Fabergé objets d'arts, rushing them in green Gladstone bags and boxes to the safety of her winter bedroom. Freddie Shirfield, the foreman at Stonor, was ordered to remove eight antique Georgian grecian lead urns from the garden walls at the Grange and to cement them to the Tudor façade on the garden side of the Park. Dutifully Freddie obeyed, working at speed with his first cousin George. The purloined urns, quite out-of-proportion, remain there to this day, absurdly small.

Amongst the booty scattered in Mama's bedroom were the many pairs of Aunt Julia's hand-made gloves, her prayer-books, several silver-lidded glass jars, a card case, an address book and a whole dressing-set of coroneted dark green morocco leather with Julia's initials surmounted by a gold crown. There was also Julia's Roman missal, which Mama signed to me with a quick flourish. But I still understood nothing of what I had witnessed. One of Jeanne's habitual cuffs to my head sent me flying from her room.

Sherman was aware of his wife's audacious theft. He also understood that Jeanne was holding Aunt Julia's gay heir Francis to ransom and blackmail. With considerable courage Sherman tried, in vain, to persuade Jeanne to return the stolen goods. He was beaten back to the short gallery from the threshold of the winter bedroom as his wife staged a fit of screaming rage and hysterical anger laced with the choicest swear words, barring the large brass door-lock with a Regency chest-of-drawers wedged beneath it. I was left, ignored, cowering with terror at her side.

In the austerity of the mid-Fifties the seaside resort of Bembridge, on the Isle of Wight, was highly fashionable, conveniently near to the enticements of the Royal Yacht Squadron at Cowes. The desirable snobbery of the Bembridge Sailing Club with its many temptations was an essential of daily life, and many of Jeanne's "old beaux" frequented both exclusive clubs—from which Jews and blacks were barred and blackballed.

A substitute for the South of France, renting a grand house on Dewcy Avenue was essential. To drive from the mainland with a quantity of the family silver, a great deal of family linen, a servant or two, and certainly the gun dogs was *de rigueur*. That it seldom stopped raining seems to have dampened no sexual enthusiasms—or extremes—whether on dingy houseboats tilting in the tides of Bembridge harbour or in the rented mansions of desirable peers, Lord St Aldwyn, Lord Malmesbury, the dashing Bellville boys. But, as Jeanne made it quite clear, Sherman was, quite simply "surplus to my needs". He remained at Stonor, quite on his own once again.

Jeanne was also courting a prestigious banker, David Colville—the fact that he was heavily married never bothered her—and any Baring bankers that she could get her hands on at Cowes. She was ever more interested in Duncan Sandys, MP, the ruthlessly successful politician and his fragile wife Diana Churchill, who she pursued mercilessly when Diana took to her solitary bedroom in a green nightgown to distance herself from Jeanne's persistent bullying. "I'm writing a life of Bismarck, so go away Jeanne, go away!" she had shouted as Mama hammered at the door.

In the Fifties Jeanne was very taken up with the various dignities of the Catholic hierarchy in London, and at the Vatican. She had maintained her pre-war friendship with Cardinal Pacelli—Pope Pius XII—and his entourage.

Now, in 1955, she insisted upon a Private Audience. I accompanied my mother on a highly unusual tour of Paris, Turin and Rome, scared of the many colourful episodes in which my mother, ever-obsessed by Royalty, involved herself so deeply,—and with maximum drama. That she travelled in great comfort and luxurious style—the Golden Arrow, the Ritz—and with mysterious assignations, quite passed me by so terrified was I.

Early morning assignations at the English College with Monsignor Tickle, and his well-stocked, heavily disguised drinks cabinet puzzled me. So did the dinners at the British Legation to the Holy See with Sir D'Arcy Osborne, Sir Douglas Howard and their male companions.

Out of earshot, Mama's threats and hisses tormented me. I was ever more timid, bewildered. My particular "Mortal Sins" dominated Mama's threats. But she was much taken up by the American Embassy, and its colourful ambassador, Clare Boothe Luce, a staunchly orthodox Catholic, close friend and political colleague of the Cold War Cardinal, Frank Spellman

Mama's attachment to the various post-war, glamorous Spanish ambassadors was a constant mania. As with the Falangist family of de Zulueta and Torre Diaz, in and around Madrid, Cádiz and Jérez de la Frontera. For a brief period I was despatched to the families of "my old beaux in Madrid, ole! Such jolly old colonels, dukes and all—absolutely devoted to *El Jefe*, Franco you know. *Viva el rey de España, ole!*" Mama was especially attached to the Marqués de Manzanedo—Pepe—and the Marqués de Nules, a stout, small statured colonel, governor of Minorca, "Spanish Guns and Uncles, ha, ha!"—these also included the Marqués of Santa Cruz, the Dukes of Alba and Primo de Rivera, assorted Domecqs, and sundry South American ambassadors.

Jeanne had surprisingly little time for her Spanish brother-in-law, Ramón, Marqués del Moral, a Falangist, and close friend of Ribbentrop and General Franco. Instead she took long-term revenge on his wife, her innocent sister Gytha, ensuring that she would be reduced to grinding poverty—and "Utter Ruin".

In 1956 Jeanne needed a "London pad" ostensibly "to launch my daughter Julia into society". I was to be presented at court to Her Majesty the Queen. For a London season, heavily chaperoned by my mother, it was essential to have a suitable base in the "right part of London".

Jeanne smoothly negotiated her "terms" with Francis Stonor at his "Rather North-of-the Park", faux Venetian palace, Number 1 Strathmore Court, perched incongruously alongside railway tracks. On the ground floor was Francis's guest flat.

Here Jeanne installed herself with me, and with Timothy Garner, a talented artist and a current boyfriend of Francis's—one of a string of exotic young lovers of varying nationalities and colour. Mama flirted with Timothy as she paid minute attention to Francis's unique collection of priceless antique vermeil, silver-gilt objets d'arts by Paul Storr and Paul Lamarie heavily embossed with crowns and coats-of-arms.

In Francis's palace above, Jeanne eyed Francis's unique collection of Baroque art and artefacts, shell-bed, antique carpets and priceless paintings. Here she dined off golden cutlery, and coroneted Royal Worcester porcelain plates.

From March until July in varying forms, the Season evolved, tea parties, cocktail parties, dances and balls, the Berkeley Dress Show. Jeanne shone at all but the female tea parties. My mother's beauty swept all before her, young men in white tie, boiled linen shirts and black tailcoats, wilting in her arms at Claridge's Hotel, the Dorchester, the Savoy, the castles of Arundel, Cliveden and Syon. Studiously Jeanne ignored the "Other Women", treating them with utmost contempt.

My mother was overwhelmed at the grandeur of the presentation at Buckingham Palace. This event, as all others, ensured that she went only to the fashionable couturiers and hat-makers of the day, her gloves made at Blenheim, her shoes from Delmans, Rayne—ever more jewellery commissioned at Cartier on Sherman's account. By now Jeanne was perfectly confident she could show off Aunt Julia's purloined amethysts and sapphires.

Between events Jeanne had become a close friend of Edith Sitwell— whom she met with the Jesuit author Philip Caraman. Jeanne's previous warm friendship with Edith's brothers Osbert and Sacheverel had been on the wane for some years; there had been verbal spats. The Sesame Club became a rendezvous for the two women .

The Spanish Embassy acted as a magnet to Jeanne, belonging as it had to her Merry del Val ancestor. She felt she came into her own here, and since long before the Civil War when her father Pedro de Zulueta was an Honorary Attaché, the embassy notoriously a nest of spies, pro-Nazi, and Falangist.

The allure of the balls staged by the Anglo-Spanish Society, in the grandest of venues, sprinkled with distinguished ambassadors, international grandees and occasional dukes was the perfect setting for Jeanne's belief in her unique grandeur. But she had encountered an unfortunate problem after the disastrous visit to the Infanta Maria Cristina, in Turin—there had been a most unseemly scene in a louche night-club involving the Infanta's husband Enrico Marone Cinzano.

Consequently Jeanne was no longer well received by her favourite princesses. And her erstwhile friend Crista refused to be cajoled. Jeanne smarted from the royal snub. Humiliatingly even she was unable to explain it away.

Mama became ever more vengeful at the protection afforded me by the stalwart, steadfast loyalty of Crista. At the end of the season of 1956 Jeanne me sent for job interviews with "my old beau that splendid oafish oarsman, Gully Nickalls, a frightfully oversexed Gun".

Uselessly I rehearsed an advertising slogan, "Britvic is GOOD for you", almost too frightened to speak. Mama, further exasperated, then organised "my dear old albino beau, SIR Edwin McAlpine (he OWNS the Dorchester Hotel you know—far too blind to be a Gun!)" into finding me a job, one that was living-in.

Dumped at a trade entrance to the Dorchester, I was interviewed as a prospective chamber maid by a heavily starched, primly correct, uniformed house-keeper. Further terrified I failed the interview again. My mother was incandescent at "your sheer uselessness, Julia!" But it would take her another year to banish me completely, with £2, "to make your way in London like the Other Women".

Meanwhile Jeanne became deeply entangled with a handsome brilliant Welsh pediatrician, Dr Jack Kempton. The recorded voice of Richard Burton rang out through the closed doors of Jeanne's boudoir and book room, intoning *Under Milkwood*. In her exasperation at my failure to become a living-in chamber maid, I was now sent to work as a volunteer in Jack Kempton's premature baby unit and as a ward orderly at Townlands Hospital for Geriatrics.

Jeanne's newest liaison caused increased grief to Sherman. His best friend Dick Ovey had become so intoxicated by Jeanne that he proposed marriage and then died prematurely. Sherman was fond of Jack Kempton, a genuinely kind man. He was less fond of "Flash Harry", Sir Malcolm Sargent, the suave conductor. One morning I heard him asking my mother about her affair with Malcolm. Shouts of scornful rage rang out through the door of Papa's bachelor bedroom as she slammed out of the door.

After the death of the parish priest Father Seyres, Jeanne devoted herself to the upkeep of the stream of chaplains who followed. Convinced that she had the Divine Right of Kings Mama insisted upon bringing her lap dogs, King Charles spaniels, to the tribune for Mass, seated on her lap.

Increasingly when Sherman had become too ill to attend Mass, Jeanne appeared fully uniformed in St John's Ambulance regalia complete with cockaded hat and medals. The congregation was hypnotised, greatly in awe of this bejewelled figure—who insisted on counting the takings of the two plates.

From the mid-Forties Jeanne had established an especial arrangement with a private nursing home at Caversham. I was the first of the family to be admitted with deep concussion in August 1946. Arm-in-arm with the then Archbishop Heenan, my mother and he had rushed to my rescue as

I fell from my bicycle onto the gravel drive, hitting my head with great force, losing consciousness as the pair came towards me.

From the late Forties Sherman became an intermittent patient at the same nursing home. Here he quickly recovered from the mysterious seizures and collapses which increasingly felled him at Stonor. Jeanne had him rushed unconscious to the nursing home, bundled-up, chauffeur driven, with her convincingly at his side.

As mysteriously as his undiagnosed seizures, Sherman made rapid progress to recovery. This stop-go pattern continued for many years—The neighbourhood, the county, Jeanne's innumerable old beaux, were quite convinced that—as she announced—Jeanne was "a Saint, a Martyr", totally devoted to the welfare of an invalid husband—and "in terrible, grinding POVERTY, *olé*!" Besides she had the hierarchy of the Roman Catholic church completely under her thumb, irresistibly attracted as they were, by the splendours of Stonor Chapel, its glorious vestments—and the sumptuous hospitality offered—but conditionally—by Jeanne.

One and all, bishops, archbishops, cardinals, monsignors, they succumbed. Additionally Jeanne had her orthodox, grandee Spanish prelate cousin Alfred Gilbey, notoriously Falangist and misogynist, at her beck and call. That the famous monsignor was gay, while also the owner of a vast gin fortune proved to be easy blackmail material. Hawknosed, aristocratic, elegantly attired, an urbane clubman and snob, Alfred was initially captivated by Jeanne's conquest of Sherman. This vain, clever, devious priest, so closely connected to her South American and Spanish family, was easy prey.

By March 1961 I had obtained a green card enabling me to sail to America to find a job at Tiffany so that I could at last meet my paternal grandmother. I was twenty-two.

My grandfather Ralph met me at the docks. He had just installed a housekeeper, Mary, from Daylight, Tennessee, at his York Town apartment, spaniel filled. I was to live in a surprisingly costly apartment with cousins at 440 East 79th Street nearby.

It was at Tiffany that a cable arrived from Mama announcing the sudden death of Jack Kempton, drowned in the Bay of Biscay. Followed by a second announcing the suicide of my first cousin James Hay—with strict instructions: "Do NOT, I repeat, do NOT write to Aunt Magda." Followed by another cable of deepest disapproval that I had attended a Protestant service at the Church of St Thomas with my uncle, John R. Drexel 3rd. Mama's text denounced my "Deep Mortal Sin".

Mildred Camoys died in Newport in 1961, after a brief illness only two days before Thanksgiving, and Mildred and Ralph's Golden Wedding. Nevertheless Thanksgiving went ahead at Stonor Lodge, then the Will reading to assembled family and executors in the Drawing Room at Stonor Lodge. A curiously worded codicil, to the disadvantage of Nadine Pepys, had only been inserted the month I arrived in New York, March 1961.

Granny Camoys's two highly unusual funerals took place both in America, and, after a lying-in-state in the drawing-room at Stonor (barred from the chapel as a Protestant), at the Pishill graveyard where her body is interred.

That Christmas I spent with Nadine and Tom Pepys in Newport, and then at 357 Benefit Street, with John Nicholas Brown and his formidable, tart wife, Anne Kinsolving. She showed me a letter from my mother ordering that the American family "completely IGNORE Julia, a worthless person, totally useless, who must find work immediately. She is to be given NO money, I repeat, NO money."

My bewilderment amused cousin Anne Kinsolving Brown. Uproarious with laughter she sent me on my way, on a Greyhound bus, with a cheap evening bag and a black astrakhan beret, my coat so shoddy the butler would only permit me into the servants' entrance. I was set to embark for home around the world by five different liners, steerage class.

Almost immediately after Mildred's death Jeanne instigated legal proceedings in the courts of Providence, Rhode Island. Ostensibly in Sherman's name, Jeanne claimed a considerably larger share of Mildred's fortune, in trusts and in cash. To achieve this Jeanne had, of necessity, to blackmail one of Sherman's sisters, the childless Nadine Pepys, living still in Newport; it was vital to co-join Nadine's signature, wrung from her by the force of Jeanne's extortionary threats of "revelation".

Not for the first time Jeanne threatened to reveal the affair that Ralph Camoys had "thrust" upon her, Jeanne, during the war. She also threatened to reveal "the consequences of your father's rape"

Nadine was powerless to resist. A kindly, shy woman, she had always been devoted to her indifferent and negligent father. Deeply attached to her only brother, Nadine was too far away from Sherman to witness his increasingly perilous state of health.

Even before the early Sixties Sherman was frequently too ill to coherently give his signature to the innumerable documents which Jeanne, together with her various lawyers, including Lord Goodman, thrust upon him, using gardeners and secretaries in tied cottages as "willing witnesses". Terrified of being forcibly evicted from their homes, they complied.

Jeanne, triumphant in her case against another of Sherman's sisters, now turned her guns on the executor of Mildred Camoys's will, John Nicholas Brown, her most patrician and upright cousin. Jeanne had a further arrow in her quill—a quick reminder that "John Nicholas raped me at Assendon Lodge in '42, *olé!*" Successfully she sued the hapless executor for misappropriation of funds, for failing to reinvest trust funds for profit. "Payback time!" Jeanne announced merrily to the assembly of all-male guests gathered round the vast table at Stonor. "Mildred Cee was always SUCH a bitch."

Jeanne's colourful words, her boasting, began to cause shivers of alarm amongst "my old beaux, Guns and Uncles". But her prediliction for Royalty, especially from Buckingham Palace and the Kingdom of Nepal, intrigued them deeply as Jeanne retold spicy tales of "my royal intimacies" (her rooms were draped with royal photographs, silver-framed and personally inscribed) "Royal Dinners and Carriages and State Visits. *Olé!*"

Seated in her boudoir or the book room, with their innumerable doors locked, immersed in estate deeds, boxes of medieval documents, surrounded by dogs and a bank of telephones, sipping Horse's Neck cocktails, issuing a stream of orders to her staff, Jeanne was in her element.

Occasionally she would spare time to play one of the grand pianos in the Hall with an old friend of Sherman's, Sir Leigh Ashton, a director of the Victoria & Albert Museum. Here they would be joined by another eccentric musical bachelor, Lord Horder. Both these men, and Jack Evelyn— whose estate of Wotton Sherman helped to administer—showed increasing concern, concerned affection for their ever-generous, forlorn host.

The contents of Wotton had arrived at Stonor in the early Fifties when its owner, Jack Evelyn had let the house to the fire brigade and appointed Sherman as his trustee. A fellow member of the St James's Club, a mathematician and poet, and a considerable hypochondriac, Jack Evelyn was a recluse who came infrequently to Stonor as a guest, and to gaze at his beautiful possessions, family portraits, paintings by George Stubbs, fine linens and antique furniture, priceless rugs and silver, prominently displayed round the house.

While Sherman was so frequently bed-ridden, or incarcerated for convenience at Dunedin nursing home, Jeanne concentrated on the gradual and steady diminishment of the Stonor Estates, converting the profits into ever more rare jewellery. The refurbishment of the Park itself escalated, and she obtained vast grants from the Ministry of Works, using her considerable influence with government ministers of both political parties.

Together with powerful gossip columnists, and high-ranking prelates, these men were seduced, one and all, by the lavishness of Jeanne's table. Deeply flattered they did as they were bid, and even more. One and all they were fascinated that Jeanne was so often in full-dress uniform. On the increasingly rare occasions when Sherman was present the guests were encouraged to ignore him, isolated and silent at the far end of the table.

During the war Mildred had sent her daughter-in-law a cookery book *The Way to a Man's Heart*. Together with *Mrs Beeton's Household Management*—with its exceptionally detailed chapter on poisons—these were Jeanne's culinary bibles, essential tools of her trade. She concentrated her entertaining on luncheons with guests separated according to rank. Those out-of-favour, tutors, governesses, Guns and Uncles, even Crown Prince Birendra of Nepal, who dared to disagree, or utter out of turn, were relegated to the nursery dining room—with a nursery meal, and Kia Ora orange juice.

In the big dining room, newly decorated (rose-pink silk damask), surrounded by courtiers, wine and port flowed. Jeanne alone drank champagne, brandy and ginger ale—and, later on, whiskey. But her propensity for male guests was sometimes overturned by actresses and singers such as Yvonne Mitchell and Eartha Kitt—and by a fierce rival, Hellbags Helen, Lady Dashwood.

Sherman had fallen heavily in love with the beautiful Eartha—who had first come to Stonor in 1955 and danced on the kitchen table. He was captivated, and by her infectious laughter and kindness. His platonic devotion was reciprocated. Under the eagle eye of Jeanne and under constant lock-and-key, Sherman's only opportunities were to escort Eartha to lunch at Brown's Hotel and to art galleries. Jeanne was enraged, ordering a minion to pursue Sherman's chauffeured Jaguar along the Embankment—"in case HE is givin' her MONEY." Despite Eartha's fame, normally an irresistible magnet, the competition of the "Other Woman" was unthinkable. However, Jeanne never fully succeeded in banishing Eartha, though she put paid to the actress Judy Campbell, Lady Iona Carrington and John Piper's formidable wife Myfanwy.

On my return from the States in 1962 I had already been banished for five years. After two weeks at the Park I was ordered to "leave immediately and find a job". Six years later in 1968 my grandfather Ralph, 5th Baron Camoys, died in Newport, Rhode Island. He was 84. In August his body, embalmed in a triple, lead-lined coffin, was flown to the chapel at Stonor. I was delegated to meet Bangpa-Pop since my mother was away at the Connaught Hotel and Papa in Suffolk.

Meanwhile serious legal problems had arisen as to the legitimate inheritance of the Camoys title; which pre-Reformation barony of writ, frequently inherited by a woman of the blood, had to be proven as legitimate at the House of Lords. Lawyers were hastily despatched to the archives in New York to verify the legality of Ralph and Mildred's marriage in a bedroom in the Sherman brownstone mansion in 1911 whilst my mother fretted with rage and consulted the Establishment's top legal brain Lord Goodman. Needless to say, my father was permitted to inherit the title.

Much mirth was caused by the lack of handles on Ralph's coffin; less mirth was caused by the re-opening of the primitive family vault beneath the altar. Since no one organised the traditional obituary card I arranged this—and a bunch of orange zinias for Bangpa's formal funeral and internment, lowered on ropes into the vault. Before this Mama ordered me to remove the top-hatted congregation for fear of ridicule. Neither a wake nor refreshments were offered.

It had taken Jeanne thirty years to achieve her peerage. Finally she became THE Baroness Camoys, wife of the reluctant 6th Baron. From this moment onwards her efforts to disperse the Stonor estate, to acquire yet more jewellery increased. As did her determination to root out and destroy any person, any relative, who held incriminating photographs, newspaper cuttings, letters, legal documents, amassed over the years.

Jeanne followed the Nazi mantra "Utter Ruin, Total Elimination" to the letter. Ruthlessly she set out to eliminate Esther Stonor, Sherman's poverty-struck Jewish aunt, and Ruby Heath, the Stonor housekeeper. Both women died swiftly in dire circumstances, completely ruined, entirely alone.

Strangely Jeanne's signature appears as "next-of-kin" on the pauper Aunt Esther Stonor's death certificate. All Esther's hoarded cuttings and documents Jeanne speedily burnt. She arranged for the old lady's burial in an unmarked pauper's grave at Pishill, enraged at her inability to persuade the Chief Rabbi of Reading to conduct a Jewish funeral. Ruby Heath, meanwhile, was slowly dying, a bullied, broken, loyal woman, in a

Newmarket Hospital. She still possessed a treasure trove of family photographs, cuttings, letters. After a brief visit from Jeanne, Ruby died within hours. Her treasures were immediately confiscated by a minion of Jeanne's—and burnt.

I had frequently visited both the poverty-struck, old ladies, gazing with fascination at their hoarded documents, horrified at the misery of their circumstances—Mama had. mercilessly, rendered me powerless to help them. Lady John Hunt gave such assistance the Red Cross could afford to the paupered Jewish tenant at Henley's crumbling Station Hotel.

Jeanne's accession to the throne of the House of Lords went dramatically to her head. She acquired ever grander cars, chauffeur-driven, heavily embossed with gold crowns—gloomy, grey-laid writing Smythsons' paper was as heavily engraved "Stonor Park", its telephone number, "Turville Heath 300" enhanced with thickly applied tar-black, four-balled coronets. The typewritten contents of such letters were habitually lethal, another of Jeanne's effective tools: bullying, threatening, suggestive and contemptuous, creating terror in the hearts of the recipients.

Sherman was now minimally on display to the public, for without him Jeanne could hardly use the exciting facilities of the House of Lords. To this end she contrived a photo shot on the steps of the Second Chamber of the new Baron and Baroness Camoys with the Duke of Kent.

Convinced she was safe, Jeanne sent "Proof of the Pudding, olé!" to the American family at Stonor Lodge. Here the doleful photograph resided on a grand piano in the company of the Duke and Duchess of Windsor.

During the years 1968 until Sherman's death on 9 March, 1976, Jeanne still had much to accomplish. She had yet to gain the actual deeds of Stonor Park itself, its freehold made out in her own name. Her frequent consultations with Lord Goodman was now making a disaster of that particular relationship.

My mother had become greatly taken up with a newly promising, friendship. In nearby Wallingford lived Dame Agatha Christie and her archaeologist husband Sir Max Mallowan. Little by little Jeanne coaxed them into lunch parties at the Park. Sir Max was particularly flattered by Jeanne's charm.

In 1974 and now well-established at the House of Lords, Jeanne no longer needed her husband—as she thought—in any guise. He too was "disposable". I had managed to see Papa on several occasions when he had been dumped at Dunedin nursing home—I could only, safely, visit him in the early morning. And I had been called by Jeanne, always in the middle of the night, to drive down to Stonor in the emergency of Sherman's dramatic collapses into unconsciousness and semi-delirium. Invariably she had a quiescent priest ministering the Last Rites.

In the latter half of 1975 Agatha Christie died, leaving the majority of her estate to her widower, Sir Max. By this time Jeanne had forcibly removed Sherman from the Park. She had announced that the Park would be sold and I at once went to see her in the book room, but she was emphatic in her decision.

Jeanne evicted her sister Barbara Bellville from the Dower House in the village, moving herself in with Sherman, taking carefully selected treasures from the Park, installing seven safes. The rest Mama left in situ, awaiting the tented sale planned with Phillips the auctioneers for the following January.

Simultaneously Jeanne assiduously courted Max Mallowan. He was mesmerised. The Dower House was "out-of-bounds" to all but a chosen few, strictly controlled by Jeanne. However she encouraged gossip columnists and selected journalists whom she wined and dined off silver-gilt heavily crested antique plates. They printed her every word, never bothering with verification of the facts with which she indoctrinated them. Inevitably scorn was poured over the hapless absentee Sherman, locked into a claustrophobic small bedroom upstairs at the four bedroomed Dower House. He was blamed for "the tragic circumstances I find myself in, reduced to grindin' poverty by keepin' Stonor".

In January 1976 a great many Stonor treasures and an even greater amount of rubbish from housemaids' cupboards, pantries and sculleries were sold by public auction on the tented lawn of the Park. The weather was freezing as I sat and watched for two days, tears streaming. Record results were achieved, and Blairmans of Mount Street were instructed by a mystery bidder to purchase family portraits, the hall lamp, and sundry items.

Early in March I left for Boston, where I had temporary, unpaid employment, as a companion to a widow. Before my departure, I went to Mass at Stonor to see Papa—it was one of his better days; he was on his feet, quite cheerful though very swollen of body. He kissed me farewell. It was the last time that I saw my father.

Sherman Stonor, 6th Baron Camoys, died suddenly in the early morning March 9, 1976. I had been in America barely two days when I was awoken with the news. My father was only 62. The curt announcement was distressing. From experience I realized that my mother had no intention of communicating with me personally. Instead I made contact with the immediate family in Newport, at "Stonor Lodge". I received a frosty reception there when I explained that I was too poor to return for my father's Requiem Mass and burial. In due course it was arranged that I would be sent a return plane ticket for 48 hours—no more.

Papa's funeral was of deep poignancy and personal heartbreak on a freezing day, drizzling, the chapel icy. My mother appeared in deepest Spanish mourning, heavily veiled—and determined not to speak to me. After Sherman's body was lowered into a grave outside the chapel, Jeanne retreated into the shuttered, deserted house, slamming the door, bolting it fast. I was both terrified and extremely worried as to the manner of Papa's death—explanation came there none. I was left to make my way with the Drexel relatives, and representatives of the King of Nepal, to an extremely shabby pub in Henley. The strict "royal" protocol was arranged on an ugly table near to a smoking fire. The following day I was returned, on my tourist ticket, like a parcel, to Boston.

In 1977 the remaining Stonor Estates and the Park were sold, some five hundred acres, several cottages and the village of Stonor. Jeanne now made it clear that, after a correct period of mourning for Sherman, she would accept Max Mallowan's proposal of marriage. Surrounded by loyal friends, the millionaire archaeologist was warned off—told that he would become Jeanne's next victim. Horrified he withdrew.

In the years following my father's death Jeanne busied herself with trying to consolidate her personal gains. Though she would live another eleven years, she gradually became a frightened, threatened woman blazing with frustrated anger.

Bored by Sherman's collection of rare porcelain, Royal Worcester, Flight, Barr & Barr, finely painted with feathers, fruit, flowers, shells, Jeanne sold it all at Christie's. She spent much time at the auction houses negotiating, wheeler-dealing, selling family portraits behind the scenes; at private galleries, trading family jewellery and antiques. Captivated, owners of the grander emporiums wined and dined the Dowager Baroness Camoys whilst she reciprocated at her suite in the Connaught Hotel, and at the Dower House, maintaining a full quota of maids, dailies and gardeners.

By 1986 Jeanne had become increasingly the victim of intense physical violence by a drug-taking male relative. Quite uninhibited, the hysterical Robert would beat Jeanne black and blue. On innumerable occasions she called the police from Nettlebed and Henley for protection. By the time they arrived Jeanne had changed her mind—and withdrew her accusations. On the occasions when I visited my mother in the early morning to find her covered with deep bruises I implored the police to act. But they had received instructions that "NO action was to be taken".

Against my wishes it was announced that my mother was to be removed from the comparative safety of the Dower House, situated outside the gates of the Park in the middle of Stonor Village. I protested but to no avail. Mama was forcibly moved to a deeply sinister, unsuitable, uncon-verted workman's cottage hidden away behind brambles down a ram-shackle, sodden lane on Maidensgrove Common. No one would be able to hear her cries for help. I too was powerless to rescue her.

This enforced move in 1986 was the consequence of a writ that Jeanne had taken out against Anne Sebba, author of a biography of Enid Bagnold. Sebba's publisher Lord Weidenfeld was considered an arch-enemy by Jeanne as he had once refused to sleep with her—the deepest of insults. She was determined to revenge herself, and to exterminate both publisher and author.

Jeanne's writ for libel was draconian and wicked. It was also ill-judged since many of the witnesses to the happenings of the neo-Nazi Thirties were available to testify to the falseness of Jeanne's extortionate claims for financial compensation—though she set her sights rather low at only £25,000 at a time when one's reputation tended to be valued at a minimum of £100,000.

In October 1987, just months away from the trial and after several false alarms, Monsignor Alfred Gilbey was decanted from the Travellers' Club to administer the Last Rites at Camoys's Cottage. He was assisted by a Polish priest who spoke no English. There, beneath an oil painting of her great grandmother's chateau of Serrant and surrounded by grandiose, elaborately embossed silver upon ebony Spanish crucifixes, Jeanne, the Dowager Baroness Camoys, took her final breath.

Acknowledgements

I owe most of all a debt of unending gratitude to my late godmother, HRH the Infanta Maria Cristina de Borbón Battenberg, Contessa Marone Cinzano. Her wisdom, devotion, extraordinary generosity and outstanding loyalty to me (through thick and thin) remained a constant in my life until her death in 1996. I am fortunate to share her name.

I received knowledge and requisite courage through the unique inspiration and personal devotion of my father Sherman Stonor, my aunts Julia Stonor, the Marquise d'Hautpoul, and Gytha Stourton, Marquesa del Moral; my cousins Father Michael Hollings, Lord (Robin) Phillimore, Frances Phillimore Gibson, Dom Julian Stonor OSB; Graham Greene, Ruby Heath, Archbishop Bruno Heim, and Archbishop David Mathew. The late HRH Prince William of Gloucester gave me continuous encouragement throughout his short life. And, as memorably in a league of his own, I owe unending gratitude to the friendship, loyalty, protection and immensely generous support through some 30 years of the late and deeply distinguished Sir John Balfour. Without Jock and Crista, both in a league of their own, this book could not have been.

With Crista I was able to retrace my mother's life during the Thirties, through her adventures during the Spanish Civil War, and onto the disastrous honeymoon which Jeanne organised for Sherman in July 1938 at her friend Count Joachim von Ribbentrop's gloomy castle, Schloss Sonnenburg, 50 miles east of Berlin at Freienwalde

Much of what my mother told me of her early life was confirmed to me by Crista who supplied many new details. However, she was genuinely frightened by my mother and her threat to reveal "secrets" in Crista's own personal life, as also those of her closest friends preferably Spanish dukes.

So dangerous did Crista's own mother, Queen Ena, consider Jeanne, that by the mid Thirties she forbade her daughter to socialise with her again, telling Crista emphatically that my mother was "beautiful, bad and very dangerous". Queen Ena forbad Crista and her sister the Infanta Beatriz to further frequent the glamorous, louche nightclubs which Jeanne took them too. To enforce her command, Queen Ena personally snubbed Jeanne by refusing to allow Crista to attend my parents' wedding in July 1936.

Nevertheless Crista remained an intimate of my mother's from the late Thirties on, a keen observer of Jeanne's activities—and through the Vatican connection, a corridor which remained open during the war—even at the safe distance of Rome, Lausanne and Geneva. Thus she was able to talk about my mother's life during these years as also during the Second World War.

It was Crista who was able to unravel my mother's astonishing boasts, based, as always, on the truth. It was Crista who endorsed the critical account of my father's all but immediate impotence in 1938 and of his attempted, but foiled, escape from the honeymoon fortress, a drama with which my mother frequently, triumphantly regaled me and many others.

For details of the lives of my great-grandparents, Viscount and Viscountess Southwell, and in particular the life of my maternal grand-mother, "Feckless Fanny" Stourton, I relied upon my cousins the Hon Mrs Pelline Eyre and her eldest sister, the Hon Mrs Douglas Woodruff, both daughters of Lord Acton, My cousin Lady Maureen Dormer and my late aunt Gytha, the Marquesa del Moral, shed light on Jeanne's upbringing and general demeanour from childhood onwards

It was especially Gytha del Moral and my mother's other half-sisters, Magda Stourton, Barbara, widow of Frank Bellville and Anne de Zulueta y de Russo, who gave detailed information about my mother's numerous boyfriends and her one true romance with Dick Sheepshanks.

In my mother's circles everyone knew about one another—not merely the bare facts but the whole intimate texture of personal lives, patterns of behaviour, sexual mores and character. Strictly adhered to was the unwritten code that all such highly sensitive information should not be divulged beyond the accepted boundaries of this exclusive—and secretive—high society club obsessed with its worldly glamour and absolute power.

Yet various of my sources, whether of her lovers of whom Jeanne boasted colourfully, ceaselessly, displaying signed photographs of several of them conspicuously at her bedside, have been from within this society. I am indebted to several who prefer not to be named for supplying vivid verification of events in my mother's life.

From my earliest childhood I regularly met a number of my mother's avowed lovers: Sir Richard Sykes, Bt, King George of Greece, his brother, Crown Prince Paul of Greece, Prince Jean Faucigny Lusinge, the

Marquess of Carisbrooke, the Marqués of Santa Cruz, the Duke of Primo de Rivera (Spanish ambassador to the Court of St James's), the Marqués Pepe de Manzanedo, Lord (Peter) Derwent, Sir Malcolm Sargent, Colonel Henry Micklem, Commander Dick Ovey, Colonel Guy de Pass, the hapless Dr Jack Kempton (who committed suicide) and the Brazilian ambassador, Raul Regis de Oliveira. There were also the bankers of social lustre, such as David Colville, Patrick de Laszlo and other useful, powerful members of the Baring and Fleming banking families, without exception wealthy members of the Royal Yacht Squadron at Cowes. Here my evidence has been at first-hand.

I was greatly helped by my godmother Crista's detailed information as to the Spanish Civil War period of my mother's life with its strong Nazi influences, the barbarism of experimental bombings. Jeanne's frequently flaunted affair with Joachim von Ribbentrop, as she boasted to Crista, had taken place from 1934. And she further boasted of her early recruitment to the Ribbentrop Büro, the richly endowed, highly sophisticated spying organisation based in London, Hamburg and Paris.

Within the glittering sophisticated social circle in which she] moved so determinedly Jeanne first met Ribbentrop at one of several and similar dinners given by her intimates, Sir Roderick Jones, and his wife Enid Bagnold. Lists printed in the Court Circular of the London *Times* testify to this. As also, in various articles, letters, to the strong pro-Nazi leanings of both Sir Roderick and Lady]ones during the Thirties.

Further details of the relationship came to me through the late Andrew Constable Maxwell. Others of the family added further corroboration. My Aunt Gytha helped me greatly to understand this era, as also my late cousin Pelline Eyre.

Sir John Balfour was the minister at the British embassy in Lisbon during the Second World War, thereafter British ambassador to the Argentine and subsequently Spain, gave me invaluable information in respect of Jeanne's activities during the Thirties and Forties; and about the incident in Rome in 1937 when she supposedly blew the safe at the British Embassy.

My late cousin Father Michael Hollings, MC, was another important source having frequently encountered my mother at close quarters within family circles. I owe him uniquely a debt of greatest gratitude As an important witness to my mother's actions, and her. successful attempts at disinheriting me, he both counselled and consoled me over several years

Only a few years Jeanne's junior, Michael was a percipient, perspicacious observer of her ambition and ambitious behaviour. No less her motives.

I have also been assisted over source maternal by Ribbentrop's biographer Michael Bloch; over the death of Dick Sheepshanks by my aunts Gytha and Barbara, and Sir Henry Chilton's son-in-law Tom DuPree, late of the Foreign Office. I was further inspired, having met the beautiful Barbara Hutton in my younger life, by her biographer Philip von Rennselaer.

For information and facts about the last will made in Sherman's name in 1974 I have been aided by the late Mrs Phyllis Messenger, widow of the head gardener at Stonor Park, Bill Messenger, who also assisted me. In connection with my American grandmother, Mildred, Lady Camoys, and my great-grandmother, Sophia Augusta Brown Sherman, I am grateful to the family lawyers, Edwards & Angell, of Newport and Providence, Rhode Island. My distinguished late cousin, John Nicholas Brown, gave me invaluable assistance in our shared family history.

My great-aunt the Condesa de Torre Diaz and her son Canon Alfonso de Zulueta de Mugaburu, gave me invaluable genealogical and related information. So too Jeanne's cousin Monsignor Alfred Gilbey As also did Diana Churchill, Lord Duncan Duncan Sandys, and Edward Slomnicki. Sister Bridget Geoffrey-Smith confirmed many facts covering the years from 1950 to 1987.

The Hon Mrs Esther Stonor, my great-aunt, gave me access to her own documentation and invaluable press cuttings prior to her murder in 1971. I am also indebted to my father's lawyers George Bellord and David Drummond, to his cousin and executor, Colonel Sir Joseph Weld. Other source material was provided by HRH the Infanta Beatriz Torlonia, Consuelo Juantorena of Madrid, Francis E. Stonor (managing director of Robert Jackson & Co of Piccadilly—he served in Alexandria and Cairo in the SOE), Charles Stonor (anthropologist and grower of the Stonor tomato), Dom Julian Stonor, OSB (Benedictine monk and author of *Stonor*), HE Archbishop Bruno Heim, Papal Nuncio, all of whom gave me invaluable information and encouragement.

So too did Timothy Garner and Clive Newbold, both companions of Francis E. Stonor. During his too-short lifetime the late HRH Prince William of Gloucester was another encouraging, illuminating source for my memoir, as were Graham Greene and Archbishop David Mathew.

Last but not least, I am grateful to my father's company sergeant-major,

George Howard of the Oxfordshire and Buckinghamshire Light Infantry; and to Dr Jack Kempton whose hospital unit at the Royal Berkshire Hospital I worked at whilst he was companion to my mother in the mid-Fifties.

JULIA CAMOYS STONOR
London 2006

Bibliography

Adolphus' Playbook for Boys and Girls, comp. James Davies, London, 1947.

Aitken, Leslie, *Massacre on the Road to Dunkirk*, Wellingborough, 1988.

Aldous, Richard, *Tunes of Glory: The Life of Malcolm Sargent*, London, 2001.

Allen, Everett S. Allen, *A Wind to Shade the World: The Story of the 1938 Hurricane*, Boston, 1976.

Almanach de Gotha, *Gotha and London*, 1887-1950.

The Anglo-American Yearbook and International Directory, Anglo-American Association, London, 1920-1937.

Annuaire de France Annuaire de la Noblesse de France: Royalty, Peerage and Nobility of Europe, 1843-1927, Paris, 1997.

Annual Register, London, 1820-1948.

The Army List, London, 1860-1944.

Bagnold, Enid, *Autobiography*, (from 1889), London, 1969.

Balfour, John, *Not Too Correct an Auriol: The Recollections of a Diplomat*, London, 1984.

Balfour, Michael, *Helmuth von Moltke: A Leader against Hitler*, London, 1972.

Ballantyne, R. M., *The Dog Crusoe*, London, 1922.

Balsan, Consuelo Vanderbilt, *The Glitter and the Gold*, New York, 1952.

Barstow, Phyllida, *The English Country House Party*, Wellingborough, Northamptonshire, 1989.

Battiscombe, Georgina, *Queen Alexandra*, London, 1969.

Beeton, Isabella, *Mrs Beeton's Household Management*, (together with a special supplement on poisons), London 1861.

Bence-Jones, Mark, *The Catholic Families*, London, 1992.

Bethell, Nicholas, *The War that Hitler Won*, London, 1972.

Bethell, Nicholas, *The Great Betrayal: The Untold Story of Kim Philby's Great Betrayal*, London, 1984.

Bloch, Michael, *Ribbentrop*, London 1992.

Blücher von Wahlstatt, Princess Evelyn, *An English Wife in Berlin*, 1920.

Blythe, Ronald, *Akenfeld: Portrait of a Village*, London, 1961.

Bokun, Branko, *Spy in the Vatican, 1941-45*, London, 1973.

Bonham-Carter, Violet, *Winston Churchill as I Knew Him*, London, 1965.

Bottin Mondain, *Paris*, 1888-1998.

Bouvier, Lee Radzowil, *Happy Times*, (autobiography), Ralph Lauren, New York, 1995.

Boyd, William, *Armadillo*, New York, 1998.

Boyle, Andrew, *The Climate of Treason: Five who Spied for Russia*, London, 1979.

Brooks: A Social History, ed. Philip Ziegler & Desmond Seward, London, 1991.

Buehrl, Marie, *Merry de Val: Cardinal Rafael Borgia: A Biography*, Rome/London, 1957.

Burke's Landed Gentry, London, 1870-1992.

Burke's Peerage, 31st edn, London, 1869.

Burke's Peerage and Baronetage, London, 1870-2002.

Burke's Royalty of Europe, London, 1968.

Burns, Jimmy, *Spain: A Literary Companion*, London, 2006.

Burrows, Gideon, *The No-Nonsense Guide to the Arms Trade*, Oxford, 2002.

Cadogan, Alexander, *The Diaries of Sir Alexander Cadogan*, ed. David Dillks, London, 1971.

Canon Law Digest, The Milwaukee, (several vols), 1935, 1937, 1938, 1941, 1943, 1949, 1976-1983, 1984-1989.

Cannadine, David, *The Decline and Fall of the British Aristocracy*, Yale & London, 1990.

Caraman, Philip, SJ, *The Other Face: Catholic Life under Elizabeth*, London, 1960.

Carter, Miranda, *Anthony Blunt: His Lives*, London 2001.

Catholic Who's Who and Directory, London, 1844-1957; 1880-1989.

Cervantes, Miguel de, *Don Quixote*, (children's edition), London, 1953.

Cesarini, David, & Kushner, Tony, *The Internment of Aliens in Twentieth Century Britain*, London, 1989, 1993.

Chadwick, Owen, *Britain and the Vatican during the Second World War*, Cambridge, 1986.

Chamberlain, Sir Austen, *Down the Years*, London, 1935.

Chamberlain, Sir Austen, *Seen in Passing*, London, 1937.

Chamberlain, Samuel, *The New England Image*, New York, 1962.

Channon, Henry "Chips", *The Diaries of Sir Henry Channon*, ed. Robert Rhodes-James, London, 1967.

Charnley, John, *Churchill: The End of Glory*, London, 1993.

Charmely, John, *Duff Cooper*, London, 1986.

Chase, David & Cheek, Richard, & Gannon, Thomas, *Newport Mansions: the Gilded Age*, Rhode Island, 1982.

Chetwode, Penelope, *Two Middle-aged Ladies in Andalusia*, London, 1963.

Chisholm, Anne, & Davie, Michael, *Beaverbrook: A Life*, London, 1992. .

Christie, Agatha, *An Autobiography (1890-1976)*, London, 1977.

Christie's Catalogue, 5 November 1991, ('The Personal Heirlooms & Jewellery of the late Julia Stonor, Marquise d' Hautpoul, former fiancée to King George V: items 1-48').

The City by the Sea: Souvenir Folder of Newport, Rhode Island, Newport, 1922.

Clifford, Colin, *The Asquiths*, London, 2002.

Cockayne, G. E., *Complete Peerage of England, Scotland, Ireland, London, 1889: Extant, Extinct or Dormant*, London, 1889.

Code Names Dictionary, ed. Richard Wightman Fox & James T. Kloppenberg, Detroit, Michigan, 1963.

Code Napoléonic, Paris, 1811.

Codice di Diritto Canonico, Rome, 1990.

A Collection's Progress: Two Retrospective Exhibitions, The John Carter Brown Library, Providence, 1968.

A Companion to American Thought, ed. By Richard Wightman Fox & James T. Kloppenberg, London, 1995.

Cooper, Artemis, *War in Egypt*, London, 1987.

Cooper, Lord Alfred Duff, *Operation Heartbreak: Mincemeat, Huelva Deception*, London 1950.

Cooper, Diana, *The Light of Common Day*, London, 1959.

Cornwell, John, *Hitler's Pope: The Secret History of Pius XII*, London 1999.

Country Life, Historic Buildings Council: Stonor, (three-part article, illus. blk & wht photographs), London, 1951; Estates Number, title page illus. Stonor Park, London, February 1989.

Cowles, Virginia, *The Astors: The Story of a Transatlantic Family*, London 1979.

Craig, Theresa, *Edith Wharton: A House Full of Rooms – Architecture, Interiors and Gardens*, New York, 1996.

Crowley, Aleister, *The Confessions of Aleister Crowley: An Autobiography*, London, 1969.

Crowley, Aleister, *The Magical Record of the Beast 666: the Diaries of Aleister Crowley 1914-1920*, London, 1972.

Dallas, Donald, *Purdey, Gun and Rifle making: the Definitive History*, London, 2000.

Darley, Gillian, *The National Trust Book of the Farm*, London, 1981.

Davenport, Marcia, *Too Strong for Fantasy: A Personal Record of Music Literature and Politics in American and Europe over Half a Century*, London, 1968.

Davies Douglas, J., & H. Lewis (eds), *An Encyclopaedia of Cremation*, London, 2005.

Debrett's Peerage & Baronetage, 1866-2005, London.

De-la-Noy, Michael, *Eddy: The Life of Edward Sackville-West*, London, 1988.

Delarue Jacques, *The History of the Gestapo*, London 1964.

Dershowitz, Alan, *Reversal of Fortune: Inside the von Bulow Case*, New York & London, 1990.

Dictionary of National Biography, London, 1900-2006.

Diplomatic Service List, 1955-2006.

Divine, David, *The Nine Days of Dunkirk*, London, 1959.

Dod's Peerage, Baronetage and Knightage of Great Britain and Ireland, London, 1841.

Domvile, Admiral Sir Barry, *By and Large: From Admiral to Cabin Boy*, London, 1936.

Dormer, Hugh, *Hugh Dormer's Diaries*, London, 1947.

Downing & Scully, *The Architectural History of Newport, Rhode Island*, American Legacy Press, Harvard Press, 1982.

Dutton, Ralph, *The Victorian Home*, London, 1954.

Dymoke, Juliet, *A Kind of Warfare*, London, 1981.

Eilers, Marlene A., *Queen Victoria's Descendants*, New York, 1987.

Faucigny-Lucinge, *Prince Jean-Louis, un Gentilhomme Cosmopolite: Mémoires d'une Famille Exotique*, (1904-1990), Paris, 1990.

Feather, Jessica, *Art behind Barbed Wire*, Liverpool, 2004.

Fleming, Kate, *Celia Johnson: A Biography*, London, 1991.

Forster, Margaret, *Daphne Du Maurier*, London, 1993.

The Forty Martyrs, pamphlets, Rome, 1970.

Fox, James, *The Langhorne Sisters*, London, 1998.

Freyberg, Paul, *Bernard Freyberg VC: Soldier of Two Nations*, London 1991.

Friedman, Dennis, *Darling Georgie: The Enigma of George V*, London, 1998.

Fusero, Clemente, *The Borgias*, trans. Peter Green, London, 1972.

Gardner, W. J. R., *The Evacuation from Dunkirk: Operation Dynamo*, London, 2000.

Garis, Howard R., *Uncle Wiggily's Fortune*, New York, 1942.

Gawthorne, P. R., *King George V, His Life and Times, 1865-1936: A Pictorial Record*, London 1940.

Glendinning, Victoria, *Edith Sitwell (1887-1964): A Unicorn among Lions*, London 1981.

Gloucester, Princess Alice, Duchess of, *The Memoirs of Princess Alice, Duchess of Gloucester*, London, 1983.

Goddard, Victor, *Skies to Dunkirk: a personal memoir*, London, 1982.

Goldhagen, Daniel Jonah, *Hitler's Willing Executioners: Ordinary Germans and the Holocaust*, London, 1996.

Graves, Charles Renke, *The Home Guard of Britain: Women in Green*, London 1940.

Graves, Charles Renke, *Pride of the Morning: 1939-1945 – personal narratives*, London, 1945.

Gregson, Jonathan, *Blood against the Snows: The Tragic Story of Nepal's Royal Dynasty*, London, 2002.

Greene, Graham, *A Sort of Life*, London, 1971.

Greene, Graham, *Doctor Fischer of Geneva, or the Bomb Party*, London, 1980.

Greene, Barbara, *Land Benighted*, London, 1938.

Greene, Barbara, *Too Late to Turn Back: Barbara and Graham Greene in Liberia*, London, 1981, 1990.

Griffiths, Richard, *Fellow Travellers of the Right: British Enthusiasm for Nazi Germany*; 1933-1939, London, 1980.

Griffiths, Richard, *Patriotism Perverted: Captain Ramsay, the Right Club and British Anti-Semitism, 1939-1940*, London, 1998.

Hagan, Toni, *Nepal*, Berne, 1961.

Hall, Rev. Charles A., *Peeps at Nature: Birds, Eggs and Nests*, London, 1932.

Halsbury, *Laws of England*, (31 vols), 1907, 1917, 1931, 1942, 1952, 1964, 1973-1987.

Halsbury, *Criminal Law, Evidence & Procedure*, (2 vols), London 1989.

Hammond, Nigel, *The Oxfordshire Village Book*, Newbury, 1983.

Hapsburg-Lothringen, Geza von, *Fabergé: Imperial Jeweller*, London, 1993.

Hebblethwaite, Peter, *Paul VI: The First Modern Pope in the Vatican*, London, 1993.

Hedges, James, *The Browns of Providence Plantation*, (2 vols), Brown University Press, Providence, Rhode Island, 1968.

Heymann, C. David, *A Woman Named Jackie*, London, 1989.

Historic Houses and Gardens, (incl. article on Stonor, Banbury, Oxon & Guildford), Connecticut, 2002.

Holloway, David (ed.), *The Thirties: A Chronicle of the Decade*, London, 1993.

Hope, Anthony, *The Prisoner of Zenda*, London, 1894.

Hope, Anthony, *Rupert of Hentzau*, London, 1898.

Howarth, Stephen, *August '39: The Last Four Weeks of Peace in Europe*, London, 1989.

Howson, Gerald, *Arms for Spain: The Untold Story of the Spanish Civil War*, London, 1998.

Hussey, Christopher, 'Country Houses Open to the Public', *Country Life*, 1950.

Ingrams, Richard & Piper, John, *Piper's Places: John Piper in England & Wales*, London, 1983.

Irish Peers Association, *Annual List*, 1976-2005.

Jackson-Stops, Gervase (ed.), *The Treasure Houses of Britain*, Washington, 1985.

Jones, Sir Roderick, *A Life in Reuters*, London, 1951.

Jowitt, the Earl, *Dictionary of English Law*, London, USA.

The Joy of Cooking, New York, 1947.

Judd, Dennis, with Fraser, Antonia, *The Life and Times of George V*, London, 1973.

Kaplan, Donald M., & Louise Kaplan, *Doomsday: The Dictionary*, London, 1963.

Kemp, Peter, *The Thorns of Memory: Memoirs*, London, 1990.

Kennedy, A. L., *The Times and Appeasement: The Journals of A. L. Kennedy, 1932-1939*, ed. George Martell, Cambridge, 2000.

Kershaw, Ian, *Making Friends with Hitler: Lord Londonderry and Britain's Road to War*, London, 2004.

Kidd, Janet Aitken, *The Beaverbrook Girl: An Autobiography*, London, 1987.

Kirby, W. Egmont, *Butterflies and Moths in the UK*, London, New York, 1909.

Kitt, Eartha, *I'm Still Here*, London, 1989.

Knightley, Philip, *Philby: The Life and Views of a KGB Masterspy*, London 1988.

Lafitte, Francois, *The Internment of Aliens*, London, 1940/1988.

Lamb, Richard, *The Ghosts of Peace, 1935-1945*, Wilton, 1987.

Lamb, Richard, *War in Italy, 1943-1945: A Brutal Story*, London, 1983.

Lamb, Richard, *The Drift to War, 1922-1939*, London, 1989.

Lamb, Richard, *Mussolini and the British*, London, 1993.

Langley, Jimmy, *To Fight Another Day (Dunkirk, 1940)*, London.

Lehmann, John, *Edith Sitwell: Selected Letters*, London, 1970.

Lord, Walter, *The Miracle of Dunkirk*, London, 1983.

Lovat, Lord, *March Past: A Memoir*, London, 1978.

Lymington, Viscount, (later 9th Earl of Portsmouth), *Famine in England*, London, 1938.

McAlpine, Alistair, *Once a Jolly Bagman: A Memoir*, London, 1997.

Martin, Brian P., *The Great Shoots*, London, 1987.

Mason, Christopher, *The Art of the Steal: Inside the Sotheby's-Christie's Auction House Scandal*, New York, 2004.

Mathew, Archbishop David, *Acton: A Biography*, London, 1934.

Mathew, Archbishop David, *Catholicism in England*, London, 1946.

Meditations by a Jesuit Father: Short Meditations for Every Day of the Year according to the Method of St Ignatius, (2 vols), Society of Jesus, London, 1883.

Mockler, Anthony, *Three Lives of Graham Greene*, London, 1994.

Moorhouse, Roger, *Killing Hitler: The Third Reich and the Plots against Hitler*, London, 2006.

Mortimer, Sir John, *Murderers and Other Friends*, London, 1994.

Muggeridge, Malcolm, *The Thirties: 1939-40*, London, 1940.

Muir, Kate, 'The Englishman who Felt Nazi-Germany Calling', *The Times*, May 1991.

Munn, Geoffrey, *Tiaras, Past and Present*, London, 2002.

My Mother the Nazi, illustrated catalogue of exhibition curated by Raul Zamudio & Julia Camoys Stonor, New York, 2005.

Nicholas, Lynn H., *The Rape of Europa: The Fate of Europe's Treasures in the Third Reich and the Second World War*, London & New York, 1994.

Nicolson, Harold, *Diaries and Letters*, 3 vols, ed. Nigel Nicolson, London, 1966.

The 1920s Scrapbook, comp. Robert Opie, London, 2003.

1936: As Recorded by The Spectator, ed. Charles Moore & Christopher Hawtree, London, 1986.

Noel, Gerald, *Ena: Spain's English Queen*, London, 1984.

Ogden, Christopher, *The Life of the Party: The Biography of Pamela Digby Churchill Hayward Harriman*, London & Boston, 1994.

Ohannessian, Griselda Jackson, *Once as It Was*, Dublin, New Hampshire, 2001.

Padfield, Peter, *Himmler: Reichsfuhrer – SS*, Basingstoke, 1980.

Page, Bruce, *Philby: The Spy who Betrayed a Generation*, London, 1968.

Philby, Kim, *My Silent War*, (intro. Graham Greene), London, 1968.

Pitt, Barrie, *1918: The Last Act*, London, 1962.

Pool, James & Suzanne, *The Secret Funding of Hitler's Rise to Power, 1919-1933*, London, 1979.

Portsmouth, Gerald, 9th Earl, *A Knot of Roots: An Autobiography*, London, 1975.

Prescett, S. John, *Strange Intelligence from Dunkirk to Nuremberg*, London, 1981.

Preston, Paul, *Doves of War: Four Women of the Spanish Civil War*, London, 2002.

Pryce-Jones, David, *Unity Mitford: A Quest*, London, 1976.

Ramsay, Captain Archibald Maule, *The Nameless War*, London, 1952.

Randall, A. L., *Newport: A Tour Guide*, Newport, 1970.

Rankin, Nicholas, *Telegram from Guernica: The Extraordinary Life of George Steer, War Correspondent*, London 2003.

Roberts, Stephen H., *The House that Hitler Built*, London, 1937.

Read, Donald, *The Power of the News: The History of Reuters*, London, 1999.

Reid, Charles, *Malcolm Sargent: A Biography*, London, 1968.

Rose, Kenneth, *King George V*, London, 1983.

Rose, Norman, *The Cliveden Set: Portrait of an Exclusive Fraternity*, London, 2002.

Rousmaniere, John, *America's Cup Book, 1851-1983*, Milan, 1983.

St Aubyn, Giles, *William of Gloucester: Pioneer Prince*, London, 1977.

St Johnston, Colonel Sir Thomas Eric, *One Policeman's Story*, London, 1948.

Salter, Elizabeth, *Edith Sitwell*, London 1979.

Sanders, Edmund, *A Butterfly Book for the Pocket, Including All Species to be Found in the British Isles*, London, 1939.

Seachlight Magazine, Partial Details Guest List of Anglo-German Fellowship Dinners, London, 1936, 1937, 1986, 1991.

Seaton-Watson, Christopher, *Dunkirk – Alamein – Bologna: Letters and Diaries of an Artillery Man*, London, 1993.

Sebba, Anne, *Enid Bagnold: The Authorized Biography*, London, 1986.

Skidelsky, Robert, *Oswald Mosley*, London, 1975.

Snowman, Kenneth, *Fabergé: Lost and Found*, London, 1993.

Social Register, New York, 1887.

Social Register, Newport, Rhode Island, 1887.

Social Register, New York and Newport, Rhode Island, 1887-2006.

Souvenir Album of Fabergé from the Royal Collection, London, 1985.

Spark, Muriel, *The Abbess of Crewe*, London, 1974.

Spears, Major General Sir Edward, *Assignment to Catastrophe*, London, 1954.

Spellman, Cardinal Archbishop, Francis, *The Road to History*, New York, 1942.

Spellman, Cardinal Archbishop, Francis, *Action this Day*, New York, 1943.

Spellman, Cardinal Archbishop, Francis, *The Foundling*, New York, 1951.

Spellman, Cardinal Archbishop, Francis, *The Card*, New York, 1963.

Stonor, Charles, *The Sherpa and the Snowman*, London, 1955.

Stonor, Francis E., *A Taste for Splendour*, (3 illus. instalments on the interior contents of his Baroque palazzo on St John's Wood roundabout), London 1961.

Stonor, Julia Camoys, 'Short Stories', *Harpers Queen Magazine*, 1977.

Stonor, Julia Camoys, 'Life Swap', BBC documentary essay, *Harpers Queen Magazine*, London, 1980.

Stonor Family Letters and Papers, 1290-1483, ed. Christine Carpenter, Cambridge, 1996.

Stonor, Dom Julian, OSB, *Stonor: History of a Catholic Sanctuary in the Chilterns from the 9th century until 1950*, Newport, Monmouth, 1951.

Storrs, Sir Ronald, *A Record of the War: The First Quarter, September-November 1939*, London, 1939.

Sykes, Christopher, *Troubled Loyalty: A Biography of Adam von Trott zu Solz*, London, 1968.

Sykes, Christopher, Nancy: *The Life of Lady Astor*, London, 1972.

Tavistock, Marquis of (Hastings William Russell), *The Fate of a Peace Effort*, High Wycombe, 1940.

Tavistock, Marquis of (Hastings William Russell), *The Years of Transition*, London, 1949.

Taylor, A. J. P., *British Prime Ministers and Other Essays*, London, 1999.

Tennant, E. W., *True Account*, (autobiography) London 1957.

Thirkell, Angela, *Pomfret Towers*, London, 1938.

Thomas, Hugh, *The Spanish Civil War*, London, 1961.

The Times, Court Circular, 14 July 1938 ('Auxilio Social' reception); Court Circular, 15 July 1938 (Wedding List and photograph of the Hon. Sherman Stonor and Miss Jeanne Stourton); Court Circular, 29 February, 2 March & 5 March 1912 (funeral of Mgr Edmund Stonor, Titular Archbishop of Trebizond).

Todd, Richard, *Caught in the Act*, (autobiography), London, 1986.

Trevor-Roper, Hugh, *The Philby Affair; Espionage, Treason and the Secret Services*, London, 1968.

Trotter, Stewart, *Love's Labour's Found: Shakespeare's Criminal Passions*, Ashford, Kent, 2002.

Uboldi, Raffaello, *King Juan Carlos: A Biography*, Rome, 1988.

Van Rensselaer, Philip, *Million Dollar Baby: An Intimate Portrait of Barbara Hutton*, New York, 1974.

Vickers, Hugo, *Cecil Beaton: The Authorized Biography*, London, 1985.

Videl, John, *McLibel: Burger Culture on Trial*, London, 1997.

Waugh, Evelyn, *Brideshead Revisited*, 1945

Waugh, Evelyn, *The Loved One*, London 1948.

Waugh, Evelyn, *Helena*, London, 1950.

Waugh, Evelyn, *Men at Arms*, 1952.

Waugh, Evelyn, *Ronald Knox*, London, 1959.

Waugh, Evelyn, *The Ordeal of Gilbert Pinfold*, London, 1957.

Waugh, Evelyn, *Edmund Campion: Scholar, Priest, Hero and Martyr*, Oxford, 1980.

Waugh, Evelyn, *The Letters of Evelyn Waugh*, ed. Mark Amory, London 1980.

The Way to a Man's Heart, (cookery book), New York, 1947.

Weale, Adrian, *Renegades: Hitler's Englishmen*, (includes an account of the British Free Corps, a Waffen SS unit formed of British nationals), London, 1994.

Webster's Royal Red Book, London, 1869-1939.

Weintraub, Stanley, *The Importance of Being Edward, King in Waiting, 1841-1901*, London, 2000.

West, Rebecca, *The Meaning of Treason*, London, 1949.

Wharton, Edith, *Here and Beyond*, New York, 1926.

Wharton, Edith, *Certain People*, New York, 1930.

Wharton, Edith, *The World Over*, New York, 1936.

Wharton, Edith, *Ghosts*, New York, 1936.

Whitaker's Almanack, London, 1918-1987.

Who's Who in Art, London, 1972.

Who's Who in France, Levallois-Peret, 2003.

Who Was Who in America, New Providence, New Jersey, 1946, 1947.

Who Was Who in Spain, 1970.

Who Was Who, London, 1897-2006.

The World Who's Who of Women, Cambridge, 1988.

Yallop, David, *In God's Name: The Events Surrounding the Death of Pope John Paul I*, London, 1984.

Genealogical tables

For the family trees and genealogy of the Camoys, Southwell, Stonor, Stourton, Merry del Val, de Zulueta and Mugaburu families, the Counts of Torre Diaz, see *Debrett* and *Burke's Peerage and Landed Gentry*; *Who's Who in Spain*, 1970; for the genealogy of John Nicholas Brown and Mildred Constance Sherman, see *The Chad Brown Workbook* (Providence, Rhode

Island, 1987); *The Browns of Providence Plantations: the Colonial Years; the Nineteenth Century*, Hedges, Brown University Press, Providence, 1968; the Historical Society of New England.

Manuscripts and Correspondence:

Personal correspondence from Graham Greene to Julia Camoys Stonor, 1950-1984; personal correspondence between HRH the Infanta Maria Cristina de Borbon Battenberg and Julia Camoys Stonor, 1955-1996; personal diaries of Julia Camoys, Stonor, 1951-2006, personal correspondence from Regimental Secretary, 43rd & 52nd Light Infantry, The Royal Green Jackets, to Julia Camoys Stonor, 1986.

Index

Also from Desert Hearts . . .

"THE PUBLIC SCHOOL CHRONICLES"

An Overseas Boy

by Peter Lazard

After Anglo-Indian George Sinclair comes of age in an English public school
he enters the shadowy worlds of espionage and voodoo in Central America
and the Caribbean. Darkly funny, this satirical thriller traces the life and
loves of an obsessive anti-hero from his Catholic school and Oxford college
to MI6, black ops . . . and murder. 'An Overseas Boy' also takes you down
the dark path of the occult, seasoned with a peppering of violence, head-
shrinking and illicit sex to create a heady cocktail -- at times sleazy, at all
times deliciously disturbing.

ISBN 1-898948-16-X • HARDBACK • £16.99

The Virgin Killers

by Nick Awde

When two Jesuit priests die violently at an exclusive Catholic prep school, an
inquisitive teacher and an investigative journalist decide to get to the bottom
of the mystery. But Hugh Weld and his ex-lover Sara Reeve soon find themselves pitted against the closed ranks of sinister lawyers, Freemasons and
English Catholics. The pair of amateur sleuths embark on a dangerous journey of discovery that leads them from the witch-haunted fells of Lancashire
to the pagan fires of the Lewes Bonfire. The action is set against the back-
drop of a country in political turmoil as voters, fearful that Britain is losing
its power to Europe, are hungry for a new regime . . .

ISBN 1-898948-15-1 • HARDBACK • £16.99

Watch out for future titles in THE PUBLIC SCHOOL CHRONICLES including:
Between the Devil and the Deep Blue Sea, *Black Pope Dead Pope*,
Death of a Public Schoolboy and *Blood Confession (a Play)*.

DESERT♥HEARTS

www.deserthearts.com
PO Box 2131
London W1A 5SU
England